STUDIES IN THE TEXT HISTORY
OF THE LIFE AND FABLES OF AESOP

AMERICAN PHILOLOGICAL ASSOCIATION
Monograph Series

L. Arnold Post, Editor

Number 7
STUDIES IN THE TEXT HISTORY
OF THE LIFE AND FABLES OF AESOP
by
B. E. Perry

STUDIES IN THE TEXT HISTORY OF THE LIFE AND FABLES OF AESOP

by

B. E. Perry

SCHOLARS PRESS

A reprint of the 1936 edition published
by Lancaster Press, Inc., Lancaster, PA, U. S. A.
B. H. Blackwell, Ltd., 50 Broad St., Oxford, England

Distributed by
Scholars Press
101 Salem St.
P.O. Box 2268
Chico, CA 95927

STUDIES IN THE TEXT HISTORY OF THE LIFE AND FABLES OF AESOP

B. E. Perry

Library of Congress Cataloging in Publication Data

Perry, B. E. (Ben Edwin), 1892-1968.
   Studies in the text history of the life and
fables of Aesop.

   Reprint. Originally published: Haverford, Pa.:
American Philological Association, 1936. (Monograph
series / American Philological Association ; no. 7)
   Includes index.
   1. Aesop. 2. Authors, Greek—Biography.
I. Title. II. Series: Philological monographs ; no.7.
PA3858.P4 1981   398.2'452   81-13575
ISBN 0-89130-534-3   AACR2

1981

Printed in the United States of America
1 2 3 4 5 6
Edwards Brothers, Inc.
Ann Arbor, Michigan 48106

TO

PROFESSOR CLARENCE P. BILL

PREFACE

The studies contained in the present volume may be regarded as in some measure preliminary to a future edition of the texts with which they deal. It is my hope that that edition, which will include the principal versions of the *Life* and *Fables* together with various other Aesopica, will be completed within the next three or four years, and that each publication will be found to contribute something to the value and interest of the other. Meanwhile, I propose to define as clearly and as adequately as possible the broad outlines of the Aesopic tradition in so far as it relates to the commonly received texts of the *Life* and *Fables*, and to the hitherto unknown but very important representatives thereof which are contained in manuscript 397 of the Pierpont Morgan Library.

Both parts of this monograph are closely related to my previous, somewhat exhaustive study of the manuscripts of the Westermann *Life* ("The Text Tradition of the Greek Life of Aesop," *T. A. P. A.* LXIV, 198–244), to which study, necessarily, numerous cross-references have been made below. Thus, in Part I, I have continued my observations upon the text history of the *Life* by describing the unique ancient version preserved in the Morgan manuscript and by discussing its relation to other texts; although I reserve for another occasion many questions relating to the ancient traditions about Aesop, to the substance of the traditional biography, and to its relation to Ahikar. The essay on the *Fables* in Part II has outgrown its original design. In the beginning I had planned to confine my attention to the Morgan text as such—hence the somewhat disproportionate length of that particular section (2a); but I soon perceived that both the Morgan manuscript and the results of my own study of the tradition in the Westermann *Life* had a very close bearing upon the history of the *Fables*, and that it would be profitable to examine the latter in the light of this new knowledge, and with the help of the copious textual data newly furnished by Chambry in his elaborate edition. Accordingly, after describing the Morgan text, I have proceeded to discuss independently, and for its own interest, each of the principal recensions of the *Fables* in turn, thereby contributing what I could to a better understanding of their nature, their date and sources, the sub-recensions within them, the parallelism with different forms of the *Life*, and, upon a few occasions, the relationships existing between certain of the individual manuscripts in which they are preserved. The latter topic, in the case of the Augustana recension at least, deserves a more thorough investigation than I have made, but I hope to return to it in the future.

A brief statement concerning the contents, date and provenience of the Morgan manuscript will be found on page 7 of the recent catalogue by Belle Da Costa Greene and Meta P. Harrsen: *The Pierpont Morgan Library, Exhibition of Illuminated Manuscripts*, New York, 1934. The manuscript comes from southern Italy and is dated by Kirsopp Lake in the last quarter of the tenth century, although he allows for the possibility that it may have been written in the early decades of the eleventh. Its identity with the long-lost Cryptoferratensis A 33, which disappeared from Grottaferrata about the time of Napoleon and which was much sought for in the nineteenth century (cf. Crusius, *Babrii Fabulae*, p. IX), was first recognized by Dr. Elinor Husselman of the University of Michigan Library, who plans to publish a fuller account of it in the near future, along with a reproduction of its unique though fragmentary text of *Kalilah and Dimnah*. The fables of Babrius contained in this manuscript have recently been published by her in the *Transactions of the American Philological Association*, LXVI (1935), 104–126. It was originally intended that the studies herewith presented, which were completed about two years ago and to which I have already

PREFACE   ix

made some references in previous articles, should be published jointly with those of Dr. Husselman, as descriptive of the various texts contained in the Morgan manuscript. This plan, however, had to be given up when it developed that my chapters on Aesop had progressed considerably beyond the limits originally set for them.

I wish to thank Miss Greene of the Morgan Library for her liberal courtesy in matters relating to the use of manuscript 397. To Professor Post, the editor of this series, my cordial thanks are due both for the unusual thoroughness with which he has examined and emended my manuscript, and for a number of valuable suggestions relating to the correction of G's text in the *Life*. Lastly, it is with pleasure that I acknowledge my deep indebtedness to the John Simon Guggenheim Memorial Foundation, through whose generosity I was enabled to spend a profitable year of study in the libraries of Europe; and to the University of Illinois which, through the medium of special funds, has supplied me in time past with much valuable equipment.

BEN EDWIN PERRY

URBANA, ILLINOIS
July 7, 1936

Abbreviated References

Chambry. *Aesopi Fabulae; recensuit Aemilius Chambry*, Budé, Paris, 1925 (unless a different title is mentioned).

G. MS 397 in the Pierpont Morgan Library, New York.

Marc. "Die Überlieferung des Äsopromans," by Paul Marc, in *Byzantinische Zeitschrift* XIX (1910), 382–421.

Text Tradition. "The Text Tradition of the Greek Life of Aesop," by B. E. Perry, in *Transactions of the American Philological Association* LXIV (1933), 198–244.

Untersuchungen. "Untersuchungen zur Überlieferung der äsopischen Fabeln," by A. Hausrath, in *Jahrbücher für classische Philologie*, Supplementband XXI (1894), 247–312.

Westermann (or West.). *Vita Aesopi; ex vratislaviensi ac partim monacensi et vindobonensi codicibus nunc primum ed. Antonius Westermann*, Brunsvigae, 1845. (Londini apud Williams et Norgate.)

W. The Westermann version of the *Life*; to be distinguished from W (= cod. Laur. conv. soppr. 627). Quoted by page and line of Westermann's text.

Zeitz. *Die Fragmente des Äsopromans in Papyrushandschriften*, by H. Zeitz. Dissertation, Giessen, 1935.

Reference List of the Principal Manuscripts Cited in Part II

(When nothing is said to the contrary the manuscript contains only the *Fables*, or the *Fables* and one of the short prefaces.)

SYMBOL IN CHAMBRY	MY SYMBOL	Class I (Augustana)
—	G	Manuscript 397 in the Pierpont Morgan Library, New York, *s.* x, *Life* and *Fables* (Plates III and IV)
Pa		Parisinus suppl. 690, *s.* xii
Pb		Monacensis 564, *s.* xiii (the so-called Augustanus)
Pc		Par. 365, *s.* xiv
Pd		Par. 1685, *s.* xv
Pe		Par. 1788, *s.* xv
Pf		Palatinus 156, *s.* xv
Pg	V (used for the *Life* only)	Vaticanus 695, *s.* xv, *Life* in the Class II version (= *W*), and *Fables* belonging to Class I
Ph		Vat. 1752, *s.* xv
		The M Recension
		(Representing the archetype of the Westermann *Life*)
—	M	Monacensis 525, *s.* xiv, *Life* and *Fables* (Plate V)
—	O	Baroccianus 194, *s.* xv, *Life* only
—	(S)	Mosquensis 436 (*olim* 285), *s.* xiv, *Life* and *Fables;* belongs mainly in Class II for both texts, but is contaminated with an ancestor of M
—	R	Vat. 1192, *s.* xiv, *Life* only (fragmentary)
—	Lo	Lollinianus 26 (Belluno), *s.* xiv, in Latin, *Life* only

Reference List

		Class II (Hausrath's "Vindobonensis")
—	S	Cf. *supra; Life* and *Fables*
Cf	B (for the *Life* only)	Brit. Mus. Add. 17015, *s.* xv, *Life* and *Fables*
Cb	P (for the *Life* only)	Pal. 269, *s.* xv, *Life* and *Fables*
Cc		Vat. 914, *s.* xv; contains only 30 fables
Cd		Par. suppl. 105, *s.* xvi
Ce		Par. 1310, *s.* xv
Cg		Vind. hist. gr. 107, *s.* xv
Ch		Vind. hist. gr. 130, *s.* xiv; probably the best text of the fables of Class II, certainly the best for the metrical fables
Ca	W (for the *Life* only)	Laur. conv. soppr. 627, *s.* xiii (the "Casinensis"), *Life* and *Fables*, both much contaminated
—	L	Leidensis Vulc. 93, *s.* xv, *Life* and *Fables;* contents mixed, but fables belong mainly to Class II
Mc	F (for the *Life* only)	Laur. 57.30, *s.* xvi, *Life* and *Fables;* probably copied in large part from L
Pg	V (for the *Life* only)	Cf. *supra*
—	λ	Lost archetype of LFV, in the *Life*

Class III (Accursiana)

La		Laur. 89.79, *s.* xv
Lf		Ambrosianus 7, *s.* xv, *Life* and *Fables*
—	N	Manuscript 100 in the Astor Collection of the New York Public Library, *s.* xiv–xv (Plate VI)

Mixed Manuscripts (Class V)

Ca	W	Cf. *supra*
Ma		Pal. 195, *s.* xv
Mb		Vat. 777, *s.* xiv
Mc	F	Cf. *supra*
Me		Ambros. 481 (= L. 43 sup.) *s.* xv, *Life* (Accursiana) and *Fables*
Mf		Par. 126, *s.* xv
Mj		Par. 2900, *s.* xv

CONTENTS

	PAGE
PREFACE	vii
ABBREVIATED REFERENCES	xi
REFERENCE LIST OF THE PRINCIPAL MANUSCRIPTS CITED IN PART II	xii

PART I

AN ANCIENT VERSION OF THE LIFE OF AESOP

1. Introduction ... 1
2. The content and nature of G as compared with the Westermann recension (*W*) ... 4
3. The presumable dates of G and *W* ... 24
4. Various ancient recensions of the *Life* prior to *W* and their connections with G and *W* ... 27
5. The texts of the papyrus fragments ... 39
    a. PSI 156 ... 40
    b. The Oxyrhynchus papyrus ... 45
    c. The Berlin papyrus ... 53
    d. The Golenischeff papyrus ... 58

PART II

STUDIES IN THE TEXT HISTORY OF THE FABLES

1. Introduction ... 71
2. The Augustana Recension
    a. Description and collation of the Morgan manuscript (G) ... 77
    b. The traditional content of the Augustana collection as it appears from a comparison of the manuscripts. Notes on the grouping of manuscripts within Class I (the Augustana). ... 146
    c. G in relation to Pb and Pa ... 153
    d. Further notes on the various manuscripts of Class I ... 155

      e. The supposed rhetorical character of the Augustana 156
  3. Cod. Monacensis 525 and Class II
      a. The manuscript tradition of the Westermann *Life* and the identity of Class II with a branch thereof (i.e. with the SBP or *B* group). Remarks upon the individual manuscripts of Class II 174
      b. The dependence of *B* upon *A* in the Westermann *Life* indicates a similar relationship in the *Fables* 185
      c. The antiquity of the *A* tradition in M and S. The probable eastern origin of the various texts (including the *Fables*) peculiar to this tradition. The fables of Pseudo-Syntipas in relation to the archetype of the *A* recension. 185
      d. Description of the fables in M and S 190
      e. Further evidence pointing to the M recension as the source of Class II 194
      f. The text of M compared with Classes II and I. 196
  4. The Accursiana Recension
      a. Date and sources 204
      b. The Planudean editorship of the Accursiana *Life* and *Fables* 217

SUMMARY 229
APPENDIX—Note on the corpus of proverbs ascribed to Aesop 231
GENERAL INDEX 234
PLATES I–VI

PART I

AN ANCIENT VERSION OF THE LIFE OF AESOP

1. INTRODUCTION

The *Life of Aesop* belongs to a species of ancient folk-literature of which very little has survived. Like the fabulous history of Alexander it is a naïve, popular, and anonymous book, composed for the entertainment and edification of the common people rather than for educated men, and making little or no pretense to historical accuracy or literary elegance. Such books are seldom treated as the literary property of any particular author, even when they are ascribed to one; hence it is not surprising that the text of our Βίβλος Αἰσώπου has undergone substantial changes at different times according to the fancy of the unknown writers and editors who have handled it. But unlike the romance of Alexander, the biography of Aesop is concerned with a cultural, not a military hero, and in this respect it is almost without parallel among the ancient Greek texts that have come down to us. For, although many popular traditions have survived concerning the doings and sayings of Homer, Hesiod, and the Seven Wise Men of Greece, yet these are either scattered and fragmentary or else, when embodied in continuous accounts such as the *Contest between Homer and Hesiod*, the *Lives* of Homer, or Plutarch's *Banquet of the Seven Sages*, have taken on something of the formal and learned character of the environment in which they were composed or through which, at any rate, they have been transmitted to us whatever their original character may have been. In comparison with these writings the *Life of Aesop*, besides being much longer, is more naïve and romantic. It gives us the portrait of a wise man as seen through the eyes of the poor in spirit, at the same time enlivened by a spontaneous and vigorous, if somewhat homely, wit. To an educated man in later antiquity this humble book may have seemed as childish and worthless as it did to J. J. Reiske, who, in an age when ancient writings were commonly judged with reference to a severely intellectual standard, called it *eine elende Kurzweile für Hanshagel;* but one need not expect a folkbook to have the style and spirit of a classic, nor even of an ordinary piece of formal literature, and for us the *Life of Aesop* is interesting not for such artistic value as it may possess—though that too, I suspect, has been unduly disparaged—but because it is one of the few genuinely popular books that have come down from ancient times.

With the exception of a few papyrus fragments, this *Life of Aesop* has hitherto been known to scholars only through the medium of its Byzantine recensions. As a result the original character of the book has been not a little obscured. In the Morgan manuscript, however—which I shall call G—we have a version which in all essentials is *ancient*, and from which, in spite of its many corruptions, we may gain a fair idea of the form in which this naïve biography was current in the early centuries of the Roman empire. It is my intention to publish in the near future a complete text of G, along with various other Aesopica; but for the present I confine myself to a general description of its nature and to a comparison of it with the Westermann version [1] on the one hand, and with the papyri on the other.

[1] So named from its first and only modern editor, A. Westermann (Braunschweig, 1845). This version, which I shall call *W*, is preserved in a dozen or more manuscripts dating from the thirteenth to the sixteenth centuries, although Westermann's edition takes no account of these, but reproduces almost exactly the mixed text peculiar to Laur. conv. soppr. 627, from which it is derived through the medium of three successive modern copies; cf. *Text Tradition*, 204. In the passages of *W* referred to in this chapter, however, it is to be understood that Westermann's text is in substantial agreement with the best manuscript tradition, except when the contrary is explicitly stated. The archetype of *W*, which is probably not older than the eleventh century, depends upon an ancient version of the *Life* similar to that contained in the Morgan manuscript (*infra*, p. 26); while the vulgate *Life* ascribed to Planudes is derived from a late and imperfect copy of *W* (*Text Tradition*, 236–239).

The *Life of Aesop* in the Morgan manuscript extends from fol. 22^r to 67^v, and is headed Βίβλος Ξάνθο<υ> φιλοσόφου καὶ Αἰσώπου δούλου αὐτ<οῦ>· περὶ τῆς ἀναστροφῆς Αἰσώπου. At the end, on fol. 67^v, the following subscription is added: Αἰσώπου γέννα, ἀνατροφή, προκοπή, καὶ ἀποβίωσις—Τὰ μετ' εὐκολίας εὑρισκόμενα καὶ εὐκαταφρόνητα πολλοῖς εἶναι δοκεῖ. See Plate IV. The connection between these sentences and the title and order of the fables in cod. Parisinus suppl. gr. 690 is discussed below in the chapter on the *Fables* (p. 167). Illustrations are found on folios 22^r, 22^v, 23^r (two), 23^v, 24^r, 46^r, and 59^v; and blank spaces for others have been left on 51 of the remaining 85 pages of the *Life*. The text has been written by at least three different though contemporary hands (ff. 1–29, 30–60, 61–112), and we may possibly distinguish a fourth.[2] Marginal notes are few in number and consist chiefly of chapter headings and the usual signs for γνώμη and σημείωσαι. These stand opposite certain gnomic passages and may, if not added merely for the reader's convenience, have been intended to serve the purposes of an excerptor, although, as it happens, the sentences thus marked do not recur in the medieval anthologies under the name of Aesop. An isolated instance of critical notation is found on 47^v, where the words ζήτ(ει) ὧδ(ε) λείπ(ει) are placed opposite an asterisk in the text indicating a small lacuna; but elsewhere the scribe shows very little concern about the readability of his text. He misspells a great many words,[3] passes in silence over obvious lacunae, and allows a large number of hopelessly corrupt words, phrases, and sentences to stand without comment. We cannot suppose, however, that all these corruptions, or any considerable part of them, are due to the copyist of the Morgan text. It is probable, in view of the complete unintelligibility of certain passages,[4] that this manuscript, or one of its ancestors, was

[2] The writing on ff. 58–60 is in a larger and somewhat more even hand that that which precedes.

[3] E.g. ει is often written for η, ο for ω and vice versa, ι for ει or η or υ, and ε for αι.

[4] For a good example, see the text of G corresponding to line 5 of the Golenischeff papyrus, *infra*, p. 60.

copied from an archetype that had become mutilated and partially illegible. Nevertheless, it is evident that much bungling has taken place somewhere along the line, since the body of the text contains a fairly large number of glosses and variant readings that have been copied in from the margins. These readings, to which some attention will be given later on, are interesting in that they give us clues to the earlier recensions of the *Life*, and to the general condition of the text in late antiquity. Lacunae of one folio each, resulting from the loss of an entire folded sheet in the fifth quire, occur after 30^v and 36^v respectively, and there is another at the end of 49^v. The examination of these passages involves a comparison of G and W.

2. THE CONTENT AND NATURE OF G AS COMPARED WITH THE WESTERMANN RECENSION (W)

In the first lacuna the lost matter corresponds to about twenty-eight lines of Westermann's text (15, 9–16, 17) and falls within the limits of a single episode; but unless the missing folio contained an unusually large amount of blank space or illustration, we must suppose that the text of G was somewhat more lengthy in this passage than that of W, as indeed is frequently the case.

The second lacuna, coming after 36^v (= West. 22, 21), has been noted by a modern librarian who writes at the bottom of the page, in what appears to be an Italian hand of the sixteenth century or later, the following: *deest folium, nempe responsum Aesopi olitori de herbis*. Aesop's reply to the gardener is about fifteen lines long in Westermann, whereas a folio leaf of the manuscript, with space for one illustration on each side, normally contains more than twice as much. This discrepancy is only partially accounted for on the assumption that Aesop's discourse was longer in G than it is in W; for the context, which I shall presently describe, shows that other matter, not preserved in W, must have been contained on the missing leaf. In W the conversation with the gardener is followed immediately by a new and much abbreviated episode, in the first three lines of which Xanthus, having met some friends at the bath, invites them to dine with him and orders Aesop to go home and boil lentils for the occasion. In G, however, the narrative is much more detailed. After the lacuna, at the top of 37ʳ, we find Xanthus speaking to Aesop as follows: βλάπτεις με περισσότερον ἢ ἔλαττον τῶν ἐπιταττομένων σοι ποιῶν. At first sight this appears to be a complaint based upon some previous actions of Aesop; but there is nothing in the preceding text of either version that can be regarded as adequate motivation for such a complaint; and if an incident furnishing that motivation had been related on the missing folio, there would scarcely have been room thereon for certain other matter, the presence of which, as we shall see, is much more clearly indicated. On the other hand, it is not unlikely, considering that the scribe of this manuscript frequently writes ει for η or ῃ, that βλάπτεις is an error for βλάπτῃς or βλάψῃς, and that we have to do, not with a complaint, but with an exhortation (<μὴ>βλάπτῃς, a possible vulgarism in syntax, or <μὴ>βλάψῃς) looking forward to future occasions generally and to the instructions that Xanthus gives to Aesop in the next sentence. Indeed, it is quite certain, however we may interpret βλάπτεις, that Xanthus' speech was of this nature, since it is clearly referred to later on in both versions.[1] The text continues: ἆρον ἐπὶ χειρῶν σου λήκυθον[2] λέντιά τε, καὶ ἄγωμεν εἰς τὸ βαλανεῖον. Αἴσωπος πρὸς ἑαυτὸν εἶπεν· " οἱ τῷ νῷ περίπικροι περὶ διακονίαν δεσπόται κακοδαιμονίας ἑαυτοῖ<ς> γίνονται παραίτιοι·

[1] Cf. West. 23,22, ἐντέταλκάς μοι ἵνα, ὅσα ἂν ἀκούω, ἐκεῖνα πράττω. As we have seen, the instructions hereby referred to have been left out in W. G at this point has no equivalent for ἐντέταλκας, etc.; but further on, in a passage which is omitted in W but which would come at 24,21, Aesop tells Xanthus that he ought not to have demanded such literal obedience: ἔδει σε οὖν μὴ ὁρίσαι μοι νόμον, καὶ διηκόνησα ἄν σοι κατὰ τρόπους χρηστούς. ἀλλὰ μὴ μεταμελοῦ, δέσποτα· ἡ γὰρ παραγγελία σου τοῦ νόμου χρησιμωτέρα ἔστω (sc. ἔσται) σοι· διδάξει γάρ σε μὴ ἐν τοῖς ἀκροατηρίοις ἁμαρτάνειν.

[2] The manuscript reads λίκυθον. In the quotations given below I have often corrected the spelling in cases where the error is obvious and involves no ambiguity of form or meaning.

ἐγὼ τοῦτον τὸν φιλόσοφον παιδεύσω, ἵνα μάθῃ πῶς αὐτὸν δεῖ ἐπιτάττειν." Here we have the explicit motivation, missing in *W*, for many of the incidents that follow in both versions. After this soliloquy Aesop takes up an empty oil-flask, along with the towels, and follows his master to the bath; and when Xanthus, after calling for the "flask" and discovering that there is no oil in it, demands an explanation, Aesop reminds him that nothing had been said about *oil* and that he had not dared to go beyond the letter of his instructions for fear of a beating.[3] To this Xanthus makes no reply, but shortly afterwards, having met some friends, he turns to Aesop with the following meticulously detailed instructions: ὕπαγε, Αἴσωπε, εἰς τὴν οἰκίαν. καὶ ἐπειδὴ διὰ τὴν μανίαν τῆς γυναικός μου συνεπατήθη τὰ λάχανα, ἀπελθὼν φακὸν ἔψησον ἡμῖν [ὄσπριον]· καὶ βάλε αὐτὸν εἰς τὸν κάκκαβον, καὶ ὕδωρ μετ' αὐτοῦ, καὶ ἐπίθες ἐπὶ τὴν μαγειρικὴν ἑστίαν, καὶ ὑπόθες ξύλα, καὶ καῦσον.[4] ἐὰν σβεσθῇ, φύσησον. ἴδε, οὕτως ποίησον. Though he tries hard, Xanthus has not succeeded in being literally exact; he has used the singular form φακόν in a collective sense instead of the plural φακούς, and so Aesop takes advantage of him by boiling only a single lentil-seed. It is quite characteristic of the Byzantine version *W* that this incident not only lacks the motivation mentioned above, but also sacrifices the spirit of the jest by leaving out all the useless specifications in Xanthus' speech; for it is precisely in these vain efforts of Xanthus to avoid any possible misinterpretation of his orders that the real humor of the incident, such as it is, consists. Here, as often in *W*, the soul of the original narrative has departed and only the skeleton remains.

It should be noted, moreover,—and this brings us back to the lacuna in G—that the Morgan version explains, as *W* does not, why Xanthus offered lentils to his friends instead of the vegetables that had been given to him by the gardener; these vegetables had been destroyed (συνεπατήθη) by his wife

---

[3] ἔδει οὖν με μηδὲν τῶν εἰρημένων πλέον ποιεῖν, ἐπ <ε>ὶ τοῦ νόμου σφαλεὶς πληγῶν ὑπεύθυνος ἤμην. The blows that Aesop fears, may have been threatened by Xanthus in the hortatory speech above mentioned.

[4] The manuscript reads κάθου.

in a fit of anger. There can be no doubt that this episode took place as soon as Aesop returned from the garden, and that it was related on the missing folio in G. It is not quite clear how Aesop aroused the anger of his mistress on this occasion, but a later passage of G suggests that he may have boasted to her of his success in having obtained the vegetables from the gardener without cost to Xanthus, and that she had trampled upon them out of jealousy and spite. The passage to which I refer reads thus: ἐξελθὼν οὖν λέγει καθ' ἑαυτόν· " νῦν καιρός ἐστιν τοῦ μετελθεῖν με τὴν μῆνιν τὴν πρὸς τὴν κυράν, ἀνθ' ὧν με ἀγορασθέντα ἔσκωψεν καὶ ἐκακολόγει, καὶ ὅτι τὰ δωρηθέντα μοι ὑπὸ τοῦ κηπουροῦ λάχανα σκορπίσασα συνεπάτησεν, καὶ οὐκ ἀφῆκεν μου τὴν δωρεὰν εὐχαρῆ τῷ δεσπότῃ μου γενέσθαι. This gives us a good idea of the episode contained on the missing leaf.

In looking back over the original contents of G, both in and beyond the lacuna, we see that the narrative of events following Aesop's conversation with the gardener and ending with the boiling of the lentils must have totalled about two pages (including 37^r entire) and that all this is passed over by *W* in five lines (West. 23,6–10).

After 49^v there is another long lacuna in the text, in spite of the fact that in this region none of the original leaves of G itself appears to be missing.[5] From this circumstance, and from the fact that the lost matter is approximately equal in amount to that which would be contained on a single folio with illustrations (or on a folio without illustrations but having a somewhat fuller text than that of *W*), one is tempted

[5] Concerning this point, Dr. Husselman writes me as follows: "As for the lacuna in the text between ff. 49 and 50 there is absolutely no indication of it in the structure of the manuscript. Ff. 45–52 form a quire in-8, and there is a complete quire (ff. 37–44) preceding it and three following it, all in-8, with no sign of any loss. If a folio is missing between 49 and 50, we should also have one missing between 47 and 48, the corresponding half of the sheet. Otherwise the folio presumed to be lost would have to have been an extra half sheet, glued into the original quire. I do not believe that that would be done unless the scribe found it necessary to supply something omitted in the copying, or to add new material. And there is no indication of such a practice elsewhere in the manuscript."

to infer that the exact pagination of the archetype from which G was copied has been preserved in G also, and that the lacuna, which shows every evidence of being unintentional so far as the scribes were concerned, was caused originally by the loss of a leaf in that archetype. The episode that has been lost in this lacuna had to do with the sexual prowess of Aesop as well as with his command of parables; hence it is natural to suppose that the leaf on which it was written, if not lost accidentally, was deliberately torn out of the codex, either by way of expurgation or for private circulation. The same fate has likewise befallen this story in the Westermann recension, where it is preserved only in two manuscripts representative of the oldest tradition (O and Lo) and where its subsequent loss, or excision, has resulted in marked disturbances to the context of the later tradition appearing in Mon. 525 and λ.[6] In order that the reader may have a clear idea of the substance of what has been lost in the lacuna of G, I print here the text of the Latin translation in Lo:

Venientes autem in domo, dixit Esopus ad dominum suum, "Ecce recuperavi domos tuas; dignus sum accipere libertatem." Sanctus respondet, "Malum cogitasti; non habeo hoc in mente." Esopus, ut hoc audivit, tristis factus est et ait intra se, "Expecta me, et ego faciam te † vidi mulier puta.†"[7]

Quadam die Esopus sustulit pallium suum et tenebat manu membrum suum ad excitandum. Uxor vero Sancti vidit eum et dixit ei, "Esope, quid est hoc?" Esopus respondet,

[6] *Text Tradition*, 208f.; *cf.* West. 35,32.

[7] The sense required would be satisfied by, e.g., *vindictam plenam*. The introductory sentences thus far have a partial equivalent in G: Αἴσωπος τῷ Ξάνθῳ λέγει· "τὸν βίον σου ἔσωσα· ἄξιός εἰμι ἐλευθερίας τυχεῖν." Ξάνθος· "οὐκ ἡσυχάζεις; τοῦτο γὰρ κἀγὼ οὐκ ἐννόουν;" ὁ δὲ Αἴσωπος λυπηθείς, οὐκ ἐπὶ τὸ <μὴ> λαβεῖν τὴν ἐλευθερίαν ἀλλ' ἐπὶ τὸ ἀχαριστηθῆναι, ἀνείχετο. καὶ εἶπεν ὁ Ξάνθος· "τὴν ἐμὴν σωτηρίδα—and here the text breaks off. O, representing the archteype of W, reads as follows: ἐλθόντος δὲ αὐτοῦ εἰς τὴν οἰκίαν, προσελθὼν αὐτῷ ὁ Ἔσωπος λέγει· "ὁ πάντα σου τὸν βίον σώσας ἄξιός εἰμι (ἀξιώσῃς μοι *cod.*) τυχεῖν ἐλευθερίας." ὁ δὲ Ξάνθος ὑβρίσας ἐδίωξεν αὐτόν, λέγων· "τί; ἐγὼ τοῦτο οὐκ ἐνεθυμούμην;" Ἔσωπος δὲ ἀχαριστηθεὶς ἐλυπήθη καὶ φησι· "ἐγώ σοι ἀνταμύνομαι (ἀταμείνομαι *cod.*)."

"Domina, habui frigus in hac nocte et adiuvat me si teneo illum in manu mea." ⁸ Videns mulier longitudinem praepucii et crassitudinem concupivit, et clamavit eum et dixit, "Esope, nunc autem si mihi facies quod volo plus gaudebis quam dominus tuus." Et ille respondet, "Scis, domina, si dominus meus hoc senserit malum mihi erit; per iusticiam reddet mihi malum meritum." Illa vero subridens dixit, "Si mecum decem vices concubueris, pallium unum dabo tibi." Esopus inquid, "Iura mihi." Illa pro magno ardore quem habebat iuravit ei. Credidit autem Esopus ei. Voluit reddere meritum domino suo, et concubuit cum ea novem vicibus et dixit, "Domina, plus non possum." Illa incensa ex ardore dixit, "Si decem vices non facis, non accipies a me aliquid." Et tunc cepit facere decimam et fecit cadere semen in coxa eius. Et ait Esopus, "Da mihi pallium; et si non, interpello pro hoc ad dominum meum." Mulier ait, "Ego te vocavi ut cultares agrum meum, tu autem transisti limitem et laborasti in extraneo campo. Fac unam vicem et tolle pallium." Veniente autem Sancto, ivit Esopus <et> ait domino suo, "Domine, iudica me insimul cum domina mea." Audiens Sanctus dixit, "Quid?" Esopus inquid, "Ego et domina mea ambulavimus in pomerium unum et vidit ramum arboris plenum malis et dixit mihi 'si potes mittere petram unam et disrumpere decem mala, do tibi pallium unum.' Tul[l]i petram et proieci[t] eam et disrupavi mala decem. Unum autem malum cecidit in stercore, et modo non vult mihi dare tunicam." Audiens haec mulier dixit viro suo, "Manifestissime de novem non est contencio, sed de decimo malo, quod cecidit

---

⁸ sustulit—mea] μονωθεὶς ἐκδυσάμενος καὶ τὰς χεῖρας ἑαυτοῦ κροτῶν καὶ τινάσσων ἤρξατο ποιεῖν τὸ ποιμενικὸν καὶ ἄτακτον σχῆμα. ἡ δὲ τοῦ Ξάνθου γυνὴ ἐκ τοῦ οἴκου αἴφνης καταλαβοῦσα φησίν· "Ἔσωπε, τί τοῦτο;" ὁ δὲ λέγει· "κυρία, εὐεργετοῦ με καὶ τὴν γαστέρα ὀφέλει" O. Since O and Lo are very closely related throughout, it is difficult to say which of these two versions is the older. I suspect, however, that Lo gives us the sense of the original passage, inasmuch as O has elsewhere rewritten the text of a few sentences merely for the sake of displaying his knowledge of ancient or poetic diction (*Text Tradition*, 233f.), and Aesop's reply in Lo is much more plausible than in O.

in stercore, non est mihi aptum; mittat iterum et disrumpat malum et tollat pallium." Iudicavit autem Sanctus ut daret ad Esopum pallium. Et [Esopus] ait dominus ad Esopum, "Eamus usque in foro, et postquam venerimus ab eo disrumpe malum decimum et tolle pallium." Uxor autem Sancti dixit, "Ita faciat, domine, et ego vere sicut praecepisti dabo ei pallium." [9]

[9] This unusual *novella* has apparently never been published before. Paul Marc, who was the first to call attention to its presence in O and Lo, cites a closely parallel story in Balzac's *Contes Drolatiques*, entitled "Comment fut basty le Chasteau d'Azay." At the end Balzac intimates—whether truthfully or in mere jest I would not venture to say—that the story he has told was an old one in France, and that it had also been localized in Austria: "This lucky adventure has been handed down from father to son, from lord to lord, in the said place of Azay-les-Ridel, where the story frisks still under the curtains of the king, which have been curiously respected down to the present day. It is therefore the falsest of falsities which attributes the dozen of the Tourainian to a German knight, who by this deed would have secured the domains of Austria to the House of Hapsburgh. The author of our days, who brought this history to light, although a learned man, has allowed himself to be deceived by certain chroniclers, since the archives of the Roman empire make no mention of an acquisition of this kind. I am angry with him for having believed that a 'braguette,' nourished with beer, could have been equal to the alchemical operations of the Chinonian 'braguettes' so much esteemed by Rabelais." (From an anonymous English translation, London 1874.) The similarity between Balzac's tale and the ancient one about Aesop is so remarkable that it is difficult to believe that there is no historical connection between them. Can it be that some unknown person, having read this story in O or Lo, or some lost MS, passed it on directly or indirectly to Balzac? Or is its circulation in modern Europe, whether oral or written, to be traced, perhaps, to one of the leaves that were torn out of the manuscripts of the *Life of Aesop?* Does it occur in the French or Italian *Novellistik* of the Renaissance? My friend, Professor Arthur Hamilton, tells me that he once read a very similar story, the reference to which unfortunately he cannot supply but which, according to his recollection, appeared in a French periodical around the year 1912. It was entitled *Le Maître de Dix*, and involved both the wager relating to 'ten' (not twelve, as in Balzac), and the pleading of the resulting dispute by means of parables before the woman's husband. In this case the lover was a Moor who had found his way into the harem of a Moslem judge. The clever device of stating a case of this nature in terms of a parable (relating to the cultivation of a field) is found also in the story of the king who makes love to the peasant's wife in the Greek version of the *Seven Wise Masters*.

Such, in outline, is the episode that has been lost in the lacuna. There remain, however, some distinct traces of it in the text beginning at the top of 50ʳ: ἐπεὶ κἀγὼ ἀκηδιώδης εἰμί, ἕως τὰ πρὸς τὸ δεῖπνον γένηται, ἐλθὲ σὺν ἐμοὶ ἔξω τῆς πύλης <ἵνα> διακινήσωμεν· ἅμα δὲ καὶ τὸ ὑπόλοιπον τινάξεις κοκκύμηλον καὶ ἐνέγκῃς τῇ κυρίᾳ σου, ἵνα τὰ ἱμάτια λάβῃς (small lacuna).[10] ὁ δεσπότης· " ἐπειδὴ σὺ νεόνητος εἶ, ἔξελθε καὶ ἴδε πρὸ τοῦ πυλῶνος ἢ οἰονιστής ἐστι δύσκολος. ἐὰν ἴδῃς δικόρονον, ἑστὼς πρὸ τοῦ πυλῶνος κάλει με· εὐφροσύνην γὰρ δηλοῖ τὸ σημεῖον τῷ εἰδότι." προελθὼν οὖν ὁ Αἴσωπος κτλ. This passage is noteworthy not only because it contains an explicit reference to the lost episode, but also because its manifold corruption is more or less typical of what we find elsewhere in the Morgan manuscript. If I am not mistaken, the original text after ὁ δεσπότης read somewhat as follows: ἐπειδὴ οἰωνιστής εἰμι, ἔξελθε καὶ ἴδε πρὸ τοῦ πυλῶνος. ἐὰν ἴδῃς κτλ. There is no point in G's νεόνητος; and O's reading, δεδόνιστός εἰμι ἔξελθε...πυλῶνος, makes perfect sense if we substitute οἰωνιστής for the meaningless δεδόνιστος. Moreover, the words τῷ εἰδότι imply that Xanthus considers himself skilled as an interpreter of omens, and that he thinks it worth while to herald the fact. ἢ οἰονιστής ἐστι δύσκολος is probably one of the numerous marginal comments that have crept into the text. Conceivably, it represents an indirect report of a variant reading, οἰωνιστής εἰμι δύσκολος (i.e. "hard to satisfy"); or perhaps δύσκολος is merely a scribal comment; in any case it should be bracketed, although it shows, I think, that οἰωνιστής, not νεώνητος, originally stood in this passage.

In addition to the three major lacunae described above, there are a number of smaller gaps in the text; but of these nothing need be said here.

Certain episodes which are extant in G but not in W have already been described. It remains to speak of other matter belonging in this category in order that, by a general survey

[10] At this point O has the following irrelevant sentence in place of Lo's ita faciat: ἡ δὲ εἶπεν· " μὴ θέλῃ, κύριε, ἵνα σὺ βάλλει ἐξ αὐτω." And the next sentence, which agrees with Lo, reads: " ἐγὼ δὲ ὡς ἐκέλευσας δώσω τὰ ἱμάτια." Lo is undoubtedly right.

of the contents of G as compared with those of W, we may exhibit in as clear relief as possible the nature as well as the substance of the older version. We may begin with a consideration of the longer and more significant passages.

The miracle by which Aesop was given the power of speech is related very briefly in W (West. 9, 8–22), without any direct discourse, and in a disinterested, matter-of-fact tone: We read that a certain priest (or priests) of Isis,[11] who had lost his way and wandered onto the estate, being hospitably received by Aesop, prayed for him out of gratitude upon his departure; that thereafter Aesop went to sleep, and that Philoxenia (or Τύχη), standing over him bestowed upon him the various gifts of eloquence and wit for which he afterwards became famous. In G the course of events is much the same in outline; but the details are different, and the whole narrative is more elaborate, more naïvely ideal, and more religious in tone. It is a priestess of Isis, not a priest or a bevy of priests, who is befriended by Aesop, and her prayer to Isis is conceived in the living spirit of that religion: " διάδημα τῆς ὅλης οἰκουμένης, Ἶσι μυριώνυμε, ἐλέησον τόνδε τὸν ἐργάτην, τὸν κακοπαθοῦντα, τὸν εὐσεβῆ, ἀνθ' ὧν εὐσέβησεν οὐκ εἰς ἐμέ, δέσποινα, ἀλλ' εἰς τὸ σὸν σχῆμα. καὶ εἰ μὴ πολυτάλαντον τὸν βίον αὐτοῦ διορθώσασθαι βούλει, ὃν ἄλλοι θεοὶ ἀφῄρηνται, τὸ γοῦν λαλεῖν αὐτῷ χάρισαι· δυνατὴ γὰρ σὺ καὶ τὰ ἐν σκότει πεπτωκότα πάλιν εἰς φῶς προελέσθαι." εὐξαμένης δὲ ταῦτα τῆς ἱεροφόρου ἡ Ἶσις, ἡ κυρία, ὑπήκουσεν· ταχὺ γὰρ ὁ περὶ εὐσεβείας λόγος εἰς τὰς τῶν θεῶν ἀκοὰς καταντᾷ.

Meanwhile Aesop, made drowsy by the noonday heat,

[11] The tradition of this passage in the Westermann recension is much confused. The oldest of the various readings within the W tradition is probably οἱ ἱερεῖς τῆς Ἴσιδος, followed later by Τύχη in place of Φιλοξενία. This is found in Mon. 525. O has οἱ ἱερεῖς τῆς Ἴσιδος and Φιλοξενία, but the latter is probably due to contamination with the SBP family. P and Laur. conv. soppr. 627, which represent the archetype of SBP, have ὁ ἱερεὺς τῆς Ἴσιδος—Φιλοξενία; but this, although in some respects a better reading, probably comes from an older source outside the W recension (*Text Tradition*, 226–230) and may be a compound. SB's reading, οἱ ἱερεῖς τῆς Ἀρτέμιδος—Τύχη is borrowed from λ (LFV), where it probably originated. For the symbols here used and the relationships between the manuscripts, see below, pp. 175ff.

decides to quit work and devote the two-hour recess, which is allowed him each day at whatever time he chooses to take it, to sleep. Accordingly he selects a suitable place in which to lie down; and here follows an elaborate *ecphrasis* in the style of the bucolic poets, of which there is no trace in W and which must have been quite effective in its way, when it was first composed and before it had become as hopelessly corrupt as it is in the Morgan manuscript. I quote the text with such emendations as occur to me, although the passage as a whole is quite beyond remedy: ἐπιλεξάμενος δέ τινα τόπον τοῦ κτήματος εὐθαλέστερον καὶ ἀπαρενόχλητον, δενδρώδη καὶ κατάσκιον, εἰς ὃν χλοερᾶς βοτάνης παμποίκιλον ἄνθος ἐπηύξανεν καὶ διὰ τὴν παρακειμένην ὕλην καὶ λιβάδα <εἰς> τὸν τόπον κατέληξεν,[12] <Αἴσωπ> ος ταῖς βοτάναις προσκλίνας καὶ τὴν γηηπόνον (τῇ γῇ πόνῳ cod.) προσβαλὼν δίκελλαν, τὸν μάνδικα καὶ τὴν μηλωτὴν πρὸς κεφαλὴν θέμενος, ἀνεπαύετο. ἔνθα [τῶν πέριξ δένδρων] ὁ ποταμὸς ἤχει. <καὶ> μαλακοῦ πνεύματος ὄντος ἀνέμου ἐπ' (ἐφ' cod.) ὄρους <τὰ> χλοερὰ τιναχθέντα φυτὰ κατέπνευσεν αὔραν τῆς πέριξ ὕλης[13] ἡδεῖαν καὶ προσηνῆ [προσέφερον]. καὶ πολὺς ἐπὶ κλάδοις ἐτετερίζετο (sic) τέττιξ, καὶ ποικίλων ὀρνέων καὶ πολυνόμων ἤχει[14] τὸ θρύλλημα. ὅπου μὲν γὰρ ἦν πολύθρους ἔνδον συμπάθεια (συνπαθῶν cod.), ἐλαίας ἐπῇδον (ἐν· παθοι cod.) μὲν οἱ κλάδοι, ἐπὶ δὲ λεπτοτάτης πίτυος ὁρμὴ ἀεροπετὴς[15] ἀπεδίδου μίμημα κοσσύφου. καὶ [μιγνυμένη σύνοδος] ἡ φωνόμιμος ἅμα πᾶσι κατέκραζεν ἠχώ. αὐτὸ δὲ τὸ κεκρα[γο]μένον ἐξ ἁπάντων εὐμελὲς ψιθύρισμα. ἐφ' ὧν ψυχαγωγούμενος ὁ Αἴσωπος εἰς ἡδὺν ὕπνον κατήγετο.

[12] A small *lemniscus* (⨪) is placed opposite and slightly above κατέληξεν; which means, I suppose, that the following passage is considered spurious or corrupt; cf. Gardthausen, *Gr. Palaeographie*² 414. Here and in what follows it is not unlikely that the confusion has resulted from the compounding of different readings or marginal additions.

[13] I have adopted Professor L. A. Post's felicitous emendation τῆς πέριξ ὕλης in place of the following reading of the manuscript: τὴν περὶ φυτῶν τῶν ἀνθέων ὕλην. As Professor Post observes, the phrase τῶν πέριξ δένδρων above is probably a marginal variant or gloss for τῆς πέριξ ὕλης; while the latter phrase in turn has been corrupted by the intrusion of another gloss on φυτά (i.e. φυτὰ τῶν ἀνθέων) which displaced the ξ of πέριξ. τήν...ὕλην for τῆς...ὕλης may be due to the influence of the accusatives αὔραν and ἡδεῖαν.

[14] πολὺν ὄρον ὑχει cod.

[15] ἀεροπετὴς Post, ἠροπῆτες cod.

This description, as a whole, is probably as old as the context in which it stands; but the verbal complexities and grammatical incongruities with which it abounds can scarcely be accounted for otherwise than by supposing them due to the infiltration of marginal notes of one kind or another.

While Aesop slept, the goddess Isis came to him in company with the nine Muses and, addressing them, said: "ὁρᾶτε, θυγατέρες, [εὐσεβείας κατακάλυμμα] τὸν ἄνθρωπον τοῦτον, πεπλασμένον μὲν ἀμόρφως, νικῶντα δὲ εἰς εὐσέβειαν (ἀμορφίαν cod.) πάντα ψόγον· οὗτός ποτε τὴν ἐμὴν διάκονον πεπλανημένην ὡδήγησεν, πάρειμι δὲ σὺν ὑμῖν ἀνταμείψασθαι τὸν ἄνθρωπον. ἐγὼ μὲν οὖν τὴν φωνὴν ἀποκαθίστημι, ὑμεῖς δὲ τῇ φωνῇ τὸν ἄριστον χαρίσασθε λόγον." εἰποῦσα[ι] δὲ ταῦτα καὶ τὸ τραχὺ τῆς γλώττης ἀποτεμοῦσα[ι], τὸ κωλῦον αὐτὸν λαλεῖν, αὐτή (ἄτε cod.) δὴ ἡ Ἶσις ἐχαρίσατο <τὴν φωνήν> [τὸν λόγον καὶ Ἕλληνα λόγων μυθικῶν εὑρέσεις], ἔπεισεν δὲ καὶ τὰς λοιπὰς Μούσας ἑκάστη<ν> τι τῆς ἰδίας δωρεᾶς χαρίσασθαι. αἱ δὲ ἐχαρίσαντο λόγων εὕρεμα (sic), καὶ μύθων Ἑλληνικῶν πλοκήν, καὶ ποιήσεις. κατευξαμένη δὲ ἡ θεὸς ὅπως ἔνδοξος γένηται, εἰς ἑαυτὴν ἐχώρησεν. καὶ αἱ Μοῦσαι δὲ ἑκάστη τὸ ἴδιον χαρισάμεναι εἰς τὸ Ἑλικῶνα (ἑλικὸν cod.) ἀνέβησαν ὄρος.

The association of Isis with the Muses is an interesting bit of Hellenistic syncretism, about which others who are better qualified may speak.[16] More important for us, since it concerns the *Leitmotif* of the entire biography, is the fact that the Muses, to which there is not a single reference in the Westermann recension,[17] are frequently alluded to in the Morgan text. Aesop, Xanthus and his wife, the scholars, and even the Samians swear by the Muses,[18] and there are other incidental allusions to them.[19] Moreover, their sig-

[16] Cf. Plut. *Is. et Osir.* 3, διὸ καὶ τῶν ἐν Ἑρμοῦ πόλει Μουσῶν τὴν προτέραν Ἶσιν ἅμα καὶ Δικαιοσύνην καλοῦσι κτλ.

[17] μοῦσαι in West. 28,8 means "arts" and has no reference to the goddesses themselves.

[18] Isis, on the other hand, is mentioned only once outside the passages already quoted, namely, by Aesop in addressing the slave dealer: μὰ τὴν Ἶσιν, πολύ σε ὠφελήσω.

[19] Aesop is said to have ἀπὸ Μουσῶν τὸ φρόνημα, and he repeatedly uses the expression ὁ προστάτης τῶν Μουσῶν instead of Apollo; see below, p. 18.

nificance in the life of Aesop is formally signalized on three different occasions: at Samos, where Aesop establishes a sanctuary of the Muses and places Mnemosyne instead of Apollo in the center of the sculptured group; at Babylon, where King Lycurgus orders a golden statue to be made of Aesop "together with the Muses"; [20] and at Delphi, where Aesop takes refuge, not at the shrine of Apollo (as in *W*), but at that of the Muses. The first and last of these three incidents are closely related and taken together belong to an important thread of motivation which underlies the whole legend of Aesop and of which there is no trace in *W*. For the Phrygian Aesop, like the Phrygian Marsyas in the ancient myth, is a champion of the native talent of the common folk as opposed to the formal learning of the aristocrats and academicians whose god is Apollo; [21] and it is the deep-seated opposition between these two types of culture that explains why Aesop is the protégé of the relatively humble, though universal Muses, to the exclusion of the aristocratic Apollo, who is usually associated with them; and why, like Marsyas, having offended that proud deity, his death is brought about at Delphi by the god's followers and with the connivance of the god himself. The popular fable-lore of Aesop and his homely wit are thought of as standing in somewhat the same relation to the Apolline formality of the academy as represented by Xanthus and his pupils, as does the wild flute-music of Marsyas to the aristocratic lyre of Apollo and the epic poets. The beginning of Apollo's anger, of which there is no hint in *W*, is thus related in G: ὁ δὲ Αἴσωπος θύσας (θυσίαις cod.) ταῖς Μούσαις ἱερὸν κατεσκεύασε αὐταῖς,[22] στήσας μέσον αὐτῶν Μνημοσύνην (-οσυνον cod.), οὐκ Ἀπόλλωνα. ὁ Ἀπόλλων ὀργισθείς (sic) αὐτῷ ὡς τῷ Μαρσύᾳ. Later (as in the Golenischeff papyrus,

[20] ἐκέλευσεν οὖν ὁ Λυκοῦργος ἀνδριάντα χρυσοῦν ἀναθῆναι (ἀχθῆναι cod.) τῷ Αἰσώπῳ μετὰ καὶ τῶν Μουσῶν· καὶ ἐποίησεν ἑορτὴν μεγάλην ἐπὶ τῇ τοῦ Αἰσώπου σοφίᾳ.

[21] *Cf.* Hausrath, *Philologische Wochenschrift* LI (1931), 67.

[22] κ. αὐταῖς] The manuscript reads κατασκευάσας; and αὐταῖς, which may be a false addition, comes after μέσον.

infra, p. 61), when the Delphians plot against Aesop, the anger of Apollo is again alluded to: ἐβουλεύσαντο οὖν ἀνελεῖν δόλῳ. καὶ τοῦ Ἀπόλλωνος μηνίοντος διὰ (δὲ cod.) τὴν ἐν Σάμῳ ἀτιμίαν, ἐπεὶ σὺν ταῖς Μούσαις ἑαυτὸν οὐ καθίδρυσεν, μὴ ἔχοντες εὔλογον αἰτίαν ἐμηχανήσαντό τι πανοῦργον, ἵνα μὴ οἱ παραδημοῦντες δυνήσονται (sic) αὐτῷ βοηθῆσαι. Accordingly, when Aesop is being led to the cliff, he takes refuge at the small shrine of his patron deities the Muses (ἐν τῷ ἱερῷ τῶν Μουσῶν) instead of at the larger sanctuary of the hostile Apollo; and this fact enables us to see for the first time the real point in the fable about the hare and the beetle, which Aesop relates to the Delphians while they are dragging him away from the shrine; for, as the eagle was made to suffer for having despised the humble asylum given by the beetle to the hare who had sought his protection, so too the Delphians may repent of their action if they violate the little shrine of the Muses by dragging away the suppliant Aesop.[23] At the end of this fable Aesop exhorts the Delphians to revere, not Apollo as in *W*, but Zeus Xenios. There is no explicit statement in either version that Apollo was responsible for avenging the death of Aesop, although that might be, and has been, inferred from the words οἱ Δελφοὶ χρησμὸν ἔλαβον κτλ. in *W* (West. 57,18); but in G we learn that this oracle did not come from Apollo but from Zeus. This solves what Hausrath (*Philologische Wochenschrift* LI [1931], 66) is pleased to call *das eigentliche Problem* suggested by the Golenischeff papyrus, namely, why Apollo, who was no friend of Aesop but, according to the papyrus, had connived at his death, should avenge that death on his followers: the vengeance came from Zeus Xenios.

The speeches of Aesop are sometimes longer in G than in *W* and what he says is often more lively and naïve. Thus, when the steward, Zenas, sends a fellow servant to summon Aesop into his presence, the latter replies with a spirited harangue

[23] Although the redactor of *W* has substituted the shrine of Apollo for that of the Muses, he nevertheless keeps Aesop's explicit allusion to the *smallness* of the shrine at the end of the fable.

upon the evils of serving a master whose authority is delegated. The dialogue runs as follows: " Αἴσωπε, ῥίψας τὴν δίκελλαν ἀκολούθει· καλεῖ σε ὁ δεσπότης." ὁ δέ φησιν· " ποῖος δεσπότης; ὁ κατὰ φύσιν ἢ οἰκονόμος; καταδήλου οὖν, καὶ διαστήσας λέγε ' ὁ οἰκονόμος' καὶ μὴ ' ὁ δεσπότης.' καὶ γὰρ καὶ αὐτὸς ὑπὸ τὸν ζυγὸν τῆς δουλείας τέτακται ὡς δοῦλος." * * * ἡ δὲ καταστροφὴ αὐτοῦ τί; ἀφ' οὗ ἤρξατο λαλεῖν περίεργος γέγονεν." ὁ δὲ Αἴσωπος ῥίψας τὴν δίκελλάν φησιν· " ὡς πονηρὰ παραδεδομένη δουλεία, καὶ πρὸς τούτῳ (ταύτην cod.) θεοῖς ἦν ἐχθρά. ' Αἴσωπε, τὸν τρίκλινον στρῶσον. Αἴσωπε, τὸ βαλανεῖον ὑπόκαυσον. Αἴσωπε, ὕδωρ πλῆσον. Αἴσωπε, τοῖς κτήμασι τροφὰς παράβαλε.' ὅσα ἐστὶν μοχθηρὰ ἢ κοπηρὰ (-ερὰ cod.) ἢ λύπης μεστὰ ἢ δούλια, πάντα τῷ Αἰσώπῳ ἐπιτάσσεται ἄγειν. μὴ γὰρ οὐκ ἔχω τὸν ἀπὸ θεῶν μοι μερισθέντα λόγον; ἐλεύσεται ὁ δεσπότης <καὶ> τῆς εὐκαιρίας <τυχὼν> κατηγορήσας αὐτοῦ μεταστήσω τῆς οἰκονομίας. νῦν δὲ ἀνάγκη ὑποτάσσεσθαι. οὕτως ἡγοῦ, σύνδουλε." παρεγένοντο δέ, καί φησιν· " ἰδοὺ, κύριε, ὁ Αἴσωπος." ὁ δὲ Ζηνᾶς φησιν· " ἀρχέμπορε, καταμάνθανε." All this is reduced in W to one short, uninteresting sentence (West. 11, 4–5): ὁ δὲ Ζηνᾶς στείλας ἐκάλεσεν Αἴσωπον καί φησι τῷ ἐμπόρῳ· " ἰδού, ὁ παῖς."

Another long harangue by Aesop is addressed to his master's wife; but, as this is partly preserved in W (West. 21,26–22,11), there is no need of reproducing it in full. G here differs from W in depicting with more sarcasm and in greater detail the stages by which Xanthus' wife would presumably make love to a beautiful slave. At the end Xanthus gives a humorous turn to the whole affair by warning his wife against Aesop's eloquence: καὶ ταῦτα μέν σοι οὕτως εἶπεν, κυρά· βλέπε μή σε ἴδῃ χέζουσαν ἢ ο<ὐ>ροῦσαν, ἐπεὶ ὄψει Αἴσωπον Δημοσθένην καθαρόν! The reference is to a previous lecture addressed by Aesop to Xanthus on the road (West. 18,14–24).

Before Aesop was brought to the house, Xanthus' wife has hoped and dreamed that the newly-purchased servant would be beautiful; but when the event proves otherwise, she complains that she has been deceived by her dream. An opportunity is thus given to Aesop to explain why dreams are sometimes deceptive, and this he does by means of an aetiological fable,—one which obviously belongs to an early Aesopic tradition, but which, so far as I know at present, is not elsewhere preserved. Aesop says: μὴ ξενίζου, κυρά, ἐπὶ τῷ ἐσκελίσθαί σε τῷ ἐνυπνίῳ, οὐ γὰρ πάντες ἀληθεῖς εἰσιν οἱ ὄνειροι. δεομένῳ γὰρ τῷ προστάτῃ τῶν Μουσῶν ὁ Ζεὺς ἐχαρίσατο τὴν μαντικήν, ὥστε καὶ πάντας τοὺς ἐν χρησμῷ ὑπερέχειν.[24] ὁ δὲ προστάτης τῶν Μουσῶν, ὑπὸ πάντων θαυμαζόμενος ἀνθρώπων, τῶν ἄλλων ὑπερφρονεῖν πάντων νομίσας,[25] ἀλαζονότερος (sic) ἦν ἐν τοῖς ἄλλοις ἅπασιν. διὸ ὁ τούτου μείζων ὀργισθεὶς καὶ μὴ θέλων τοῦτον παρὰ ἀνθρώποις τοσοῦτον ἰσχύειν, ἔπλασέν τινας (τε cod.) ὀνείρους ἀληθεῖς, οἵτινες ἔλεγον ἐν τοῖς ὕπνοις τὰ μέλλοντα γίνεσθαι. ἐπιγνοὺς δὲ ὁ μείζων τῶν Μουσῶν ὡς οὐδεὶς αὐτοῦ (-ὸν cod.) χρείαν ἔχει τῆς μαντικῆς ἕνεκεν, ἠρώτησεν τὸν Δία καταλλαγῆναι αὐτῷ καὶ μὴ ἀκυρῶσαι αὐτοῦ τὴν μαντικήν. ὁ δὲ καταλλαγεὶς αὐτῷ [καὶ], οὕτως ὀνείρους ἑτέρους ἔπλασεν εἰς τοὺς ἀνθρώπους ὅπως αὐτοῖς καθ᾽ ὕπνους ψευδῆ δεικνύωσι (-ύουσι cod.), ἵνα πλανηθέντες τὴν ἀκρίβειαν πάλιν ὑπὸ τὴν τοῦ πρωτοτύπου καταφύγωσι μαντείαν. διὰ ταύτην τοίνυν τὴν αἰτίαν ὁ προπλασθεὶς ὄνειρος, ἐὰν ἐπιστῇ, ἀληθινὸν ἐμφαίνει τὸ ἐνύπνιον.[26] ὥστε οὖν μὴ θαυμάσῃς (-εις cod.) ὅτι ἄλλα μὲν καθ᾽ ὕπνους ἑώρακας, ἄλλα δὲ ἀπέβη (ἐπέβη cod.)· οὐ γὰρ ἦν ὁ πρότερος ὃν ἐθεάσω, ἀλλὰ σοί (σὺ cod.) τις τῶν ψευδηγόρων παρέστη ψεύδεσιν ἐξαπατῶν ἐνυπνίοις. We learn from Plato that aetiological fables of this kind were quite in the manner of Aesop;[27] and the few such that have survived in the traditional corpus are among the most genuine and best attested by ancient authors.[28]

As a professional philosopher Xanthus is a sorry figure.

[24] ὥστε...ὑπερέχειν] This clause in the manuscript follows ἄλλοις ἅπασιν below, but I can make no sense of it in that position.

[25] It may be suspected that the phrase τῶν ἄλλων...νομίσας is a variant reading for ὑπὸ...ἀνθρώπων. In the text as we have it, νομίσας must be taken in the sense of εἰωθώς.

[26] ἐμφαίνοντὸ ἐνύπνιον cod.

[27] In the Phaedo (60c) Socrates, in commenting upon the strangely close connection between pleasure and pain, says: καί μοι δοκεῖ, εἰ ἐνενόησεν αὐτὰ Αἴσωπος, μῦθον ἂν συνθεῖναι ὡς ὁ θεὸς βουλόμενος αὐτὰ διαλλάξαι πολεμοῦντα, ἐπειδὴ οὐκ ἐδύνατο, συνῆψεν εἰς ταὐτὸν αὐτοῖς τὰς κορυφάς, καὶ διὰ ταῦτα ᾧ ἂν τὸ ἕτερον παραγένηται ἐπακολουθεῖ ὕστερον καὶ τὸ ἕτερον.

[28] Cf. Hausrath, Pauly-Wissowa VI, 2, 1718.

Throughout both versions he is repeatedly humiliated by Aesop in the presence of others. The climax, however, is reached when, being publicly asked by his fellow-citizens to explain a portent, he finds himself unable to do so. His despair under these circumstances, and his consequent resolve to commit suicide, are described at great length in G and with more dramatic effect than in W, where the story is reduced to about seventeen lines (West. 39,20–40,2). G reads as follows:

οἱ δὲ Σάμιοι εἰς ἀγωνίαν γενόμενοι οὐκ εἰς ὀλίγην συμφορὰν ἀπετράπησαν, μέγα τι τὸ σημεῖον νομίσαντες εἶναι. καὶ εὐθέως μάντεις καὶ ἱερεῖς (sic) παρεκάλουν ὅπως τὸ σημεῖον τὸ γενόμενον διαλύσωνται. μηδενὸς οὖν δυναμένου τὸ σημεῖον διαλύσασθαι, ἀναστάς τις ἐκ τοῦ πλήθους πρεσβύτης ἔφη· " Ἄνδρες Σάμιοι, τούτοις μέλλομεν προσέχειν οἵτινες τὸ (τι cod.) ἀπ' ἀρχῆς γαστέρα πληροῦνται <καὶ> εὐσχημόνως τὸν βίον διακυβεύουσιν. ἀγνοεῖτε δὲ ὅτι οὐκ ἔστιν εὔκολον σημεῖον ἐπιλύσασθαι· εἰ μὴ γάρ τίς ἐστιν ἔμπρακτος παιδείας σημεῖον οὐ καταδιέρεται (sc. καταδιαιρεῖται). παρ' ἡμῖν δέ ἐστιν Ξάνθος ὁ φιλόσοφος ὃν ὅλη ἡ Ἑλλὰς οἶδεν· αὐτοῦ δεηθῶμεν ἵνα τὸ σημεῖον διαλύσηται." καθεζομένου δὲ τοῦ Ξάνθου ἐπεφώνουν καὶ ἐδέοντο παρακαλοῦντες ὅπως διακρίνῃ (-ει cod.) τὸ σημεῖον. ὁ δὲ Ξάνθος ἔστη εἰς τὸ μέσον καὶ μηδὲν εὑρίσκων κατὰ νοῦν εἰπεῖν ἔλαβεν διωρίαν ὅπως τὸ σημεῖον ἐπιλύσῃ. μελλούσης δὲ τῆς ἐκκλησίας λύεσθαι ὁ ἀετὸς πάλιν καταπτὰς ἔβαλεν πάλιν τὸ δακτύλιον εἰς δημοσίου δούλου κόλπον. ἠρώτων (-ουν cod.) δὲ τὸν Ξάνθον καὶ περὶ τοῦ δευτέρου σημείου λύσιν διαγνῶναι· ὑποσχόμενος δὲ ἐξῆλθεν σκυθρωπός. καὶ εἰσῄει οὖν εἰς τὸν ἴδιον οἶκον καὶ φησι· " μέλλω πάλιν Αἰσώπῳ (-ου cod.) χάριν ἔχειν ὥστε (ὡς γὰρ cod.) τὴν τοῦ σημείου λύσιν λαβεῖν." εἰσελθὼν οὖν φησιν· " κάλει τὸν Αἴσωπον." καὶ εἰσῆλθεν δέσμιος.[29] ὁ δὲ Ξάνθος λέγει· " λύσατε αὐτόν." Αἴσωπος λέγει· " οὐ βούλομαι λυθῆναι." Ξάνθος· " ἀλλὰ λύω σε ἵνα καὶ σύ τι λύσῃς (-εις cod.)." Αἴσωπος· " οὐκοῦν ἰδίας μου χρείας ἕνεκα λύεις με." Ξάνθος λέγει· " παῦσαι, Αἴσωπε, [τὸ λεγόμενον,

[29] The redactor of W overlooks the fact that Aesop was in prison, when he represents him on this occasion as coming to Xanthus of his own accord and offering to help him (West. 39,26–28). This inconsistency was noted by the author of the later SBP recension (whence Planudes), who tried to remedy the difficulty by adding the statement that Aesop was set free immediately after being put in prison.

ἐπίλυσον] λῆξον [30] τῆς ὀργῆς." Αἴσωπος λυθεὶς εἶπεν· " τί βούλει, δέσποτα; " ὁ Ξάνθος διηγήσατο τὸ σημεῖον. Αἴσωπος ὑπέσχετο. τῇ δὲ ἑξῆς Αἴσωπος θέλων αὐτὸν λυπῆσαι λέγει· " δέσποτα, εἴ τι περὶ λόγου ζητήματος, ἑτοίμως ἔχω ἀποκρίνασθαι, περὶ * * * οὐδὲ διηγήσω· ἀμήχανόν ἐστιν, οὔτε γάρ εἰμι μάντις." ἀκούσας δὲ ὁ Ξάνθος καὶ ἀφελπίσας, καὶ τοὺς Σαμίους αἰσχυνόμενος, ἐλογίσατο ἑαυτὸν διαχειρίσασθαι. καί φησιν· " ὁ χρόνος ἤδη πεπλήρωται τῆς διαλύσεως τοῦ σημείου καὶ οὐχ ὑποφέρω τὸ[ν] ὄνειδος (-ον cod.), ὅτι φιλόσοφος ὢν τὴν ὑπόσχεσιν οὐκ ἐδυνήθην πληρῶσαι." ταῦτα εἰπὼν ὁ Ξάνθος, νυκτὸς γενομένης, σχοινίου εὐπορήσας ἐξῆλθεν τῆς οἰκίας. ὁ δὲ Αἴσωπος κοιμώμενος εἰς τὸ δωμάτιον εἶδε (ἴδεν cod.) τὸν δεσπότην ἄωρον προερχόμενον, αἰσθόμενος δὲ ὃ ἤμελλεν ποιεῖν συνηκολούθησεν αὐτῷ, οὐ μνησικακήσας περὶ τοῦ χρυσίου. ἰδὼν δὲ αὐτὸν ἔξω τῆς πύλης γενόμενον καὶ ἀπό τινος δένδρου βρόχον (βρόγχον cod.) κάμψαντα, καὶ μέλλον <τα> τὸν αὐχένα ὑποβαλεῖν, μακρόθεν Αἴσωπος κέκραγεν· " ἐπίμεινον, δέσποτα." ὁ δὲ ἐπιστραφεὶς καὶ ἰδὼν τὸν Αἴσωπον πρὸς τὸ λάμπον τῆς σελήνης συντρέχοντα, [καὶ] φησίν· " κατελήφθην ὑπὸ τοῦ Αἰσώπου. Αἴσωπε, τί με ἀπὸ τῆς δικαίας ὁδοῦ μετεκαλέσω;" Αἴσωπος εἶπε· " δέσποτα, ποῦ ἡ φιλοσοφία σου; ποῦ σου τὸ τῆς παιδείας φρύαγμα; ποῦ σου τὸ τῆς ἐγκρατείας δόγμα; ἔα, δέσποτα. οὕτως εὐχερῶς καὶ ἀψύχως ἐπὶ θάνατον ἔσπευσας, ἵνα κρεμάμενος τὸ ἡδὺ ζῆν ἀπολέσῃς; μετανόησον, δέσποτα." Ξάνθος· " ἔα με, Αἴσωπε· διάξω γὰρ τὸν μετ' ἀρετῆς θάνατον ἢ τὴν ἐπονείδιστον ἐν βίῳ ζωὴν ἀκλεῶς κτήσομαι." Αἴσωπος· " κατάλειπε τὸν βρόχον (βρόγχον cod.), δέσποτα. ἐγὼ σοι πειράσομαι τὸ σημεῖον διαλύσασθαι." Ξάνθος εἶπεν· " τίνι τρόπῳ; [πειράσομαι] " Αἴσωπος εἶπεν· " ἀπάγαγέ με εἰς τὸ θέατρον ἅμα σοὶ καὶ πλάσσου τοῖς ὄχλοις εὔλογον πρόφασιν ἀπὸ τοῦ σημείου διὰ τὸ κόσμιον τῆς φιλοσοφίας, καὶ ἐμὲ πρόβαλε ὡς αὐτὸς διδάξας. ἐπιλύσομαι ἐγὼ καὶ εὐκαίρως προσκληθήσομαι λέγειν." ταῦτα εἰπὼν ἔπεισεν μετατραπῆναι. ἐλθὼν δὲ τῇ ἑξῆς ὁ Ξάνθος ἤρξατο λέγειν οὕτως· " ἐπεὶ ὁ ἡμέτερος κανὼν λογικῆς φιλοσοφίας μέτρα περιέσπασεν * * * ἐχρῆν [με] διὰ πάσης σπουδῆς ἀπὸ τῆς ἐμῆς οἰκίας καὶ ταύτην γενέσθαι τὴν λειτουργίαν. ἐγὼ μὲν οὖν ἐπὶ τῆς ἐμῆς ἀξίας [οὔτε γάρ ποτε σημειολύτην ἴδον ἢ ἡμέρα τὸ σκότος ἐφιμήσθην], ἐπεὶ φιλόσοφός

[30] It is possible that λῆξον should be bracketed instead of τὸ λεγόμενον ἐπίλυσον.

εἰμι, δώσω ὑμῖν δοῦλον ὃν εἰς τὰ τοιαῦτα φιλοσόφως προετρεψάμην, ὃς τὸ σημεῖον ὑμῶν διαλύσεται (-ειτα cod.)."

The longer passages thus far quoted will serve to show how much new material has been recovered in G, and how significant for our understanding of the ancient *Life* that material often proves to be.

Incidents which are abrupt or poorly motivated in *W* take on a new meaning when read in the older context preserved in G. Numerous examples of this have already been noted, but a few others may also be mentioned. The appearance of Xanthus and his pupils in the market-place, where Aesop and other slaves are being sold, is quite fortuitous in *W*; we are told merely that he went there, not why. From G, however, we learn that Xanthus' wife, while riding by on a litter, had been attracted by the cries of the auctioneer and, upon returning home, had urged her husband to buy her a new slave. Accordingly, Xanthus, after indulging in a little philology (ὀλίγα φιλολογήσας), goes to the market-place for that purpose. His wife, as appears later, had hoped to provide herself with a manservant who should be handsome and therefore a possible lover. It is fitting that she, and not Xanthus (as in *W*), should take the initiative in the purchase of the new servant. Again, in the story of Aesop's attempt to find a man who can mind his own affairs (West. 29,7–32,9) certain motivating sentences are missing in *W* but preserved in G: Aesop's words σύ μοι δοκεῖς κακεντρεχέστερος εἶναι, at West. 29,5, imply the previous use of the epithet κακεντρεχής on the part of the pupil who has been denouncing Aesop to his master; in G this pupil has just finished saying <ὁ> φιλολοίδορος καὶ κακεντρεχὴς δοῦλος οὗτος ὀβολοῦ ἄξιος οὐκ ἔστιν. Soon afterwards Xanthus tells Aesop what he may expect if the man that he brings to dinner proves to be in any way meddlesome: ἐάν τι περιεργάσηται, τὸ πρῶτον σιωπήσω, τὸ δεύτερον συγγνώμην δώσω, τὸ τρίτον δαρήσῃ. Although these conditions are not stated in *W*, they are nevertheless clearly implied; for when the stranger commits his first offence by saying too much

Xanthus *nods* to Aesop "ἔχω ἅπαξ," on the second offense "ἴδε, δύο," and on the third "ἰδού, τρίτα," after which Aesop is flogged. In *W* Lycurgus speaks as follows to Hermippus, when he learns that the latter has disobeyed his orders by saving the life of Aesop (West. 45,16f.): εἴθε ἠδυνάμην τὴν σήμερον ἡμέραν αἰωνίαν ποιῆσαι, ἐὰν ἀληθεύῃς κτλ. These words are beside the point, since they emphasize the joy of Lycurgus (which has already been fully described) instead of his gratitude to Hermippus. G reads <εἴθε> ἠδυνάμην ἣν λέγεις σαυτοῦ (-ὴν cod.) ἐσχάτην ἡμέραν αἰῶνα ποιῆσαι κτλ; and the reference here is to the words, omitted in *W*, by which Hermippus had prefaced his confession of disobedience: δέσποτα βασιλεῦ, ἡ σήμερον ἐσχάτη εἶναί μοι οἶδα (*sic*).

A few sentences which are corrupt in all the manuscripts of *W* can be restored to meaning by comparison with G. Thus, at West. 10,15f., the correct reading is somewhat as follows: "καὶ μάλα," φησίν. <ὁ δεσπότης· "διὰ τί; εἰ> οἱ θεοὶ χολωθέντες ἀνθρώπῳ πρὸς ὀλίγον <χρόνον ἀφείλαντο τὴν φωνὴν αὐτοῦ, νῦν δὲ> πάλιν διαλλαγέντες ἐχαρίσαντο." And at 33,27, in order to make sense, we should read: παραχωρήσατε <τὴν τῆς ὕβρεως (*sc.* κρᾶσιν) τοῖς νέοις· ἔχεις γὰρ ἀκροατήρια> ἐν οἷς δεδώκατε ἀπόδειξιν, although G has τὸν τῆς ἀκηδίας (*sc.* σκύφον), and is otherwise somewhat more correct.

Many interesting features of style belonging to the older version have disappeared in *W* through the desiccating process of syncopation and paraphrasing. Sometimes it is the humor of the original passage that has been lost (*cf. supra*, p. 6), sometimes a speech pregnant with ethical characterization, or again a colorful epithet, a vigorous phrase in the language of the ancient comedy, or a proverb. We read without interest in *W* that Aesop's master ordered his fellow slaves to be flogged, and thereupon quoted to them the verse beginning ὅστις καθ' ἑτέρου δόλια μηχανεύεται κτλ.; but the irony of G's version is more real: "ἔκδυσον αὐτούς!" δερόμενοι δὲ ἐκεῖνοι ἔγνωσαν ἀσφαλῶς ὅτι ὁ κατ' ἄλλου μηχανευόμενος κακόν κτλ. When the steward Zenas hurries to his master with the news that Aesop has suddenly recovered his speech, he prefaces the announcement by saying that a portent (πρᾶγμά τι τερατῶδες) has taken place on the estate. Hereupon the master inquires what the portent was: "Has a tree borne fruit out of season, or a four-legged animal given birth to an anthropoid?" In W Zenas replies prosaically: "No, Aesop has become talkative." [31] But in G the dialogue continues thus: Ζηνᾶς λέγει· "οὐχί, δέσποτα." ὁ δέ· "τί οὖν νομίζεις τερατῶδες εἶναι; ἀνάγγειλόν μοι τἀληθῆ." ὁ δὲ Ζηνᾶς εἶπεν· "Αἴσωπος ὁ σαπρός, ὃν ἀπεπέμψω εἰς τὸν ἀγρὸν σκάπτειν, ὁ προγάστωρ—" ὁ δὲ κύριος· "τί τέτοκεν;" ὁ δέ· "οὔ τι τοιοῦτον,[32] ἀλλά" κτλ. The preparations that Xanthus makes to drink up the sea are so convincing that his opponent is actually alarmed for a moment, and exclaims: πολλά μοι κακά! ἀληθῶς ἐκπίνει τὴν θάλασσαν; When Aesop stands up in the assembly of the Samians to explain the portent, the crowd greets him with an interesting variety of banter: ἀχθήτω ἄλλος σημειολύτης ἵνα τοῦτο τὸ σημεῖον (i.e. Aesop) διαλύσηται ... τὸ τέρας τῆς ὄψεως αὐτοῦ! βάτραχός ἐστιν, ὗς τροχάζων, ἢ στάμνος κήλην ἔχων, ἢ πιθήκων πριμιπιλάριος,[33] ἢ λαγυνίσκος εἰκαζόμενος, ἢ μαγείρου σκευοθήκη, ἢ κύων ἐν γυργάθῳ. Seeing that the Delphians were all of the same complexion and like so many vegetables, Aesop said to them, in the words of Homer:

οἵη περ φυλλῶν γενεή, τοίη δὲ καὶ ἀνδρῶν.[34]

When Aesop explains to Xanthus that he was not laughing (καταγελῶ) at him personally, but at his teachers, Xanthus exclaims: κατάρατε, εἰς τὸ κοινὸν τῆς Ἑλλάδος βλασφημῶν λέγεις. ἐν Ἀθήναις γὰρ ἐσχόλασα παρὰ φιλοσόφοις, ῥήτορσι, γραμματικοῖς. ἔξεστιν οὖν σοὶ εἰς τὸν Ἑλικῶνα τῶν Μουσῶν εἰσελθεῖν; And Aesop replies, ἐὰν μηδὲν λέγῃς χλευάζεσθαί σε δεῖ. This self-conscious professional pose of Xanthus (τὸ τῆς παιδείας φρύαγμα) is more

[31] This syncopation is probably older than the archetype of W; infra, note 3, chap. 4.
[32] I have transposed the words τι τοιοῦτον hither from their position after ἐγέννησεν in the manuscript, where they make no sense. See note 3, chap. 4.
[33] πριμηπηλάριον cod.
[34] The manuscript reads: οἱ ὥσπερ φύλλον γένοιτο πρὸς δὲ καὶ ἀνδρῶν οἴυται (!)

elaborately portrayed in G than in W. The friends of Croesus who are scarcely mentioned in W, advise him as follows in G ἄγωμεν εἰς τὴν νῆσον (sc. Samos)· χειρωσώμεθα αὐτήν, καὶ ἑλκύσωμεν εἰς τὸ Ἀτλαντικὸν πέλαγος, καὶ θῶμεν εἰς ὑπόδειγμα τοῖς λοιποῖς δήμοις, μὴ ἑτέρῳ φανείη τηλικούτῳ ἀντιλέγειν βασιλεῖ. But a kinsman says to him: ὄμνυμί σοι τὸ ἁγνὸν διάδημα ᾧ σὺ αὐτὸς καθοπλίζει (-ίσει cod.), [ἐπειδὴ ἑτέρου] οὐ δυνήσῃ Σαμίους παραλαβεῖν κτλ. In the absence of Aesop, Lycurgus summons his friends and asks them whether they can solve the riddle proposed to him by Nectenabo; and when they are unable to do so, he sits on the ground and weeps. That is W's version, told in two short sentences; the following is G's: ἐκέλευσεν τοὺς φίλους ἀνελθεῖν, ἐν οἷς καὶ Ἕρμιππος, ἔφη τε αὐτοῖς· " δύνασθε λῦσαι τὸ τοῦ πύργου ζήτημα, ἢ πάντας τραχηλοκοπήσω; " The poor fellows apologize for being unable to solve the riddle, and their death is ordered immediately. Finally, we may note at random such unusual expressions as ἑπτασφόνδυλα ῥήματα, ὑποκαίεις σπινθῆρσι λόγων, ὁ ἄγροικος ὡς Χάρυβδις [δελφῖνος] ἤρξατο καταπίνειν (sc. τοὺς ἰχθύας), ἱπποπόρνη, βούπαιδες, Δημόκρατε! νὴ τὴν Νέμεσιν, ὡραίως ἐπενόησας μὰ τὴν σκοτίαν σου, ἐπ' ἐμαυτὸν θησαυρίζω κακά, ἡ Μοῦσα κρίνεται ἐν θεάτροις, ἐν δὲ κοιτῶσιν Κύπρις, ἐδάρη ἐπιμελῶς κτλ., none of which are in W.[35]

3. THE PRESUMABLE DATES OF G AND W

The Berlin papyrus, which Schubart assigns to the end of the second or the beginning of the third century after Christ (*infra*, p. 53), shows that the *Life of Aesop* must have been current at that time in approximately the same form as we now have it. The other papyrus fragments, dating from the fourth and seventh centuries, belong obviously to the same general tradition, as do likewise G and W. The archetype of all these texts (which was probably not the earliest form in

---

[35] Some of the words and phrases which seem to have been taken from the old Attic comedy may have come down through a written tradition of the *Life* from the fifth or fourth century. At any rate, one does not get the impression that they have been added to the text through a pedantic love of display, since they are usually natural and effective in their context.

which the biography of Aesop had appeared, but which may have been derived in part from a written tradition reaching back as far as the fifth century B.C.)[1] can hardly be older than the first century B.C. This may be inferred from the fact that in G an important rôle is assigned to Isis, who is represented as the mother of the Muses and a deity of universal potency, and from the unusual number of Latin words that appear in the text.[2] Beyond this I am unable to point to any reliable *terminus post quem*. I think it probable, however, in view of the general character of the book, that the archetype of which we have been speaking was composed sometime in the second century after Christ. At that time the cult of Isis was widespread and powerful and many authors who wrote in Greek, whatever their nationality, were familiar also with Latin. The contemporary activity of Babrius (?) and the paroemiographers, the collection of fables made by Nicostratus,[3] the fondness shown by such writers as Lucian and Maximus of Tyre for Aesopic and proverbial lore generally, and the popularity of all kinds of biography, make it easy to understand why the *Life of Aesop*, like that of Homer, should have received new attention at this time. Moreover, the second century is a period in which romantic interest in the past is very pronounced and in which there is a distinctly popular trend in literature in spite of the affectations of *litterati*, as one may see from the numerous fragments of sentimental romance dating from this period and from the subject-matter of such writers as Apuleius and Lucian. But if I am

[1] Aristophanes (*Vespae* 1447ff., quoted *infra*, p. 172) refers explicitly to the story (West. 53ff.) that the Delphians accused Aesop of having stolen a φιάλη from the temple of Apollo, and that Aesop on that occasion related to them the fable about the eagle and the beetle. While this, and similar early allusions, do not prove that a book about Aesop existed in the fifth century, yet they render it likely. Certainly in the Alexandrian age, if not sooner, the numerous legends about the famous Aesop must have been committed to writing by someone.

[2] E.g. ἀκουμβήσομεν, ἄγειν = agere, μάππα, πριμιπιλάριος, δηνάριον, ἀσσάριον, λέντιον, οὐά (frequent).

[3] *Cf.* Christ-Schmid, *Gr. Lit.*[6] II, 682.

right in supposing that the Berlin papyrus belongs to the same modified edition of the *Life* that was laid under contribution by the redactor of the SBP recension (*infra*, p. 30), and hence that a double tradition existed as early as the time of the papyrus, then it is likely that the archetype of the two traditions belongs to the early rather than to the later part of the second century. All this, of course, is highly speculative; the most that one may say with certainty is that the *Life of Aesop*, in the oldest form that we know it (i.e. in G), must have been composed, or rewritten, at some time between 100 B.C. and 200 A.D.

That *W* depends upon a text very similar to G, though of course not G itself, will be evident to anyone who has followed the comparisons made above. The archetype of this recension (*W*) cannot be dated with certainty, but to judge from the manuscript tradition, it is probably not older than the eleventh century. We may perhaps think of it as an early product of the Byzantine renaissance, roughly contemporary with Symeon Seth's translation of *Kalilah and Dimnah*, the original Greek version of the *Book of Syntipas* by Michael Andreopoulos, and the Aesopic fables falsely ascribed to Syntipas, with all of which texts it is closely associated in the manuscripts (*infra*, pp. 186ff.)—so much so that the entire group would seem to belong to a single corpus originating in eastern Asia Minor (perhaps at Trebizond or Melitene) in the reign of the first Alexios Komnenos (1081–1118). In the twelfth-century manuscript, Par. suppl. 690, the older version of the *Life* typified by G appears to have been deliberately left out (*infra*, p. 167), and from that time on no traces of it are found in any of the manuscripts of Aesop. The discarding of the old *Life* at about this time may be partially explained as due to the greater popularity of the new Westermann recension. If a scribe of the *Fables* decided to include the *Life* at all, he chose either the Westermann recension or, following the example of Par. 690, the brief notice about Aesop ascribed to Aphthonius.

4. VARIOUS ANCIENT RECENSIONS OF THE *LIFE* PRIOR TO *W*, AND THEIR CONNECTIONS WITH G AND *W*

G is only one of several more or less different texts that were current in late antiquity and that differed substantially from *W* in much the same way as G does. Traces of other texts are found in the papyri, in *W* (especially in the SBP recension), in cod. Vind. theol. gr. 128, and in G itself. The Golenischeff papyrus (VII *saec.*) shows, in comparison with G, a distinct tendency to abbreviate;[1] whereas the Oxyrhynchus papyrus (IV–V *saec.*) agrees more closely with the Morgan text and contains, in greater measure than the Golenischeff papyrus, matter for which there is no equivalent in G.[2] It is probable, therefore, that some of the abbreviation in *W* did not originate with the author of its archetype, but was already present in the text upon which *W* was based; and the same may also be true to some extent of certain other stylistic features of *W*, especially the substitution here and there of indirect for direct discourse, a tendency which seems to have begun already in the Golenischeff papyrus.[3] Whatever may

---

[1] *Cf.* lines 13, 30, 55, 57, 64–65, 72–73 (*infra*, pp. 60f., 63f.).

[2] See lines 21–22, 32, 45–47 (*infra*, pp. 47f.).

[3] *Cf.* lines 20f. where the papyrus agrees with *W* against G in reporting the thoughts of the Delphians indirectly.

I have not noted any *sure* instance in which an abbreviated reading in *W* appears also as a variant in G, but I think it probable that a case in point is to be found in the dialogue between Zenas and his master which has been partially quoted and restored above (p. 23). The full text of G with its own punctuation reads as follows: ὁ δὲ Ζηνᾶς ἔφη· τερατῶδές τι πρᾶγμα συνέβη ἐν τῷ κτήματί σου· ὁ δὲ λέγει· μή τι δένδρον πάρωρον καρπὸν ἤνεγκεν; ὁ δὲ εἶπεν· οὐχὶ δέσποτα· ἀλλὰ τετράπουν ἀνθρωπόμορφόν τι ἐγέννησεν· λέγει ὁ κύριος αὐτοῦ· τί τοιοῦτον; Ζηνᾶς λέγει· οὐχὶ δέσποτα. ὁ δέ· τί οὖν νομίζεις τερατῶδη εἶναι· ἀπάγγειλόν μοι τἀληθῆ· ὁ δὲ Ζηνᾶς εἶπεν· Αἴσωπος ὁ σαπρός...ὁ προγάστωρ· ὁ δὲ κύριος, τί τέτοκεν· ὁ δὲ οὔ· ἀλλὰ νωδὸς ὢν ἐλάλησεν. The restoration of this passage after ἐγέννησεν is not difficult: λέγει...αὐτοῦ must be deleted as totally irrelevant, and τι τοιοῦτον belongs after οὐ and before ἀλλά in the last line. With these emendations the text may be read as it stands, by merely placing a question mark after ἐγέννησεν. But it is quite awkward thus to prolong the dialogue by reading two such similar questions, with their answers, in place of one (i.e. μή τι δένδρον...ἤνεγκεν <ἢ> τετράπουν...ἐγέννησεν; Ζ. λέγει οὐχί, δέσποτα); and

be the exact truth about these matters, it is interesting to note that some of the readings of the text from which W was derived, and also of that from which the redactor of SBP interpolated his recension of W,[4] have been copied into G as variants. In illustrating these points it will be worth while to call attention at the same time to certain other variant readings which throw light upon the tradition previous to W, and especially those which mark a cleavage between G or GW on the one hand and the source of SBP's interpolations on the other. The following table, though far from complete, will give the reader some idea of the *varietas lectionum* in the ancient texts:[5]

the words ὁ δὲ εἶπεν οὐχί, δέσποτα, ἀλλά bear a very suspicious resemblance to the phraseology by which W abridges the entire text commencing after ἐγέννησεν and ending with τέτοκεν (viz. ὁ δέ, οὔ, φησιν, ἀλλ' Αἴσωπος κτλ. West. 10,12). In short, I believe that ὁ δὲ εἶπεν...ἀλλά stood originally, like many other readings in G, either in the margin of G's archetype or, more probably, in that of some manuscript still further back; and that they were intended to indicate a variant tradition whereby everything from ἐγέννησεν through τέτοκεν was abridged just as in W. This variant tradition would then read somewhat as follows: μή τι δένδρον πάρωρον καρπὸν ἤνεγκεν ἢ τετράπουν ἀνθρωπόμορφόν τι ἐγέννησεν; ὁ δὲ εἶπεν· "οὐχί, δέσποτα, ἀλλ' Αἴσωπος νωδὸς ὢν ἐλάλησεν" (or, possibly,—Αἴ. λαλεῖν ἀρξάμενος στωμύλος γέγονεν as in W). The words λέγει ὁ κύριος αὐτοῦ, which must be deleted in any case, are probably a marginal notation which was made after the variant ὁ δὲ...ἀλλά had crept into the text, and by a reader who wished to explain the resulting ambiguity; it cautions us not to understand ἀλλά...ἐγέννησεν as part of the speech of Zenas, as we should otherwise be likely to construe these words. The present passage is typical of many others in G, in that it has resulted from an accumulation of marginalia reaching back into the tradition two or more stages prior to G itself.

[4] *Text Tradition*, 226–230.

[5] Ahikar is herein cited from the translations given by J. Rendel Harris in *Apocrypha and Pseudepigrapha of the Old Testament*, edited by R. H. Charles, Oxford, 1913, vol. II, pp. 715–779. For Vind. 128, an excerpt from the old *Life of Aesop*, see Westermann's edition, pp. 4f. The papyri are edited below, pp. 40ff.

Cf. West.	G	Arch. of W	Arch. of SBP	Remarks
7,5	καὶ πρὸς τούτους ἐλάττωμα μεῖζον εἶχε τῆς ἀμορφίας τὴν ἀφωνίαν· ἦν δὲ καὶ νωδὸς καὶ οὐδὲν ἠδύνατο λαλεῖν	πρὸς τούτους δέ, ἦν καὶ βραδύγλωσσος καὶ βομβόφωνος, φαῦλός τε καὶ δεινὸς πανουργίᾳ	τὸ δὲ χαλεπώτερον, ἦν καὶ βραδύγλωσσος,... δεινὸς πρὸς κακουργίαν σφόδρα (as W)	G's reading is apparently a compound of two different versions, one of which reappears only in W, the other only in SBP. Further, cf. Text Tradition, 227f.
8,10f.	Ἀγαθόποι, δὸς τὰ σῦκα· ἄλλος ἑρμᾶ (sic), φέρε τὰ σῦκα	δός μοι τὰ σῦκα	φέρε τὰ σῦκα	Cf. Text Tradition, 227
8,14f.	ὁ δὲ φησιν λέγει αὐτῷ· ἐπικατάρατε κτλ.	καὶ φησιν ὁ δεσπότης· λέγε μοι, ἐπικατάρατε	As W, but with σύ after μοι	W may have come from a text which, like G, had a double reading; cf. infra (West. 40,8)
31,17	ὡς Χάρυβδις δελφῖνος (sic) ἤρξατο καταπίνειν	ὡς δελφὶς ἤσθιε (not ὡς ἀδελφός, as in West.)	ἤσθιε	δελφῖνος looks like a corrupted variant on Χάρυβδις, though it may possibly be an error for δελφῖνας
40,8–18	Two long and somewhat different versions, one after the other, of Aesop's prefatory speech to the Samians concerning outward appearances vs. character (ὄψις and νοῦς)	Both speeches retained, but in a much abbreviated form	As W	G preserves the readings of two distinct ancient traditions, and W was based upon a text which had the same compound. The first speech in G is probably the older, as it is the better. Originally there could have been only one speech
45,16f.	ὄφειλον εἰδύναμεν (sic)... ποιῆσαι	εἴθε ἠδυνάμην... ποιῆσαι	εἴθε εἰ δυνατόν μοι ἦν... ποιῆσαι	Either ὄφειλον is a gloss or variant, or <εἴθε> ἠδυνάμην is a variant, which G took from a text similar to W's source

Cf. West.	G	Arch. of W	Arch. of SBP	Remarks
46,2	διέθηκεν (= διηύθυνε?) διὰ λόγων ἐνουθέτει	ἐνουθέτει	ἐνουθέτει	
52,10	σοφίαν καὶ παιδίαν	σοφίαν	σοφίαν	παιδίαν Berlin papyrus. G has added παιδίαν from a text similar to the papyrus
26,21–27,9	Not present	Not present	The reconciliation of Xanthus' wife brought about by Aesop	This episode, like the two others cited below, is undoubtedly ancient; but it was absent in the tradition represented by G and the source of W. See Text Tradition, 222f.
36,12–38,8	Not present	Not present	Two episodes corresponding to chapters 13 and 14 in Westermann	These also are ancient, though preserved only through SBP. Here again we see that the source of SBP's interpolations was a text in many respects different from G and the source of W
47,14	προσπορίζεται	προσπορίζεται	πορίζει (= Vind. 128)	Vind. 128 and the source of SBP's interpolation represent a tradition differing from GW
51,34	Λυκοῦργος	Λυκοῦργος	Λυκοῦρος	Λυκωρ[ος] Berlin Papyrus. The form Λυκοῦρος in SBP appears to be derived from a text similar to the papyrus and different from GW. Cf. infra, pp. 57f.

LIFE OF AESOP

Cf. West.	G	Arch. of W	Arch. of SBP	Remarks
53,6	ὁ δὲ Αἴσωπος μηδὲν ἑαυτοῦ συνειδὼς (sic), κλαίων ἔφησεν· ἀπολέσθαι θέλω ἐάν τι τοιοῦτον εὑρεθῇ εἰς ἐμέ	τοῦ δὲ ἀπολέσθαι λέγοντος ἐὰν καταγνωσθῇ (or something very similar; the MSS vary. Cf. infra, p. 69)	τοῦ δὲ ἀρνουμένου καὶ δυσχυριζομένον μηδὲν εἰδέναι	]ηδεν ειδεναι κ[αι] λεγορ[τος Gol. Pap. The source of SBP's reading was a manuscript similar to the papyrus and different from GW, which is more complete. Cf. Text Tradition, 229. δυσχ. μ. εἰδέναι appears to be a variant for G's μηδὲν ἑαυτῷ συνειδὼς which W omitted
8,4	ἐπιζητήσῃ	ζητήσῃ	ἐπιζητήσῃ	The agreement of SBP with G against the archetype of W is quite exceptional. In some cases it may be due to borrowing on the part of SBP from an old text which had the same reading as G and the source of W, but which had been changed by the redactor of W's archetype. In other cases it is probable that SBP's source agreed with G against the source of W. Note how, in two of the parallel passages here cited (13,24 and 35,15), SBP appears to have combined the reading of G with that of W
8,27	τοῦτο	ὁμοίως	τοῦτο	
13,24	πρὸς ἑαυτούς	εἰς ἀλλήλους	πρὸς ἀλλήλους	
17,24f.	τῷ ἐμπόρῳ	τῷ σωματεμπόρῳ	τῷ ἐμπόρῳ	
35,15	πλῆθος ἅπαν	πλῆθος τῆς πόλεως	πλῆθος ἅπαν τῆς πόλεως	
39,7	ἀπολάβῃς	λάβῃς	ἀπολάβῃς	
48,10	προσκαλεσάμενος	συγκαλέσας	προσκαλεσάμενος	
54,14	φιλήσας	φιλωθείς	φιλήσας (φιλήσας Gol. Pap.)	

32   The Life and Fables of Aesop

Cf. West.	G	Arch. of W	Other texts	Remarks
30,25	οἶδας Ξάνθον τὸν φιλόσοφον	Ξάνθον οἶδας τὸν φιλόσοφον	Ξανθο]ν οιδας τον φιλοσοφον Ox. Pap. 2083	Exceptional
44,23	Ἥλιος	Αἶνος	Αἶνος Vind. 128	Note the similarity of G to the source of W
46,13f.	τοὺς ἐχθροὺς εὔχου ζῆν καὶ ἁρμοστεῖν καὶ πένεσθαι, ἵνα κατὰ πάντα ἀδυνατῶσι	Essentially the same as G (om. ζῆν)	Absent in Vind. 128 and Ahikar	
(46,15)	Absent. (But the passage generally is corrupt and defective)	Absent	ἐν βασιλικῇ αὐλῇ ἐάν τι ἀκούσῃς, τοῦτο ἐναποθανέτω σοι, μὴ σὺ ἐν τάχει ἀποθάνῃς Vind. 128. Son, if thou hear any word in the royal gate, make it to die and bury it in thy heart Ahikar (Armenian)	Here, as in the preceding citation, the text of the *Life* from which Vind. 128 was excerpted agrees with Ahikar against GW. An equivalent of this sentence is found in all the principal versions of Ahikar including the ancient papyrus from Elephantine (v saec. B.C.); but mention of the 'royal gate' survives only in the Armenian and Slavonic texts. In the GW tradition the omission is probably due to error
47,13f.	εἰδὼς ὅτι καὶ τὸ κυνάριον οὐρᾷ ἄρτον προστορίζεται, κἂν τὸ στόμα πληγὰς ὑπάγει	εἰδὼς ... προστορίζεται only, with slight variants from G	εἰδὼς ὅτι καὶ τῷ κυνὶ ἡ οὐρὰ ἄρτον πορίζει, τὸ δὲ στόμα πληγάς Vind. 128 and, in substance, all the chief versions of Ahikar	Merely an omission in W or in W's source

Life of Aesop

Cf. West.	G	Arch. of W	Other texts	Remarks
(48,9)	ὁ δὲ λαμπρῶς αὐτὸν ἔθαψε πενθήσας χρόνον τινά	Omitted	ὁ δὲ Αἴσωπος λαμπρῶς αὐτὸν ἔθαψεν πενθήσας Vind. 128 (πενθήσας is omitted in Westermann's transcript, p. 5). Not in Ahikar	
52,20	οὐδὲν γὰρ ἀνάξιον (a correct reading)	Probably οὐδὲν ἄξιον. For the variants cf. infra, p. 69	οὐδὲν γὰρ ἄξιον Gol. Pap.	W's erroneous reading appears to have come from a text similar to the papyrus
52,20f.	ταῦτα ἀκούσαντες	= G	Evidently omitted in Gol. Pap.	
54,3	λυπούμενος	λυπούμενος	Omitted in Gol. Pap.	
54,6	καὶ πολλὰ δακρύσας ὁ φίλος αὐτοῦ ἀφίκετο (read ἀφίστατο)	ὁ οὖν φίλος πρὸς αὐτὸν ἔφη (a perverse alteration by which the friend is made to utter the words elsewhere spoken by the Delphians themselves)	Omitted in Gol. Pap.	

From the foregoing comparisons it will be seen that the source of *W*, in so far as we can test it, is decidedly closer to G than to the other discernible ancient traditions; for, apart from the agreement in smaller variants, both texts lacked three episodes which were present in the source of SBP's interpolations, and both had in common at least one very conspicuous double reading (West. 40,8–18). It is true that *W* contains some important matter that is not preserved in G, but the absence of this in the Morgan manuscript is probably accidental. Thus, although the story about the first ἀπερίεργος (West. 29,16–30,10) has been left out of G, its presence in the tradition is, nevertheless, clearly implied by the context. For, in the first place, the words ἐάν τι περιεργάσηται κτλ. (*supra*, p. 21) look forward very definitely to the episode in question, as we see from *W*; and, in the second place, G's text is erroneous and contradictory in that it represents the rustic wood-carrier (i.e. the second ἀπερίεργος) as being found in the market-place [6] instead of in the country on his way to the city. That Aesop met the rustic outside the city is explicitly stated in *W* [7] and clearly implied in G; whereas the mention of the market-place, as appears from *W*, belongs only with the story about the first indifferent man, who was sitting down and reading on the edge of a large crowd gathered about a fight. It was only after Aesop had failed to find the right kind of man in the city that he went outside. Again, the last of the apologues that Aesop related to the Delphians (ἀνήρ τις ἐρασθεὶς τῆς ἰδίας θυγατρός, West. 57,7–14), though alluded to in G, is accidentally omitted therein: μέλλων δὲ ἀπὸ τοῦ κρημνοῦ ῥίπτεσθαι ἔτι ἕτερον λόγον εἶπεν (lacuna) ἄνδρες Δελφιοι, ἠβουλόμην Συρίαν, Φοινίκην, Ἰουδαίαν μᾶλλον κυκλεῦσαι ἢ ἐνθάδε παρ' ὑμῶν ἀναγκασθῆναι ἀποθανεῖν ὑπὸ δυστήνων δουλαρίων. Here it seems to be implied that there

---

[6] ἀπελθὼν εἰς τὴν ἀγορὰν ἐζήτει ἄνθρωπον ἀπερίεργον (lacuna) καὶ δὴ θεωρεῖ ἄνθρωπον τὸ μὲν ἰδέσθαι ἄγροικον, πολιτικὸν δὲ τοῖς ἤθεσιν, ὀνάριον ἐλαύνοντα κτλ. In *W* we are told that this man was going to the city; in G his exact destination is not mentioned, but he is hurrying along in order to sell his faggots, obviously toward the city.

[7] τῇ δὲ ἐπαύριον ἔξω τῆς πόλεως ἀπελθὼν ἐζήτει κτλ. (West. 30,10).

was some plausible analogy between traveling through Syria, Phoenicia, and Judaea (Sicily only in *W*) and the substance of the story that has just been told; but it is by no means easy to see what this analogy could have been if the story here omitted was as brief and as apparently out of line with the application as it is in *W*.⁸ Can it be that we have in *W* only the beginning of the original tale? The father's attack upon his daughter, together with the allusion to travel in Syria and Phoenicia, reminds one of the romance of Apollonius of Tyre, or (less precisely) of Matthidia in the Pseudo-Clementine *Recognitiones* (VII, 15); hence, it is not difficult to imagine that the story which Aesop told the Delphians on this occasion related to some young woman who had wandered about in voluntary exile suffering many hardships in order to avoid the incestuous advances of her own father at home. Such a story would be relevant to Aesop's situation—in danger at the very shrine of the Muses—and at the same time would account for the otherwise meaningless allusion to foreign travels.

Alongside of G*W* we may recognize, as a substantially different edition of the old *Life*, the source from which SB*P* took the three episodes that are not present in G. It is clear that these episodes have not been omitted by mistake in the G*W* tradition, because there is no sign of textual disturbance such as might have been caused by their accidental loss, and the context of the biography reads just as well, and in fact better, without them. The first episode, which tells how Xanthus' wife deserted him and was later reconciled by Aesop, is in ill accord with the context because the wife does not leave her husband until it has been completely demonstrated to her that she has no real ground for complaint—that

---

⁸ The story reads as follows in *W*:... ἕτερον ἔφη λόγον· "ἀνήρ τις ἐρασθεὶς τῆς ἰδίας θυγατρὸς καὶ εἰς ἔρωτα τρωθείς, ἔπεμψεν εἰς τὸν ἀγρὸν τὴν γυναῖκα αὐτοῦ, τὴν δὲ θυγατέρα κρατήσας ἐβιάσατο. ἡ δὲ ἔλεγε· ' πάτερ, ἀνόσια πράττεις. ἤθελον μᾶλλον ἑκατὸν ἀνδράσι με παρασχεῖν ἢ σοί.' τοῦτο κἀγὼ πρὸς ὑμᾶς, ὦ Δελφοί· προῃρούμην Σικελίαν κακοπαθῶν κυκλεῦσαι ἢ ἐνθάδε παραλόγως ὑφ' ὑμῶν ἀποθανεῖν." It is easy to see the application of ἤθελον...σοί to Aesop's mistreatment by the Delphians, but what about Σικελίαν κακοπαθῶν κυκλεῦσαι?

Aesop, and not Xanthus, as she had supposed, was the one who held her in less esteem than the family dog. In some ancient version of the *Life* this story might well have stood in place of the scene whereby Xanthus proves his innocence (West. 26,1–21). Likewise the other two episodes (chapters 13f. in West.) are organically superfluous, and their absence in G makes possible a closer and more logical connection between the incidents that precede and follow.[9] We may be sure, therefore, that the three episodes of which we have been speaking did not belong in the ancient recension represented by G*W*.

Concerning the edition represented by the source of SBP's interpolations, we can of course know very little. Although the three odd episodes that it contained may be as old as any of the others, yet we do not know where they were placed in the narrative: if they stood in the same contexts as they do in SBP, we should not hesitate to say that this edition was an interpolated version of that which is typified by G*W*, but it is equally possible that they took the place of other similar episodes in G*W*. The Byzantine redactor of SBP is

[9] The sequence of events in G is as follows: Aesop, having saved Xanthus from the consequences of his rash wager to drink up the sea, asks for his freedom and is refused (West. 35,31). In his resentment he declares that he will avenge himself on Xanthus; and this he does by lying with the latter's wife (*supra*, p. 8). After Xanthus has settled the dispute between Aesop and his mistress, which had been put to him in the form of a parable relating to cuckoo apples, he proposes to take a walk with Aesop before dinner, both for the sake of exercise and in order that Aesop may bring his mistress the extra cuckoo apple. Accordingly, before setting out, Xanthus, who says that he is careful about omens, asks Aesop to report to him whether he sees a pair of crows or only one. The result of this ὀρνεοσκοπία is that Aesop, having seen the favorable omen of two crows, is flogged, while Xanthus, who has seen only one, receives an unexpected invitation to dinner. At this point SBP inserted chapters 13 and 14 into *W*, each of which is entirely unconnected with the context and separated from it by time intervals of several days (West. 36,12, leaves out μεθ' ἡμέρας δέ τινας, which is in all the manuscripts); whereas in G, chapter 15, which tells how Xanthus took a walk with Aesop and how they came among the tombstones and began to read the epitaphs, follows immediately after the ὀρνεοσκοπία, where it belongs. In short, the whole series of incidents is more closely related and better motivated in G than in SBP. *Cf.* note 10.

somewhat more likely to have been responsible for an awkward compounding of episodes than an ancient editor; and yet even in G*W* there are a few incidents that do not fit well in their context,[10] not to mention the double version of Aesop's speech to the Samians (*supra*, p. 29). Besides all this, when we bear in mind the fact that in matters of phraseology G and the manuscripts through which it is descended were almost what might be called variorum editions, we need have little hesitation in concluding that different editions of the *Life* were current at a very early period, and that they varied considerably in respect to the episodes that they contained as well as in phraseology.

Although the papyrus fragments, owing to their brevity, cannot be confidently assigned to either of the two editions above defined, it is nevertheless probable that the Oxyrhynchus papyrus, in view of its remarkable similarity to G, is more closely related to the G*W* tradition than is the Golenischeff papyrus; and that the latter text, which shows some agreement

[10] I am thinking of chapter 11 (West. 32,16–33,18), where Aesop deceives Xanthus, who wanted to avoid a crowd while bathing, by telling him that there was only one man at the bath, explaining afterwards that by "only one man" he meant only one *intelligent* man. This act of roguery would be more plausible if it had been committed some time before, when Aesop was doing everything he could to outwit his master and to teach him not to demand such literal obedience (*cf. supra*, p. 6), but that series of acts, among which chapters 13f. also belong, was brought to a logical conclusion at the end of chapter 10, where Xanthus admits that Aesop has triumphed over him, and begs him earnestly to quit fooling thereafter and to serve him in good faith. This Aesop promises to do: οὐκέτι με μέμψει, δέσποτα· γνώσῃ δὲ εὔνοιαν οἰκέτου. These words appear to be sincere. They should be followed, not by chapter 11, in which Aesop twice offends his master without any provocation, but by chapter 12, in which he does Xanthus the great favor of saving his entire fortune. Thereafter in G*W* there is no more fooling on Aesop's part, and whatever he does against his master's interest is directly provoked by the ungenerous acts of Xanthus himself. Indeed this latter part of the *Life* is marked by a distinctly more serious tone than the first ten chapters, and this new tone is very noticeably interrupted by chapters 11, 13, and 14. I believe, therefore, that chapter 11, as well as chapters 13f., belonged originally in another part of the biography—the part in which Aesop was studiously engaged in outwitting his master at every turn. That particular aspect of Aesop's behavior naturally invited a multiplicity of illustrations.

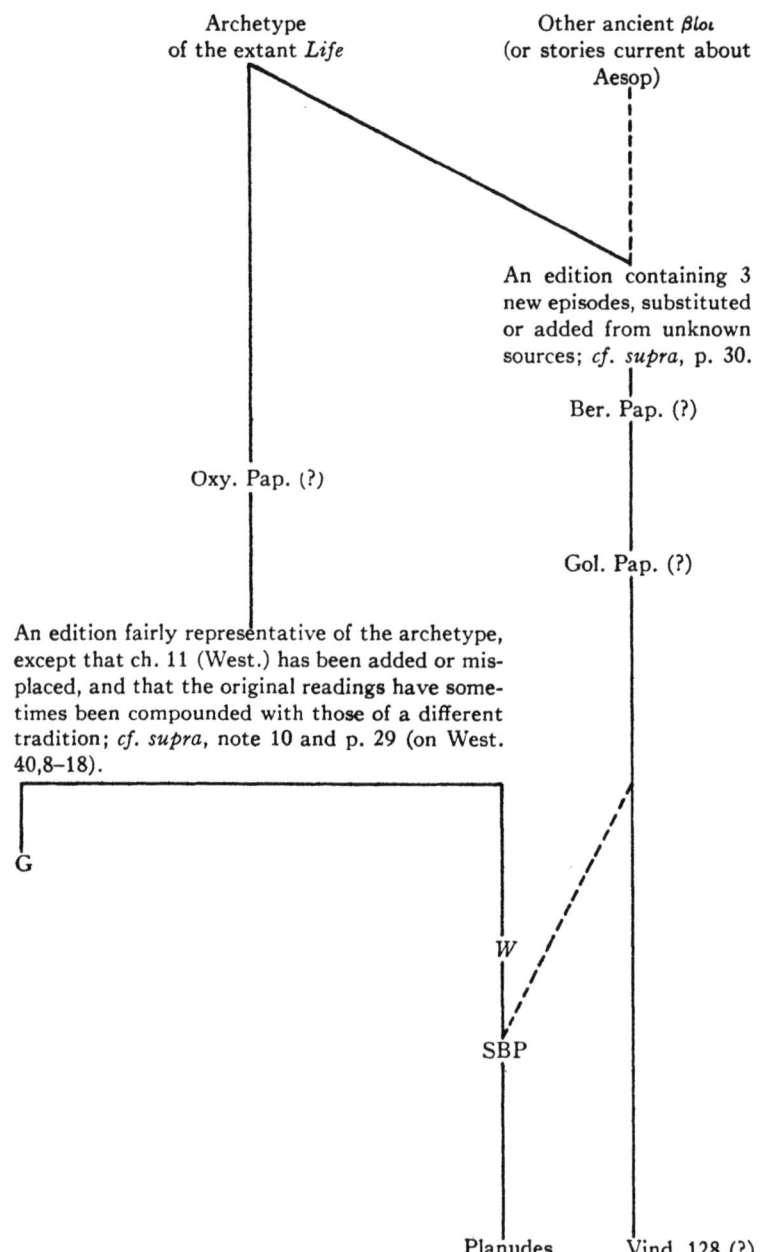

with SBP's variations from WG (*supra*, p. 31) and which is apparently a briefer text than G, had some definite kinship with the version from which SBP extracted the three episodes above described, and probably also a considerable number of smaller variants.[11] Concerning the Berlin papyrus, *cf. infra*, p. 53.

The accompanying diagram indicates what I believe to be the main outlines of the ancient tradition in so far as they can be plausibly inferred from the scanty evidence at present available.

5. THE TEXTS OF THE PAPYRUS FRAGMENTS

New material for the restoration and interpretation of the papyrus fragments is afforded by both G and *W*. For getting at the text tradition of the latter version, including SBP, Westermann's text, upon which previous editors and critics of these fragments have had to rely, is very inadequate; it has no critical apparatus worth mentioning, and since it depends entirely [1] upon a single mixed manuscript (i.e. W, = Laur. conv. soppr. 627), it often fails to give any clue to the oldest reading. Accordingly, although the contribution of *W* to our understanding of the papyri is relatively small as compared with that of G, I have nevertheless thought it worth while in editing the relevant passages to supply a rather full critical apparatus, which is intended to include all the variants that may be thought to have any traditional value. In doing so, I have ignored many erroneous or unique readings of the inferior manuscripts, though never when they seem to show any kinship with the papyri; and in all cases I have been at pains to record the readings of the two main families of manuscripts, MO (or MR) and SBP. W [2] and λ

---

[11] *Cf. Text Tradition*, 227, note 38.

[1] Except that, from 11,18–22,21, Westermann reports the readings of Mon. 525 in his notes at the bottom of the page.

[2] Here, and below in the critical notes to *W*, W stands for Laur. conv. soppr. 627, to conform with the terminology used in my *Text Tradition*. A stemma of the manuscripts together with an explanation of the symbols is given below in part II (pp. 175f.).

(= LFV or LF), on the other hand, are merely compounds of these two main traditions. The oldest text of *W* is represented by MO and MR, and it is upon the basis of those manuscripts (especially M, since O and R, though basically older, are often corrupt or contaminated) that the text given below rests. Essential but inexact agreement of manuscripts is sometimes indicated by parentheses, as in the first variant below, where S reads καὶ τὸ δὴ χαλεπώτερον and P τὸ δὲ χαλεπότερον, as contrasted with πρὸς ἐπὶ τούτοις δέ of Mλ.

a. PSI 156

The small fragment which here follows appeared for the first time in the *Pubblicazioni della Società Italiana* (*Papiri Greci e Latini*) II (1913), no. 156, where the text was reproduced without comment. The papyrus was acquired at Luxor, and the date tentatively assigned by the editors is the fourth century. Though unidentified by the original editors, it was soon afterward recognized by Crusius as belonging to the *Life of Aesop*, and in 1919 was reedited and commented upon by P. Collart in the *Revue de Philologie* (XLII, 38–46). In reproducing the text, I have tried to keep the lines in approximately the same position relative to each other as they have in PSI. This arrangement indicates that, as Collart observes, the loss is greater on the left-hand side for the recto and on the right for the verso. Indeed, it would appear that the right-hand extremity of the recto and the left of the verso were close to the margin of the page. The most plausible restorations that I have been able to make (lines 2f., 3f., 10f., 12f., 24f.) favor the assumption of about forty-two or forty-three letters to the line. The reconstruction of this papyrus is especially difficult and hazardous, because the text of *W* is very unreliable in this part of the *Life*, and there is a considerable lacuna in the corresponding part of G. Moreover, the wording of the papyrus must often have differed from both G and *W*. For these reasons, and also because it is impossible without the aid of a facsimile to measure the gaps accurately, I have been more cautious than others in proposing restorations. The supplements of Collart, clumsily copied from Westermann's text, and based on the mistaken assumption that fully forty letters are missing in each line, are worthless and misleading; and although Zeitz has made some plausible restorations and has proceeded on much sounder principles than Collart, yet he too has been led astray by Westermann's text, certainly in lines 3 and 16, and probably elsewhere. Except for the uncertain matter which has been accidentally lost in G's lacuna, there is practically nothing in the papyrus that does not have a substantial equivalent in the Morgan manuscript, whereas *W* has no equivalent for lines 5–7 of the papyrus.

TEXT OF PSI 156
Recto

[ελαττω-
1 μα μειζον ειχε της αμορφιας τη]ν αφωνει[αν ην γαρ νωδος
2 και ουδεν ολως εδυνατο λαλειν] τουτον ο[υ]ν ο δ[εσποτης
3 κατα παντα σιγηλον εχων και α]ποιητον της π[ολιτικης
4 εργασιας επεμψεν εις εν τω]ν κτηματων α[υτου σκαπτειν
5   ]. μον αυτου κ[
6   ].σε..ει εις την π[ολιν
7   ]..οτον υπο δε την ωρα[ν
8   κ]ατηντησεν εις τα εαυτου[κτηματα
9 γεωργος δε τις τρυγη]σας καλλιστα συκα επικ[αλλυνας
10 ηνεγκε τω του Αισωπου δε]σποτη και φησιν λαβε [δεσποτα
11 απο των σων καρπων πρωιμο]ν οπωραν ο δε ειπεν[
12   Αγαθ]οπου λαβε ταυτα τα σ[υκα και
13 φυλαξον οταν δε επανελθ]ω και αριστησω παραθε[ς μοι
14   ]..[   ]...[

Verso

15   ].ευχαρ[
16   ] . [   ] πιων [εβαλεν τους δακτυλους εις το στομα
17 και σπαρ]αξας εαυτον [ανεβαλεν το υδωρ οπερ επιεν
18 ουδενος γα]ρ ετερου γευσα[μενος ην
19   ]. γευσασθαι τ[ων συκων

20   το] αυτο ποιησατωσαν κ[αι
21   θ]αυμασας αυτου το νοερον[
22   ]αι οι δε δουλοι εις εαυτου[ς τι ποιησωμεν Ερμα
23   πιωμεν κα]ι̣ κατω μη χαλασωμεν τ̣[ους δακτυλους αλλα παρα
24   τας γωνιας α]μα τω πειν α<υ>τους το χ[λιαρον χολοποια οντα
25   τα συκα προσ]ανελυσαν κα̣[ι ν]αυτι[α]σα[ντες ευθυς το υδωρ
26   ανεβαλον κ]α̣ι τα συκα αυτοματως [ἀνεδραμον ταυτα ο
27   δεσποτης ιδ]ων φησιν [ιδε τα] συκ[α

CORRESPONDING TEXTS OF G AND W

G: (-1-14) καὶ πρὸς τούτοις ἐλάττωμα μεῖζον (μείζων cod.) εἶχε τῆς ἀμορφίας τὴν ἀφωνίαν· ἦν δὲ καὶ νωδὸς καὶ οὐδὲν ἠδύνατο λαλεῖν. τοῦτον ὁ δεσπότης κατὰ πάντα σιγηλὸν (συγητὸν cod.) ἔχων καὶ ἀποίητον τῇ πολιτικῇ ἐργασίᾳ ἔπεμψεν εἰς τὸν ἀγρόν—lacuna. (-15) ἰδὼν παρακείμενον ξέστην ἔλαβεν αὐτὸν καὶ διὰ τῶν νευμάτων ᾔτησεν ὕδωρ χλιαρόν, καὶ λεκάνην παραθεὶς εἰς τὸ μέσον Αἴσωπος (16) καὶ (δὲ cod.) πιὼν, ἔβαλεν τοὺς δακτύλους εἰς τὸ στόμα (17) καὶ σπαράξας ἑαυτὸν ἀνέβαλεν τὸ χλιαρὸν ὅπερ ἔπιεν· (18) οὐδαμῶς γὰρ ἦν γευσάμενος. (19) διὰ δὲ τῆς πολυπειρίας δοὺς ἀπόδειξιν, (20) τοῦτο ἠξίωσε καὶ τοὺς συνδούλους αὐτοῦ ποιῆσαι, ἵνα γνωσθῇ τίς ἐστιν ὁ φαγὼν τὰ σῦκα. (21) θαυμάσας δὲ ὁ δεσπότης τὸ ἐνθύμημα αὐτοῦ ἐκέλευσεν καὶ τοὺς ἄλλους (22) πιόντας ἐμέσαι. οἱ δὲ δοῦλοι εἰς ἑαυτούς· " τί ποιήσωμεν, Ἑρμᾶ; (23) πίομεν (l. πίωμεν) καὶ μὴ κάτω τοὺς δακτύλους βάλωμεν, ἀλλὰ παρὰ (24) τὰς γωνίας." ἅμα δὲ τῷ (τὸ cod.) πιεῖν αὐτοὺς τὸ χλιαρόν, χολοποιοῦντα (25) τὰ σῦκα ἐπέπλευσαν ἄνω, καὶ ἅμα τῷ (τὸ cod.) χαλάσαι τὸν δάκτυλον (26) ἀνέδραμον (-ων cod.) τὰ σῦκα. ὁ δὲ δεσπότης (27) ἔφη· " ὁρᾶτε πῶς κατεψεύσασθε τῷ μὴ δυναμένῳ λαλῆσαι ; "

W: (-1) πρὸς τούτοις δέ, ἦν καὶ βραδύγλωσσος καὶ βομβόφωνος, φαῦλός τε καὶ δεινὸς πανουργίᾳ. (2) τοῦτον οὖν ὁ δεσπότης (3) ὡς ἄχρηστον ὄντα τῆς πολιτικῆς (4) ὑπηρεσίας ἐξέπεμψεν αὐτὸν εἰς ἕν τῶν κτημάτων αὐτοῦ σκάπτειν. (7-8) καὶ δή ποτε παραγενομένου αὐτοῦ ἐπὶ τὸν ἀγρόν, (9) γεωργός τις τρυγήσας κάλλιστα σῦκα (10) ἤνεγκεν τῷ τοῦ Αἰσώπου δεσπότῃ, καί φησιν· " λάβε, δέσποτα, (11) ἀπὸ τῶν σῶν καρπῶν ὀπώραν πρώιμον." ὁ δὲ τερφθεὶς εἶπε· " νὴ τὴν σωτηρίαν μου, (12) καλὰ σῦκα." καί φησι τῷ οἰκέτῃ· "' Ἀγαθόπου, λάβε καὶ (13) φύλαξόν μοι αὐτά· μετὰ δὲ τὸ λούσασθαι καὶ ἀριστῆσαι παράθες μοι τὴν ὀπώραν.... (15–16) καὶ λαβὼν ξέστην καὶ ὕδατι χλιαρῷ συγκεράσας, λεκάνην τε παραθεὶς καὶ πιών, ἐχάλασε τοὺς δακτύλους ἐπὶ τὸ ἴδιον στόμα (17) καὶ σπαράξας ἑαυτὸν ἀνέβαλε τὸ ὕδωρ μόνον ὃ ἐπεπώκει· (18) οὐδενὸς γὰρ ἦν ἑτέρου γευσάμενος. (20) ἐδέετο δὲ καὶ τοὺς κατηγόρους ὁμοίως ποιῆσαι, καὶ ἐπιγνώσῃ τὸν βεβρωκότα τὰ σῦκα. (21) ὁ δὲ θαυμάσας αὐτοῦ τὸ νοερὸν ἐπέταξε καὶ τοῖς ἄλλοις (22) ποιῆσαι ὁμοίως. οἱ δὲ δοῦλοι (23) ἐβουλεύσαντο τοὺς δακτύλους πέμψαι παρὰ τὰς γνάθους καὶ κάτω μὴ χαλάσαι. (24) ἅμα δὲ τῷ πιεῖν αὐτοὺς τὸ χλιαρὸν ὕδωρ καὶ συγκύψαι τὰ σῦκα χολοποιὰ ὄντα (25) προσανέβλυσαν (26) καὶ αὐτομάτως ἀνέδραμον. τότε ὁ (27) δεσπότης εἶπε· "τί κατεψεύσασθε τοῦ μὴ δυναμένου λαλεῖν;"

Variants in W: πρὸς ἐπὶ τούτοις δὲ Μ(λ) τὸ δὲ χαλεπώτερον WB (SP) evanuit lectio cod. O ‖ πανουργίᾳ Μ <παν?>ουργίας Ο πρὸς κακουργίαν σφόδρα WB(SP) ‖ 2–4 τοῦτον...σκάπτειν] ὀνούμενος τοίνυν αὐτός γε ἀπεστάλθη παρὰ τοῦ δεσπότου ὡς ἄχρηστος πάντα τῆς τοῦ ταμείου ὑπηρεσίας εἰς ἱμερὴν γεωργεῖν, inepte Ο ‖ 2 ὁ δεσπότης Μ ὁ δ. αὐτοῦ LFV ὁ κύριος αὐτοῦ BPW(S) ‖ 3 ὄντα om. Μ ‖ τ. π. ὑπηρεσίας Μλ εἰς ὑπηρεσίαν αὐτοῦ WP(SB) ‖ 7–8 καὶ δή ποτε ΜΟλ ἐν μιᾷ οὖν τῶν ἡμερῶν SBPW ‖ παραγενομένου (-μενος P)...ἀγρόν ΜΡ παραγενόμενος ἀπ' ἀγροῦ Ο παραγενομένου τοῦ κυρίου ἐπὶ τὸν ἀγρόν SBλW ‖ 10 ἤνεγκεν τὸ τοῦ Ἐσώπου δ. Ο προσήνεγκεν αὐτῷ ΜΒΡλW(S) ‖ 11 ὀπώραν πρώϊμον ΜΟ π. ὀπώραν SBPW ‖ πάνυ τερφθεὶς SBPW ‖ ἐπὶ τούτοις post τερφθεὶς SBWλ τὴν τῶν ἰσχάδων ὥραν Ο om. Μ ‖ εἶπε SBPWλ ἔφησε· Ο om. Μ ‖ 12 καλὰ Μ κάλλιστα SBPWλ θειμύρη πάμπαν ἐμοῖ ταῦτά γε τυγχάνει Ο ‖ καί φησι Μ εἶτα λέγει SBPW ‖ αὐτοῦ post οἰκέτῃ SBPWλ om. ΜΟ ‖ 12–13 λάβε...μετὰ δὲ Μ λάβε ταῦτα καὶ φ. καὶ μετὰ LFV λαβὼν τ. φ. καὶ μ. SBPW orationem obliquam ac prorsus suam habet Ο ‖ με post λούσασθαι SBλW ‖ καὶ ἀριστῆσαι om. SBPλ ‖ τὴν ὀπώραν Μ hunc fructum Lo ταῦτα SBO αὐτά Wλ(P)... 15–16 ὕδατι χλιαρῷ Μ χλιαρὸν ὕδωρ SB θερμὸν χλιερὸν (sic) W θ. χλίον LVO(P) ‖ πιὼν τὸ θερμὸν WP(λ) ‖ 17 τὸ ὕδωρ μόνον MOSB τὸ ὕδωρ καὶ μόνον ἐκ τοῦ στόματος (στομίου W) αὐτοῦ WPλ ‖ 18 οὐδενὸς...γευσάμενος] νήστης γὰρ ἦν SB ‖ ἑτέρου ΜΟ ἄλλου WPλ ‖ τὸ παράπαν (τὸ om. W) ὁ Αἴσωπος post γευσάμενος ΡλW ‖ 20 ἐδέετο...ποιῆσαι Μ(ΟΡλ) ἐδέετο δὲ ἵνα καὶ οἱ κατήγοροι αὐτοῦ τοῦτο ποιήσωσι W(SB) ‖ καὶ ἐπιγνώσῃ ΜΟ καὶ ἐν τούτῳ γνώσῃ W(Ρλ) ‖ 21 ὁ δὲ MOSB ὁ δὲ δεσπότης αὐτοῦ WPλ ‖ αὐτοῦ τὸ νοερὸν MOSB τ. ν. τοῦ Αἰσώπου Wλ(P) ‖ 22 ποιῆσαι ὁμοίως ΜΟ ὁ. π. WPλ τοῦτο ποιῆσαι SB ‖ 25 πρὸς ἀνέβλυσαν Ο προσαν......Μ προσανέλυσαν LFV (P) προσανέκαμψαν SB πρὸς τὸ στόμα ἀνήλθοσαν W ‖ 26 αὐτομάτως (M)OSB om. rell. ‖ ἀνέδραμον ἔξωθεν WPλ ‖ 26–27 τότε ὁ. δ. εἶπε ΜΟ ταῦτα (δὲ add. W) ὁ δ. αὐτῶν ἰδὼν εἶπε ΡλW τότε ὁ κύριος αὐτῶν αἰσθανόμενος τὸ σκαιώρημα λέγει αὐτοῖς SB.

NOTES

1. The reported reading of the papyrus is]. αρων ει[. The editors may easily have mistaken φ for ρ. ει for ι appears in l. 55 of the Oxy. pap. (*infra*, p. 49).

2-4 (ἔπεμψεν). Restored from G.

2. The editors read ὁ α[ὑτοῦ κύριος, on the analogy of Westermann's text (from SBP); but G and probably also the archetype of W have ὁ δεσπότης, and ạ and δ̣, when indistinct, are very easily confused.

3. πολιτικῆς is the reading of W as well as of G, though it does not appear in Westermann's edition—hence the failure of Collart and Zeitz.

4. ἐν τῶ]ν κτ. α[ὑτοῦ. Herein the papyrus agrees with W against G.

5. τὸν οἰκονό]μον αὐτοῦ κ[ύριον (or καλέσας, κατέλιπε, or καί)? The sense of the missing words may be that Aesop was put under the charge of the overseer, Zenas. Collart's παραγενο]μένου τοῦ κ[υρίου, taken from a part of Westermann's text that corresponds to lines 7-8 of the papyrus, is impossible from the standpoint both of sense and of palaeography; *cf.* Zeitz p. 28. Zeitz suggests πρόθυ]μον αὐτοῦ κ[ατέλιπεν; but for πρόθυμον, on the analogy of Planudes, there is no traditional authority.

6-8. This passage, for which there is only a partial equivalent in W, is thus plausibly supplemented by Zeitz; ὁ δὲ δεσπότη]ς ἐ[σή]ει εἰς τὴν πόλ[ιν . . . .] . .οτον· ὑπὸ δὲ τὴν ὥρα[ν τῶν σύκων ὁ δεσπότης αὐτοῦ ἀπ]ήντησεν εἰς τὰ ἑαυτοῦ [κτήματα. I prefer κατήντησεν because the word is more frequent in the Aesopica, and because the letter before the first η, according to Collart's report, is not π, but one which (like τ) extends below the line.

9. ἐπικ[αίρια Zeitz.

11-12. W's reading, νὴ...οἰκέτη, is too long to insert in the lacuna, especially when accompanied by SBP's πάνυ and ἐπὶ τούτοις; we need something like "καλά, νὴ τὸν Ἑρμῆν." καί φησιν· "'Αγαθόπου. Zeitz reads [πάνυ τερφθεὶς ἐπὶ τούτοις· "'Αγαθ]όπου, which omits the most essential part of W's text, and contains only one word (τερφθεὶς) that can confidently be referred to its archetype.

12. The papyrus is said to read]ηπου; *cf.* Collart *ad loc.*

13. There is no traditional authority for the noun λουτροῦ, which Zeitz takes from Planudes' paraphrase (μετὰ τὸ λουτρόν).

13-15. The intervening text relates how Agathopous and his friend ate the figs and thereafter accused Aesop of having done so, and how Aesop, when about to be flogged, implored his master by signs to wait a moment, that he might prove his innocence.

15. The identity of the extant letters seems to be quite uncertain, and restoration would be futile in any case.

16. Zeitz reads τὸ θερμὸν ἐκ]πιών: the only authority for ἐκπιών is J. J. Reiske (not Schneider) in Westermann; and θερμόν, which is not in G, is probably a late accretion in W (see apparatus). Here again restoration is useless.

17. The papyrus reads]αξιος, emended to]αξας by Collart and Zeitz. For the supplement cf. G.

19. Zeitz conjectures δῆλόν με μ]ὴ γεύσασθαι τ[ῶν σύκων, which probably gives us the right sense. Here and in the next line G appears to have paraphrased the direct discourse of the papyrus.

21–22. Note that νοερόν agrees with W against G. On the analogy of G one is tempted to read [ἐκέλευσε τοὺς ἄλλους πιόντας ἐμέσ]αι, but that is probably too long.

22–24. Reconstructed from G. W has paraphrased by indirect discourse.

24. πειν is probably an error for πιεῖν. The papyrus also reads ατους for αὐτούς.

24–25. Zeitz proposes τὸ χ[λιαρὸν ὕδωρ καὶ συγκύψαι ἐμεσί[αν ἔλυσαν. This ignores W's τὰ σῦκα χολοποιὰ ὄντα, for which there is an exact equivalent in G, while συγκύψαι occurs only in W. Since there is not space enough for both phrases, the former only must be retained. Moreover, προσανέλυσαν, though unusual, has the support of several manuscripts in W, whereas ἐμεσίαν ἔλυσαν is without traditional authority.

25. I have adopted ναυτιάσαντες from Zeitz; but there is probably no connection between this and the ναυτίαν of Planudes. In the next line αὐτομάτως, for which Zeitz finds an equivalent only in Planudes (αὐτομάτην), is simply the traditional reading of W, although it does not appear in Westermann's text. I have added εὐθύς merely to fill out the line.

27. ἰδ]ών . . . σῦκ[α Zeitz.

b. Oxyrhynchus Papyrus 2083

No. 2083 of the *Oxyrhynchus Papyri*[3] dates from the late fourth or early fifth century, and contains a portion of the *Life of Aesop* corresponding to West. 30,21–31,18. Through

[3] *Oxy. Pap.* XVII (1927), 95–99.

the kindness of the editor, the late Professor Hunt, I have been able to obtain the facsimiles of this text which are reproduced on Plates I and II. With the aid of G the papyrus can be reconstructed throughout with considerable probability, at least as far as the sense of the missing words is concerned, and not infrequently also, as in lines 1–4, even to the letter. The number of letters in each line was approximately thirty, as Professor Hunt rightly estimated. This is confirmed by many of the new restorations. Some lines, however, must have contained as much as four or five letters more than others, since they do not all extend an equal distance to the right of the page (on the recto), and the spaces between the words vary in length and frequency. In a very few cases the lines as I have restored them contain as many as thirty-four letters, or as few as twenty-eight, but usually the number ranges from twenty-nine to thirty-one. I have kept Professor Hunt's supplements in lines 10, 14, 21, 28, 32, 34, 35, 41, 46, 53, 58, 59, 61, 64, 65, and 69. The text of *W*, which follows that of the papyrus, includes at the beginning a few lines of the immediately preceding context.

Recto   G

          [αιφνιδι-
1 ως γενομενος ανεξοδους ημας πο]ιηση

2 [εαν γαρ σημερον κριθας φαγης ε]ιτά αυτις
3 [γενηται αιφνιδιον τι εναντιο]ν ουτε
4 [χορτον ουτε κριθας εξεις] φαγειν ο Αι
5 [σωπος νη τας Μουσα]ς απεριεργος ειναι μοι

6 [φαινεται ο α̅ν̅ο̅ς̅ ο]υτος [πρ]οσελευσομαι

7 [προς αυτον προσελθ]ων δ[ε α]υτω πατεριω

8 [λεγει χαιροις ο δ]ε αντησπασατο Αι

μή τις ἀσθένεια ἐπιδράμῃ ἢ χειμὼν αἰφνιδίως γενόμενος ἀνεξόδους ἡμᾶς ποιήσῃ. ἐὰν γὰρ σήμερον κριθὰς φάγῃς εἶτα γένηται αἰφνίδιόν τι ἐναντίον, οὔτε χόρτον οὔτε κριθὰς ἔξεις φαγεῖν." Αἴσωπος ἀκούων ταῦτα πρὸς ἑαυτὸν εἶπεν· " νὴ τὰς Μούσας, ἀπερίεργός μοι φαίνεται ὁ 'α̅ν̅ο̅ς̅ οὗτος· προσελεύσομαι πρὸς αὐτόν." εἶτα προσεγγίσας λέγει· " πατερίων, χαίροις." ὁ ἄγροικος ἀντησπάσατο. Αἴσωπος

LIFE OF AESOP 47

9 [σωπος εφη προς αυτο]ν ποσου τα ξυλα δω
10 [δεκα εφη ασσαριω] Αισωπος ως και αληθης
11 [εστι οσου προεθετο] τοσουτου τετιμηται

12 [ειτα λεγει Ξανθο]ν οιδας τον φιλοσοφο̄

13 [ουχι τεκνον δια τ]ι οτι ουκ ειμι περι

14 [εργος Αισωπος αγα]θα σοι γενοιτο εκει

15 [νου ειμι δουλος τ]ουτο γαρ αν εγω σε εξη
16 [τησα ποτερον δ]ουλο[ς ε]ι η ελευθερος
 <τί δέ μοι τοῦτο διαφέρει; Αἴσωπος λέγει>

17 [αληθως απεριε]ργος νη τους θεους
18 [πατεριων πεπ]ραται σου τα ξυλα ελασον
19 [ουν εις την] οικιαν Ξανθου το οναριον
20 [ο αγροικος εφη] αλλα τη οικιαν ουκ οιδα

21 [ο δε Αισωπο]ς οιδας τα του φιλοσοφου
22 [ο ξενος ουχι ου] γαρ ειμι π[[ρ]]ολυπραγμων
23 [Αισωπος ακολουθ]ει μοι πατερ ηγαγεν αυ

24 [τον και καθελων] τα ξυλα εδωκεν αυτω

25 [ευθυς την τιμην] και φησιν αυτω πατερ
26 [ιων ο δεσποτης] μου ερωτα σε διπνησαι
27 [παρ αυτω κ]αταλιπε εις το μεσαυλιον

28 [το οναριον κ]αι τευξεται επιμελειας
29 [συ δε εισελθων κ]ατακλιθητι ο δε θελων

λέγει· "πόσου τὰ ξύλα;" ὁ ἄγροικος εἶπεν· "ιβ ἀσσαρίων." Αἴσωπος λέγει· "ἀληθῶς, ὅσου προέθετο τοσούτου καὶ πωλεῖ." εἶτα λέγει· "πατερίων, οἶδας Ξάνθον τὸν φιλόσοφον;" ὁ ἄγροικος εἶπεν· "οὐχί, τέκνον." Αἴσωπος λέγει· "διὰ τί;" ὁ ἄγροικος εἶπεν· "ὅτι οὐκ εἰμὶ περίεργος· ἀκούω γὰρ αὐτόν." Αἴσωπος λέγει· "πολλά σοι ἀγαθὰ γένοιτο. ἐκείνου εἰμὶ δοῦλος." ὁ ἄγροικος εἶπεν "τοῦτο γὰρ ἐγώ σε ἐξήτησα, πότερον δοῦλος εἶ ἢ ἐλεύθερος; τί δέ μοι τοῦτο διαφέρει;" Αἴσωπος λέγει· "ἀληθῶς ἀπερίεργός ἐστιν· πατερίων, πέπραταί σοι τὰ ξύλα. ἔλασον εἰς τὴν οἰκίαν Ξάνθου τὸ ὀνάριον." ὁ ἄγροικος εἶπεν· "ἀλλὰ τὴν οἰκίαν οὐκ οἶδα ποῦ ἐστιν."

Αἴσωπος λέγει· "ἀκολούθει μοι καὶ μαθήσῃ." καὶ ἤγαγεν αὐτὸν εἰς τὴν οἰκίαν καὶ καθεῖλεν τὰ ξύλα καὶ ἔδωκεν αὐτῷ τὴν τιμὴν καὶ εἶπεν· "πατερίων, ὁ δεσπότης μου ἐρωτᾷ σε δειπνῆσαι παρ' αὐτῷ· κατάλιπε οὖν τὸ ὀνάριον εἰς τὸ μεσίαυλον (sic) καὶ ἐπιμελείας τεύξεται." ὁ ἄγροικος εἰσελθὼν εἰς τὸ δεῖπνον

30 [λαμβανειν το] διπνον ουτε περιεργα   καὶ μὴ περιεργασάμενος
31 [σαμενος εκ] ποιας αιτια[s] καλειται   ἐκ ποίας αἰτίας καλεῖται
32 [ουτ ουν ει αυ]τος καλειτ[αι] εισηλθεν   εἰσῆλθεν
33 [ουτως ως ην συν] τω πηλω και τοις υπο   οὕτως σὺν τῷ πηλῷ ὡς ἦν καὶ τοῖς ὑποδήμασιν.
34 [δημασιν ον ι]δων ο Ξανθ[ος] λεγει Αι   ὁ Ξάνθος εἶπεν· "οὗτός ἐστιν
35 [σωπε εισηλθ]ε τις

Verso   G

36 απε[ριεργος ο Ξανθος ιδων οτι επαγγελ]   ὁ ἀπερίεργος; ὁ Ξάνθος ἰδὼν ὅτι ἐπαγγέλλεται

37 λετα[ι μεγα περι αυτου εφη τη γυναικι]   Αἴσωπος τὰ μέγιστα περὶ αὑτοῦ λέγει τῇ ἑαυτοῦ γυναικί·

38 κυρι[α θελεις τον Αισωπον δαρηναι η δε] "κυρά, θέλεις τὸν Αἴσωπον παιδευθῆναι;" ἡ γυνὴ τοῦ Ξάνθου

39 ειπε [τουτο ευχομαι ο Ξανθος ειπε συ]   λέγει· "τοῦτο εὔχομαι." ὁ Ξάνθος εἶπεν· "ποίησον οὖν ὡς λέγω σοι,

40 ουν ανα[στηθι και την λεκανην τω ξενω]   καὶ ἀναστᾶσα τὴν λεκάνην τῷ ξένῳ
41 προσενεγκο[ν] ως νι[ψουσα αυτου τους πο] προσένεγκε ὡς ὀφείλουσα νίψαι αὐτοῦ τοὺς πόδας.

42 δας απο τ[ης] αξιας [επιγνους οτι οικο]   κἀκεῖνος ἀπὸ τῆς ἀξίας σου ἐπιγνώσεται ὅτι οἰκο-

43 δεσποινα [συ] ει ου[κ εασεται αλλ ερει]   δέσποινα εἶ καὶ οὐ μὴ ἐάσηταί σοι, ἀλλ' ἐρεῖ σοι·

44 αυτη δουλος ουκ [εστι και φανη περι]   'κυρά, δοῦλος οὐκ ἔστιν ἵνα μου νίψῃ τοὺς πόδας,' καὶ φανήσεται περίεργος

45 εργος εξ αναγκης [και Αισωπος δαρησεται] καὶ Αἴσωπος δαρήσεται."
46 η δε θελουσα τω Α[ισωπω κακα γενεσθαι]   ἡ γυνὴ τοῦ Ξάνθου
47 αμα δε και μισουσα [αυτον ευθυς περι]   διὰ τὸ μῖσος τὸ πρὸς τὸν Αἴσωπον περι—

48 ζωσαμενη λεντιον[και ετερον βαλου]   ζωσαμένη λέντιον καὶ ἕτερον βαλοῦ—

49 σα κατα του ωμου πρ[οσεφερε λεκανην]   σα περὶ τοὺς ὤμους προσέφερεν τὴν λεκάνην

LIFE OF AESOP   49

50 τω αγροικω ο ξενο[s ιδων αυτην και νοη]
51 σας οτι η δεσποινα[εστιν προς εαυτον]

52 εφη Ξανθος εστιν[φιλοσοφος ει ηθελε]

53 Ξανθος μου τους ποδας υ[πο τινος παιδα]
54 ριου η δουλου πλυθηναι [επεταξεν αν ει δε]

55 αυτος μοι τειμην παρα[σχων την αυτου γυ]
56 ναικα ηναγκασεν νιψαι[εμαυτον ου]

57 καταγγελλω περιεργον[και δη προτει]

58 νας τους ποδας φησι ν[ιψον και νιψα]

59 μενος αναπιπτει ο Ξα[νθος ειπεν δο]

60 θητω τω ξενω πρωτω πι[ειν οινομελι]

61 ο απεριεργος παλιν προς εὑ[τον ειπε τους]
62 δεσποτας πρωτους εδ[ει πιεῖν αλλ εμοι]

63 τιμην παρεσχεν ουδ[εν ουν βουλομενος πε]

64 ριεργαζεσθαι λαβων επ[ιεν και ειπεν]

65 ακρως νη τους θεους[μετα δε τουτο]
66 εισηνεχθη λοπας ιχ[θυων και ο Ξανθος]

67 ειπεν τω [ξ]ενω πρω[τος εσθιε ο δε ξενος]

68 τους ιχθυ[α]s ως δελφ[ις λαβων κατεπι]

τῷ ξένῳ. ὁ ξένος νοή—
σας ὅτι ἐστὶν ἡ οἰκοδέσποινα πρὸς ἑαυτὸν
εἶπεν· "Ξάνθος ἐστὶ φιλόσοφος, εἰ ἤθελεν
τοὺς πόδας μου ὑπὸ
δούλου πλυθῆναι ἐπιτετάχει (sic) ἄν. εἰ δέ
μοι τιμὴν παρέχων τὴν γυναῖκα
τὴν ἑαυτοῦ ἠνάγκασεν νίψαι μου
τοὺς πόδας, ἐμαυτῷ
ἀτιμίαν οὐ περιβάλλω, οὐ περιεργάσομαι,
ἀλλὰ προτείνοντός μου τοὺς πόδας
νίψημαι (sic)." καὶ δὴ νιψά—
μενος ἀνεπάει (sic). ὁ Ξάνθος
εἶπεν· "σοφῶς, νὴ τὰς Μούσας,"
<καὶ εἶπεν>
τῷ ξένῳ πρώτῳ δοθῆναι πιεῖν
οἰνόμελι.
ὁ ξένος πρὸς ἑαυτὸν εἶπεν. "τοὺς
οἰκοδεσπότας ἔδει πρῶτον πιεῖν,
ἀλλ' ἐμοὶ
τὴν τιμὴν παρέχων ὁ φιλόσοφος
πρώτῳ διετάξατο δοθῆναι πιεῖν·
οὐ
περιεργάσομαι οὖν." καὶ λαβὼν
ἔπιεν.

ὁ Ξάνθος ἐπέτρεψεν δεῖπον εἰσε-
νεχθῆναι. εἰσήχθη λοπὰς ἰχθύων.
ὁ Ξάνθος
τῷ ἀγροίκῳ εἶπεν· "ἔσθιε." ὁ ἄγροικος
ὡς Χάρυβδις δελφῖνος (sic) ἤρξατο
καταπίνειν.

69 νε ο δ[ε] Ξανθος γε[υσαμενος αυτων]   ὁ Ξάνθος γευσάμενος
70 και θελων εκκαλεσα[σθαι τον αγροικον]   καὶ θέλων ἐκκαλέσασθαι
                                          τὸν ἄγροικον—

W (cf. West. 30, 16ff.)

ὁ δὲ χωρικὸς τῷ ὀναρίῳ φησί· " περιπάτει, ὅπως ταχέως φθάσωμεν εἰς τὴν πόλιν καὶ πραθῶσι τὰ ξυλάρια ἀσσαρίων δώδεκα, καὶ ἕξεις σὺ δύο εἰς χόρτον καὶ κριθήν, κἀγὼ δύο εἰς ἐμαυτόν, τὰ δὲ ὀκτὼ τηρήσωμεν εἰς ἑτέρας τύχας, μή τις ἀσθένεια ἐπιδράμῃ ἢ αἰφνιδίως γένηται χειμών." (4–5) Αἴσωπος δὲ ἐν ἑαυτῷ λέγει· " τί ταῦτα; τῷ ὀναρίῳ διαλέγεται, ὡς μᾶλλον ἀπερίεργός ἐστιν· (6–7) ἀσπάσομαι αὐτον." καὶ ἀσπασάμενος (8) " χαῖρε" φησίν. ὁ δὲ ἀντησπάσατο. Αἴσωπός (9–11) φησι· " πόσου τὰ ξυλάρια;" ὁ χωρικὸς ἔφη· " δώδεκα ἀσσαρίων." (12) Αἴσωπος λέγει· " Ξάνθον οἶδας τὸν φιλόσοφον;" (13–14) ὁ δέ φησιν· " οὔ, τέκνον." Αἴσωπος λέγει· " διὰ τί;" ὁ ξένος ἔφη· " ἐγὼ ἄγροικός εἰμι, οὐδένα ἐπίσταμαι." (14) ὁ δὲ Αἴσωπος, " ἐκείνου," (15) φησί, " δοῦλός εἰμι." ὁ ξένος ἔφη· " τί ἠρώτησά σε (16) πότερον δοῦλος εἶ ἢ ἐλεύθερος; (17–22) ἐμοὶ τί διαφέρει;" Αἴσωπος ἔφη· " ἀγαθά σοι γένοιτο, (23) ἀκολούθει μοι κἀγώ σοι δώσω τὸ ἀργύριον μετὰ καὶ τοῦ ἀρίστου." ἀγαγὼν δὲ αὐτὸν (24) εἰς τὴν οἰκίαν καθεῖλε τὰ ξυλάρια δεδωκὼς (25) τὸ τίμημα καί φησιν· (26) " ὁ δεσπότης μου ἐρωτᾷ <σε> παρ' αὐτῷ ἀριστῆσαι." (29–30) ὁ δὲ ἄγροικος οὐ περιεργασάμενος (31) διὰ ποίαν αἰτίαν καλεῖται, (32–33) εἰσελθὼν σὺν τῷ πηλῷ καὶ τοῖς ὑποδήμασιν (34) οὕτως ἀνέπεσεν. ὁ δὲ Ξάνθος ἔφη· (35–36) " τίς οὗτος;" Αἴσωπος ἔφη· " ἄνθρωπος ἀπερίεργος." (36–40) ἰδὼν δὲ αὐτὸν ἐκεῖνος ἄγροικον ὄντα λέγει τῇ ἑαυτοῦ γυναικί· " κυρία, ὑποκρίθητί μοι ἵνα δαμάσω τὸν Αἴσωπον· καὶ ἀναστᾶσα, βαλοῦσα ὕδωρ εἰς τὴν λεκάνην (41) πρόσφερε τῷ ξένῳ ὡς νίψουσα αὐτοῦ τοὺς πόδας· (42–45) ἴσως εὐλαβηθεὶς φανῇ περίεργος καὶ ὁ Αἴσωπος δαρήσεται." (46–50) ἡ δὲ θέλουσα τὸν Αἴσωπον τυφθῆναι ὑπεκρίθη, καὶ λαβοῦσα λέντιον προσέφερε τῷ ξένῳ (50–52) τὴν λεκάνην. ὁ δὲ θεασάμενος καὶ γνοὺς ὅτι ἐστὶν ἡ οἰκοδέσποινα, φησὶ πρὸς ἑαυτόν· (52–58) " πάντως τιμῆσαί με θέλει, καὶ διὰ τοῦτο αὐτοχείρως νίπτει μου τοὺς πόδας· εἰ δὲ ἤθελέ μου τοὺς πόδας ὑπὸ δούλου νιφθῆναι εἶχεν ἂν ἐπιτάξαι." καὶ προτείνας (58–59) τοὺς πόδας ἔφη. " νίψον, κυρία," καὶ νιψάμενος (59–60) ἀνέπεσεν. ὁ δὲ Ξάνθος φησί· "δοθήτω (60) τῷ ξένῳ πρῶτον οἰνόμελι." (61-62) ὁ δὲ ξένος πρὸς ἑαυτόν. "αὐτοὺς μὲν ἔδει πρῶτον πιεῖν, (62-64) ἐπεὶ δὲ αὐτοῖς οὕτως δοκεῖ οὐ περιεργάσομαι." (64-66) καὶ λαβὼν ἔπιεν. ἀριστώντων δὲ αὐτῶν παρετέθη ἰχθύων λοπάς. ὁ Ξάνθος (67-68) τῷ ξένῳ λέγει· "φάγε." ὁ δὲ ὡς δελφὶς ἤσθιε τοὺς ἰχθύας. (69-70) ὁ δὲ Ξάνθος ἐπαφορμιζόμενος λέγει τῷ μαγείρῳ· "διὰ τί κακῶς ἤρτυσας;"

Variants in W: ὁ δὲ χωρικὸς...ἐρωτᾷ (26)] desunt in SBP || ἔξεις Ολ   ἔξης M   ἐξῆς W || σοι pro σὺ W || μή...ἐπιδράμῃ] μή τις ἡμῶν ἀσθενήσῃ M || ἐπιδράμῃ W   περιδράμει Ο   om. LFV || ἡ W   ἡ καὶ M   καὶ Ο || αἰφνιδίως MO   αἰφνίδιος W(λ) || χειμὼν γένηται M || 4-5. Αἴσωπος...λέγει] Αἴσ. δὲ ἐν ἑαυτῷ λογιζόμενος M   Ἔσωπος λέγει ἐν ἑαυτῷ Ο   ὁ δὲ Αἴσ. ἐν ἑαυτῷ W   Αἴσ. ἐν ἑαυτῷ ἔλεγε LFV || ὡς codd.   τίς West. || 6-7 ἀσπ. αὐτὸν om. O || καὶ ἀσπ.] καὶ ἐλθὼν ἔφη V || 8 φησίν] λέγει αὐτῷ Ο || χαῖρε εἰπὼν post ἀντησπάσατο MλW   om. Ο || 9-10 φησι OW   ἔφη M   εἶπε LFV || πωλεῖς post ξυλάρια M || ὁ χ. ἔφη om. Ο || 12 λέγει Mλ   ἔφη WO || 13-14 ὁ δὲ...ἔφη] ὁ δέ, οὔ. διὰ τί; ἔφη. καὶ ὁ ξένος Ο || 14 ὁ δὲ Αἴσ. M   ὁ Ἔσωπος ἔφη Ο   ὁ (ὁ om. W) Αἴσ., add. φησί post ἐκείνου, Wλ || 15 ὁ ξ. ἔφη MW   καὶ ὁ ξ. πρὸς αὐτὸν Ο || καὶ τί W || τί ἠρώτησά σε (σε om. OW) MOW   ἐγὼ ἐρωτῶ σε LFV || 17-22 Αἴσ. ἔφη MW   Αἴσ. λέγει LFV   Ἔσωπός φησι, sed infra post γένοιτο, Ο || τοῦ M   om. rell. || 26 ἐρωτᾷ παρ' (ἐπ' MW) αὐτῷ ἀριστῆσαι MOW   κελεύει σοι (σοι om. P) ἵνα μετ' αὐτοῦ ἀριστήσῃς (-ησις P) SP   σε καλεῖ ἵνα μετ' αὐτοῦ ἀριστήσεις B || 31 διὰ codd.   ἐπὶ West. || κέκληται SBP || 32-33 εἰσελθὼν MOWλ   ἐλήλυθε καὶ εἰσελθὼν μετὰ τῶν λοιπῶν (μ.τ.λ. om. P; ἐν τῷ οἴκῳ S) BPS || 35-36 τίς ἐστιν οὗτος SBP || ἀπερίεργος ἄνθρωπος M || 36-40 ἰδών...ὄντα] ὁ δὲ Ξάνθος SBP || ἵνα δαμάσω MλW   ὅπως τύψω (τυπτήσω P) BP || καὶ ἀναστᾶσα... δαρήσεται] ὅπερ γάρ σοι ἐπιτάσσω ποίει.   καὶ λέγει αὐτῇ εἰς ἐπήκοον πάντων κυρία, βάλλουσα ὕδωρ εἰς τὴν λεκάνην νίψον τοὺς πόδας τοῦ ξένου.   ἔλεγεν (ἔλεγον SB) γὰρ πάντως (pro γ.π., πάντες B, οὖν S) εὐλαβηθήσεται ὁ ξένος καὶ ὁ Αἴσ. τυφθήσεται B (P), et S nisi quod ad init. ἵνα καὶ σὺ ὃ ἐπιτάσσει ποιεῖ legitur pro ὅπερ...ποίει || κ. ἀναστᾶσα MO   ἡ δὲ ἀν. καὶ W   σὺ δὲ ἀν. κ. West. || βάλε...λεκάνην καὶ πρόσφερε Ο   καὶ ὕδωρ εἰς λ. βαλοῦσα προσέφερε W || 41 νίψουσα W   νίπτουσα Ολ || 46-50 ἡ δὲ...λεκάνην] ἡ δὲ βαλοῦσα (βαλλοῦσα SB) ὕδωρ εἰς τ. λ. προσέφερε τοῦ νίψαι τοὺς πόδας αὐτοῦ (τοῦ ξένου B) SBP || 50-52 πρὸς ἑαυτόν Ο   καθ' ἑαυτόν (ἑαυτοῦ P) SBPW   om. Mλ || 52-58 εἰ δὲ...προτείνας τοὺς πόδας om. West. || εἰ δὲ ἤθελε MOλ   εἰ γὰρ ἐβούλετο SB(P) || δούλου MO   δούλων (S)BPW || 58-59 ἔφη MS   φησί OBPλW || 64-66 παρετέθη MO   παρετίθη W   παρέθηκεν SBP   περιετέθη LFV || ἰχθύων λοπάς Ο   ἰχθύς MF   ἰχθῦς WLV   ἰχθύν SBP || 67-68 ὡς δελφὶς MOLF   ὡς ἀδελφὸς WV   om. SBP || 69-70 ἐπαφορμιζόμενος MλW   ἀφορμισάμενος Ο   περιεργαζόμενος SB(P).

NOTES

Owing to his dependence upon Westermann, the latest editor, Zeitz, makes false supplements in lines 5, 6, 7, 11, 17, 18, 27, 33, 36, 37, 38, 39, 40, 42, 43, 45, 47, 48, 49, 52, 54, 56, 60, 68, and 70. I have refrained from commenting upon these systematically.

14. There is room for ἔφη after Αἴσωπος if we allow thirty-four letters to the line.

16. After ἐλεύθερος a line has evidently been omitted in the papyrus by accident; G's reading fills the gap perfectly.

20. τη papyrus; read τὴν.

21–22. These lines appear to be superfluous and out of place; hence we may suspect that the text of the papyrus, like that of G, was occasionally interpolated from other sources.

26. The papyrus has διπνῆοαι, the o being crossed out.

35. The last half of this line has been left blank for no apparent reason. On the assumption that nothing was omitted I have adopted Professor Hunt's supplement; but if we assume a lacuna in the text of the papyrus, which is not unlikely, then it is better to restore with Zeitz as follows (cf. W): "Αἴ[σωπε, εἰπ]ὲ, τίς [οὗτος ;" Αἴσωπος ἔφη· " ἄνθρωπος] ἀπε[ρίεργος."

36–37. ἤγγει]λε τὰ [μέγιστα etc. is also possible.

39. Note that G's ποίησον...σοι is a needless addition, that it is retained in substance by the archetype of W (ὑποκρίθητι), and that SBP appears to have changed it back to a form nearer that of G.

44. Either αὕτη or αὐτῇ may be read.

47. σφόδρα might do as well as εὐθύς; but some such word is necessary in order to fill out the line.

54 and 57–8 (προτείνας τοὺς πόδας). Zeitz (p. 33) is mistaken in supposing that Planudes alone agrees with the papyrus in respect to the substance of these lines; there is a full equivalent in all the manuscripts of W, but it is omitted accidentally in Westermann's text. Cf. supra, under W.

68. The reading ὡς ἀδελφός, which appears in West., and which has given the commentators (Hunt, Zeitz, and Hausrath) much trouble, is merely an error peculiar to the manuscripts W and V. The original reading of W was δελφίς (MOLF), and G has the equivalent δελφῖνος. The readings of LF, M, and S, as reported by Zeitz second hand from Marc, do not stand in this passage at all, but at West. 54,32.

c. Berlin Papyrus No. 11628

The complete text of this fragment has recently been published by Zeitz, although twelve lines of it (33–44) were reproduced in facsimile by Schubart in his *Griechische Palaeographie* (1925) I, 131 (= Müller's *Handbuch d. kl. Alt.* Bd. I, Abt. 4, erster Hälfte). The date of the papyrus, according to Schubart, is the late second or early third century after Christ. The lines normally contained between 17 and 20 letters, and are easily restored except in the first column. The reading Λυκωρος, which seems to be the source of SBP's Λυκοῦρος, as contrasted with Λυκοῦργος in GW, suggests that the Berlin papyrus does not belong to the ancient edition typified by GW, but to that which we have described above (p. 35) as the source of SBP's interpolations. Some slight confirmation of this may be seen in the reading παιδείαν in line 53, which appears in G as a variant on the σοφίαν of GW. Since παιδείαν does not appear in SBP, we cannot be sure that it stood in the source of SBP's interpolations; but since we have at least one sure instance in which the second member of a compound reading in G can be traced to that source (*supra*, p. 29), it is probable that παιδίαν belongs in the same category.

TEXT

	Col. 1	G
1	]ωσω	ὁ δὲ βασιλεὺς ἀκούσας περιχαρὴς ἐγένετο, δόξας εὑρηκέναι νίκας. καὶ παρα-
2	παραγενομε]νω	γεναμένου (sic) τοῦ Αἰσώπου ἔφη αὐτῷ
3	[Αισωπω εφη ετι ε]ν η[μιν]	ὁ βασιλεὺς Νεκταναβών· "ἔτι ἐν ἡμῖν
4	[επιλυσον καγω] φορους	ἐπίλυσον κἀγὼ παράσχω φόρους
5	[τω Λυκωρω παρεξ]ομαι	Λυκούργῳ, λέξον (λέγον cod.) ἡμῖν
6	[ειπε ο ουτε εωρακαμε]ν ου	ὃ οὔτε ἴδομεν οὔτε
7	[τε ακηκοαμεν ο δε Αισ]ω	ἠκούσαμέν ποτε." ὁ δὲ Αἴσωπος
8	[πος εφη αποκριθησομ]αι	ἔφη· "δός μοι τριῶν ἡμερῶν καὶ ἀποκριθήσομαί σοι." καὶ ἐξελθὼν ἀπὸ τοῦ

9]ναι	βασιλέως διελογήζετο (sic) ἐν ἑαυτῷ ὁ Αἴσωπος· "ὅτι περ ἐὰν εἴπω, φήσωσιν (sic) εἰδέναι αὐτό." πανοῦργος δὲ ὢν ὁ Αἴσωπος καθέξεται καὶ τυποῖ ἑαυτῷ δανείου γραφὴν τοιαύτην· †τῷ Νεκταναβῷ δανεισάμενος παρὰ Λυκούργῳ χίλια τάλαντα χρυσίου χρόνου ἐν οἷς τὸν παρελθόντα παρεσχηκέναι.† μετὰ δὲ τὰς τρεῖς ἡμέρας ἦλθεν ὁ Αἴσωπος πρὸς τὸν βασιλέα Νεκταναβῶν καὶ εὗρεν αὐτὸν μετὰ τῶν
Lacuna	
10]<π>ροσ	φίλων προσ-

Col. 2

11 δεχομε<ν>[ον πρ]ος <το> απο-	δεχόμενον (-ου cod.) πρὸς τὸ ἀπο-
12 ρησαι αυ[τον εκ]βα[λων]	ρῆσαι. ὁ δὲ Αἴσωπος ἐκβαλὼν τὸ χειρόγραφον ψευδῆ ἔφη·
13 ουν εις μεσο[ν α]νεγνω	"ἀνάγνωτε
14 το δανιον οι δε [ε]φασαν	τὸν κοινὸν τοῦτον." οἱ δὲ φίλοι τοῦ βασιλέως Νεκταναβῶν ἔφησαν
15 [ψ]ευδομενοι κ[αι ε]ωρακε	ψευδόμενοι· "τοῦτον καὶ ἑωράκαμεν
16 ναι και ακηκο[εν]αι εν	καὶ ἀκηκόαμεν πολλάκις."
17 τυπους ο δε Αισω[π]ος χαι	ὁ δὲ Αἴσωπος ἔφη· "χαίρω
18 ρω φησιν επ<ε>ι υ[μεις] και μαρ	μαρτυρούντων.
19 [τυρ]ειτε αποδο[τ]ε ουν	ἀποδοθήτω παραυτὰ
20 τα χρηματα [η γ]αρ προ	τὰ χρήματα· ἡ γὰρ προ-
21 [θεσ]μια παρηλ[θεν] της	θεσμία παρῆλθεν τῆς ?
22 [απο]δοσεως ο δε [Νε]κτα	ἀποδόσεως." ὁ δὲ βασιλεὺς Νεκτα-
23 [νεβο]ς αγανακτ[η]σας [ε]	ναβῶν ἀκούσας ἔφη·
24 [λεξε π]οθεν υμ[εις μ]αρ	"πόθεν μαρτυρεῖτε
25 [τυρει]τε περ[ι ου ο]υ[τε] ε	περὶ τῶν (sic) ἐγὼ οὐκ ἐποφείλω;" οἱ δὲ εἶπον· "οὔτε
26 [ωρακα]μεν ουτε [ακηκο]α	οἴδαμεν οὔτε ἠκούσαμέν
27 [μεν ο] δε Αισωπ[ος εφη ει]	ποτε." ὁ δὲ Αἴσωπος ἔφη· "εἰ (τί cod.)
28 [ταυτα] δοκει ου[τω] λ[ε]λυ	ταῦτα ὑμῖν οὕτως δοκεῖ, λέλυ-
29 [ται το] προβλη[μα ο] δ[ε]	ται τὸ πρόβλημα." ὁ δὲ
30 [Νεκτ]α[ν]εβος ειπ[εν μα]	Νεκταναβῶν ἔφη· "μα-

LIFE OF AESOP 55

31 [καριο]ς Λυκωρ[ος εχ]ων
32 [τοιαυτ]ην σοφια[ν εν] τη

κάριος Λυκοῦργος
ἐν τῇ βασιλείᾳ αὐτοῦ τοιαύτην σοφίαν
κεκτημένος." (-ένους cod.)

Col. 3
33 εαυτου βασιλεια δους [αυ]
34 τῳ φορους ετων τρι[ων α]
35 πεπεμψε ο δε Αισωπ[ος πα]

36 ραγεναμενος εις Βα[βυ]
37 λωνα διηγησατο α[υτω]
38 τα πραγματα εν τη [Αι]
39 γυπτω επεδωκατ[ο δε]
40 χρηματα εκελευσε[ν]
41 ουν ο [Λ]υκωρος ανδρ[ιαν]
42 τας α[υ]του ανατεθη[ναι]
43 και εικονας χρονο[ν]

44 δε <τι> να συνβιωσα[ς] τω [βα]
45 σιλει [α]πεταξατο βουλ[ο]

46 μενος την Ελλαδα [εκ]
47 πλευσαι ομοσας αυτω
48 συνστεφεις εις τη<ν> Βα
49 βυλωνα κακει βι[ω]σασθ[αι]
50 τον λοιπον χρον[ο]ν π[ε]
51 [ρ]ιερχομενος τας πολε[ις]
52 επεδεικνυετο την α[υτου]
53 παιδειαν παρεγενε[το]
54 δε και εις Δελφους

δοὺς δὲ αὐ-
τῷ φόρους ἐτῶν τριῶν
ἔπεμψεν αὐτὸν (-ων cod.) μετὰ ἐπιστολῶν
εἰρηνικῶν. ὁ δὲ Αἴσωπος
παραγενάμενος εἰς Βαβυ-
λῶνα διηγήσατο τῷ Λυκούργῳ
πάντα τὰ πραχθέντα ἐν Αἰ-
γύπτῳ, καὶ ἀποδέδωκεν αὐτῷ τὰ
χρήματα. ἐκέλευσεν
οὖν ὁ Λυκοῦργος ἀνδριάντα χρυσοῦν
ἀχθῆναι τῷ (τὸ cod.) Αἰσώπῳ μετὰ
καὶ τῶν Μουσῶν, καὶ ἐποίησεν ἑορτὴν
μεγάλην ὁ βασιλεὺς ἐπὶ τῇ τοῦ Αἰσώπου
σοφίᾳ.

ὁ δὲ Αἴσωπος ἀπετάξατο τῷ βασιλεῖ
ἀπελθεῖν θέλων
εἰς Δελφούς,
ὀμώσας (sic) αὐτῷ πάλιν
ὑποστρέφειν πρὸς αὐτὸν ἐν Βα-
βυλῶνι (-νυ cod.) καὶ βιῶσαι
τὸν λοιπὸν χρόνον. πε-
ριερχόμενος δὲ τὰς λοιπὰς πόλεις
ἐπεδείκνυτο τὴν ἑαυτοῦ σοφίαν
καὶ παιδίαν. παρεγένετο
δὲ εἰς Δελφούς

W (cf. West. 51, 19ff.)

(1–7) Ἀρεσθεὶς οὖν ὁ Νεκτεναβὼ εἶπεν· "Αἴσωπε, φράσον ἡμῖν ὃ
οὔτε εἴδομεν οὔτε ἠκούσαμεν." ὁ δέ (8–11) φησι· "ἔνδοτέ μοι ἡμέρας
τρεῖς καὶ ἀποκριθήσομαι." πανοῦργος δὲ ὢν τυποῦται συγγραφὴν

δανείου τοιαύτην· δεδανεισμένον τὸν Νεκτεναβῶ παρὰ Λυκούργου τάλαντα χίλια, προσθεὶς χρόνον τὸν παρεληλυθότα. μετὰ δὲ τὰς τρεῖς ἡμέρας ἦλθεν ὁ Αἴσωπος καὶ εὗρε τὸν Νεκτεναβῶ μετὰ τῶν φίλων ἐκδεχόμενον. (12–23) εἰσελθὼν δὲ ἐπέδωκε τὸν χάρτην. οἱ δὲ πρὸ τοῦ τὴν δύναμιν γνῶναι ἔφασαν τοῦτο ἐπίστασθαι. ὁ δὲ Αἴσωπος ἔφη· "χάριν ἔχω· ἡ γὰρ προθεσμία τῆς ἀποδόσεως παρῆλθεν." ἀναγνοὺς δὲ ὁ Νεκτεναβῶ εἶπεν· (24–29) "ἐμοῦ μηδὲν χρεωστοῦντος Λυκούργῳ ὑμεῖς μαρτυρεῖτε;" οἱ δὲ εἶπον· "οὔτε εἴδομεν οὔτε ἠκούσαμεν." Αἴσωπος ἔφη· "εἰ ταῦτα οὕτως δοκεῖ, λέλυται τὸ ζήτημα." ὁ δὲ (30–35) Νεκτεναβῶ ἔφη· "μακάριος Λυκοῦργος, ἔχων τοιαύτην φιλοσοφίαν ἐν τῇ βασιλείᾳ αὐτοῦ." δοὺς δὲ αὐτῷ φόρους ἐτῶν δέκα ἀπέπεμψεν. ὁ δὲ Αἴσωπος (36–40) παραγενόμενος εἰς Βαβυλῶνα διηγήσατο Λυκούργῳ πάντα τὰ ἐν Αἰγύπτῳ πραχθέντα, ἀποδοὺς καὶ τὰ χρήματα. ὁ δὲ Λυκοῦργος ἐκέλευσεν (41–50) ἀνδριάντα χρυσοῦν ἀνατεθῆναι τοῦ Αἰσώπου, καὶ ἐτίμησε μεγάλως εὐφημοῦντα αὐτόν. μετ' ὀλίγον δὲ χρόνον τῷ βασιλεῖ συνταξάμενος ἐβουλεύσατο εἰς τὴν Ἑλλάδα πλεῦσαι, ὀμόσας αὐτῷ πάλιν ὑποστρέψαι εἰς Βαβυλῶνα κἀκεῖ τὸν λοιπὸν βιῶσαι χρόνον. (51–54) περιερχόμενος οὖν τὰς πόλεις τῆς Ἑλλάδος καὶ τὴν ἑαυτοῦ ἐπιδεικνύμενος σοφίαν παρεγένετο ἐν Δελφοῖς.

Variants in W: 1–7 οὖν om. M || ἐπὶ τούτῳ (-οις B) post οὖν BPW || εἶπεν Αἰσώπε MSW   λέγει Αἰσώπε P   ἔφη Αἰσ. B   προσεκαλέσατο τ. Αἰσωπον καὶ φησι R || τι post ἡμῖν W   τις M   πρᾶγμα PV   πράγματα (ἅπερ) B || εἴδομεν (οἴδαμεν P) οὔτε ἠκούσαμεν MBPV   ἠκ. οὔτε εἴδομεν (ἴδομεν R) WRS || 8–11 φησι om. R   ἔφη BP || ἔνδοτε...ἀποκρ.] αὔριον περὶ τούτου ἀποκριθήσομαι ὑμῖν BP || ὁ Αἴσωπος post ὧν BPWV || ἐτυπώσατο R || τοιαύτην RSW   ταύτην M   om. BP || δεδανεισμένον (-μένῳ LF) τὸν N. MLF   τὸν τε N. δ. W   τῷ (om. P) Νεκτεναβῶ δεδανεισμένα (-μένο R, -μένην B) SBPRV || Λυκούργου W   Λυκούργῳ RV   Λυκούρου SLF   abscissum in M   Λυκούρῳ P   Λυκήρῳ B (unde Planudes) || χίλια τ. BP || προσθεὶς...παρεληλ. om. BPV || προσθεὶς καὶ MLF || μετὰ...ἡμέρας] πρῶτας δὲ γενομένης BP || τὰς R   om. rell. || ἦλθεν...εὗρε] ἐλθὼν εὗρε BP || ὁ R   om. rell. || φίλων αὐτοῦ BPR || ἐκδεχόμενον om. BP || Αἴσωπον post ἐκδ. W || 12–23 καὶ εἰσελθὼν BP || Αἴσωπος post δὲ W || δέδωκε MB || τὸ χαρτίον WR   τὸ ἔγγραφον BP || γνῶναι R   διαγνῶναι MWLF   ἀναγνῶναι BPV || ὁ...ἔφη] καὶ ὁ Αἰσ. πρὸς αὐτοὺς R || εἰς τοῦτο post ἔχω BPV || δὲ MRW   οὖν BPV || τὴν ὁμολογίαν post οὖν (δὲ) BPVW || λέγει BPV || 24–29 ἐμοῦ μ. χρ. Λυκούργῳ (Λυκούρῳ P, Λυκήρῳ B) WBP   ἐμοῦ μ. Λυκούργῳ χρ. S   ἐ[μοῦ Λυκούργῳ] μ. χρ. M   ἐμοὶ μ. Λυκούργῳ χρεωστοῦντι R   οἴδαμεν SP || ἠκούσαμεν οὔτε ἴδμεν R || Αἰσ.... δοκεῖ] R   Αἴσωπος εἶπεν οὐκοῦν εἰ ταῦτα οὕτως [δοκεῖ?] M   Αἰσ. εἶπεν εἰ τ. οὕτως δ. S   εἶπεν δὲ (οὖν W) πρὸς αὐτοὺς ὁ Αἰσ. εἰ (καὶ εἰ B) τ. οὕτως ἔχει

LIFE OF AESOP 57

(ἔχει οὕτως P, οὕτως δοκεῖ W) BPW || ὁ δὲ N. ἔφη MSW   ὁ δὲ βασιλεὺς ἔφη R   ἔφη δὲ N. BP || 30-35 μακάριος...αὑτοῦ] RWF(MLS)   μ. ἐστι Λυκοῦργος (Λυκῆρος B) ὅτι τοιαύτην σοφίαν (φιλοσοφίαν V) κέκτηται ἐν τῇ αὑτοῦ β. BV   μ. εἰ Λύκουρε ὅτι αὑτην φιλοσοφίαν κέκτησαι ἐν τῇ σαυτοῦ β. P || δοὺς δὲ] καὶ δοὺς BP || δέκα ἐτῶν W   δ. ἐνιαυτῶν B   ἐνιαυτῶν δ. P || ἀπέστειλεν αὐτόν BP || 36-40 ἐν Βαβυλῶνι BP || Λυκούργῳ W   Λυκούρῳ S   om. R   Λυκούρῳ τῷ βασιλεῖ M   τ. β. Λυκούρῳ (Λυκήρῳ B) BP || ἅπαντα BP || ἀποδοὺς αὐτῷ BPW || 41-50 τοῦ Αἰσώπου RS   τῷ Αἰσώπῳ rell. || καὶ...αὐτόν] R cf. G   om. rell. || μετὰ δὲ χρ. ὀλίγον BP || ἀποπλεῦσαι M || ἐπωμώσας BP || πάλιν om. RS || κἀκεῖσε BP || τ. ὑπόλοιπον αὐτοῦ χρ. β. B   τ. ὑπολ. χρ. τῆς ζωῆς αὐτοῦ β. P || περιερχόμενος SBPλ   περιερχομένου RW   abscissum in M || οὖν MRSWLF   δὲ BPV || πόλεις πάσας BP || ἐπιδεικνύμενος Mλ-SBP   ἐπιδεικνυμένου RW || παρεγένετο καὶ MLFBP

NOTES

3. Zeitz reads]τη[
6-8. οὔτε...Αἴσωπος Zeitz; cf. infra, 15-16, 25-27.
9-10. It is clear that the substance of G and W, i.e. the making of the false document and the indication of its nature, however briefly related, could not possibly have been contained in the narrow space of these two lines (ca. 33 letters); we must therefore conclude that there was a lacuna in the text of the papyrus itself.
10-11. Zeitz supposes that another line of writing stood in the papyrus after no. 10 and at the bottom of the column; but the similarity of .ρος + δεχομε. to G's προσδεχόμενον can hardly be accidental, and the resulting sense is perfect.
11. After]ος Zeitz indicates that at least one letter has been lost; <τὸ> is therefore plausible.
13-17. Restored by Zeitz.
15-16. The papyrus reads ε]ορακαναι.
18. Zeitz suggests that ἐπὶ is for ἐπεί; cf. δάνιον for δάνειον in 15. υ[μεις] και (or μοι) Perry; Zeitz reads υ[ ]ιαι.
18-19. μαρτυρεῖτε Zeitz, μαρ[...]ειται papyrus.
19-23 (ἀγανακτήσας). Restored by Zeitz.
23-24. [ὀφείλειν μ]ηδὲν Zeitz, who admits, however, that the papyrus reads]ηθεν and that the space is very narrow for ὀφείλειν.
25-27 (Αἴσωπος). Restored by Zeitz.
25.]ται for]τε papyrus.
27. Αἰσωπ[ός φησι εἰ] Zeitz.
28-32. Restored by Zeitz.
31-32. Λυκῶρος (accent?) probably represents the traditional reading which passed, by interpolation, into the archetype of SBP in the form Λυκοῦρος. From the latter comes B's corrupt Λυκῆρος,

thence transmitted to Planudes (*cf. Text Tradition*, 236ff.). Herein the source of SBP's substituted reading agreed with the Berlin papyrus against G*W*. Note further that the papyrus agrees with G in reading σοφίαν, whereas the archetype of *W* changed to φιλοσοφίαν in accordance with the editor's preference for that term, and with his designation of Aesop as φιλόσοφος (*cf. infra*, p. 189). On the other hand the editor of the SBP archetype (as represented by B) has abandoned *W*'s original φιλοσοφίαν, and has taken σοφίαν (+ κέκτηται) from an older version closely resembling G and the papyrus. S in this region (West. 50ff.) very frequently deserts the SBP tradition to which it normally adheres, and follows, as here, the older MOR family. P and V get φιλοσοφίαν from λ; and V, which regularly depends upon λ up to West. 40, thereafter crosses frequently to SBP, whence its agreement with B in respect to ἐστι, ὅτι, κέκτηται. These relationships, complex though they are, are certain; in many cases, however, the manuscripts of *W* have been contaminated in such a way that the oldest reading can only be surmised.

33–37. Restored by Schubart.

36. παραγενάμενος]. Note the agreement in error between G and the papyrus.

38. Schubart adds <τὰ> after πράγματα; but πράγματα may be an error for πραχθέντα.

40–41. Thus Zeitz; Schubart reads ἐκέλευσε [δὲ] ὁ Πολύκωρος, for which there is no authority in the tradition; *cf.* also Λυκωρ[ος] in l. 31.

41 (ἀνδριάντας)–44 (βασιλεῖ) Schubart.

45–55. Thus Zeitz.

48. Read ὑποστρέφειν, or ὑποστρέψειν (Zeitz).

53. Note G's double reading: σοφίαν (= *W*) καὶ παιδίαν (= the papyrus). The papyrus reads παραγενε[το

d. The Golenischeff Papyrus

In the *Revue de Philologie* for 1885 (pp. 19ff.) [4] H. Weil published twenty-seven lines from a papyrus which had been acquired shortly before that time by W. Golenischeff in Cairo. This papyrus is now in the Museum at Moscow. The complete text has been carefully edited by G. Zereteli, at first in *Sammlung von Aufsätzen W. Lamansky* (St. Petersburg, 1907;

[4] Reprinted in the author's *Études de Littérature et de Rythmique Grecques*, Paris, 1902.

vol. I, 41–54), a publication which is not accessible to me, and more recently in *Papyri Russischer und Georgischer Sammlungen* (Tiflis, 1925) edited by G. Zereteli and O. Krueger, vol. I, 114–125. The text given below is taken from the latter publication. The twelve-page pamphlet by Filomena Potente (Naples, 1930) entitled *Il Papiro Golenischef*[5] contains nothing new or critical; but a few new supplements have recently been proposed by C. F. Kumaniecki in *Aegyptus* XIII (1933), 51f., and by Zeitz in his dissertation, and of these some account has been taken in the notes below. Zereteli dates the papyrus in the seventh century and gives a detailed description of it. The part of his description that is most relevant to our purpose reads as follows: "Ein langes Papyrusblatt, von dem rechts und links soviel weggebrochen ist, dass es in der Mitte der Kolumne etwa 2 cm. Breite hat und nur einzelne Buchstaben aufweist. Am meisten ist von rechts verloren gegangen, an der linken Seite fehlen nur 6 Buchstaben auf jeder Zeile. Oben und unten sind 2,5 cm. breite Ränder erhalten . . . die Buchstaben sind mit gleichmässig grobem Federdruck geschrieben und da sie recht eng aneinander gereiht sind, scheinen sie zusammenzufliessen." The statement that more has been lost on the right-hand side of the papyrus than on the left is applicable only to the verso; for the text as Zereteli prints it, and as a study of the contents clearly shows, lacks only about six letters on the right of the recto and as many on the left of the verso, whereas the major lacunae are on the opposite side of the page. The restoration of line 5, which is practically certain, shows that there were approximately fifty or fifty-two letters to a line. The restorations of single words within the extant portions of the papyrus are those of Zereteli, except that in line 70 I write μου βαλων for μ[. . . .].ων. The text of *W* is added after the notes on the papyrus.

[5] Reviewed by Hausrath in *Philologische Wochenschrift* LI (1931), 65–67; but my acquaintance with it is first-hand.

TEXT
Recto

1 [περιερχομενος δε τας π]ολεις επεδεικνυτο την εαυτου σ[οφιαν]
2 [κ(αι) παιδιαν παρεγενετο δε ε]ις Δελφους κακει επεδεικνυτο ο[ι δε οχ-]
3 [λοι ει κ(αι) ηδεως ηκροων]το κατ αρχας ουδεν αυτω παρειχον [ιδων δε]
4 [ο Αισωπος λαχανα τινα το]ις ανοις ομοχρωμα εφη προς αυτο[υς οιη]
5 [περ φυλλων γενεη τοιη δε κ]αι ανδρων ετι δε κ(αι) αυτοις προσκ[ρουσας]
6 [ειπεν ω Δελφοι ομοιοι εστ]ε ξυλω εν θαλασση φ[ε]ρομ[ε]νω [εκεινο]
7 [γαρ θεωρων τις εκ πολλου διαστη]ματος υπο κυματων φερομ[ε]ν[ον δο-]
8 [κει τινος αξιον ειναι επαν δ]ε εγγιστα ελθη ελαχιστον ο[ν ευρι-]
9 [σκει κ(αι) μηδενος λογου αξιον ο]μοιως δε καγω απο πορρωθ[εν υπαρ-]
10 [χων της υμετερας πολεως κατεπ]λησσομην δοκων υμας π(α)ν[τως μεγα-]
11 [λους ειναι νυν δε ηττονας ευρον] υμας των αλλων ανων π̱λα̱ν̱[ηθεις]
12 [ην ειχον υπερ υμων πρωην διανοια]ν· ουδεν γαρ αξιον υμ[εις ποι-]
13 [ειτε των γονεων οι δε Δελφοι ε]φησαν τινε[ς] γαρ [οι] γ[ο]ν[εις] η[μων ησ-]
14 [αν ο δε δουλοι ει δε αγνοειτε μαθη]τε εθος ην αρχ[ην π]αρα τοι̱ς̱ [Ελλη-]
15 [σιν ινα πεμπωσι πολιν καταλαβ]οντες τω [Α]πολλωνι̱ δεκ[ατον με-]
16 [ρος των λαφυρων απο ειδους εκασ]του οιον απο προβατω̱ν̱ [εκατον]

G

(1) περιερχόμενος δὲ τὰς λοιπὰς πόλεις ἐπεδείκνυτο τὴν ἑαυτοῦ σοφίαν (2) καὶ παιδίαν· παρεγένετο δὲ εἰς Δελφοὺς καὶ ἤρξατο κατεπιδείκνυσθαι. οἱ δὲ ὄχλοι (3) ἡδέως μὲν αὐτοῦ ἠκρόοντο (sic) τὰς καταρχάς, οὐδὲν δὲ αὐτῷ παρεῖχον. ἰδὼν δὲ (4) ὁ Αἴσωπος λαχάνοις τοὺς ανους ὁμόχροας ἔφη πρὸς αὐτούς· " οἱ (5) ὥσπερ φύλλον γένοιτο πρὸς δὲ καὶ ἀνδρῶν οἴηται " *** (6) " ξύλον ἐν θαλάσσῃ φερόμενον. ἐκεῖνο (ἐκεῖνοι cod.) (7) γὰρ θεωροῦντες ἐκ πολλοῦ διαστήματος ὑπὸ κυμάτων φερόμενον δοκοῦμέν (8) τι ἄξιον εἶναι, ἔπειτα ἐγγίσαντες αὐτῷ καὶ προσελθόντες ηὕρομεν ἐλάχιστον (9) καὶ μηδενὸς λόγου ἄξιον. ὁμοίως δὲ κἀγὼ πόρρωθεν ὑπάρχων (10–11) τῆς πόλεως ὑμῶν κατεπλησάμην (sic) ὑμᾶς πλουσίους καὶ μεγάλους ταῖς ψυχαῖς ὄντας· ἰδὼν δὲ ὑμᾶς τῶν ἄλλων ανων ἥττονας καὶ γένει καὶ πόλει πεπλάνημαι (-με cod.) (12) ἔχων (ἔχον cod.) περὶ ὑμῶν φαύλην διάλυσιν· οὐδὲν γὰρ ἀνάξιον (13) τῶν γονέων ποιεῖτε (-ῆτε cod.)." ταῦτα ἀκούσαντες οἱ Δέλφιοι πρὸς αὐτὸν εἶπον· " τίνες ἡμῶν ἐγνώσθεις (sic)." (14) ὁ δὲ Αἴσωπος· "δούλων· εἰ δὲ ἀγνοεῖτε, μάθετε. νόμος ἦν ἀρχαῖος παρὰ τοῖς Ἕλλησιν (15–16) ἵνα ἐὰν πόλιν καταλάβωνται τῶν λαφύρων

17 [δεκα απο βοων το αυτο μερος και] ἀπο αλλων τετραποδων απο χ[ρημα-]
18 [των απο σωματων ανδρων κ(αι) γυ]ναικων· εκ τουτου υμεις εγενν[ηθητε]
19 [ανελευθεροι οντες ταυτα ει]πων ο Αισωπος περι εκδημιαν [εγενε-]
20 [το οι δε Δελφοι περι Αισ]ωπον λογιζομενοι οτι εαν εις ετ[ερας πο-]
21 [λεις ελθη χειρονα αυ]τους κακολογησει εβουλευσαντο [ανελειν]
22 [αυτον δολωι Απολλω]νος συνεργουντος αυτοις δια την ατ[ιμιαν]
23 [την εν Σαμωι επει συν τ]αισ θ̄ Μουσαις ου καθιδρυσεν αυτῳ [·φοβου-]
24 [μενοι δε μηπως οι παραδημου]ντες ξενοι βοηθησωσιν αυ[τω φανε-]
25 [ρως μεν ουδεν εποιησαν π]αρατηρησαμενοι δε τον δουλο[ν αυτου]
26 [προ της πυλης σκευη φερο]ντα κ(αι) αφυπνωκοτα· ενεκρυψαν [φιαλην]
27]χρυσην εις τα στρωματα] αυτου εκ του ιερου αραντες· ο [δε Αισω-]
28 [πος αγνοων τα συνεσκευασμενα αυτωι] ω[δευ[σεν επι την Φω[κιδα οι]
29 [δε Δελφοι επιδραμοντες κ(αι) κρατησ]αντες τον Αισωπο[ν ειλκον]
30 [εις την πολιν του δε αρνουμενου μ]ηδεν ειδεναι κ(αι) λεγον[τος αδι-]

δέκατον μέρος τῷ Ἀπόλλωνι πέμπουσιν, οἷον ἀπὸ βοῶν [ἀπὸ] ἑκατὸν (17) δέκα, ἀπὸ αἰγῶν τὸ αὐτό, καὶ ἀπὸ τῶν ἄλλων τὸ αὐτό, ἀπὸ χρημάτων (18) ἀπὸ ἀνδρῶν, ἀπὸ γυναικῶν. ἐκ τούτων ὑμεῖς γεννηθέντες (19) ἀπελεύθεροί ἐστε ὁμοίως τοῖς δεδεμένοις· ἐκεῖθεν γὰρ ὄντες πάντων Ἑλλήνων καθεστήκατε (-ται cod.).'' ταῦτα εἰπὼν περὶ ἀποδημίαν ἐστέλλετο. (20–21) οἱ δὲ ἄρχοντες ἰδόντες αὐτοῦ τὸ κακόλογον ἐλογίζοντο· '' ἐὰν αὐτὸν ἀφῶμεν ἀποδημῆσαι, περιελθὼν εἰς ἑτέρας πόλεις πλεῖον ἀτιμοτέρους ἡμᾶς ποιήσει.'' ἐβουλεύσαντο οὖν ἀνελεῖν (22–23) δόλῳ. καὶ τοῦ Ἀπόλλωνος μηνίοντος διὰ (μηνύοντος δὲ cod.) τὴν ἐν Σάμῳ ἀτιμίαν, ἐπεὶ σὺν ταῖς Μούσαις ἑαυτὸν οὐ καθίδρυσεν, (24) μὴ ἔχοντες εὔλογον αἰτίαν, ἐμηχανήσαντό τι πανοῦργον, ἵνα μὴ οἱ παραδημοῦντες δυνήσονται αὐτῷ βοηθῆσαι. (25–27) παρατηρησάμενοι ἐπὶ τὴν πύλην τὸν δοῦλον αὐτοῦ ἀφυπνωκότα (-οκότα cod.) ἐπολέμουν, καὶ <εἰς> τὰ σκεύη φέροντες ἐκ τοῦ ἱεροῦ ἐνέκρυψαν φυάλην (sic) χρυσῆν. ὁ δὲ Αἴσωπος (28–29) ἀγνοῶν τὰ συν<ε>σκευασμένα εἰς τὴν Φωκίδα ὥδευεν. ἐπιδραμόντες δέ τινες τῶν Δελφῶν, δήσαντες αὐτὸν εἰς τὴν πόλιν εἷλκον. (30) βοῶντος (-τως cod.) δὲ αὐτοῦ· '' τίνος οὖν ἕνεκεν δέσμιόν με ἄγετε (-ται cod.); '' οἱ δέ· '' χρήματα ἔκλεψας ἐκ τοῦ ἱεροῦ.'' ὁ δὲ Αἴσωπος μηδὲν ἑαυτοῦ (sic) συνειδώς (-δών cod.), κλαίων ἔφησεν· '' ἀπολέσθαι θέλω ἐάν τι τοιοῦτον εὑρεθῇ

31 [κεισθαι οι Δελφοι εκτιναξαντες α]υτου τα σκευη ευρισκ[ουσι την]
32 [χρυσην φιαλην εκεινην του Απολλωνος] κ(αι) επεδεικνυον [αυτην]
33 [πασι τοις εν τη πολει μετα πολλου θορυβου κ(αι)] θυμου κ(αι) κρα[υγης πα-]
34 [ραδειγματιζοντες αυτον ο δε Αισωπος εδεε]το εξαφεθη[ναι οι δε]
35 [ουκ επειθοντο αλλ ενεκλεισαν αυτον εν τω δεσ]μωτηριω[Αισωπος]
36 [...................................το μελ]λον εκφυ[γειν..]
37 [....................................]αυτου τι[νος...]
38 [..................................] Αισωπο[......]
39 [...................................]ιλικησ[......]
40 [................................]σ ο δε Α[ισωπος]
41 [.................................]ν προς τ[......]
42 [..................................ε]πεθυμ[......]
43 [..............................π]ρος το μ[νημα..]
44 [................................ε]πυθετ[ο.......]
45 [........................... καλη]ν τε κ(αι) α[γαθην]
46 [...............................] καγω τ[......]

εἰς ἐμέ." (31) οἱ Δελφοὶ ἐκτινάξαντες τὰ σκεύη ηὖρον τὴν (32) φιάλην ἐπιδεικνύμενοι (33) τῇ πόλει καὶ μετὰ βίας καὶ θορύβου (34-35) παραδειγματίζοντες αὐτόν. ὁ Αἴσωπος λογιζόμενος ἐξ ἐπιβουλῆς συγκεκρυφέναι, ἠρώτα τοὺς Δελφούς. οἱ δὲ οὐκ ἐπείθοντο. Αἴσωπος λέγει· "θνητοὶ γεγονότες ὑπὲρ θεοὺς μὴ φρονεῖτε." οἱ δὲ ἐνέκλεισαν (-ησαν cod.) αὐτὸν εἰς φυλακὴν τιμωροῦντες. (36) Αἴσωπος μὴ εὑρίσκων μηχανὴν τῆς σωτηρίας ἔφη· "νῦν ἐγὼ θνητὸς ἄνθρωπος ὢν πῶς δυνήσομαι τὸ μέλλον ἐκφυγεῖν;"[6] (37) παραγενομένου δὲ φίλου αὐτοῦ τινος καὶ (38-39) παρακαλέσαντος τοὺς φύλακας εἰσῆλθεν πρὸς αὐτὸν (40) καὶ κλαίων (-ον cod.) ἔλεγεν· "τί γέγονεν τὰ ἡμῶν;" ὁ δὲ (41) λόγον αὐτοῦ εἶπεν· "γυνή τις ἄνδρα κατορύξασα καθημένη πρὸς τὸ μνῆμα (42) αὐτοῦ συνεχομένη ἔκλαιεν. ἀρωτριῶν (sic) δέ τις ἐπεθύμησεν ἰδὼν (43) αὐτὴν συγγενέσθαι αὐτῇ, καὶ ἀφῆκεν τοὺς βόας ἑστῶτας ἐν τῇ ἀρούρῃ (sic). ἐλθὼν δὲ πρὸς αὐτὴν (44) ἔκλαιεν προσποιούμενος. παυσαμένης δὲ ἐκείνης ἐπύθετο· 'τί κλαίεις;' (45) ἔλεγεν ὁ ἀροτρεύς· 'σοφὴν τε καὶ ἀγαθὴν γυναῖκα κατώρυξα. (46) ὅταν δὲ κλαύσω

[6] After ἐκφυγεῖν G has the following irrelevant material, which I have omitted above: μὴ πολλὰ μόχθει θυμὸς ἀσθενὸν ὂν ἔσω τῆς ψυχῆς ὀφθαλμὸς πρὸ ὁρᾷ· οὐκ ἄνευ τῆς αἰτίας ἄλλως ποιεῖ τῶν Δελφῶν(!).

47 [................................αυτ]αις λυπ[αις....]
48 [..................................]ως εκειν[ην....]
49 [...τ]ην γυν[αικα..]
50 [.......................................]πο του[......]
51 [.................................απηλα]σεν ο δ[ε.....]
52 [..]σ[......]

Verso

53 [η δε γυ]νη επυθετο αυτου δια τι κλαιεις[...................]
54 [......]σ κ(αι) επερωτας· ολος γαρ ολοφυρο̣[.................]
55 [......]τυχην· ο δε φιλος εφη τω Αισ[ωπω τι γαρ σοι εδοξεν ξενω]
56 [οντι υβ]ριζειν τους Δελφους εν τη ιδ[ια αυτων πατριδι που]
57 [σου η φι]λοσοφια· που σου ο σεμνος λογο[s ο δε παλιν αυτω ετερον λο-]
58 [γον ειπε γ]υνη τις ειχετο θυγατερ[α παρθενον μωραν αυτη ηυχ-]
59 [ετο πασι τ]οι̣ς̣ [θ]εοις εφ εκαστης ημερας [την θυγατερα νουν εχειν]
60 [ευχομενης] δε α[υ]της πολλακις η παρ[θενος ηκουσεν κ(αι) δη ποτε]

κουφίζομαι τὴν λύπην.' ἡ δέ· 'ἐστέρημαι κἀγὼ ἀνδρὸς ἀγαθοῦ, ὡσαύτως δὲ πράττουσα ἀποτείνω τῆς λύπης τὸ βάρος.' (47) ὁ δὲ πρὸς αὐτὴν εἶπεν· ' εἰ τοίνυν περιεπέσομεν ταῖς αὐταῖς συμφοραῖς καὶ (48) τύχαις, τί (ὅτι cod.) οὐκ ἐπιγινώσκομεν ἀλλήλους ; ἐγὼ δὲ ἀγαπήσω σὲ ὡς ἐκείνην, σὺ δὲ (49) ἐμὲ ἀγάπησον ὡς ἄνδρα.' ταῦτα λέγων (λεγόντων cod.) ἔπειθεν τὴν γυναῖκα. (50) ἐν ὅσῳ δὲ συνεγένετο αὐτῇ (51) ἔλυσέν τις αὐτοῦ τοὺς βόας καὶ ἀπήλασεν. ὁ δὲ ἀρωτήρ (sic) (52) ἐπιστὰς καὶ μὴ εὑρὼν αὐτοῦ τοὺς βόας, ἐκ ψυχῆς ὀδυρόμενος ἀνέκραγεν. (53) ἡ δὲ γυνή, ' τί κλαίεις ;' ὁ δὲ ἀρωτήρ, ' ὦ γύναι, ἄρτι ἔχω κόψασθαι.' (54) ὥστε καὶ σὺ ἐρωτᾷς με διὰ τί κατολοφύρομαι (-με cod.), βλέπων αὐτὸς τὴν κατέχουσάν (55) με τύχην ; " ὁ δὲ φίλος λυπούμενος πρὸς αὐτὸν ἔφη " τί γάρ σοι <ἔδοξεν> (56) ὑβρίζειν αὐτοὺς ἐν τῇ ἰδίᾳ αὐτῶν πατρίδι (-δη cod.) καὶ πόλει, καὶ ταῦτα ὑπὸ τὴν αὐτῶν ὄντος σου ἐξουσίαν ; ποῦ (57) σου ἡ παιδεία ; ποῦ σου τὸ φιλόλογον ; σὺ πόλεσιν καὶ δήμοις γνώμας ἔδωκας καὶ εἰς σεαυτὸν ἄφρων γέγονας ; " ὁ δὲ προστέτακεν αὐτῷ λόγον ἕτερον· (58) " γυνή τις εἶχεν θυγατέρα μωρήν. αὕτη (59) πᾶσι τοῖς θεοῖς ηὔχετο τὴν θυγατέρα νοῦν λαβεῖν· (60) εὐχομένης δὲ αὐτῆς ἡ παρθένος πολλάκις ἤκουσεν. καὶ δή ποτε εἰς ἀγρὸν ἦλθεν· ἡ δὲ καταλιποῦσα τὴν μητέρα

61 [προκυπτ]ουσα αν[ω τ]ης αυλε<ι>ου [θυρας ειδεν ονον θηλειαν υπο]
62 [ανο͞υ βι]α[ζο]μεν[ην] κ(αι) προσελθ[ουσα τω ανο͞ω ειπε τι ποιεις ο δε]
63 [ταυτη ε]ντιθη[μι] νουν· αναμν[ησθεισα δε η μωρα των της μητρος ευχ-]
64 [ων εφη α]υτω [ενθες] κ(αι) εμοι νουν· [ο δε υπακουσας αυτικα κατα-]
65 [λιπων τη]ν ονον [διε]παρ[θε]ν[ευ]σεν αυτη[ν . . . . περι-]
66 [χαρης γε]νομενη [π]ρος την μητερα [. . . .]
67 [. . . . . ι]δου υπηκουσαν σου οι θεοι των[ευχων . . . .]
68 [. . . . οι] θεοι των ευχων· μου ειπε μ[οι] τε[κνον . . . .]
69 [προκυψ]ασα επανω της αυλε<ι>ου ανηρ τι[ς μακρον πυρρον νευρωδες]
70 [εχων εσ]ω κ(αι) εξω μ[ου βα]λων νουν μοι δε[δωκε η δε μητηρ ακουσασα]
71 [εφη ω τ]εκνον απωλεσας κ(αι) ον ειχες προτ[ερον νουν τουτο δη συν-]
72 [εβη κ(αι) ε]μοι φιλε· απωλεσα γαρ ο[ν ει]χον [προτερον νουν . . . .]
73 [εισελθο[ντες δε οι Δελφοι αποσπασαν[τες . . . .]
74 [. . . . . .] δεον δισε βληθηναι κα[τα τω]ν [κρημνων . . . .]
75 [. . . . εψ]ηφισαμεθα σε αξιον οντα ως ι[εροσυλον . . . .]

(61) ἔξω τῆς ἐπαύλεως <ἐ>ῖδεν ὄνον βιαζομένην ὑπὸ (62) ἀνο͞υ, καὶ ἠρώτησεν τὸν ἄνο͞υ· 'τί ποιεῖς;' ὁ δέ· (63) 'νοῦν ἐντίθημι αὐτῇ.' ἀναμνησθεῖσα ἡ μωρὰ τῆς εὐχῆς (64) ἔφη· 'ἔνθε<ς> καὶ ἐμοὶ νοῦν.' ὁ δὲ ἐν τῇ τρυφῇ (στύφει cod.) ἠρνεῖτο λέγων· 'οὐδέν ἐστιν ἀχαριστότερον (ἀχάριστον ἱερὸν cod.) γυναικός.' ἡ δέ· 'μὴ λόγον ἔχῃς (ἔχεις cod.), κύριε, καὶ ἡ μη͞ρ μου εὐχαριστήσει (-είσει cod.) σοι μισθὸν δοῦσα ὅσον ἂν θέλῃς· εὔχεται γὰρ ἵνα νοῦν ἔχω.' (65) ὁ δὲ διεπαρθενεύσατο αὐτήν. ἡ δὲ (66–67) περιχαρὴς πρὸς τὴν μη͞ρα δραμοῦσα εἶπεν· 'νοῦν ἔχω, μη͞ρ.' ἡ μη͞ρ φησίν (68) 'οἱ θεοὶ ἐπήκουσάν μου τῶν εὐχῶν.' ἡ κόρη· 'ναι, μη͞ρ.' ἡ δέ· 'πῶς ἔσχες νοῦν, τέκνον;' ἡ δὲ μωρὰ ἐξηγήσατο· (69) 'μακρὸν γὰρ πυρρὸν νευρῶδες (70) ἔξω ἔσω (ἐάσω cod.) τρέχον ἔσω μοι ἐνέβαλεν.' ἀκούσασα δὲ ἡ μη͞ρ ἐξηγουμένης τῆς θυγατρὸς αὐτῆς, (71) ἔφη· 'ὦ τέκνον, ἀπώλεσας καὶ ὃν πρῶτον εἶχες νοῦν.' ὁμοίως καὶ (72) ἐμοὶ συνέβη, φίλε· ἀπώλεσα γὰρ καὶ ὃν πρῶτον εἶχον νοῦν εἰς Δελφοὺς εἰσελθών." καὶ πολλὰ δακρύσας ὁ φίλος αὐτοῦ ἀφίστατο (ἀφίκετο cod.). (73) οἱ δὲ Δέλφιοι εἰσελθόντες πρὸς τὸν Αἴσωπον ἔφησαν· (74) "ἀπὸ κρημνοῦ σε δεῖ (δια cod.) βληθῆναι σήμερον· οὕτως γάρ σε (75) ἐψηφίσαμεν ἀνελεῖν, ἄξιον ὄντα καὶ βλάσφημον, ἵνα μηδὲ ταφῆς ἀξιωθῇς· ἑτοίμασαι σεαυτόν."

76 [παρακα]λων δε αυτους [α]κουσαι[..................επιτρε-]
77 [ψαντω]ν αυτων εφη· ο̣τε̣ [ην ομοφωνα τα ζωα μυς χερσαιος φιλιασας]
78 [τον βα]τραχον εκαλεσεν [αυτον επι δειπνον κ(αι) εισηγαγεν εις ταμι-]
79 [ειον πλ]ουσιου ο[π]ου αρτο[s.........................]
 [80–97.; see notes]

Αἴσωπος ἰδὼν αὐτοὺς ἀπειλουμένους ἔφη· (76) " λόγον ἀκούσατε."
οἱ δὲ ἐπέτρεψαν (77) αὐτὸν λέγειν. ὁ δὲ Αἴσωπός φησιν· " ὅτε ἦν τὰ
ζῷα ὁμόφωνα, μῦς φιλιάσας (78) βατράχῳ ἐκάλεσεν αὐτὸν ἐπὶ δεῖπνον
καὶ εἰσήγαγεν αὐτὸν εἰς ταμιεῖον (79) πλούσιον πάνυ, ἐφ' ᾧ ἦν ἄρτος,
κρέας, τυρός, ἐλαῖαι κτλ.

NOTES

1. So restored by Zereteli.
3. εἰ καὶ ἡδέως αὐτοῦ ἠκροῶν]το Zeitz. καὶ is regularly abbreviated in the papyrus.
4–5. *Iliad* 6, 146. Restored from G. Weil was able to read more of line 4 than Zereteli; he reads αν̅ο̅ις—προς αυτους οι[. The omission of the Homeric quotation in *W* may have been due to the corruption which appears in G.
6–7. ἐκεῖνο—διαστή]ματος Zereteli. κιματων papyrus.
7–8. Zeitz reads θεωροῦντες...δοκοῦμεν...ὁρῶμεν on the assumption that ἔλθῃ refers to ξύλον; that is possible, but the phrase from Planudes which he cites in support of this interpretation is without value, because it originated with Planudes himself. On the other hand both G and *W* represent the spectator as approaching (προσελθόντες, προσέλθωμεν), and this provides a better analogy to Aesop's experience.
8. εγγυστα papyrus.
10. Thus Zereteli.
11–12. πλαν[ηθεὶς—διάνοια]ν Zereteli.
12. The right reading was probably οὐδὲν γὰρ ἀνάξιον; cf. G. ὧδε, which Zeitz substitutes for οὐδὲν is Westermann's correction of W's ὁ δὲ, which in turn is probably an emendation of οὐδέν.
16. ἀπὸ εἴδους ἑκάσ]του Zereteli.
18. ἀπὸ—γυ]ναικῶν. Thus Zeitz, from *W*.
19–21. Thus Zereteli.
22. There is no need of assuming, with Zeitz, that the aid of Apollo on this occasion was a story invented (for self-justification) by the Delphic priesthood. The enmity between Apollo and Aesop lies at the foundation of the legend, and is in accord with the whole tenor of the biography; cf. *supra* p. 15.

23. καθιδρευσεν papyrus.
23–24. φοβούμενοι δὲ μὴ (μήπως Zereteli) οἱ παρό]ντες Weil and Zereteli.
24–25. φανερῶς οὐδὲν ἐποίησαν Zereteli. I add μέν with Zeitz.
26. απυπνωκοτα papyrus.
29–30. Αἴσωπο[ν ἀπῆγα] [γον. ἀπαρνουμένου δὲ αὐτοῦ μ]ηδὲν Kumaniecki; but this leaves the line somewhat too short, and εἷλκον is better authenticated than ἀπήγαγον. Zeitz, following Planudes, reads Αἴσωπο[ν ἀνέκριναν ὡς ἱεροσυληκότα, etc.; but for this there is no traditional authority. The text of the papyrus is here abbreviated, as comparison with G and W shows. Note that SBP at this point has interpolated from a manuscript similar to the papyrus.
30–31. I have written ἀδικεῖσθαι because it makes good sense, but the real reading may have been ἀπολέσθαι; cf. W.
32. χρυσῆν φιάλην τοῦ Ἀπόλλωνος] Zereteli.
33. ἐν—καὶ] Zereteli, from W.
34. εξαφηθηναι papyrus.
35. οἱ δὲ συλλαβόμενοι αὐτὸν ἐνέκλεισαν ἐν τῷ δεσ]μωτηρίῳ Kumaniecki; but συλλαβόμενοι tells what we have already been told, and with this supplement the line has only forty-seven letters. I have taken οἱ δὲ οὐκ ἐπείθοντο from G.
36–52. The context in which these isolated words belong may be seen in the text of G, where their equivalents are underlined.
53. αυτω papyrus.
56. Three or four more letters are needed for the restoration, unless the line was abnormally short.
59. ἡμέρας [νοῦν αὐτῇ χαρίσασθαι] Kumaniecki from W; cf. G.
61–64. ἐξελθ]οῦσα ἀν[ω τ]ῆς αὐλε<ί>ου [θύρας εἶδε τὴν ὄνον ὑπ'] [ἀνδρὸς βι]α[ζο]μέν[ην] κ(αὶ) προσελθ[οῦσα ἔφη· "τί ποιεῖς;" ὁ δὲ] [" τῇ ὄνῳ ἐ]ντίθη[μι] νοῦν." ἀναμν[ησθεῖσα δὲ ὧν ἡ μήτηρ ηὔχετο] [λέγει α]ὐτῷ Kumaniecki.
61. αυλεου papyrus.
66–67. [π]ρὸς τὴν μητέρα [αὐτῆς μετὰ περιχαρείας] [λέγει ἰ]δού Kumaniecki. Since μετὰ π. was presumably the reading of the SBP archetype, it may have been taken from a text similar to the papyrus; cf. supra, pp. 31, 37–39. But the restoration of these lines remains very uncertain.
69. προκύψ]ασα Zereteli. αυλεου papyrus.
71–72. πρότ[ερον—ἐ]μοί Zereteli.
71. απολεσας papyrus.
74. δί<σ> σε Zereteli.
76. παρακα]λῶν Zereteli.
80–97. These lines dealt partly with the fable of the frog and

the mouse (77–87), and partly with that about the eagle and the beetle (*ca.* 92ff.); but the fragments are so scanty that it is useless to compare them with other texts. See Zereteli, p. 125.

W (*cf.* West. 52, 9ff.)

(1–2) Περιερχόμενος οὖν τὰς πόλεις τῆς Ἑλλάδος καὶ τὴν ἑαυτοῦ ἐπιδεικνύμενος σοφίαν, παρεγένετο ἐν Δελφοῖς. (2–3) οἱ δὲ ὄχλοι ἡδέως μὲν αὐτοῦ ἠκροῶντο, οὐδὲν δὲ αὐτὸν ἐτίμησαν. (4–6) προσκρούσας δὲ πρὸς αὐτοὺς ἔφη· " ὅμοιοί ἐστε ξύλῳ ἐν θαλάσσῃ φερομένῳ· (6–7) ἐκεῖνο γὰρ θεωροῦντες ἐκ πολλοῦ διαστήματος ὑπὸ κυμάτων φερόμενον (8–9) δοκοῦμέν τινος χρυσίου ἄξιον εἶναι, ἐπειδὰν δὲ ἐγγυτάτω προσέλθωμεν ἐλάχιστον ὁρῶμεν. κἀγὼ δὲ πόρρωθεν ὑπάρχων (10–11) τῆς ὑμῶν πόλεως κατεπλησσόμην ὑμᾶς ὡς μεγάλους, ἐλθὼν δὲ πρὸς ὑμᾶς, ὦ Δελφοί, εὗρον ὑμᾶς ταπεινοτέρους τῶν ἄλλων ἀνθρώπων. πεπλάνημαι οὖν (12–13) καλὴν ἔχων ὑπὲρ ὑμῶν διάνοιαν. οὐδὲν <ἂν> ἄξιον ποιεῖτε τῶν προγόνων ὑμῶν." ταῦτα ἀκούσαντες οἱ Δελφοὶ ἔφησαν· " τίνες γάρ εἰσιν οἱ πρόγονοι ἡμῶν;" (14–16) ὁ δέ, " ἀπόδουλοι· εἰ δὲ ἀγνοεῖτε, μάθετε. νόμος ἦν παρὰ τοῖς Ἕλλησιν ἐὰν πόλεις καταβάλωνται τῶν λαφύρων τὸ δέκατον μέρος πέμπειν, ἀπό τε βοῶν, (17–19) προβάτων, αἰγῶν καὶ τῶν λοιπῶν κτηνῶν, ἀπὸ χρημάτων, ἀπὸ σωμάτων ἀνδρῶν τε καὶ γυναικῶν. ἐκ τούτων οὖν ὑμεῖς γεννηθέντες ἀνελεύθεροί ἐστε, ἐκεῖθεν γεννηθέντες τῶν Ἑλλήνων δοῦλοι καθεστήκατε." ταῦτα εἰπὼν ὁ Αἴσωπος περὶ ἐκδημίαν ἐγένετο. (20–24) οἱ δὲ Δελφοί, λογισάμενοι ὅτι ἐὰν εἰς ἑτέρας πόλεις ἀπέλθῃ ὁ Αἴσωπος χεῖρον αὐτοὺς κακολογήσει, ἐβουλεύσαντο δόλῳ αὐτὸν ἀνελεῖν καὶ ὡς ἱερόσυλον αὐτὸν καταδικάσαι. (25–27) παρατηρησάμενοι οὖν τὸν δοῦλον αὐτοῦ πρὸ τῆς πύλης τῆς πόλεως σκεύη φέροντα ἐνέκρυψαν εἰς τὰ στρώματα ἣν ἔλαβον φιάλην χρυσῆν ἐκ τοῦ ἱεροῦ τοῦ Ἀπόλλωνος. ὁ δὲ Αἴσωπος (28–30) ἀγνοῶν τὰ συνεσκευασμένα αὐτῷ ὥδευσεν εἰς τὴν Φωκίδα. οἱ δὲ Δελφοὶ δραμόντες ἐκράτησαν αὐτὸν καὶ εἰσήγαγον (30) εἰς τὴν πόλιν. διαπορουμένου δὲ τοῦ Αἰσώπου, " τί τοῦτο;" ἔφησαν, " ἃ ἔκλεψας ἐκ τοῦ ἱεροῦ ἡμεῖς διαβεβαιούμεθα." τοῦ δὲ ἀπολέσθαι λέγοντος ἐὰν καταγνωσθῇ, (31–32) ἐκτινάξαντες αὐτοῦ τὰ σκεύη εὗρον τὴν χρυσῆν φιάλην τοῦ Ἀπόλλωνος, ἐπεδείκνυόν τε (33–35) πᾶσι τοῖς ἐν τῇ πόλει, μετὰ θορύβου καὶ ταραχῆς περιβομβίζοντες αὐτόν. ὁ δὲ Αἴσωπος αἰσθόμενος τὴν ἐπιβουλὴν πολλὰ ἐδέετο ἀπολυθῆναι. οἱ δὲ ἐνέκλεισαν αὐτὸν εἰς φυλακήν.... (52–55) ἡ δὲ γυνὴ εὑροῦσα αὐτὸν ὀλοφυρόμενον ἔφη ' πάλιν κλαίεις ; ' ὁ δέ· ' ἄρτι ἐν ἀκριβείᾳ τῷ ὄντι πενθῶ.' καὶ ἐκεῖνος μὲν οὕτως. σὺ δὲ βλέπων τὴν ἔχουσάν με ἐξ ἐνέδρας τύχην διὰ τί ὀδύρομαι ἐρωτᾷς ; " (55–57) ὁ δὲ ἐπ' αὐτῷ λυπούμενος ἔφη. " τί γάρ σοι ἔδοξεν ὑβρίζειν τοὺς Δελφούς ; ἡ τοιαύτη σου σοφία εἰς τὸ ὑβρίζειν πολίτας κατέληξε, καὶ μάλιστα ἐν τῇ ἰδίᾳ πατρίδι ; " (57–59) ὁ δὲ Αἴσωπος πάλιν αὐτῷ ἕτερον λόγον εἶπε· " γυνή τις εἶχε θυγατέρα παρθένον μωράν. πάντοτε οὖν ηὔχετο τὴν θυγατέρα νοῦν ἔχειν. (60–61) εὐχομένης δὲ αὐτῆς παρρησίᾳ ἡ παρθένος ἤκουσε καὶ τὸν λόγον κατέσχε. μεθ' ἡμέρας δέ τινας σὺν τῇ μητρὶ εἰς ἀγρὸν ἐξελθοῦσα καὶ τῆς προαυλίου προκύψασα θύρας, εἶδεν ὄνον θήλειαν ὑπὸ (62–63) ἀνθρώπου βιαζομένην. καὶ προσελθοῦσα τῷ ἀνθρώπῳ εἶπε· ' τί ποιεῖς ; ' ὁ δέ φησι· ' νοῦν αὐτῇ ἐντίθημι.' ἀναμνησθεῖσα δὲ ἡ μωρὰ (63–65) ὅτι καθ' ἑκάστην ἡ μήτηρ αὐτῆς νοῦν αὐτῇ ηὔχετο, παρεκάλει λέγουσα· ' ἔνθες, ἄνθρωπε, κἀμοὶ νοῦν. καὶ γὰρ ἡ μήτηρ μου πολύ σοι πρὸς τοῦτο εὐχαριστήσει.' ὁ δὲ ὑπακούσας, καταλιπὼν τὴν ὄνον διεπαρθενεύσατο αὐτήν. ἡ δὲ (66–68) ἀναβᾶσα πρὸς τὴν μητέρα εἶπεν· ' ἰδού, μῆτερ, κατὰ τὴν εὐχήν σου νοῦν ἔλαβον.' ἡ δὲ μήτηρ αὐτῆς φησιν· ' ἐπήκουσάν μου τῶν εὐχῶν οἱ θεοί.' ἡ μωρὰ ἔφη· ' ναί, μῆτερ.' ' καὶ πῶς,' φησιν, ' οἶδας, τέκνον ; ' (68–70) ἡ δὲ εἶπεν· ' ὁ τοῦτόν μοι ἐνθεὶς μακρὸν πυρρὸν νευρῶδες ἔξω καὶ ἔσω ἐντρέχον ἐνέβαλέ μοι, κἀγὼ ἐτερπόμην.' ἡ δὲ μήτηρ ἀκούσασα (71–75) ἔφη· ' ὦ τέκνον, ἀπώλεσας καὶ ὃν πρῶτον εἶχες νοῦν.' " ὁ οὖν φίλος πρὸς αὐτὸν ἔφη· " σὲ οἱ Δελφοὶ ἀνέκαμψαν ψηφισάμενοι ὡς βλάσφημον καὶ ἀλαζόνα καὶ ἱερόσυλον ἀπὸ κρημνοῦ βληθῆναι, ἵνα μηδὲ ταφῆς τύχῃς." ταῦτα αὐτοῦ ἐν τῇ φυλακῇ τῷ Αἰσώπῳ λαλοῦντος, ἐλθόντες οἱ Δελφοὶ καὶ ἐκβαλόντες τὸν Αἴσωπον ἐκ τῆς φυλακῆς εἷλκον μετὰ βίας ἐπὶ τὸ κρημνίσαι αὐτόν. (76–79) ὁ δὲ Αἴσωπος παρεκάλει αὐτοὺς ἐπὶ τὸ ἀκοῦσαι αὐτοῦ. ἐπιτρεψάντων δὲ αὐτῶν, ἔφη· " ὅτε ἦν ὁμόφωνα τὰ ζῶα, μῦς βατράχῳ φιλιωθεὶς ἐκάλεσεν αὐτὸν εἰς δεῖπνον καὶ ἀπήγαγεν αὐτὸν εἰς ταμεῖον πλουσίου, ὅπου ἦν ἄρτος κτλ.

Variants in W: **1** cf. supra p. 57 (on Ber. pap.). **2–3** ἐτίμησαν αὐτόν SBP αὐτὸν ἐτίμων R || **4–6** προσκρούσας...ἔφη] ὑπολαβὼν δὲ ἔφη αὐτοῖς BP || πρὸς om. RV || ὁ Αἴσωπος post αὐτοὺς W || ὦ ἄνδρες Δέλφιοι ante ὅμοιοι BP || **6–7** τῶν κυμάτων ML || **8–9** δοκοῦμέν τινος ἅ <ξιον χρυσίου εἶναι ? >M χρυσίου om. L hiat lacuna in B δ. πολλοῦ τινος χρυσίου ἄξιον εἶναι P || ἐπὰν P || ἐγγυτάτω PSW αὐτῷ ἐγγυτάτω M ἐν ἐγγυτάτω R αὐτὸ ἐγγίσαι L ἐγγὺς V || ἐλάχιστον εἶναι V || κἀγὼ δὲ LV periit lect. cod. M ἔτι

Life of Aesop

δὲ κἀγὼ R   κἀγὼ οὖν BPW || **10–11** τῆς ὑμῶν π. MRW   τ. π. ὑμῶν BPλ || μεγίστους W || Δελφοι RS   om. BP || ταπεινοτέρους τ. ἄλλων ἀνθρώπων (τ. ἄλλων amissis in M) MRλS   ἀχρειοτέρους ἀπάντων τῶν ἀνθρώπων ὄντως B   ἀχρειώτερον ἀπάντων ἀ. ἑώρακα (omissis εὗρον ὑμᾶς) P   ταπ. τ. ἀ. ἀνθρώπων καὶ ἀχρειοτέρους ὄντας W || πεπλάνημαι...καθεστήκατε (**19**) om. P   tantum πεπλάνημαι B || οὖν MRλ   om. WSV || **12–13** οὐδὲν ἀνάξιον L   periit lect. in marg. M   οὐδὲν ἄξιον R   ὁ δὲ ἄξιον W   οἱ δὲ οὐδὲν ἄξιον V   καὶ γὰρ ἄξια S || ποιεῖτε...ἐκράτησαν αὐτὸν (**29**)] ἐποίησαν αὐτὸν V || τοῖς προύχουσι καὶ τοῖς προγόνοις R   ταῦτα...ἔφησαν om. R || οἱ ἐν Δελφοῖς W || τίνες...ἡμῶν om. R || ἦσαν S || **14–16** ἀπόδουλοι ὁ δὲ M   σύνδουλοι ὁ δὲ R   ὁ δὲ σύνδουλοι W   ὁ δὲ om. SL   ἀπόδουλοι MSL || εἰ...μάθετε] <......>φησί M || πόλεις καταβάλωνται W   π. καταβάλλοντε R   π. καταβάλλωνται S   πόλις καταβαλῆται (-εῖται L) ML || τὸ δωδέκατον ML || **17–19** ἐλεύθεροί ἐστε οὐχί R || καθεστήκατε RSW   καθίστασθε ML || ταῦτα... ὅτι] ταῦτα ἀκούσαντες οἱ Δελφοὶ εἶπον πρὸς ἀλλήλους BP || **20–24** ὅτι...κακολογήσει R   ὅτι καὶ ἐὰν εἰς ἑτέρας πόλεις ἐπέλθοι Αἴσωπος χείρων αὐτοὺς κακολογίσει S   ὅτι καὶ εἰς ἑτέρας π. ἀπελθὼν ὁ Αἴσωπος χεῖρον αὐτοὺς κακολογήσει L(M?)   ἐὰν οὗτος εἰς ἑ. π. ἀπέλθει πλεῖστα ἡμῶν κακολογήσει (κ. ἡμᾶς B) BP   ὅτι καὶ ἐὰν εἰς ἑτέρας ἀπελθὼν Αἴσωπος πόλεις χείρονα αὐτοὺς κακολογήσας W || ἐβουλεύσαντο...ἀνελεῖν] καὶ παραχρῆμα ἐβουλεύσαντο ὅπως δόλῳ ἀνέλωσιν αὐτὸν BP || ἀνελεῖν δόλῳ (om. αὐτὸν) W || αὐτὸν post ἱερ. om. RP || καταδικάσουσιν P   κατεδίκασαν L || **25–27** παρατηρησάμενοι...φέροντα] παρατηρησάμενοι δὲ τὸν τοῦ Αἰσώπου δόλον P   π. τόν τε Αἴσωπον δόλῳ B   π. οὖν τ. δοῦλον αὐτοῦ ὑπήντησαν πρὸ τ. π. τῆς π. σκεύη φέροντα R || ἐνέκρυψαν... Ἀπόλλωνος] καὶ ἀπέκλεισαν αὐτόν. τὰ δὲ σκεύη ἔκρυψαν εἰς τὰ στρώματα μετὰ καὶ τῆς φυάλης τοῦ Ἀπόλλωνος, πρὸς τὸ ποιῆσαι σκευὴν κατὰ τοῦ Αἰσώπου, ὡς ἄτε χρυσῆν οὖσαν R   ἐνέκρυψαν (ἀν-B) εἰς τ. στ. αὐτῶν (αὐτῶν om. B). φυάλην (φιάλλην P) χρυσῆν ἥνπερ ἀνελάβοντο (ἀνέλλαβον B) ἐν τῷ (ἐκ τὸ B) τοῦ Ἀ. ἱερόν BP || ἔκρυψαν ML || στρώματα αὐτοῦ M || **28–30** τὰ ὑπ' αὐτῶν συσκευασθέντα (σκευασθέντα P) εἰς αὐτὸν BP || ὤδευσεν MRLP   ὤδευεν SBW   τὴν om. SBP || δραμόντες οὖν οἱ Δελφοὶ BP   οἱ δὲ Δελφοὶ εἰσδραμόντες W || καὶ... πόλιν om. BP || **30** τί τοῦτο] fort. cum διαπορουμένου coniungendum   τὸ τί ἂν εἴη τοῦτο BP || ἃ MλS   σὺ R   ἵνα τί BPW || ἔκλεψας...διαβεβαιούμεθα] ἀνόσιε (om. B), τὸ τοῦ Ἀπόλλωνος ἱερὸν εἴληφας BP || ἡμεῖς RV   καὶ ἡμεῖς ML   ἡμεῖς δὲ S   ἃ ἡμεῖς W || διαβεβαιωσόμεθα L || τοῦ...καταγνωσθῇ] τοῦ δὲ ἀρνουμένου καὶ διισχυριζομένου μηδὲν εἰδέναι (εἶναι B) BP   τοῦ δὲ ἀρνουμένου καὶ διισχυριζομένου μηδὲν εἰδέναι, ἔτι δὲ ἀπολέσθαι λέγοντος ἐὰν καταγνωσθῇ W   τὰ δὲ (sic) ἀπολέγεσθαι λέγοντες ἵνα καὶ διαγνωσθῇ S || **31–32** ἐκτινάξαντος West.—αντες codd. || αὐτοῦ BPλW   τούτου S   ἐκεῖνοι M   οἱ τὴν σκεωρίαν ποιήσαντες R || τὰ σκεύη RVSB(P)   τὸ στρῶμα ML || τὴν τοῦ Ἀ. χρ. φ. BP || ἐπεδείκνυόν τε ML   ἐπιδεικνύοντες RSV   καὶ λαβόντες (συλλαβόντες P) οἱ Δελφοὶ (-φοὶ W) ἐπεδείκνυον BPW || **33–35** τοῖς ἐν τ. π. πᾶσιν (πάσῃ P) BP || πολλοῦ θορύβου BPW || περιβομβίζοντες MS   περιβαβίζοντες L   περιμείζοντες R   περικομίζοντες (-ζων W) WV   om. BP || αὐτόν codd. αὐτὴν West. || αἰσθόμενος...πολλὰ] ἐπιγνοὺς τῆς ἐπιβουλῆς τὸ ἔνεδρον BP || αὐτοῖς post ἐδέετο B   αὐτὸν P || οἱ δὲ...φυλακήν] οἱ δὲ συλλαβόμενοι αὐτὸν εἰς φυλακὴν ἔβαλον (ἀνήγαγον εἰς τὴν φ. B) PB   οἱ δὲ αὐτὸν συλλαβόμενοι ἐνέκλεισαν εἰς φ. W || **52–55** hanc fabulam om. P, et (inter alia) V || ἐλθοῦσα καὶ εὑροῦσα WB || ὀλοφυρόμενον om. R || ἔφη RSBW   φησι ML || φησι post ὁ δέ SBW   ἔφη R   om. ML || ἐν ἀκριβείᾳ τῷ ὄντι RSW   τῷ ὄντι ἐν ἀληθείᾳ Β   ἐν ἀλ. τῷ ὄντι L   verba abscissa perierunt in M || πενθῶ RSW   κλαίω MLB || καὶ...οὕτως om. B || ἐπισχοῦσαν W || λύπην pro τύχην R || 55–57 ὁ δὲ...Δελφούς] ὁ δέ φησι καὶ ἵνα τί σὺ καθύβρισας τ. Δελφούς Β   om. P || ἡ τοιαύτη...κατέληξε om. MLS || εἰς τὸ ἀτιμάζειν R   ἐν τῷ ὑβρίζειν Β || κατήντησεν R || 57–59 ὁ δὲ...εἶπε om. SBPW || γυνή...νοῦν (71)] hanc fabulam om. B, infra in alieno loco (West. p. 56) habent SPW || καὶ πάντοτε (om. οὖν) R || τ. θυγατέρα ν. ἔχειν] τῇ θεᾷ νοῦν αὐτῇ (-τὴν P) χαρίσασθαι PW || 60–61 παρρησίᾳ codd.   παριοῦσα vel παροῦσα Reiske apud West. || ἡ μωρὰ post παρθένος add. PW || ἤκουσε RSL   ἢ <κουσε?> M   ἤκουε PW || καὶ τ. λόγον κατέσχε LS   κ. τῶν λόγων κ. R   periit lect. cod. M   τῶν λόγων (τὸν λόγον P) καὶ κατεῖχε WP || μεθ' ἡμέρας δέ τινας R   μ. ἡμέραν δὲ ML   μ. ἡμέρας δὲ SPW || ἄνθρωπε post ποιεῖς PW || ὁ δὲ ἔφη W   om. West. || 63–65 ἑκάστην ἡμέραν P || νοῦν αὐτῇ PW   ν. αὐτὴν ἔχειν L   ν. αὐτῇ ἔχειν M   ν. ἔχειν αὐτῇ R   ν. αὐτὴν προσλαβεῖν S || ἄνθρωπε ἔνθες PW || ἡ γὰρ μήτηρ W || σοι MRSP   σε LW || πρὸς τοῦτο MPSW   εἰς τ. L ἐν τούτῳ R || ἐπακούσας W   ἀκούσας P || καὶ καταλιπὼν W(P)   καὶ om. MLS   κατέλιπε (add. καὶ post ὄνον) R || διεπαρθενεύσατο ML   διεπαρθένευσε SPWR || αὐτήν MRLS   τὴν κόρην (τῇ κόρῃ W) φθείρας αὐτήν PW || 66–68 ἡ δὲ μετὰ περιχαρίας (-είας P) ἔρχεται π. τ. μ. αὐτῆς λέγουσα PW || εἶπεν] ἔφη R || μῆτερ μου W || κατὰ τῶν (τῶν om. W) εὐχῶν PW || αὐτῆς om. W || λέγει pro φησιν PW || ἐπήκουσαν W   ὑπήκουσαν P   εἰσήκουσαν R   ἤκουσαν S ἤκουσα (om. q. s. usque ad ἔφη ὦ τέκνον) L   periit lect. cod. M || τ. εὐχῶν om. PW   τῆς εὐχῆς (post θεοί) R || ἡ μωρὰ ἔφη MS   ἡ δὲ μ. ἔφη P   ἡ δὲ ἔφη W   ἡ δέ R || καὶ πῶς φησιν MRS   ἡ δέ, καὶ ποίῳ τρόπῳ PW || οἶδας, τέκνον RS   <οἶδας, τέκν?>ον M   τοῦτο ἔγνως PW || 68–70 ἡ δὲ...ἐνέβαλέ μοι] καὶ ἡ μωρά, ἄνθρωπός τις μακρὸν πυρὸν (ποῖρον P) καὶ δύο στρογγύλα νευρώδη ἔθηκεν ἐν τῇ κοιλίᾳ μου ἔσω βαλὼν καὶ ἔξω ἐντρέχων (ἔξωθεν τρέχων P) ἐνέβαλέ μοι (με W) PW || ἐνθεὶς M   ἐντιθεὶς SR || ἢν post ἐντιθεὶς et παχὺ post μακρὸν R || πυρὸν codd. || ἔξω κ. ἔσω ἐντρέχον (τα suprascr. al. m.) M   ἔσω κ. (καὶ om. R) ἔξω ἐντρέχων RS || κἀγὼ δὲ (δὲ om. P) ἡδέως εἶχον PW || μήτηρ αὐτῆς R || ἀκούσασα καὶ ἰδοῦσα PW || 71–75 ὃν πρῶτον RPW   ὃν πρότερον ML   ὅνπερ S || ὁ οὖν...ἔφη om. BP || ὁ οὖν SW   ὁ δέ R   ὁ γοῦν L   abscissum in M || πρὸς τὸν Αἴσωπον (om. ἔφη) R || σε] χθὲς S   χθὲς γὰρ B   χθὲς δὲ P || Δελφοὶ SPWR || ἀνέκαμψαν ψηφισάμενοι (ψ. om. L) MWS(L)   ἐψηφίσαντο R   συνεψιφήσαντο Β(P) || ἐπὶ κρυμοῦ ῥιφῆναι (ῥιφένε P) σε BP || ἵνα... τύχῃς om. BP || ταῦτα οὖν WS || ἐν...Αἰσώπου om. BP || τοῦ Αἰσώπου R || λέγοντος pro λαλοῦντος BP || ἐλθόντες...ἐκβαλόντες ML   συνῆλθον οἱ Δελφοὶ καὶ ἐκβαλόντες (ἐκβάλλοντες S ἐξέβαλον R) WSR   ἰδοὺ καὶ οἱ Δελφοὶ (-ιοι P) συνῆλθον κ. ἐκβαλλόντες (-ῶντες P) BP || ἐκ MLSP   ἀπὸ WBR || ἕλκοντες R || ἐπὶ MRLW   εἰς SBP || τῷ M || αὐτὸν om. BPM || κατακρημνίσαι W(SBP) || 76–79 ὁ δὲ...αὐτοῦ] om. L   ὁ δὲ Αἴσωπος εἶπε (ἔφη P) πρὸς αὐτούς BP || Αἴσωπος om. R || ἐπὶ τὸ om. M || ἐπιστρεψάντων W   ἐπακουσάντων L || ἐπιτρεψάντων...ἔφη om. BP || ὁμόφρονα SBP || μῦς βατράχῳ φιλιάσας S(BP)   μ. βάτραχον φιλήσας W || γοῦν post μῦς M || αὐτὸν post ἐκάλεσεν om. BPR || καὶ ἀπαγαγὼν (προαγαγὼν B) εἰς ταμεῖον πλουσίου (π. τινος P) ὅπου ἦν μέλι...BP || ταμιεῖον SW

PART II

STUDIES IN THE TEXT HISTORY OF THE *FABLES*

1. INTRODUCTION

The text tradition of the Greek fables ascribed to Aesop presents a large and complicated problem. Not only are there a great many manuscripts to be reckoned with,[1] but

[1] Chambry (p. 1) says that he knows of the existence of 94 MSS of Aesop's fables. In addition to these and to six or eight others mentioned by Hausrath (*Philologische Wochenschrift* XLVII [1927], sp. 1541, 1543) and by Marc (398) I may add the following:
  1. New York Public Library, Astor Collection, cod. 100, s. XIV–XV (Plate VI). This is a very carefully written manuscript in which errors of any kind are rare. It contains 127 fables corresponding exactly in order and identity with the first 127 fables in Laurentianus 89.79 (= La in Chambry) and Ambrosianus 7 (= Lf). The text, which I have compared throughout with Chambry's apparatus, is somewhat closer to Lf than to La, but in no way inferior to either.
  2. Cambridge, Library of Trinity College, cod. 1032, s. XV. This contains 32 fables, according to the catalogue by M. R. James, vol. III, p. 6.
  3. *Ibid.*, cod. 1158, s. XVII, contains 52 fables beginning Αἰ δρῦες κατεμέμ-φοντο τὸν Δία. This is probably copied from the well-known Bodleian manuscript, Auct. F. 4,7 (= Ba in Chambry). See James, III, p. 175.
  4. *Ibid.*, cod. 1408, s. XVI, contains 58 fables. This manuscript (noted by Marc, 415, n. 2) is very closely related to Par. suppl. gr. 105, since it has the same peculiar form of interpolated *Vita; cf. infra*, p. 163. I am indebted to the kindness of Professor D. S. Robertson for sending me some useful notes on the fables contained in this manuscript.
  5. Norfolk, Holkham Hall, in the library of the Earl of Leicester, cod. 278 in S. de Ricci's *Handlist of MSS in the Library of the Earl of Leicester at Holkham Hall*, Oxford, 1932. Through the kindness of Mr. C. W. James I have been able to secure photographs of a large part of this MS. It is a faithful copy, made apparently by some Italian humanist in the 16th, or possibly 15th, century, of Laur. conv. soppr. 627 (the so-called Casinensis), the numbered pages of which MS are recorded in the margin. The contents consist of the Westermann *Life* followed by the Aphthonian *Preface* (*cf. infra*, p. 163) and, according to the description in the library catalogue by Sir Frederick Madden, 200 fables. The Casinensis (Ca) contains 199 fables, and since my photographs include only the first nine

the majority of them are in some degree mixed as regards their contents and sources. The fables themselves, moreover, appear in different versions according to the manuscript or group of manuscripts in which they are found. In copying the text of a well-known classical author it is unusual for a scribe to depart very far from the single manuscript before him; he may occasionally substitute readings or corrections from a second or a third manuscript, but he rarely attempts to rewrite the text himself or to omit, add, or combine substantial

fables and the last nine, I am unable to say whether the discrepancy is due to the presence of an extra fable or to an error in counting.

6. Bologna, University Library, cod. 2839 (*olim* 106), *s*. xv. This contains 61 fables belonging to the Accursiana recension; *cf.* V. Puntoni in *Stud. Ital. d. Fil. Cl.* iv (1896), 376.

7. Lucca, R. Biblioteca Pubblica, cod. 1426, *s*. xv. Contains fables of Aesop according to the very brief notice by T. W. Allen, "Notes on Gr. MSS in Italian Libraries," *Class. Rev.* iv (1890), 105.

8. Modena, Biblioteca Estense, cod. 252 (ii, 33), *s*. xvi (1526). This has 61 fables, apparently belonging to the Accursiana recension; *cf.* Puntoni in *Stud. Ital. d. Fil. Cl.* iv (1896), 525.

9. Padua, University Library, cod. Sem. 753 (*olim* B 7), *s*. xv. Contains 60 Accursiana fables; *cf.* A. Mancini in *Stud. Ital. d. Fil. Cl.* N. S. v (1927), 162.

10. Pesaro, Biblioteca Oliveriana, cod. 1647, *s*. xv. Contains 61 fables; *cf.* Mazzatinti, *Inventari dei Manoscritti delle Biblioteche d'Italia* xlviii (1931), 186.

11. Rome, Vatican Library, cod. Chisianus gr. 21 (R iv 21), *s*. xv. Contains 60 Accursiana fables.

12. Udine, Bibliotheca Archiepiscopalis Utinensis, cod. 6 in Cosattini's catalogue, *s*. xv. Contains 151 fables; see below, p. 165.

13. Vienna, in the Staatsbibliothek, cod. suppl. 99. This is said to contain 61 fables. The age of the manuscript is not indicated in the handwritten list of supplements at the library, and I did not see the manuscript itself.

14. At Constantinople, in the Old Seraglio, there is a manuscript of the sixteenth century containing "Aesop's Fables with the Life of him by Planudes," according to S. Gaselee, *The Greek MSS in the Old Seraglio at Constantinople*, Cambridge 1916, p. 9.

Hausrath (*l.c.*) allows that Chambry knew and used Ambrosianus 481, but lists Ambros. L 43, which is the same manuscript, among those unknown to Chambry.

Some fables of Syntipas are contained on ff. 125ff. of cod. Marcianus x 9, *s*. xv, beginning Λαγωός τις ἐδίψα. As I recall, these are not mentioned in the catalogue.

portions according to his own fancy. In the transmission of the Aesopic fables, on the other hand, as in that of popular lore generally, such loyal adherence on the part of scribes to a single manuscript source is the exception rather than the rule. Besides the fact that the text of a single fable is sometimes, though perhaps not very frequently, compounded of two or three different sources, there is a tendency among Byzantine copyists to make up each his own collection of fables, drawing some of them from one manuscript collection and others from others, a practice which has likewise become traditional in the popular modern editions and translations of "Aesop's Fables," and which, apart from being easy and natural in the case of such small textual units, is due in the final analysis to the fact that a definitive edition of the *Fables* never existed, at least none that was universally recognized as such and as coming from the pen of Aesop himself.

But in spite of the varying contents of the manuscripts, and of the mixing of sources, it is nevertheless easy to distinguish, among the fables themselves, at least four different recensions, upon one or more of which every known manuscript of any consequence either entirely or in large part depends.[2] These are (I) the Augustana recension, so called from its best known representative manuscript, the *Augustanus* or *Monacensis* 564; (II) the collection typified by cod. Vind. hist. gr. 130; (III) the Accursiana, named after its first modern editor, Bonus Accursius; and (IV) the so-called Bodleian paraphrase, dependent largely upon Babrius. The groups of manuscripts which represent these several recensions are designated by Chambry (pp. 29–30) as Classes P, C, L, B, or nos. I, II, III, IV respectively. In referring to them hereafter, I shall use sometimes the Roman numerals and sometimes the terms

[2] See Friedrich Fedde, *Über eine noch nicht edirte Sammlung äsopischer Fabeln, nach einer Wiener Handschrift*, Programm, Breslau, 1877; A. Hausrath, *Jahrb. f. class. Phil.*, Supplementband XXI (1894) pp. 296ff. (= *Untersuchungen*); idem, in Pauly-Wissowa, *R.-E.* VI 2 (1909), 1734, and *Phil. Wochenschrift*, XLVII (1927), sp. 1539; P. Marc, *Byz. Zeitschr.*, XIX (1910) pp. 409ff.; Chambry, *Aesopi Fabulae* 5–24.

'Augustana' and 'Accursiana' (sc. *recensio*). It is with regard to the greater part of its contents that a manuscript is assigned to this or that group, since many of them overlap their own group to the extent of having taken a few fables from other recensions. A fifth group is composed of manuscripts the contents of which, on the whole, do not represent a distinct recension, but have been drawn in varying proportions from two or more of the other recensions. A thorough study of the text-tradition of any one of the four recensions above mentioned would necessarily have to take into account the relevant parts of manuscripts belonging to this mixed group.

In publishing the fables belonging to all four classes separately, and in giving us in his elaborate critical apparatus the variant readings of some forty-seven different manuscripts, Chambry has done a most valuable service to Aesopic scholarship. Thanks to his edition, it is now possible for one who is interested in the history of the transmission of these fables to consult in a convenient and classified form the greater part of the data with which he must work.

Other important data may be gathered from the text-history of the *Life of Aesop*. The advantage of studying the *Life* and *Fables* together in their bearing one upon the other was recognized long ago by Hausrath and Marc, although their knowledge of the text-history of the *Life* was very inadequate. The outlines of the manuscript tradition in the *Life* are probably not a great deal simpler than those in the *Fables*, but, owing to the comparatively small number of manuscripts involved, and to the continuous nature of the text, they can be traced more easily, and with greater precision, than is the case in the *Fables;* and since the scribes and redactors who copied or edited the *Life* are usually the same persons who copied or edited the *Fables*, whatever we can learn about their dates and methods of workmanship in the *Life* is bound to be of significance for the study of the *Fables* also. My own study of the *Life*, which has been carried on quite independently of the views of Hausrath and Marc, was undertaken originally without any intention of applying the results to the problem of the *Fables;* and it was not until I had completed my investigations in this field, and had drawn up my stemma of the manuscripts, that I decided to examine the tradition of the fable collections, at certain points, in the light of the relationships that I had already established for the *Life*. In so doing I have been led to the same *general* conclusions concerning the dates and interrelationships of Classes I, II, and III, as those already reached by Fedde and Hausrath; although, as will appear hereafter, there are a number of important points upon which I disagree with the latter and with his pupil, Marc.

The general conclusions regarding Classes I–III, to which I have referred, may be stated briefly as follows: Class I, the Augustana, is the oldest of the three recensions and (loosely speaking) the principal source of the other two. The approximate date of its origin cannot be fixed with certainty (see pp. 156f.). Class II derives all its prose fables from I, and the changes introduced by its editor are almost entirely verbal and inconsequential. The forty verse fables in Class II come indirectly from the so-called Bodleian paraphrase of Babrius (Class IV). These views on Class II, though essentially correct, are subject to the modifications and extensions described below, pp. 174ff. Class III, the Accursiana, is derived partly from II (fables 1–62, *infra* Table VII), partly from I (fables 63–71; 80–127), and partly from IV and other miscellaneous sources (fables 72–79). It is the work of a learned Byzantine scholar who lived at about the time of Planudes (in my opinion, Planudes himself; see pp. 217ff.). Such are the general relationships between Classes I–III which are assumed throughout the greater part of the following somewhat intricate study. To set forth in detail the proofs for these relationships would be merely to repeat what has already been satisfactorily done by Fedde and Hausrath; but if the reader is inclined to doubt the validity of their demonstrations, he may find an abundance of additional corroborative evidence both in my *Text Tradition* and throughout the present volume, where, however, it is necessarily either incidental or implicit in some other demonstration. All of us who have worked in this field, except Chambry, are agreed that the propositions outlined above are fundamentally true; and the cardinal heresy of Chambry—that the Accursiana is an ancient instead of a Byzantine recension, and that it owes nothing to Class II, which he imagines to be later, yet not Byzantine—is refuted in a chapter below dealing with that subject (pp. 204ff.).

In general, it has become quite evident to me, thanks to the recovery of the old Augustana *Life* in the Morgan manuscript and to a closer knowledge of the tradition in the Westermann *Life*, that the two texts, *Life* and *Fables*, have, in the broad outlines of their evolution and apart from Class IV, an almost exactly parallel history as far back as either can be traced in our manuscripts. Some important aspects of this parallelism have already been noted by Marc (who, however, has made some errors, especially with reference to Class I); but it can be followed much farther than Marc has indicated, and its full extent will become apparent only after we have studied all three recensions one by one, and have pointed out the subdivisions (i.e. the lesser recensions) within them. See Summary, pp. 229f.

My purpose in tracing the parallel traditions of *Life* and *Fables* is to clarify the manuscript traditions, and in other ways to contribute what I can to our knowledge of the individual recensions as such. Consequently I have stopped short of a complete study of the tradition. A great deal still remains to be done if one considers it advisable to define the complex relationships of the manuscripts in stemmas worked out in detail on the evidence of complete collations. While such an undertaking might be worth while in the case of the Augustana, it is my feeling that it would be largely a waste of effort if applied to the other recensions. The prose fables of Class II have no artistic value of their own and they can never be trusted as witnesses to the text of their source in Class I; while Class III, besides being still further removed from the ancient text, has been preserved so well and in so uniform a tradition that an editor may almost as well follow one of several obviously good manuscripts as another. On the other hand, it is important to know whether the Accursiana recension was made by an unknown writer in the third century (Chambry) or by Maximus Planudes at the beginning of the fourteenth; whether the Augustana collection is composed mainly of schoolboys' exercises (Hausrath), or whether it represents an ancient edition or combination of editions which was no more the peculiar product of the schools of rhetoric than were the other classical texts used therein; whether the prose fables of II come directly from I, as hitherto supposed, or, as I believe, from an intermediate recension typified by cod. Mon. 525; when and where the latter recension originated, and what other texts are to be associated with it in time and place; what value we must attach to the newly recovered Morgan text of the *Fables*, in view of the fact that it is found in the oldest of all our manuscripts, and what light this text throws upon various phases of the tradition in and beyond Class I. It is with questions of this sort, and not with any one particular thesis, that the following chapters are concerned.

2. THE AUGUSTANA RECENSION

a. Description and collation of the Morgan manuscript (G)

The Morgan text of the *Fables* (= G) extends from f. 67^v–108^r and is headed Αἰσώπου μῦθοι κατα στοιχεῖον ὠφέλιμοι: Μῦθος ᾱ (*sic*). The number of fables that are actually extant in the manuscript, in whole or in part, is 226. Of these, four (nos. 46, 51, 66, and 75 in Table I below) are fragmentary or incomplete owing to the loss of leaves after 77^v and 80^v. More or less different versions of essentially the same fable are represented by nos. 23 and 202, 31 and 238, 62 and 177, 86 and 180, 99 and 173, 189 and 233, and probably [71] and 220. The numbering of the fables in the margin begins anew with each of the twenty-four alphabetical divisions. Marginal notes in uncials are found on ff. 68ᵛ, 70ʳ, 74ᵛ, 75ᵛ, 76ʳ, 76ᵛ, 77ʳ, 81ᵛ, 85ᵛ, 86ʳ, 86ᵛ, 87ᵛ, 100ᵛ, 103ᵛ, 107ᵛ. These are of little or no importance in themselves except when they consist of readings accidentally omitted in the body of the text. Some of them are grammatical notes on the declension of nouns, others paraphrases or glosses on the text, a few seem quite irrelevant or unintelligible; no one of them, so far as I can discover, reflects any variant reading in the other manuscripts as reported by Chambry. The following examples will serve to illustrate the character of these jottings: 75ᵛ δωρᾶν ξένιον ἀναθήσω, followed after a space by ἑκατὸν θυσίας βοῶν, stands opposite τοῖς θεοῖς ηὔχετο ἑκατόμβην ποιήσειν in fable 34. 76ᵛ, opposite no. 39: τὰ εἰς ῆρ ὀξυτόνων ὅσα μεν ἔχει τὸ τ̄ διὰ τ̆ ῆ κλίνεται καμπτήρος ἀροτήρος σεσημειω πατέρος ἀστέρος. 86ᵛ, δερματοκόπτας is a noteworthy gloss on τοὺς σκύτεις (sic). On f. 68ʳ, at the end of the first fable, the following unintelligible notations, written in uncials, seem to have been copied from the margin of the archetype into the body of the text: ἔνοι ἀποβολήν· ἀποτμηθῆναι· ἔνοι ὑπολαβεῖν ἀποτμηθῆναι· ὡς οἰμ(αι), ὁμολογίας· ὁ εἰς τὰς συνθήκας καὶ εἰς τὰ ὅρκια τῆς φιλίας ὠμώσεις ὅρκου ἀσεβήσας καὶ παραβάς:—100ᵛ, in the top margin, ὅτι τὸν ἐλέφαντα δέδοικεν φοβεῖ τὸ χοιρίδιον has reference to fable 224 (= Ch. 146), which in the manuscript is found six folios later on at the top of 106ᵛ. Here the scribe appears to have copied a note that was already glossed in his archetype; if so, the note itself must be of still earlier origin. Indeed it is probable, in view of the numerous corruptions in these insignificant notes and the fact that they have been transmitted at all, that the tradition of the text in G's immediate ancestors was as literal and faithful as it was unintelligent, and that such meddling with the contents as is indicated by the presence of a few duplicate, or otherwise suspicious-looking, fables is likewise due to G's predecessors two or more stages back. Certainly the scribe of G was no scholar with a penchant for emendation, or a desire to improve his book by drawing on

THE FABLES 79

other sources, but rather an ignorant man engaged in transcribing a single codex. The text is full of orthographical errors and corrupt readings which any schoolboy could have emended, although there are not so many hopelessly corrupt passages in the *Fables* as there are in the *Life*.

After 77^v one leaf of the manuscript has been lost and after 80^v two leaves. The number and identity of the missing fables can be determined with considerable probability by reference to the other manuscripts of Chambry's Class I, which, in the corresponding regions, are nearly all in close agreement.[1] The lacuna after 77^v begins in the middle of fable 46 (Βορέας καὶ Ἥλιος) and ends in the second line of Γεωργὸς καὶ ὄφις, which fable must have been the second one beginning with Γ, since that which immediately follows is designated as no. 3 in the margin. Thus, apart from the first line of Γεωργὸς καὶ ὄφις, only one fable in Γ has been lost, namely Γαλῆ καὶ Ἀφροδίτη. The total number of fables beginning with Β in the manuscripts of Class I is, according to Chambry's edition, seven; since four of these (counting no. 46) are extant in G, it appears that only three complete fables in B have been lost. This gives us a presumable total of four fables that have disappeared entirely in the lacuna, and the amount of text represented by these particular fables (see Table I) closely approximates to the average contents of one folio in the manuscript. Measuring by Chambry's edition, the total number of lines presumably lost in G is 46, while the average number of Chambry's lines to a single *page* of the manuscript in this region is about 22.[2] It is evident, therefore, that only one leaf (i.e. two pages) has been lost at this point and that its contents were, in all probability, the same as those which intervene in the manuscripts Pa, Pb, Pe and Pg.

The same method of reckoning as that employed above, leads to the conclusion that two leaves containing eight fables

[1] See Table I below.
[2] 77^v has 21 of Chambry's lines; 78^r, 22; 79^r, 23; 79^v, 22½; 78^v has an abnormally large margin.

in all have been lost after 80ᵛ. This lacuna begins just before the epimythium of no. 66 and ends in the twelfth line of Ἔλαφος καὶ λέων (= Cham. 103). The latter fable, according to the numbers in the margin, was third in the series beginning with E; the other two that have been lost entirely are presumably the same as those given in Pa, Pb, Pe, and Pg. The total number of fables in Δ occurring in the other manuscripts of Class I is twelve; but one of these (Cham. 97), which is not a fable but a χρεία concerning Diogenes, is found only in Pe; another, also a story about Diogenes (Cham. 98), is found only in Pa and Ca; and still another, a rhetorical ἠθοποιΐα (Cham. 62), is extant only in Pb and Ma. Our best guide amid this diversity is Pb, since that manuscript is, as we shall see, closer throughout to G than any of the others. Since Pb has ten fables in Δ, of which four are extant in G, it is probable that G has lost six fables beginning with Δ. This reckoning includes Pb's ἠθοποιΐα but not the unique fables in Pe and PaCa. The total number of Chambry's lines in the eight fables which are thus assumed to have been lost in G, is ninety-three; and this approximates rather closely to the amount of text contained on two average leaves of the manuscript. Without the ἠθοποιΐα (15 lines) the contents of the lost pages cannot be satisfactorily reconstructed.

Explanation of Table I

To the following table, which gives a full perspectus of the contents and order of G in comparison with other manuscripts of Class I, I have added, from a complete collation with Chambry's text, all the variant readings of the Morgan manuscript that seemed to me to be noteworthy either for their own sake or for the sake of comparison with other texts. The variants that do not appear here consist mainly of such smaller additions, omissions, and manifest errors as are peculiar to G. Here and there I have corrected the accents and breathings of the manuscript and have added iota subscripts, but only where error or neglect could without question be inferred, and never when the reading or the tradition was conceivably affected thereby. The agreement of the manuscripts of Class I with G is indicated by a cross. This is inclosed in parentheses (×) when the agreement is substantial but not exact, as for example in 1,19, where Pb has ἔτι πτηνοὶ ἀτελεῖς for G's ἔτι πτῆναι ἀτελεῖς against Pa's ἔτι ἀτελεῖς οἱ πτηνοί. Movable ν is ignored. Each fable in G begins with the same letter as the title given at the left, unless otherwise indicated. The agreements with G of manuscripts outside Class I have been only partially indicated, though Ma, Mb, and Ca are cited quite regularly. Occasionally I have used the symbols C, L, and m in the right-hand margin to designate the consensus of all, or nearly all, the manuscripts of Classes II, III, and V (mixed group) respectively. The facts here reported about the manuscripts other than G are taken entirely from Chambry, except that I have checked the readings of Pb with Sternbach's collation in *Wien. Stud.* XVII (1896), pp. 75ff., and have upon occasion consulted the editions of Pb by Schneider (1812) and of Pa by Sternbach (1894).

TABLE I

No.	Chambry Title	Chambry Line	Chambry Reading	G No.	G Reading	Order of fables in the MSS of Class I and their agreement with the readings of G								Agreement of other MSS Remarks
						Pa	Pb	Pc	Pd	Pe	Pf	Pg	Ph	
3	Ἀετὸς καὶ ἀλώπηξ			1		11	1	–	1	–	1	–	1	Ma 11
		1	φιλίαν πρὸς ἀλλήλους ποιησάμενοι αὐτῆς ποτε		= Chambry	×								
		5	⟨τοσοῦτον⟩		ποτε αὐτῆς μᾶλλον		×						×	Me
		9	τῇ ἀμύνῃ		τῆς ἀμύνης	×	×							Ma Mb
		19	ἔτι πτηνοὶ ἀτελεῖς οἱ πτηνοί		ἔτι πτῆναι ἀτελεῖς	×	×							
		20	προσδραμοῦσα		δραμοῦσα		(×)							Ma
5	Ἀετὸς καὶ κολοιός			2		12	2	–	4	8	–	1	–	Ma 12
		2	τοῦτο (Pb)		τοῦτον	×			×	×		×		All MSS except Pb
		7	τὰ ὀξύπτερά		τὰ εἰς ὀξύπτερά	×			×	×				
		11–12	τῷ μηδὲν		τὸ μηδὲν	×				×				Ma
4	Ἀετὸς καὶ κάνθαρος			3		13	3	–	5	9	2	–	2	Ma 13
		1	τῶν βοηθησόντων		= Chambry					×	×			Ma Me Mh Cb Cc Ch
		10	τὸν Δία		Δία	×			×	×	×			
		10	Διός		θεοῦ									
		12–13	ἐν τοῖς ἑαυτοῦ κόλποις		ἐν τοῖς κόλποις αὐτοῦ		×							Ma
		17	τὰ ᾠά		om.	×	×		×	×	×		×	Ma Cb Cd Ch

82

						14	4	-	6	10	3	2	3	
8	Ἀηδὼν καὶ ἱέραξ	6 7	καὶ ὃς ὑποτυχών	4	καὶ ὡς ἐπιτυχών	X X	X	-	-	-				Ma 14
10	Ἀθηναῖος χρεωφει- λέτης			5		15	5	-	-	11	4	3	4	Ma
		1 3	χρεωφειλέτης ἀνήρ δοῦναι		ἃ. χρεοφειλέτης παρέχεσθαι		(X)					(X)		(Me Mf) (παρασχέσθαι Pe Pf Pg Ph Me Mf)
		3–4 5 7 7	προσαγαγών προσελθόντος γὰρ om.		προσαγαγών προελθόντος om. ἐστὶν before θήλεα	X X	X X					X		
17	Αἰπόλος καὶ αἶγες ἄγριαι			6		16	6	-	-	11	-	4	-	On Pe, cf. Chambry p. 6
		3 6 7 8 17 17	εἰσήλασε παραβάλλων παρασωρεύων ἰδιοποιήσασθαι δηλοῖ μὴ δεῖν		ἔλασεν περιβάλλων περισωρεύων ἐξιδιοποιήσασθαι διδάσκει μηδέν	X	X X					X X		
14	Αἴλουρος καὶ ὄρ- νιθες		ὑποκρίνωνται	7	ὑποκρίνονται	17	7	-	8	12	-	5	-	μὴ δὲ Pb Pg
									X					Ma 15

TABLE I—*Continued*

No.	Title	Chambry Line	Reading	G No.	G Reading	Pa	Pb	Pc	Pd	Pe	Pf	Pg	Ph	Other MSS Remarks
19	Αἴσωπος ἐν ναυπηγίῳ			8		18	8	—	9	13	—	—	—	
		1	*om.*		*ποτε* after Αἴσωπος									
		2	σκωπτόντων (Hudson)		σποπούντων	X	X		X	X				Mb
							X		X					Mb
		5	τρίς		τρεῖς		X		X					
		8	αὐτῇ		αὐτῆ	X	X		X	X				
		8	καὶ τὸ τρίτον		κ. τρίτον	X	X		X	X				Mb
40	Ἀλώπηξ καὶ τράγος v. 2 (*i.e.* second version)			9 v.2		2 v. 1	9 v. 2	—	2 v. 2	14 v. 3		6 v. 2	11 v. 2	Ma 2 v. 1
		6–7	ὁ δὲ – ἐπιθυμίαν		τοῦ δὲ ἀμελητὸς καθαλλομένου διὰ τὸ μόνην ὁρᾶν τότε τὴν ἐπιθυμίαν									*Cf.* Pg and Pe
					om.		X							
		7	τὴν before δίψαν		ἐὰν γ. θελήσῃς									
		10	εἰ γὰρ θελήσεις											
		11	προσερείσαι ἐγκλίνας		προσερίσας ἐγκλῖναι							(X)	(X)	προσερείσας ἐγκλῖναι Pg Ph
		12	ἀναβιβάσω		ἀνασπάσω					X		X	X	
		14	ἀλλομένη		ἀναλλομένη				X	X		X	X	ἀνελομένη Pa Pi Ma
		14	τὸν νότον		τοῦ νώτου									Ma
		17	παραβαίνουσαν		παραβαινούσης							X		All MSS
		19	<ἂν>		*om.*									
		23	ἐπιχειρεῖν		ἐγχειρεῖν	X							X	Pi Ma

84

				1	10	–	3	15	12	7	12	
42	Ἀλώπηξ <μηδέ- ποτε θεασαμένη λέοντα>	10										Ma 1
		3	διεταράχθη				X	X	X	X	–	Ma
		3	καί									Ma Mb
		6	προσελθοῦσα		X			X	X	X	X	προελθοῦσα Pg Ma
		6	διελέχθη		X				–	8	–	Ma Mb etc.
24	Ἀλιεὺς αὐλῶν	11		19	X		10	16	–			Ma 16
		3	προβλήματος αὐτομάτως		X			XX				Ma
		3–4	(ω in margin)									
		4–5	ἐξαλεῖσθαι πρὸς αὐτόν		XX		X	X		X	X	And all others except Pa
		8	τοῦ δικτύου		X		X			X	–	Ma
37	Ἀλώπηξ καὶ βάτραχος	12		20	12	–	11	–	–	9	–	Ma 17
23	Ἀλιεῖς <λίθον ἀγρεύσαντες>	13		21	13	–	12	–	7	10	7	
		3	τῶν μὲν ἰχθύων ὀλίγον	X	X							
		5	οὐ τοσοῦτον οὐχ οὕτω μᾶλλον									
		9–10	πάντως παθεῖν τι καὶ λυπηρόν πάντως τι καὶ λυπηθῆναι		XX		XX		(X)	XX	(X)	All MSS (Me Mf)

Table I—Continued

No.	Chambry Title	Chambry Line	Chambry Reading	G No.	G Reading	Pa	Pb	Pc	Pd	Pe	Pf	Pg	Ph	Other MSS Remarks
39	Ἀλώπηξ καὶ πίθηκος ⟨περὶ εὐγενείας ἐρίζοντες⟩			14		22	14	1	–	–	–	–	–	
		2	διεξιόντος		διεξιόντων									
		3	κατά τινα τόπον		κατά τι	×	×							
		3–4	ἀνεστέναξεν		ἐστέναξεν	×								
		4	ὁ πίθηκος		om.	(×)								
		4	ἐρομένης		ἐρωτωμένης									
		5	εἶπεν		ἔφη	×	×							κλαίων Pa²
		6	κλάεων		κλαίων		×							κλάεων Pa¹
		8	σε		om.		×							
32	Ἀλώπηξ καὶ βότρυς			15		23	15	2	–	–	–	11	–	(Ma 158 aliter)
		1	ἀπό τινος		= Chambry	×		×						
		2	ἠβουλήθη		ἐβουλήθη			×						
12	Αἴλουρος καὶ ἀλεκτρυών			16		3	16	3	13	–	5	12	5	Ma 3
		4	αὐτούς		om.		×	×	×		×	×	×	Me Mf
		5	ὠφελείᾳ		ὠφέλειαν		×	×				×		
		7	ἀλλὰ καί		= Chambry			×						Mf
		7	om.		τε καί after ἀσεβής							×	×	Mf 'libri excepto Pg', Me
		8	ἐπεμβαίνων		ἐπιβαίνων		(×)	×			(×)	(×)	(×)	
		11	εὐπορῇς		εὑρήσεις		(×)	(×)				(×)		
		11–12	οὐχ ἧσσον ἔδομαι		οὐ κατέδομαι	×			×			×		κατεδοῦμαι Pb
		13–14	προαιρουμένη		προελομένη									προελομένη all MSS except Pa Pd

41			17		24	17		14		13	13	13	
41	Ἀλώπηξ κόλουρός												Ma 18
	8	<μή>σοι		ἢ σοὶ									Mc (Cb Cd) Cb Ce
	11	ποιοῦνται		ποιοῦντες									
26	Ἀλιεύς καὶ μαινίς		18		4	18				—	—	—	Ma 4
	1	ἀνήνεγκε		ἀνήνεγκεν		X							
	3	ὅτι		παροῦσα (after μικρά)									Ma
	3	συλλαμβάνειν		συλλαβεῖν		XX							
	4	ἐγώ		ἔγωγε		XX							
	5	ἄν		ὅτι.	X								
	5	χειρί		χερσίν		X							
	6	διώκουμι		διώκειν οὐ δύναμαι									
	8	τὸ		τοῦ									
31	Ἀλώπηξ καὶ βάτος		19		5	19	4	15	—	14	14	14	Ma 5
	3	ὅτι		εἶγε		X	XX	XX		XX	XX	XX	Pi Mb Me Mf
	4	χείρονι		χείρον		(X)	(X)	(X)		(X)	(X)	(X)	Mb Me Mf
	4	ἐχρήσατο (Pa)		ἐχρήσατο καὶ αὐτοῦ τοῦ προκειμένου									(Ma Mb Me Mf)
35	Ἀλώπηξ καὶ κροκόδειλος		20		6	20	5	16	—	11	15	10	Ma 6
	5–6	εἰ γεγυμνασμένος		ἢ ἀναλωμάτων			(X)			(X)	(X)	(X)	(Mb) See Chambry
22	Ἀλιεύς καὶ θύννος		21		7	21	6	17	—	8	—	8	Ma 7
	2	συνέλαβον		ἔτηρον									Cf. Pc Pf Ph Me Mf
	2	δὲ		ὅτι.		X							

Table I—Continued

No.	Chambry Title	Line	Reading	No.	G Reading	Pa	Pb	Pc	Pd	Pe	Pf	Pg	Ph	Other MSS Remarks
34	Ἀλώπηξ καὶ δρυτόμος			22		25	22	7	18	–	–	16	–	Ma 19
		1	φεύγουσα		διαφεύγουσα									
		2	ἱκέτευε		καθικέτευεν									
		7	κατεκρύπτετο		κατακέκρυπτο									Cf. Pb Pc Pd Pg
		16	ἐπαγγελομένους		ἐπαγγελαμένους									
21	Ἀλεκτρυόνες καὶ πέρδιξ			23		26	23	–	–	–	6	–	6	
		7	ἦ		om.									
		9	ὑπ' αὐτῶν		ὑπὸ τούτων		X				X		X	Me Mf
		11	φέρουσι				X							Me
		11	τὰς τῶν		τὰς ἐκ τῶν									
		12	om.		ἀλλὰ (after αὐτοὺς)									Ma
30	Ἀλώπηξ ἐξογκωθεῖσα τὴν γαστέρα			24		27	24	8	19	–	–	–	–	
		2	ποιμένων		om.									
		6	ἐπυνθάνετο τὴν αἰτίαν		om.									
28	Ἀλκύων			25		28	25	–	20	–	10	17	–	
		3	παραθαλαττίοις		περιθαλαττίοις									
		8	ἐπικλύσασαν		ἐπικλύσαν	X						X		

88

27	Ἁλιεὺς ⟨ὕδωρ τύπτων⟩			26		29	26	–	–	–	9	
		5	οἰκούντων τις		οἰκῶν τις	×			21			θολοῦντα καὶ Pa
		6	θολοῦν καὶ		θολοῦν τε καὶ							Pb Pd Pf Ph
												Me Mf
43	Ἀλώπηξ πρὸς μορμολύκειον			27		8	27	9	–	15	15	Repeated in Pa after no. 29
		5–6	ὁ λόγος εὔκαιρος] after ἀλόγιστον		before πρός		×					
55	Ἀνὴρ φέναξ			28		30	28	–	–	–	–	
		1	νοσῶν		ὧν	×						ἑκατόμβην Pb
		2	ἑκατὸν βόας		κατατόμβην	×						
		6	κατέκαυσεν		κατεσκεύασεν							
		10	καὶ ὃς		καὶ ὡς							
56	Ἀνθρακεὺς καὶ γναφεύς			29		31	29	10	22	–	17	
		1	οἰκίας		οἰκίαν	×						
		3	ὅτι		καὶ (after γένηται)	×		×	×			
		5	γναφεύς		γναφεὺς							
		6	ὅτι		ἔστιν (after παντελῶς)							
53	Ἀνὴρ ναυαγός			30		32	30	11	–	–	18	Cf. Pb and Ma
		2	νηὸς		νεὼς	×	×	×××				
		5	εἰ περισωθείη		ἂν περισωθείη	×	×					×
		6	σὺ		ὅτι							Me Mf
		13–14	τοὺς… δέεσθαι		ὅτι.							Ma

TABLE I—Continued

No.	Chambry Title	Line	Reading	No.	G Reading	Pa	Pb	Pc	MSS of Class I Pd	Pe	Pf	Pg	Ph	Other MSS Remarks
52	Ἀνὴρ μεσοπόλιος καὶ ἑταῖραι			31	Cf. infra, no. 238	33	31	—	41 v. 4	—	—	152 v. 4	—	
		2	ὑπῆρχεν		om.									
		4	περιαιρουμένη			X	X							
		7	φαλακρὸν		περιχρουμένη φαλακρότερον									
45	Ἀνδροφόνος			32	inc. Ἄνθρωπον	9	32	12	—	—	—	18	—	
		3	αὐτῷ		αὐτοῦ		X	X				X		Ma
		3	ἐπὶ δένδρου		ἐπί τι δένδρον		X					X		Ma
		5	δράκοντα		ἔχιν									
		5	διαιρούμενον		διαιρούμενον		(X)	(X)				(X)		Ma (κροκόδειλος Pb Pc Pg)
		6	ἐν...αὐτὸν		ἐν δὲ τούτῳ ὑποδεξάμενος αὐτὸν κορκόδειλος			X						
		9	ἐστι		om.									
51	Ἀνὴρ κομπαστής			33		34	33	—	—	1	—	—	—	
		3	πολλὰ		πολλὰ μέν	X	X							
46	Ἀνὴρ ἀδύνατα ἐπαγγελλόμενος			34		35	34	13	—	2	18	—	19	
		1	ἐπειδὴ		ἐπεί									

60	Ἄνθρωπος καὶ σάτυρος	6	προσφαγήματος	35	προσφαγημάτων	36	35	—	3 v.2	—	—	—
		11	ὅτι		ὅτι.	X							Ma
50	Ἀνὴρ κακοπράγ-μων			36		37	36	—	4	19	—	—
54	Ἀνὴρ πηρός	3	τῷ ἱματίῳ		τῶν ἱματίων	X	X		X	X	19	—
		7	προσενεγκεῖν	37	προσενεγκεῖν	38	37	23	5				Me Mf / Ma 28
64	Ἀρότης καὶ λύκος	4	λύκου		κυνός	X	X	X	X	—	X	—
		4	ἐστίν	38	εἴη	X	X	X					Ma Ca / Ma Ca
						39	38	24	6			
350	Χελιδὼν καὶ ὄρνιθες	1	ἀπῆγε		ἀπήγαγεν	X	X		X			—
		6	ἀρότης		ἀρότηρ							
		10	ἐπαγγέλλονται		ἐπαγγέλλονται							
				39	inc. Ἄρτι	40	39	—	75 v.2	139 v.2	146 v.2		v. 2 inc. χελιδὼν
		3–4	ταῖς ἐξοφόρους δρυσὶν		τὰς ἐξοφόρους δρῦς	X	X					
		6	συλλαμβάνωσιν		συλλαμβάνονται	(X)							(—ωνται Pa)
		7	γελασάντων		ἐγγελασάντων							
		7	αὐτῆς ὡς ματαιο-λογούσαν		αὐτῆς ὡς ματαιο-λογούσης							
		10	ἀγρεύουσαν		ὄρνεα							

TABLE I—Continued

No.	Chambry Title	Chambry Line	Chambry Reading	G No.	G Reading	Pa	Pb	Pc	Pd	Pe	Pf	Pg	Ph	Other MSS Remarks
65	Ἀστρολόγος	1	ἑσπέρας	40	ἑσπέραν	41	40	—	—	—	20	—	21	
		2	ἐπισκοπῆσαι		ἐπισκοπεῖσθαι	×					×		×	Me Mf Mj
		4	φρέαρ		τὸ φρέαρ	×					×		×	Me Mf Mj
		5	τῶν στενάγμων		τῶν στεναγμὸν	×								
		10	παραδόξος		περιδόξης		(×)							περὶ δόξης Pb
		10	ἀλαζονεύονται		ἀλαζονεύοντες		×							
36	Ἀλώπηξ καὶ κύων	2	ἀρνίον	41	ἄρνιον	42	41	14	—	—	16	20	16	
		2	ἀναλαβομένη		λαβομένη	(×)	(×)					(×)	(×)	(Mb)
		4	αὐτὸ		αὐτόν	×	×					×	×	Mb
83	Γεωργὸς καὶ παῖδες αὐτοῦ			42	inc. Ἀνὴρ	10	42	—	25	7	—	—	—	
		2	εἶναι		ποιῆσαι αὐτῆς (apparently changed from an original αὐτοῖς)		×							Mb
		7	αὐτοῖς						×					
		7	ἀπεδίδου		ἀπεδίδουν		×							
		8	τοῦτο μὲν ἔγνωσαν		ὁ λόγος δηλοῖ		×							
68	Βάτραχοι ⟨ἐν λίμνῃ⟩	1	αὐτῶν	43	om.	43	43	15	26	17	21	21	22	
		3	συνεβούλευεν		συνεβούλευεν		×							
		3	ἀμελητί		ἀμέλητος			(×)			(×)		(×)	Ma

			44	44	44	16	27 v.4	18	22	22	23	
66	Βάτραχοι <αἰτοῦντες βασιλέα>											
		2			εἰς							
		3	πρὸς αὐτῶν		×	×			×			
		5	om.		(×)	(×)						
		5										
		5	ἐνέδωσαν ὡς										
		7			×	×					×	
		11	καθ' αὐτῶν										
		12	κατεσθίονται										
70	Βόες καὶ ἄξων		45	45	45	17	28 v.4	19	23			
		3		σὺ κέκραγας μοχθούντων ἑτέρων	σὺ τί κράξεις ἕτερον μοχθούντων	×						
		4			×							Ca Mj
												Ma Mb Ca
73	Βορέας καὶ Ἥλιος		46	46	46	18	29 v.4	20	24			
		3	ἀποδύσῃ	ἐκδύσει								ἐκδύσῃ Pb Pg
		6	περιττοτέραν	περιττότερον	×	(×)	(×)		×	(×)		
		7	<ὁ Βορέας>	om.	×	×	×			×		
		7	αὐτὸν παρέδωκε	μετεπαρέδωκεν This fable ends with the word πρῶτον (= Chambry, line 8), followed by a lacuna at the end of f. 77ᵛ; cf. supra, p. 79	(×)							(μετεπαρέδωκε Pa)

TABLE I—*Continued*

No.	Chambry Title	Line	Reading	G No.	G Reading	Pa	Pb	Pc	Pd	Pe	Pf	Pg	Ph	Other MSS Remarks
293	Παιδίον ἐσθίον σπλάγχνα		inc. Βοῦν	[47]		47	47	19	—	21	—	25	—	
75	Βοταλὶς καὶ νυκτερίς			[48]		48	48	—	—	22	23	26	—	
74	Βουκόλος καὶ λέων			[49]		49	49	20	—	23	—	27	—	
76	Γαλῆ καὶ Ἀφροδίτη			[50]		50	50	21	30 v. 5	24	—	28	—	
81	Γεωργὸς καὶ ὄφις ⟨τὸν παῖδα αὐτοῦ ἀποκτείνας⟩			51	inc.—το δεινοπαθήσας (=Cham. line 2)	51	51	22	—	25	—	29	—	
		5 12	τοῦ μὲν καταλλαγάς		τοῦ μὲν ὄφεος μεταλλαγάς	×	×	×		×		×		
80	Γεωργὸς καὶ κύνες			52		52	52	23	—	26	—	30	—	Ma Mb
		2 3 7 10	καὶ πρόβατα ἡμῖν δηλοῖ ὅτι δεῖ		om. βρώματα ἡμῖν ἐστιν διδάσκει δεῖν	×	×					××		Mb, cf. Ma

86	Γεωργοῦ παῖδες ⟨στασιάζοντες⟩			53		53	53	24	—	—	27	—	31	—		
		3	πράγματος													
		4	δέσμην													
		6	κατὰ πᾶν βιαζόμενοι			xx	xx	x					x			
		12	ὅσον													
		12	εὐκαταγώνιστος			xx	xx	x								
173	Κοχλίαι		inc. Γεωργοῦ	54		54	54	25	—	—	27	—	32	—		
89	Γυνὴ καὶ θεράπαιναι			55		55	55	26	—	—	—	—	27	xx	Ca Ma Ma Mb	
		2	ἀλεκτροφωνίαν											xx		
		6	πραξάσαις τοῦτο					xx			xxx		xx	x x (x)		
		8	ἐπὶ τὸ ἔργον ἤγειρεν													
91	Γυνὴ μάγος			56		56	56	27	—	—	28	—	33	28		
		1	ἐπῳδάς…μηνυμάτων	ἐπῳδὰς καὶ καθέσεις θείων μηνυμάτων		x		x						x	Ca	
		2	διετέλει…τούτων	ὅτι												
		7	ἤ	οὐ												
		7–8	ἐπαγγελλομένη	ἐπαγγέλλουν												

TABLE I—Continued

No.	Chambry Title	Line	Reading	G No.	G Reading	Pa	Pb	Pc	Pd	Pe	Pf	Pg	Ph	Other MSS Remarks
87	Γραῦς καὶ ἰατρός			57	*inc.* Γυνή	57	57	—	—	—	—	34	29	
		3	ἐκείνης		*om.*	×								
		3	καθ' ἕκαστον		καθ' ἐν ἕκαστον ὑφηρεῖτο	×	×							
		4	ὑφαιρόμενος		*om.*									Mb
		5	καὶ											
		8–10	νῦν δὲ . . . ἔφη		κἀκείνη ἔφη. πρότερον μὲν ἐβλεπον ἅπαντα									
		10	οἰκίας		οἰκίας μου		×					×		
90	Γυνὴ καὶ ὄρνις			58		58	58	28	31	—	—	35	—	
		4	ποιησάσης		ποιούσης	×		×				×		Mb
		6	τινές (Pd)		οἱ πλείονες	×	(×)	×				×		
77	Γαλῆ καὶ ῥίνη			59	*inc.* Γυνή (for Γαλῆ)	—	59	—	—	27	24 v.2	36	24 v.2	
		2	ῥίνην		ῥίναν									ῥίνα Pb
		4	ἀπέβαλε		ἀπέβαλλεν		(×)			×		×		
		6	φιλονεικίαις		φιλονικίᾳ		×							
		7	καταβλάπτοντας		καταβάλλοντας καὶ βλαπτομένους									
78	Γέρων καὶ θάνατος			60	*inc.* Γεωργός	—	60	—	32	28	25 v.3	37	25 v.3	
		1	Γέρων		Γεωργός									
		2	τῆς ὁδοῦ		*om.*		(×)		×	×		×		Ma Mb
		4	παρακαλεῖται		προσκαλεῖται θανεῖν δὲ ἐγὼ οὐ θέλω (after ἄρῃς)		×							(Pb omits ἐγώ)
		5	*om.*											
		6	μῦθος		λόγος									

84	Γεωργὸς καὶ τύχη		61	59	61	—	—	29	26 v. 2	38	26 v. 2	
		2	αὑτήν		τὴν γῆν				×			Ca τῇ γῇ Pb
		2	ὡς		om.				×			
		2	παρ' αὑτῆς		ὑπ' αὑτῆς		×						
		3–4	τὰ ἐμὰ δῶρα		τὸ ἐμὸν δῶρον		×				×		Ca ὅπερ Pb
		4	περιτιθείς		προστιθεὶς		(×)						
		4	ἃ ἐγώ		ἅπερ ἐγώ		×						
		4	σοι		om.								
		6	χείρας...μέμψη		χρῄας μοχθηρὰς ἐξαναλωθῇ οὐ τὴν γῆν ἀλλὰ τὴν τύχην μέμψεσθαι	×							See Chambry for partial agreements with other MSS, esp. Pb
		7	λόγος		μῦθος		×						
		7	ἐπιγινώσκειν		γινώσκειν	×	×				×		
		8	χάριτας		χάριτας μεγάλας		×						
82	Γεωργὸς καὶ ὄφις ⟨ὑπὸ κριοῦ πεπηγώς⟩		62	174 v. 2	62	102 v. 2	—	30	—	112 v. 2	—	Pb and G each have two versions of this fable; for the second see below, no. 177
		1	Γεωργός τις		inc. Γέρον								
		2	κόλπον		Γέρον κόλπους					×			(τοὺς κόλπους Pe) Ma
		6–7	τὰ μέγιστα		om.								
		7	φιλανθρωπεύονται		φιλανθρωπεύονται								

97

TABLE I—Continued

No.	Chambry Title	Line	Reading	G No.	G Reading	MSS of Class I								Other MSS Remarks
						Pa	Pb	Pc	Pd	Pe	Pf	Pg	Ph	
96	Δημάδης ὁ ῥήτωρ	1	Δημάδης ἀντέχεσθε	63	Δημάδης ἀνέχεσθαι	61	63	30	–	–	–	40	–	Ma
		10												Ma Cf. ἀνέχεσθε Pc
95	Δελφῖνες καὶ φά- λαιναι καὶ κωβιός			64		60	72	29	–	–	29 v. 2	39	30 v. 2	Concerning the misplacement of this fable in Pb, see below, after no. 72
		2–3	ἐστί...ἰχθύς		om.		×							
		3	καί...διαλύειν		καὶ αὐτὸς ἐπειρᾶτο διαλύειν		×							
		5	μαχομένους		μαχομένους		×							Mb Ca
178	Κυνόδηκτος			65	inc. Δηχθείς	62	64	31	–	31	–	41	31	Cf. Pb
		1	περιῄει ζητῶν ὑποτυχών		περὶ ἐζήτει ὑποτυχὼν δὲ ὁ δηχθείς		×							
		3												
		4–5	ὑπό...κυνῶν		ὑπὸ πάντων κυνῶν ἐν τῇ πόλει									
		6	πονηρία		φύσις		×							

				66	inc. Δύο	64	65	32	–	32	–	42	–	
255	Ὁδοιπόροι καὶ ἄρκτος													
		1–2	αὐτοῖς ἐπιφανείσης ἕτερος		ἐν τῇ ὁδῷ φανήσης εἷς (for εἷς)		(X)(X)	(X)						(Ma)
		3	καὶ ἐνταῦθα ἐκρύπτετο		κακεῖ κατεκρύπτετο		X							
		4	κατὰ		ἐπί		(X)	X						Ma
		5	αὐτῷ		αὐτοῦ									
		6	συνεῖχε		αὐτὸς συνῆχεν αὐτάς		(X)							
		7	ὑποχωρησάσης		ἀπαλλαγήσης	X	(X)					(X)		(Ma Mb)
		8	ὁ		om.									
		8	ἐπυνθάνετο αὐτοῦ		ἐπυνθάνε τουτὸν τοῦ ἑτέρου									
		9	τοῦ λοιποῦ τοιούτους		τοιούτους τοῦ λοιποῦ. The epimythium is lost in the lacuna that here follows; cf. supra, p. 80		(X)							(τοιούτους Pb)
248	Νεανίσκοι καὶ μάγειρος		inc. Δύο	[67]		65	66	33	–	33	–	43	32	
257	Ὁδοιπόροι καὶ πέλεκυς		inc. Δύο	[68]		66	67	34	33	34	30	–	33	
115	Ἐχθροὶ δύο		inc. Δύο	[69]		67	68	35	34	35	31	44	34	
67	Βάτραχοι ⟨γείτονες⟩		inc. Δύο	[70]		68	69	–	35	36 v. 2	32	45	35	

TABLE I—*Continued*

No.	Chambry Title	Chambry Line	Chambry Reading	G No.	G Reading	Pa	Pb	Pc	Pd	Pe	Pf	Pg	Ph	Other MSS Remarks
101	Δρῦς καὶ κάλαμος		*inc.* Δρῦς (Pb)	[71]		(221)	70	—	—	37 v. 2	—	—	—	No. 221 in Pa, though essentially the same fable, corresponds with no. 213 in Pb, = 220 in G
62	Ἄνθρωπος λέοντα χρυσοῦν εὑρών		*inc.* Δειλός	[72]		—	71	—	—	—	—	—	—	Elsewhere only in Ma
95	See above		*inc.* Δελφῖνες	64		60	72	29	—	—	29 v. 2	39	30 v. 2	Pb inserted this fable here at the end of Δ, probably because it had been accidentally omitted above
236	Μελισσουργός		*inc.* Εἷς	[73]		69	73	36	—	39	36	46	36	Pe's no. 38 (= Cham. 97) is unique
306	Πίθηκος καὶ δελφίς		*inc.* Ἔθος	[74]		70	74	—	—	40	—	47	—	
103	Ἔλαφος ⟨ἐπὶ νάματος⟩ καὶ λέων			75	*inc.* -πρὸς ἑαυτὴν (Cham. line12).	71	75	—	—	41	—	48	—	
		13	προδοθήσεσθαι ἔμελλον		ᾠόμην προδοθήσεσθαι		×					×		(Ma Mb)

				76		72	76	37	–	42	35	–	37	
106	Ἔλαφος πηρωθεῖσα													
		1	τὸν ἕτερον τῶν ὀφθαλμῶν		τὸν ἕταιρον ὀφθαλμὸν	X	(X)			X	X		X	(ἕτερον Pb)
		4–5	πρὸς τὴν θάλασσαν		ἐν τῇ θαλάσσῃ		X							And the others except Ca
		6, 7–8	παραπλέοντες καὶ...ὡς		πλέοντες καὶ (after a blank space of about 3 cm.)	X	X							
		9	φυλαττομένη		ἐφυλαττόμην	X		X						Mb Ca
		11	παρὰ		περὶ									Ca
		13	σωτήρια...ἐπισφαλῆ		ἐπισφαλῆ νομιζόμενα σωτήρια	(X)					(X)		(X)	(Me Mf)
105	Ἔλαφος καὶ λέων ⟨ἐν σπηλαίῳ⟩			77		73		38	–	43 v. 2	36	49	38	
		2	καὶ		om.	X								Me Mf Ca
		4	ἔγωγε		ἐγὼ		X	XX			X	X	XX	Mb Me Mf Ca
		6–7	ἐλάττονος...ἐμβάλλουσιν		ἐλάττονον κινδύνων ἑαυτοὺς εἰς μείζονα κακὰ ἐνσείουσιν									See Chambry for partial parallels in other MSS, esp. Pb Pc Pg Ma
104	Ἔλαφος καὶ ἄμπελος			78		74		39	–	44	37	50	39	
		3	τις		om.									
		4	ὁ		ὡς	X	XX	XX		X	XX	XX	XX	Repeated in Pa after 91 (=91a)
		4	ἀκόντιον		ἀκοντίῳ	X							X	Mb Ca
		5	ἔφη		εἶπεν									τοῦ θεοῦ Pa 91a
		8	θεοῦ		θεῶν									

TABLE I—*Continued*

No.	Chambry Title	Line	Reading	G No.	G Reading	Pa	Pb	Pc	Pd	Pe	Pf	Pg	Ph	Other MSS Remarks
309	Πλέοντες			79	*inc.* Ἐμβόντες (*sic*)	75	79	40	–	–	38	–	40	
		5	ἐπαγγελλόμενος		ἐπαγγελάμενος		(×)							-ελάμενος Pb
		9	κυδύνου		ὀπ.	×	×	×					×	
		11	γεγησομένου		ἐσομένου		×						×	
		11	ὀπ.		πάλιν κλαύσωμεν									
		13	ἐννοουμένους		ἐννοούμενοι									
13	Αἴλουρος καὶ μύες			80	*inc.* Ἔν τινι	76	80	41	–	45	–	51	–	Ma
		5	ἔγνω		ὀπ.	×								
241	Μυῖαι			81	*inc.* Ἔν τινι	77	81	–	–	–	39	52	41	Ma Ca (Ma)
		3	ἐδύναντο		ἠδύναντο		×							
		4	ἀποπνιγόμεναι		ἀποπνιγομένων	×								
		6	λιχνεία		λιχνία									
38	Ἀλώπηξ καὶ πίθηκος <βασιλεὺς αἱρεθείς>			82	*inc.* Ἐν	78	82	42	–	46	40	–	42	
		1	ὀρχησάμενος καὶ		ὀπ.	×		(×)			(×)		(×)	Mb
		7	ἀτημελήτως		ἀμελητὸς						×			Mb
		8	ἐνεδρεύσασαν		ἐνεδρεύσασα		×	×			×			
		9	μωρίαν		τύχην									
		11	ἀπερισκέπτως		ἀπροσκέπτως									

102

					83	79	83	—	47 v. 2	41	53	43	
270	Ὄνος καὶ ἀλεκτρυὼν καὶ λέων	3			inc. Ἕν τινι			—				—	
		4–5	παρὰ δὲ πτύρεσθαι τοὺς λέοντας ἀποδιώξων		καὶ τοὺς λέοντας πτύρεσθαι ἀποδιῶξαι ὅτι					X	X		Ma (Pb Mb) Ca
		7–8	Ὁ δέ...αὐτόν									X	Me Mf
307	Πίθηκος καὶ κάμηλος				inc. Ἕν		80	84	43	48	—	—	—	
		1	ὠρχήσατο ὅτι		ὠρχεῖτο εἴτε ἐκ τούτου σφαλλομένους (after ἁμιλλωμένους)		(X)	(X)						(Mb Ca)
		7												(Ma)
150	Κάνθαροι δύο				inc. Ἕν τινι	81	85	—	49 v. 2	—	54	—	
		3	ἕτερον		φίλον	X							Ma
		5	ἱκανῶς		ἱκανὴ	X							
		6	εὕροι		εὕροι								
		8	πολλὴν...μένων		πολλὴν μὲν τὴν κόπρον, ὑγρὰν δέ, μένον		X				X		Ma
		8–9	ἐτρέφετο ἐνταῦθα		ἐνταῦθα ἐτρέφετο								
		11	ᾐτιᾶτο		ᾐτιᾶτο								Ma
		12	ἐμέ		ὅτι								Ma

TABLE I—Continued

No.	Chambry Title	Chambry Line	Chambry Reading	G No.	G Reading	Pa	Pb	Pc	Pd	Pe	Pf	Pg	Ph	Other MSS Remarks
94	Δέλφαξ καὶ πρόβατα			86	*inc.* Ἔν τινι	82	86	44	—	50	—	—	—	
		4	τῷ		τὸ	×								
		4	μὲν		γὰρ	×		×		×				Ca
		4	*om.*		οὐ (before συνεχῶς)					×				Ma
		4	συλλαμβάνει		λαμβάνει	×								
		7	τὸ γάλα		ταῦς ἄρνους	×		×		×				Ca
		7	τὰ κρέα		= Chambry	×								Mb (Ma)
158	Κίχλα			87	*inc.* Ἔν τινι	83	87	45	—	51	42	55	44	
		4	ἔφη		εἶπεν									
		5	σωτηρίας		ζωῆς		×			×				Ma
		6	Ὁ λόγος		*om.*					×				
		7	εὔκαιρός ἐστιν		ἑαυτὸν									
288	Χὴν χρυσοτόκος			88	*inc.* Ἑρμῆς	84	88	—	—	52	—	—	—	
		8	προίεται		προίεμεν									
109	Ἑρμῆς καὶ ἀγαλματοποιός			89		85	89	46	—	53	—	56	—	
		2	*om.*		ὁρᾷ (before εἰς)	×	(×)	(×)		(×)		(×)		
		4	εἰπόντος...δραχμῆς		τοῦ δὲ εἰπόντος δραχμῆς		×	×		×		×		δραχμῆς codd.
		5	πόσον		πόσον ἐστίν	×								
		5	*om.*		καὶ (before θεασάμενος)	×	×	×						
		8	πόσου		*om.*		×					×		
		9	τοῦτον		τοῦτο									
		11	παρά		περί		×	×				×		

104

													Ma (Ma)	Me Mf Cf. Pa Pg
111	Ἑρμῆς καὶ Τειρεσίας					—		90	—	—	—	46	×	×
		2-3	πρὸς αὐτὸν εἰς ἄστυ	90	εἰς αὐτὸν ὡς ἄστυ									
		4	om.		περὶ (before τῆς)									
		7	παρῄνει λέγειν		παραινεῖ λέγων			×						
		7	om.		αὐτῷ (after λέγων)									
		9	παριστάμενον...		om.									
			πρὸς											
		10	τούτου		τοῦ							47	×	×
		12	ἔφη		εἶπεν									
118	Ἔχις καὶ ὕδρος			91		86	—	91	—	—	—	57	×× ×	×××
		2	ὅτι		εἴ γε									
		5-6	τοῦ ὕδατος... γῆς		τῆς γῆς καὶ τοῦ ὕδατος			××						
		6	γίγηνται		γένηται			×				44	×	×
		7	μίσους		μίσους									
		8	παρεθάρσυνον		παρεθάρσυναν	×								
		9	ἐνστάσης		ἐνστάσης							45	×× ×	×
		10	μηδὲν		οὐδὲν									
		11	ἐκεκράγεσαν		κεκράγεσαν			(×)						
		13	παρὰ		περὶ									
		14	γε		om.			×						
276	Ὄνος καὶ κυνίδιον			92	inc. Ἔχων	87	—	92	47	—	54	—		
		2	ἐδείπνει		δειπνοίη			×××			×			
		2	διεκόμιζε		ἐκόμιζε									
		3	παρέβαλλεν		παρέβαλεν	×		×××	××					
		4	ἐλάκτιζεν		ἐλάκτισεν	×						47		
		4	ὃς		ὡς									
		5	ἀπαγαγεῖν		ἐπαγαγεῖν									
176	Κύνες δύο			93	inc. Ἔχων	88	—	93	—	—	55	—	60	×
		1	ἐδίδασκε		ἐδίδαξεν			××			×			
		2	θηρευτῆς		θηρευτικὸς									
		2	ἐπ'		πρὸς									
		3	ἐκ τούτου μέρος		τοῦτο δὲ ἐκ μέρος									
		5-6	παρ' ἕκαστα... ποιῶν		om.									

TABLE I—*Continued*

No.	Chambry Title	Line	Reading	G No.	G Reading	MSS of Class I Pa	Pb	Pc	Pd	Pe	Pf	Pg	Ph	Other MSS Remarks
117	Ἔχις καὶ ῥίνη			94		89	94	—	—	—	46	—	48	
		8	κερδαίνειν		κερδαίνειν		×				×		×	Mb Me
		8	προσδοκῶντες		προσδοκῶσιν		×							
300	Πατὴρ καὶ θυγα- τέρες			95	*inc.* Ἔχων	90	95	—	—	56	49	63	51	
		3	ὡς		πρός		×							Ma
		7	πρός		καὶ πρός	×	×			×	×		×	Ca
		8	εἰπούσης		*om.*	×	×			×	×		×	Ma
		10	ἥλιος		ὁ ἥλιος					×				
		11	δὲ		*om.*									
		13–14	Οὕτως...πταίουσιν		*om.*									
49	Ἀνὴρ καὶ γυνὴ ⟨ἀργαλέα⟩			96	*inc.* Ἔχων	—	96	48	—	—	48	64	50	
		1	πάντας τοὺς οἰκεί- ους		πάντα									Mb πᾶν Pf
		5	ἀνελθούσης		ἐλθούσης		×	×						πάντω Pg
		10	συνδιέτριβες		συνέτριβες		×	×						Mb
		11	καὶ ἐκ τῶν		καὶ τῶν						×	×	×	Mb
		12	γνωρίζονται		γνωρίζεται									Mb
116	Ἔχις καὶ ἀλώπηξ			97		91	97	49	—	57	—	58	—	
		1	ἐπὶ		ὑπὸ									
		1	ὑπὲρ ποταμὸν		ἐπὶ ποταμοῦ	×	×(?)	×						
		2	παροῦσα		παροῦσα									
		3	νηός		νεώς									
		4	ἐγχειρήσαντα		ἐνευρήσαντα									

106

		98		92	98	–	–	58	43 v.2	59	45 v.2	
108	Ἔριφος καὶ λύκος <αὐλῶν>											
	5–6	καὶ ἐξελθόντες	om.							×		
	6	κατεδίωκον	ἐδίωκον					×				
	6	ὁ λύκος	om.									
2	Ἀγαλματοπώλης	99	inc. Ἑρμῆν	170 (aliter)	99	98 (aliter)	–	59	93 (aliter)	61	–	Repeated below in G, no. 173
	1	Ξύλινόν τις Ἑρμῆν (= Pa Pc Pf)	Ἑρμῆν τις ξύλινον		×					×		Mb
	2	ἐκκαλέσασθαι	ἐγκαλέσασθαι τινα					×				Ca
	3	ἐβόα	βοᾷ					×		×		
	3	ἀγαθοποιὸν δαίμονα	ἀγαθὸν θεόν		×			×				Mb
	4	παρατυχόντων τινός	περιτυχόντων τις		×			×				
	4	εἰπόντος	ἔφη		×			×				
	5	Ὦ... τοιοῦτον	ὦ ἄνθρωπε, τί τοῦτον οὕτως εὐεργέτην δέον ἐστὶν σε (after ἀπολαύειν)		×			(×)		(×)		Mj (Mb) (τοῦτον Pe Pg Mb).
	6	δέον			×			×		×		Mb
	6	om.			×					×		
	7	ἀπεκρίνατο	κἀκεῖνος ἀπεκρίνατο		×			×		×		Mb
	7	ὅτι... τινος	λέγων ὅτι ταχίας τινός		×		×			×		Mb
	7	ὠφελείας	om.									
	9–10	δέομαι πρός... εὔκαιρος	ἐπιδέομαι ὁ λόγος δηλοῖ ὅτι διδόασιν κατὰ τῶν ἀμείνων θράσος οἱ καιροί		(×) (×)					×		Mb Me Mj Ca (—διδόασι κ.τ. ἀμεινόνων τὰ φράσῃ οἱ κ. Pb)

107

TABLE I—Continued

No.	Chambry Title	Line	Reading	No.	G Reading	Pa	Pb	Pc	Pd	Pe	Pf	Pg	Ph	Other MSS Remarks
125	Ζεὺς καὶ Προμηθεὺς καὶ Ἀθηνᾶ καὶ Μῶμος			100		93	100	50	—	—	—	—	—	
		4	ἀρξάμενος		αὐξανόμενος	×	×							
		5	μή		ὅτι	×								
		6	τοῦ τύπτει		τοῦ τύπτειν		×	×						τὸ τύπτειν Pa
		9	τὸν οἶκον		τῷ οἴκῳ		×	×						Ma (ἐν τ. οἴκῳ)
		9	τροχοῖς		τροχοὺς	×	×	×						Ma
		10	πονηρός		πονηρῷ		×	×						Ma
		10	γείτων		γείτονι		×	×						Ma
163	Κολοιὸς καὶ ὄρνεα			101	inc. Ζεὺς	94	101	51	—	—	50	65	52	
		2	παραγενήσεται		παραγενήσονται		×⁴	×						Ma Me Mf Mj
		4	ἐνέστη		ἀνέστη		×	×				×		
		12	ἀποδώσωσιν		ἀποδώσουσιν									Ma
		12	ὅτι		οὕτως (before εὑρίσκονται)									
110	Ἑρμῆς καὶ γῆ			102	inc. Ζεὺς	95	102	52	—	—	51	66	—	
		5	προστετάχεναι		προστετάχθαι									Ma
		5	ὅσον		ὥστην									
		6	αὐτὸ		αὐτὴν	×	×	×			×	×		
		6	κλαίοντες		προσκλαίοντες									m

⁴ Pb has περιγενήσονται according to Sternbach.

											Ma Ml χύσιν Pa no. 96 τρυγίαν Pf Ph Mj m	
112	Ἑρμῆς καὶ τεχνῖται			103	*inc.* Ζεὺς	96 and 101	–	–	–	–	53	
		4–5	ὑπολειφθέντος χύσιν		ὑπολιπόντας θυίαν	×(101)	103	–	–	–	×	
		5										
		6	σκυτέας		σκυτεύς							
												Ma
122	Ζεὺς καὶ Ἀπόλλων			104		97	103	53	–	–	–	–
		4	τῷ		τὸ	×						
140	Ἵππος καὶ βοῦς καὶ κύων καὶ ἄνθρωπος			105	*inc.* Ζεὺς	–	104	–	–	–	–	67
		1	ποιήσας		ζῳογονήσας							
		1	αὐτὸν		*om.*							
		3	κατεσκεύαζε		κατεσκεύασεν							
		6	*om.*		δέξηται (after σκέπῃ)							
		7	οἰκείων		ἰδίων							
		10–11	ὑποδέξεσθαι		ὑποδέξασθαι							×
		14	*om.*		αὐτῷ after τινα							
		18	χρόνου		Χρεισμοῦ							××
		18	δὲ εἰς		δὲ καὶ εἰς							
		19	τοὺς		ἐπὶ							
		21	ἀνύοντας		διανύοντας							
			Τούτῳ...τις		οὗτος ὁ λόγος χρή-σετο ἄντις							οὗτος ὁ λόγος ἁρ-μόττει Pg

TABLE I—Continued

No.	Title	Chambry Line	Reading	G No.	G Reading	Pa	Pb	Pc	MSS of Class 1 Pd	Pe	Pf	Pg	Ph	Other MSS Remarks
126	Ζεὺς καὶ χελώνη			106	*inc.* Ζῶα	98	105	—	—	—	—	—	—	
		1	Ζεὺς ... ἑστία		Ζῶα πάντα ἰστία om.									
		2	ὑστερησάσης				✕							
		3	ἦλθε		ἦλθε									
		5–6	τὸν οἶκον ... περι-φέρειν		αὐτὸν οἶκον βαστά-ζουσαν φέρειν									Ca
		8	οἰκεῖν		οἴκωι							53	54	
120	Ζεὺς καὶ ἀλώπηξ			107		99	106	—	—	—	—	—	—	
		1	ἀγασάμενος		ἐργασάμενος									
		4	ἕξιν		ἕξιν		✕							
		4–5	γλισχρότητα ἐν φορείῳ		ἐμφορείῳ									
		5	παρὰ		περὶ									
		9	ἀποκατέστησεν		ἀπεκατέστησεν	✕								
		11	γοῦν		γὰρ									
121	Ζεὺς καὶ ἄνθρωποι			108		100	107	54	—	—	54	68	55	Me Mf
		2	ποιήσας ἴσον		ἴσον ποιήσας		✕	✕				✕	✕	m
		2	ἐνέχεεν ἑκάστῳ		ἑκάστῳ ἐνέχεεν	(✕)	✕	✕			(✕)	(✕)		(Mb Me Mf)
		3	πληροθέντας		πληροθέντος									
		7–8	Πρός ... εὔκαιρος		om.									
119	Ζεὺς καὶ αἰσχύνη			109		—	108	55	—	—	—	69	—	No. 101 in Pa = 96; see above
		1	διαθέσεις		διανοίας									
		2	ἐπέθηκε		ἐπέθηκεν		✕					✕		
		3	ἀμηχανῶν		μὴ σχῶν									μὴ ἔχων Pc
		8	πόρνους		μάχλους									

110

132	Ἥρως	2	ἀναλισκομένου τὴν οὐσίαν δια-φθείρων	110	ἐξαλισκομένου τὴν θυσίαν διαφθείρων τὴν οὐσίαν	102	109	56	–	–	–	71	57	ἐξαλισκομένου Pc (τ. θ. διατρίβων τ. οὐσίαν Pb) τὰς θυσίας διαφθείρων Ph
		4					(X)						X	
131	Ἡρακλῆς καὶ Πλοῦτος			111		103	110	57	–	–	–	70	56	Ma
		3	τελευταῖον		τελευταῖον	X								
		4	κύψας		κύψας		X	X				X		Ma Me Mf
		6	π. ἀσμένως		ἀσμένως προσαγορεύσας		X	X				X		
		7	ὑποβλέπεται		ἀποβλέπεται									ἀπεβλέπετο Pc
		9	τό		ὅπ.									
243	Μύρμηξ καὶ κάνθαρος			112	inc. Θέρους	104 and 235	111	–	–	–	–	72	–	
												143 v. 2		
		6	ὅτε		ὡς ὅτε	X X (X) 235	(X)							Cd
		6	τῆς		καὶ τῆς		(X)					X		Cd
		7	ἐκλυθείσης		κλυθθῆσης									Cd
		8	καὶ		ὅπ.	X 104	X							
		8	τροφῆς		τροφῶν									
		9	ἔφη		ὅπ.	X 104	X						X		
		10	ἐμέ		με									
133	Θύννος καὶ δελφίς			113	πρὸς αὐτὸν λιποψυχοῦντα	105	112	58	–	–	–	73	58	
		5	αὐτὸν λιποθυμοῦντα			X	(X)	X (X)						
		5–6					(X)					(X)	(X)	(m.)

111

TABLE I—Continued

No.	Chambry Title	Chambry Line	Chambry Reading	G No.	G Reading	MSS of Class I Pa	Pb	Pc	Pd	Pe	Pf	Pg	Ph	Other MSS Remarks
135	Ἰατρὸς καὶ νοσῶν	3	κλυστήρσιν	114	κλυστῆρι	106	113	59	—	—	57	74	59	
		4	τούτων		τοῦτον	×		×			×	×	×	Mb
		5	ἔδει		δεῖ		×	×					×	
		5	om.		ἐστιν (after ὠφελος)			×			×	×	×	Ma Mb Me Mj
		5	om.		αὐτῷ (after δὲ)									Me Mf Mj
138	Ἰξευτὴς καὶ ἀσπίς	3	συνάψας	115	ἀνάψας	107	114	60	—	—	58	75	60	
		7	δῆξιν		δὰξ		×	×						
		10	ἐπιβουλὰς ῥάπτοντες		βλάπτοντες									
151	Καρκῖνος καὶ ἀλώπηξ			116	om. ἀνέλαβεν	108	115	61	—	—	60	76	62	
		2	μόνος ἐνέμετο				×							
		3	συνέλαβεν											
147	Κάμηλος καὶ Ζεύς			117		109	116	62	—	14 (altera pars)	59	77	61	
		1	τοῖς		om.									m
		6	περισσοτέρων		περισσότερον	×	×	××		××	××	×	×	m

154	Κάστωρ		118		110	117	—	—	—	61	78	63	
		1		ἐστὶ ζῷον								
		1		λίμνῃ								Me Mj
		1		νεμόμενον	(×)	(×)				×		×	(γενόμενον Pb γιγνόμενον Pa Pf)
		3		διώκει	×	×						
		6		διαφυλάξαι	×	×						
		10		τῇ σωτηρίᾳ								Cb Ch
155	Κηπουρὸς <ἀρ-δεύων λάχανα>		119		111	118	63	—	—	—	—	—
		4		Κἀκεῖνος ἔφη								
		4		ἐστί, after μήτηρ		×						
156	Κηπουρὸς καὶ κύων		120	om. ἐστὶν after μητρυιᾷ	112	119	64	—	—	62	79	64	Pf 42 according to Chambry, but that is probably a misprint; cf. Chambry, no. 106 (= Pf 42)
		2		ἐκεῖ	×							
		2		Ὁ δὲ κύων = Chambry								
		3		ὑπ' ἀπ'	×		××					
		7		εἰς πρὸς								
157	Κιθαρῳδός		121		113	120	—	—	—	63	—	65
		2		ἐνόμισεν αὐτὸν	ὥστε αὐτὸν	×	(×)						(ὥστε αὐτὸν νομί-σαι Pb)
		3		σφόδρα εἶναι	εἶναι σφόδρα		×						Mb

TABLE I—Continued

No.	Chambry Title	Line	Reading	G No.	G Reading	Pa	Pb	Pc	Pd	Pe	Pf	Pg	Ph	Other MSS Remarks
159	Κλέπται καὶ ἀλεκτρυών			122		114	121	65	–	–	64	80	66	
		1	ἄλλο		om.									
		5	ἐγείροντα		ἐγείραντα									
		6	μᾶλλον		μάλιστα	×		×						Mb
		7	ἡμᾶς...κλέπτειν		ἐξετέρῳ ἀγῆμας οὐκεᾶς ἡμᾶς κλέπτειν									
162	Κολοιὸς καὶ κόρακες			123		115	122	66	–	–	65	81	67	
		1	τῷ		πόσῳ									
		2	τοὺς ὁμοφύλους		τὰς ὁμοφύλους		×					×		Ma Cd
		5	ἀπελαθείς		ἀπελαθεῖς	×	×	×			×	×	×	Ma
		11	ξένοι		ξένους									m Cd
166	Κόραξ καὶ ἀλώπηξ			124		116	123	67	–	–	–	82	–	
		2	καὶ		om.	×	×	×				×		Ma
		2	κρέατος		κρέως	×		×				×		
		4	καὶ		om.			×				×		
		5	ἐγένετο		γένοιτο		×					(×)		(Ma)
		6–7	ἀποβαλών		βαλών		(×)					×		Ma
		9	οὐδὲν ἂν ἐδέησας		οὐδὲν ἐδέησεν									Ma
		9	βασιλεῦσαι		βασιλεύειν									Ma
171	Κορώνη καὶ κόραξ			125		117	124	–	–	–	–	–	–	

114

161	Κολοιὸς καὶ ἀλώπηξ			126		118	125	–	–	–	66	83	68	
		2	σῦκα									(×)		(συκαῖ Pg)
		7	[Πρὸς ἄνδρα φιλό-νεικον]		συκαῖ Πρὸς ἄνδρα ψευδο-λόγον ὁ λόγος εὔκαιρος									
172	Κορώνη καὶ κύων			127		119	126	68	–	–	69	–	–	Mj
		1	Ἀθηνᾶ θύουσα τοὺς ἐχθροὺς		ἑστιῶσα τοὺς πολλοὺς	×	×	××			××			Mb Mj
		7												
168	Κόραξ καὶ ὄφις			128		120	127	69	–	–	–	84	–	Mh Cd
		4	εὕρηκα ἄνδρα		εὑρὼν ἀνδρὸς									
		6												
164	Κολοιὸς καὶ περιστεραί			129		121	128	×	–	–	–	–	69	
		3	μὲν αὐτοῦ... αὐτὸν ἐπιθυμήσας τῷ		ὅτι αὐτὸν ἐπιθυμῆσαι ζητῶν τὸ	×								
		5–6				××								
		9												
		12												
160	Κοιλία καὶ πόδες			130		122	129	–	–	–	68	–	–	ἐπιτυχεῖν ζ. Pb
		4	ὑμῖν παράσχωμαι		ὅτι προσλάβωμαι	(×)	(×)	(×)						
		4												
165	Κολοιὸς φυγάς			131		123	130	–	–	–	67	–	70	L and m
		2	κάλῳ ἔδωκεν παρὰ ἀνθρώπων περιπεσόντες		ὅτι. δέδωκεν περὶ ἀνθρώπους περὶ τυχόντες	×	×	–			××		×	Mj
		2												
		7												
		12												

Table I—Continued

No.	Chambry Title	Line	Reading	G No.	G Reading	Pa	Pb	Pc	Pd	Pe	Pf	Pg	Ph	Other MSS Remarks
188	Κύων <λέοντα διώκων> καὶ ἀλώπηξ			132		125	131	71	—	—	70	86	—	
		2	ὁ λέων		ἐκεῖνος		×	×			×	×		Mb Me Mf Mj
		2	τούπίσω		τὰ ὀπίσω							×		Mb Me Mf Mj
186	Κύων κρέας φέρουσα			133		126	132	72	—	—	—	—	—	
		3	ἀφεῖσα		ἀφήσασα									Ma
		4	ὡς		εἰς		×							Ma
		4	αὐτῇ		αὐτήν									Ma
		5	ἐφικομένη		ἐφικομένην			×						
		5	οὐδὲ		μηδὲν			×						
185	Κύων <κοιμώμενος> καὶ λύκος			134		127	133	73	—	—	71	87	—	
		1	πρὸ		πρὸς		×	×						
		1	om.		τοῦτον (after δὲ)	(×)	×	×			×			αὐτὸν Pc
		5	ἀφῇς με		ἀφῇ αὐτὸν						×			Mj
		6	καταβουθήσῃ με		καταβουθήσεται		×	×			(×)	×		Cf. Pa
		6	πεισθεὶς τότε		πεισθεὶς αὐτῷ τότε									Mb Mj
		8	ἐκάλει		κατεκάλει									
177	Κύνες λιμώττουσαι			135		128	134	74	—	—	72	—	—	Mb Cd
		3	ἀλλήλαις		ἀλλήλους	×		×			×			Mb Me Mf Cd
		5	πρὶν		om.									
183	Κύων καὶ λαγωός			136		129	135	—	—	—	—	88	—	
		3	με		μή	×								Cd

116

190	Κώνωψ καὶ ταῦρος			137		130	136	75	–	–	–	–
192	Λαγωοὶ καὶ βάτραχοι			138		133	137	76	–	–	91	–
		1	τῆς		om.	X	X	X	–	–		Ma Ca
		4	αὑτοὺς βαθέα		ἑαυτοὺς βαθέα		X	X	–	–	X	εὕρεται Ma
		6	αὑτοὺς		τοὺς ἑτέρους							
		7	εὕρηνται		εὕρηται							
194	Λάρος καὶ ἰκτῖνος			139		134	–	–	74	–	–	–
		1	αὐτῷ		αὐτοῦ				X			
199	Λέων ⟨ἐρασθεὶς⟩ καὶ γεωργός			140		135	138	77	–	–	92	Ma
		3	ἀρνήσασθαι		ἀρνεῖσθαι	X	X	X	–		X X	
		3	τι		om.							
		13–14	καθεστήκεσαν		καθεστήκασιν							
202	Λέων καὶ βάτραχος			141		136	139	78	75	–	93	αὐτῷ Pa
		3	om.		αὐτοῦ (before μικρόν)	X		X X				Me Mf
		3	αὐτὸν		om.				X		X	
		7	εὔκαιρος		om.							
197	Λέων ⟨γηράσας⟩ καὶ ἀλώπηξ			142		137	140	–	–	–	–	Ma κατακλεισθείς, all other MSS Cf. Pb
		3	τι		τὸ κατακλιθῇς							
		3	κατακλιθεὶς (Schneider)									Ma Ca
		4	προσεποιεῖτο νοσεῖν		προσεποίητο νοσοῦντα							
		11	ἐξιόντος		ἐξιόντων							

TABLE I—Continued

No.	Chambry Title	Line	Reading	G No.	G Reading	Pa	Pb	Pc	Pd	Pe	Pf	Pg	Ph	Other MSS Remarks
212	Λέων καὶ ταῦρος			143		138	141	79	—	—	—	94	—	
		4	αὐτὸν		om.									Ma
		7	αὐτὸν...δι ἦν		διακ̀			×						
		8	οὐδὲν		οὐδὲ ἐν		×							
		8	ἀλόγος		ἀλόγος		×							
		9	οὐχὶ		οὐχ									
198	Λέων <ἐγκλεισθείς> καὶ γεωργός			144		139	142	80	—	—	76	—	—	
		2	αὐλείαν		αὐλίαν	×								
		2	ὃς		ὡς	×								
		7	ἐβούλου		ἐβούλειου	×								Ca
203	Λέων καὶ δελφίς			145		140	143	—	—	—	77	—	72	
		1	ἐπὶ		ἐν	×	×				×		×	m
		2	[ὡς]		om.	×					×		×	m
		4	θαλαττίων		θαλασσίων		×							m
		5–6	ἐπὶ πολὺν		μετ' οὐ πολὺν						×			οὐ μετὰ π. Pf Ph
		6	ἐπεκαλεῖτο		ἐπεκάλει καὶ (before ἠτιᾶτο)	×								m
		8	om.		om.	×	×				×		×	
		9	ὁ λέων		om.	×								
		9	'Ο δὲ...εἶπεν		om.	×								m
		11	γῆς		= Chambry									
		11	ἐπιβαίνειν (Chambry)											m
		12	Οὗτος		'Ατὰρ οὖν		×							

118

214	Λέων <μῦν φοβηθεὶς> καὶ ἀλώπηξ			146		141	144	—	—	33	—	—	95	—
		2	πανταχόθεν		παντοχοῦ	X	X			X			X	Ma Ca
		2	περιελίττετο		περιελίττετο									
		3	ὠνείδιζεν		ἐμειδίασεν									
		4	ηὐλαβήθη		ἐφοβήθει	(X)	(X)			(X)			(X)	δ. δεῖν Pa
		5	ἐφοβήθην		ἔλαβήθη									
		7	διδάσκει		διδάσκει δεῖ									
201	Λέων καὶ ἄρκτος			147		142	145	—	—	—	—	—	96	—
		1	νεβρὸν εὑρόντες		νεβρὸν σύροντες	X					79				(τῶν δ. νεύρων μέ-
		4–5	τὸν δὲ ... κείμενον		τὸ δὲ νεῦρον μέσον κείμενον	(X)	X				v. 2				σων κειμένων Pa)
		9	ἀποφερομένους		ἐπιφερομένους									
205	Λέων καὶ λαγωός			148		143	146	81	34	—	78	—	97	—
		7	ἔγωγε		ἔγωγε	X	X	X X	X		X			
		7	ὅτι		ὅτι									
		7	ἀφείς		παραφείς									
210	Λέων καὶ ὄνος καὶ ἀλώπηξ			149		144	147	82	—	—	80	—	98	—
		1	κοινωνίαν		κοινωνίας	X X X	X X	X X			X		X X X	Ma Mb
		2	σπεισάμενοι		στειλάμενοι									Ma Mb Me
		4	ἐξ ἴσου		ὅτι.									Ma Mb
		9	τίς		καὶ τίς									Ma Mb
		10	Ἡ ... συμφορά		αἱ ... συμφοραί									Mb
207	Λέων καὶ μῦς <ἀντ-ευεργέτης>			150		145	148	83	—	—	—	—	—	Ca
		9	κατεγέλασας		κατεγέλας	(X)		X						
		10	ἐστί		ἔστιν τις									Mb Ca
		12	οἱ		καὶ οἱ									

TABLE I—Continued

No.	Chambry Title	Line	Reading	G No.	G Reading	Pa	Pb	Pc	Pd	Pe	Pf	Pg	Ph	Other MSS Remarks
209	Λέων καὶ ὄνος ⟨ὁμοῦ θηρεύοντες⟩			151		146	149	84	—	—	81	—	73	
		2	θήραν		θήρας	×		×						
		6	συλλαβόντος		συλλαμβάνοντος	×		×					×	
		7	ἐξεδίωξεν		ἐξεδίωκεν									
		8	σε after ᾔδειν		ὅτι.									
215	Λῃστὴς καὶ συκάμινος			152		147	150	—	—	—	—	99	—	
		2	ἡμαγμένον		ἐπημαγμένον									
		5	ὡς		ἕως							×		
		6	ἀπὸ		ἐπὶ									
		9	ἀπεργάσω		ἀπειργάσατο									
218	Λύκοι καὶ πρόβατα			153		148	151	—	35	—	—	—	—	
226	Λύκος καὶ ἵππος			154		149	—	—	—	—	82	—	74	
		1	κριθὰς εὗρε		= Chambry	×								εὗρε κριθάς Pf Ph Me Mj
		5	αὐτοῦ		αὐτὸν									

222	Λύκος καὶ ἀρήν			155		150	152	–	–	–	–	–	Ma
		2	μετά (= Ma)		ἀπό	×							
		8	μηδὲ τότε γεγενῆσ-		μηδὲ τῇ γαίαν γε-								
			θαι		γενέσθαι								
		9	πρὸς αὐτόν		om.		×						
		10	οὐχ <ἧττον>		οὐ κατέδομαι								
			κατέδομαι										
		11	ἤ		om.								
		11	om.		τοὺς πάντας (be-								
					fore ἀδικεῖν)								
225	Λύκος καὶ ἐρωδιός			156		151	153	85	–	–	–	–	Mb Ca
		3	ἐκβαλεῖν (Pa)		ἐξελεῖν		××	×					Ca
		4	τήν		τόν								
		4–5	ὡμολογημένον		ὡμολογημένον	(×)							
221	Λύκος καὶ αἴξ			157		152	154	86	–	83	–	–	Ma Mb
		3	αὐτῇ		αὐτήν	×	××			×			m Ca
		4	ἐστι		om.	×		××		(×)			(ἀπεκρίθη Pf)
		5	ἀπεκρίνατο		= Chambry	×		×		×			
		8	ἀνόητοι		ἀνόητοι								
224	Λύκος καὶ γραῦς			158		153	155	87	–	–	–	–	Mb 112
		5	ἐγίγνετο		ἐγένετο		×	×					
		9	οὐκ...ἀκόλουθα		ἀκόλουθα τὰ ἔργα								
					οὐκ ἔχουσιν								
231	Λύκος <κεκορεσ-			159		154	156	88	–	–	–	–	Mb 113
	μένος> καὶ πρό-	4	εἴπῃ		om.	×							
	βατον	4	αὐτό. <Τὸ> δὲ		αὐτὸς δὲ		×						
		5	ἀρξάμενον		ἀρξάμενος								
		7	ἀπόλουσθε		ἀπολλύσθαι		×						
		10	ἀλήθεια		ἡ ἀλήθεια		×						

TABLE I—Continued

No.	Chambry Title	Chambry Line	Chambry Reading	G No.	G Reading	MSS of Class I Pa	Pb	Pc	Pd	Pe	Pf	Pg	Ph	Other MSS Remarks
232	Λύκος ⟨τετρωμένος⟩ καὶ πρόβατον			160		156	157	89	—	—	85	—	—	
		1–2	ἐβέβλητο...καὶ δή		ἐβούλετο τροφὴν ἑαυτῷ περιποιεῖσθαι· καὶ δὴ									
		4	Ἐὰν γάρ...εὔρησω		om.			×			×			Me Mf
		5	Τὸ δὲ ὑποτυχὸν		ὁ δὲ ὑποτυχὼν						×			m
		7	ὁ λόγος εὔκαιρος		om.									
234	Μάντις			161		158	—	90	—	—	86	100	—	
		3	εἰσί		εἶσαν	(×)		(×)			(×)			(ἦσαν Pa Pc Pf)
		5	ᾔει		ἔτι	×								
		8	προεμαντεύον		προεμαντεύσας									
		9	Τούτῳ		Οὕτω									
		10	τοὺς...διοικοῦντας		οἱ τῶν βίον φαῦλος διοικοῦντων									
295	Παῖς καὶ κόραξ		inc. Μαντευομένης τινός	162	inc. Μαντευομένη τινι	159	—	—	—	—	—	—	—	Not found elsewhere
		1	om.		ἔτι before νηπίον καὶ τὴν ἐπιτήδειον τροφήν									
		6	καὶ τὰς...τροφάς		πῶμα									
		7	πῶμα		βρέγματος									
		9	βρέγματος		Ὁ λόγος δηλοῖ ὅτι τὸ πετρωμένον ἀπαρευχείρητόν ἐστιν									
			om.											

122

235	Μέλισσαι καὶ Ζεύς			163	παράσχῃ τινα ἀποβάλλειν	160	161	91	–	–	–	101	–	Ma 110
		3	παράσχηται τινα (Ma) ἀποβαλεῖν			×	××	××				×		
		6												
		6												
237	Μηραγύρται			164		161	162	–	–	–	87	102	–	m
		2	αὐτοῦ		αὐτοῦ τοῦ ὄνου	×	×				×	×		Ma
		6	οτι.		ἂν (before εἴ[η])									
		7	ποτε (Pa)		ἀλλ'									
		8	καίπερ		καὶ περὶ									
		9	οὐκ ἀπαλλάττονται		οὐ καταλλαγέντες									
239	Μύες καὶ γαλαῖ			165		162	163	–	–	–	–	103	–	Ma Ca
		5	φανῆναι		εἶναι	×	×					×		
		7–8	ἐπί... καταφεύγοντες		= Chambry									
242	Μύρμηξ			166		163	164	92	–	–	–	104	–	
		2	τοῖς ἰδίοις		οὐ μόνον τοῖς ἰδίοις	××		××						
		2	οὐκ		οτι.									
		8	πυροὺς		πόρους τε									
240	Μυῖα			167		164	–	93	–	–	–	–	–	
247	Ναυαγὸς καὶ θάλασσα			168		165	166	94	–	–	–	–	–	
		1	εἰς τὸν		εἴς τινα		×	×						Ma Mb
		1–2	ἐκοιμᾶτο...κόπον		διὰ τὸν κόπον ἐκοιμᾶτο		×	×						Ma Mb
		8	με (after αἰφνίδιον)		μου		×	×						Ma Mb
		8	ἐπέρχονται		ἐμπίπτοντες									

TABLE I—Continued

Chambry			G		MSS of Class I								Other MSS Remarks
No.	Title	Line	Reading	No.	Reading	Pa	Pb	Pc	Pd	Pe	Pf	Pg	Ph	
249	Νέος ἄσωτος καὶ χελιδών			166		—	—	95	—	—	—	106	—	
		2	ἐλθοῦσαν		ὀρθεῖσαν	×		×				×		Ma Mb
		5	καί...γενομένου		ὅτι.	(×)		(×)				(×)		(Mb)
		6	ἐρριγωμένῃ		ἐρριγωμένῃ πᾶν τὸ περὶ καιρὸν									(Ma Mb Ca)
		8	πάντα...ἐπι- φαλὴ		δρώμενον ἐπι- φαλὲς									
		9	τυγχάνουσιν		τυγχάνει									Ca
250	Νοσῶν καὶ ἰατρός			167			—	—	—	—	89	107	—	
		3–4	Ἀγαθόν...ἔφη		ὅτι.			×			×	×		Mj
		5	ἔφη, ἀγαθόν		ἀγαθὸν ἔφασκεν εἶναι						×			Ma Mb
		7	τοῦτο		τοῦτο εἶναι									
251	Νυκτερὶς καὶ βάτος καὶ αἴθυια			168		—	167	96	—	—	90	—	—	
		1	ἀλλήλας		ἀλλήλους	×	×	×			×			m
		2	σπεισάμενοι		στειλάμεναι			×			×			Mb Me Mf
		2–3	νυκτερὶς ἀργύριον		νυκτερὶς ἀργύριον	×		×			×			
		6	νηός		ἀργυρίου νεώς	×								
		6–7	πάντα...διεσώθη- σαν		ὅτι.	×		×			(×)			
		7	καί		ὅτι.		ἐπί	×			ἐκ			
		8	κατὰ (Schneider)		ἀπό		(×)	(×)						
		8	οἰομένη...εὑρήσειν		οἰομένη ὅτι εὑρή- σειν									(ποτε εὑρήσειν Pb ὅτι εὑρήσει Pc)

124

252	Νυκτερὶς καὶ γαλαῖ	3–4 5 6	πάντας...πτηνοῖς πεσοῦσα πάλιν ὅπως μὴ θύσῃ (Pa)	172	πᾶσι...πτηνοῖς πάλιν π. ὅπως μεθῇει	169	–	–	97	–	91	108	–	m Ca Ma Mj Ca ὅτ. μὴ θουνῄσεται Pg Mb Ca
		7	διεχθραίνειν		διεχθρεύειν				×		×	(×)		
									ὁ. μεθῇ		ὁ. ἑάσῃ			
2	Ἀγαλματοπώλης			173	inc. Ξυλινόν τις Another version of no. 99.	170	99 (aliter)		98		93	61 (aliter)	–	(aliter : inc. Ἑρμῆν)
		1–2	καὶ εἰς ἀγορὰν		τοῦτον ott.	(×) ἐν πόλει					×			
		2	μηδενὸς...προσιόντος ὄντα		ott.				×					
		6 7 10	ἀπεκρίνατο δέομαι εὔκαιρος		ott. κἀκεῖνος ἔφη ἐπιδέομαι ott.		×		×		×	×		m Ca
254	Ξυλευόμενος καὶ Ἑρμῆς			174		171	168	–	99	–	92	109	–	
		3	ὁ		ott.				×			×		Ma
		5–6 9 20 23	Τοῦ...εἶναι ἀνεκόμισε ἀποκατέστησεν Ὁ λόγος δηλοῖ ὅτι		ott. ἐκόμισε ἀπεκατέστησεν Οὕτω πολλοὶ τῶν ἀνθρώπων		×		××		××	×		m Ca

TABLE I—Continued

No.	Chambry Title	Chambry Line	Chambry Reading	G No.	G Reading	Pa	Pb	Pc	Pd	Pe	Pf	Pg	Ph	Other MSS Remarks
262	Ὁδοιπόρος καὶ Τύχη			175		172	169	100	—	—	—	110	—	
		3	οὔπω		οὐδέπω							×		Mb
258	Ὁδοιπόροι			176		173	170	101	—	—	94	111	75	
		4–5	ὡς ... δένδρον		ὡς ἀνωφελές τι τοῦτο καὶ ἄκαρπον ἄνους ἐστὶν τὸ δένδρον									See Chambry's apparatus
		6	ἔτι											Ma
82 v. 2	Ὁδοιπόρος καὶ ὄφις			177 v. 2	G and Pb are unique in having two different versions of this fable; see above, no. 62	174 v. 2	171 v. 2	102 v. 2	—	(30 v. 1)	—	112 v. 2	—	Ma 122 Ca 130
		1	ὥρᾳ		om.		×	×				×		Ma Ca
		5	καὶ ... ἔδακε		δὰξ εἰς τὴν ἑαυτοῦ γαστέραν ἀνήνεγκεν	××	×	(×)				(×)		Variants complex; see Chambry
		5	ὅς		ὡς									Ca
		9	τῷ		τὸ									Ma
		10	μή		om.									

126

				178	175	172	103		95			
259	Ὁδοιπόροι καὶ φρύγανα							—		—		
		2	ἐνθένδε			ἔνθεν δὲ						
		2	πόρρωθεν			ἀπὸ πόρρωθεν						Ma
		4	ἀνέμου			ἀνέμου						
		5	ἀπεκαραδόκουν			ἐπεκαραδόκουν	×					
		6	ὑπολαμβάνοντες			ὅτι.	×					
		7	Ἐγγὺς...ἰδόντες			ἐξενεχθέντων δὲ	(×)					Ma
						αὐτῶν καὶ ἰδόντες						
		8	ὅν			ἦν						
261	Ὁδοιπόρος καὶ Ἑρμῆς			179	176	173	104	—	96	113	—	
		1	ἐάν		×	×	×					
94 v. 2	Δέλφαξ καὶ ἀλώπηξ			180	177	174	—	—	97	—	—	
						inc. Ὄνῳ						
		4	αὐτὸς μόνος			μόνος αὐτὸς	×		×			m Ca
		5	Ὁ δὲ			ὅτι.	(×)		×			Me Mf
		8	ἐμοὶ			ἐμὲ	×					Mb
		9	θῦσαί με θέλει			με θύσει						Mb etc.
		12	ἑαυτούς			ὅτι.						Mb Ca
274	Ὄνος καὶ κηπουρός			181	178	175	—	37	98	114	—	
		2	τοῦ κηπουροῦ		×							
		7	ἰδών			τῷ κηπορῷ						
		8	ὑπό			εἰδώς	(×)	(×)	(×)			(Me Mf)
		11	ἀξιωθήσομαι			παρὰ						
						τεύξωμαι						

TABLE I—Continued

| | Chambry | | | G | | MSS of Class I | | | | | | | | Other MSS |
No.	Title	Line	Reading	No.	Reading	Pa	Pb	Pc	Pd	Pe	Pf	Pg	Ph	Remarks
266	Ὄνος ἅλας βαστάζων			182		179	176	—	—	—	—	115	—	
		1	ἔχων		γέμων							×		Ma
		2	Ὀλισθήσας		ὀλισθῶν		×							Ma
		2	ἅλατος		ἁλός							×		Mb
		3	τούτῳ		τοῦτο							×		
		6	τὸν σπόγγον									(×)		(τὸν σπόγγον Pg)
		7	δυνάμενον		δυνάμενος	×								Ma
		7	ἐξαναστῆναι		ἐξανίστασθαι	×	×					×		Ma Mb
		9	διά		om.									
142 v. 6	Ὄνος καὶ ἡμίονος			183		180	177	—	—	—	—	—	—	
		3	ἐγένοντο (Ca)		ἐγένετο	×	×							
		3	κατά τι ὄρος		κατάφορος	×	×							Mb
		3	ὑποφέρειν μ. δ.		μὴ δυνάμενος ὑποφέρειν		×							Mb Ca
		5	δυνήσηται		δύνηται	×								
		11	τῷ ὄνῳ		om.		×							
		15	ἀπολλῦσιν		ἀπολλύουσιν									Ca
267	Ὄνος βαστάζων ἄγαλμα			184		181	178	—	—	—	—	116	—	
		2	om.		καί (after συναντώντων)	×								
		4	προϊέναι		προσιέναι	×								

128

265	"Ονος <ἄγριος καὶ ὄνος ἥμερος>			185	182	179	–	–	–	–	99	117	–	
279	"Ονος καὶ τέττιγες	4	ὀπίσω (Pa)			ὄπισθεν		X^5	–	–	–	×	×	–	m
		1	ἤσθη...εὐφωνία	186	183	180 v.2	ἴσθη ἐπὶ τῇ εὐφωνίᾳ τῇ τροφῇ τῆς δρόσου				100	–		
		4	δρόσον											
263	"Ονοι πρὸς τὸν Δία			187	184	181			38	–	–	–	–	
		1	τῷ				τὸ		××					
		7	νῦν				τοῦ νῦν							L, and m except Mb
278	"Ονος καὶ ὀνηλάτης			188	185	182	om. εἰς		–	–	–	–	–	
		2	ἀτραπὸν											
		2	διά			××			–	–	–	–	–	
282 v.1	"Ονος <χωλαίνων προσποιούμενος> καὶ λύκος			189	186	183	See no. 233 below		–	–	–	–	–	Ca Ca Mb
		9	ὡς		×		ὡς							
		11	ἰατρικῆς				ἰατρικὴν					×		
		11	ἐπελαβόμην				ἐπεβαλόμην								
268	"Ονος <ἐνδυσάμενος λεοντῆν> καὶ ἀλώπηξ			190	187	184			–	–	–	–	–	
		3	γὰρ				om.							Ma
		4	τὸν ὄνον		×	××	αὐτὸν							Ma
		6	τύφους				τυφλοῖς							Ma
		7	τινες				om.							Ma

[5] Pb has ὄπιθεν according to Sternbach.

TABLE I—*Continued*

No.	Chambry Title	Line	Reading	No.	G Reading	Pa	Pb	Pc	Pd	Pe	Pf	Pg	Ph	Other MSS Remarks
272	Ὄνος καὶ βάτραχοι			191		189	185	—	—	—	—	119	—	
275	Ὄνος καὶ κόραξ καὶ λύκος			192		190	186	—	—	—	102	—	—	
		5	ἑαυτὸν		αὐτὸν	×	×				×			Mb
		5	αὑτὸ		αὐτῷ	×								
		8–9	[καὶ-προσώπων]		ὅτι.							×		
271	Ὄνος καὶ ἀλώπηξ καὶ λέων			193	αὐτοῖς περιτυχόντος	191	187	105	—	—	103	120	—	m Ca
		2	π. αὐτοῖς		πρώτην		×	×				×		
		8	πρῶτον		ἀναπόλλυνται									Mb Ca ἐναπόλύντες Pf
		11	συναπολλύντες											
287	Ὄρνις καὶ χελιδών			194	καὶ ταῦτα ἐκθερμάνασα ὅτι.	194	188	—	—	—	106	121	—	Ma Mb Ca (Ma) etc.
		1	ταῦτα				××				××	××		
		1	ἐθέρμανε											
		2	καί...θερμάναι											
284	Ὀρνιθοθήρας καὶ κορύδαλος			195		195	189	107	—	—	104	—	—	
		1	ἵστη		ἵστα	×	××	×			×			Me Mb
		2	ἤρετο		ἠρώτα		(×)							Mb
		6	ἔφη		ὁ κορύδαλος ἔφη		××							m
		6	Ὦ οὗτος		ἔφη									Mb
		6	οὐ		ὅτι.									(χαλεπὰ ποιῶσι Pb)
		8	οἶκοι		καὶ οἶκοι		(×)	××			×			
		9	χαλεποὶ ὦσιν		χαλεπὰ ποιοῦσιν									

130

285	Ὀρνιθοθήρας καὶ πελαργός			196		196	190	106	—	—	—
		2	ἀπεκαραδόκει		ἐθεώρει		×				Mb Ca
		2	ταῖς		τοῖς		(×)				Mb Ca
		3	ἐπικαθισαντος		καθήσαντος		××				(καθίσαντος Pb)
		5	αὐτὸς		ὅτι.		××				Mb Ca
		7	κατεσθίει		ἀναιρεῖ		(×)				Mb Ca
		7	ἀπεκρίνατο		ἔφη		××				Mb Ca
		8	μὴ φαῦλος σὺ εἰ		σὺ φαῦλος ὑπῆρχες						
		8–9	δι' αὐτὸ…κολά- σεως		διὰ τοῦτο κολάσεως ἄξιος						
149	Κάμηλος τὸ πρῶ- τον ὀφθεῖσα			197	inc. Ὅτε	197		—	—	107	—
		1	πρῶτον		πρῶτος		××				Ca L m
		5	τοῦτο		τοσοῦτο		××				(L)
		5	χαλινῶν		χαλινοὺς		(×)				
		6	αὐτὴν		ὅτι.		(×)				
		6	ἔδωκαν		δεδώκασιν (after		××				
		8	ὅτι.		μεγάλος καταπραΰνει)						
291	Ὄφις καὶ καρκίνος			198		198	192	—	—	108	122
		2	ἁπλῶς		ἁπλόσας		××				Mf
		2	καὶ		ὅτι.						(Mb)
		2	ὁ δὲ		ὁ δὲ ὄφις		××				Mb
		4	τὰ πρὸς αὐτὸν		κατ' αὐτὸν		××			×	(×)
		5	Διόπερ		διόπερ ὁ καρκίνος		εἶδεν				
		7	ἀνεῖλε καὶ		ὅτι.		××				
		7	ἰδὼν		ἴδεν		××				
		8	εἶπεν		καὶ ἔφη		××				
		8	ἔχρῆν		χρὴ						
		9	ὅτε δέ σου		ἀλλ' ὅτε σου						
		9	<ἂν> ἀνήρησο		ἐπήκουες						

TABLE I—Continued

No.	Chambry Title	Line	G No.	G Reading	Reading	Pa	Pb	Pc	Pd	Pe	Pf	Pg	Ph	Other MSS Remarks
290	Ὄφις καὶ γαλῆ καὶ μύες		199			199	193	—	—	—	109	—	—	
		2		καταναλισκόμενοι αὐτοὺς...ἰδόντες	καταναλίσκοντο	(X)	(X)							
		3		τότε	om.	X	X							
		4		τῶν (before δημαγωγῶν)	om.		X							Mb
		6			om.		X							
		7		παρεισβάλλοντες	παρακυλλοῦντες ἑαυτοῖς	(X)	(X)							(Mb)
		7		αὐτοί			X							(Mb)
292	Ὄφις πατούμενος καὶ Ζεύς		200			—	194	—	—	—	—	123	—	
		3		σε	om.		X							Mb 170
		5		ἐπιβαίνουσιν ἀνθιστάμενοι	ἀμυνόμενοι							(X)		ἐπιβαίνοντες Pb
294	Παῖς καὶ σκορπίος		201			200	195	108	—	—	—	124	—	
		1		τοῦ	om.		X							
		2		οἰηθείς	νομίσας	X	X							Ma Ca
		3			αὐτοῦ (before τὴν χεῖρα)		X								
		3		αὐτόν	αὐτοῦ	X	X					X		
		3		ὅς	ὡς		X							Ca
		4		ἐπάρας εἶπεν	ἔπληξεν, εἶπεν		(X)							
		5		ἃς συνείληφας ἀκρίδας ἀπολέσῃς	ἃς κατέχω τὰς ἀφᾶς ἀκρίδας ἀποβάλλεις									
		6		om.	ἡμᾶς (after λόγος)		X	(X)				(X)		(Ca) ἡμᾶς after δίδασκει Pc Pg Ca
		7		τοῖς	om.		X					X		Ca

132

21	Ἀλεκτρυόνες καὶ πέρδιξ			202 (=23)	inc. Πέρδιξ πιτρασκομένη, τοῦτον, etc. This is a repetition of no. 23 above, though mutilated at the beginning	26	23	–	–	–	6	–	6
297	Παῖς κλέπτης καὶ μήτηρ			203									
		1	ὑφελόμενος αὐτῷ		ἀφελόμενος αὐτὸν								
		2	ἐπιπληξάσης		ἐκπληξάσης	201	196 v. 2	–	–	–	111	125	–
		3	μᾶλλον		καὶ		X				X	X	Mb
		4–5	Ἔτι δὲ... ἐκείνη		ἔτι μᾶλλον ἐκείνη ἀπεδέξατο		(X)						Mb
		5	om.		δὲ (after προϊών)		X X						
		5–6	ὡς νεανίας ἐγένετο		ὁ νεανίας		X X				X	X	Mb Me Mf
		7	περιαγκωνισθεὶς		περὶ ἀγκωνισθεὶς		X						
		8–13	καὶ στερνοκοπουμένης... εἶπεν		τῆς δὲ μητρὸς καὶ στερνοποιουμένης, ὁ νεανίας εἶπεν, θέλω τι εἰπεῖν τῇ μητρί μου εἰς τὸ οὖς. ἡ δὲ ἐλθοῦσα πρὸς αὐτὸν ταχέως ἐκεῖνος ἐπελάβετο τοῦ ὠτὸς αὐτῆς καὶ αὐτὸν ἐξέκοψεν. τῆς δὲ κατηγορούσης αὐτὸν ὡς δυσσεβεῖ ἐκεῖνος ἔφη		(X)				X	X	Mb Me Mf
		14	ἐπέπληξάς μοι		ἐπέπληξάς με		X X X						
		15	ὡς		om.								
		16	κολαζόμενον		κωλυόμενον								

TABLE I—Continued

No.	Chambry Title	Chambry Line	Chambry Reading	G No.	G Reading	Pa	Pb	Pc	MSS of Class I Pd	Pe	Pf	Pg	Ph	Other MSS Remarks
302	Περιστερὰ διψῶσα			204		202	197	–	–	–	112	126	–	
		3	ἑαυτήν		αὐτῇ		(X)							
		3	om.		ἐμπεσεῖν καί (after πίνακι)		(X)							
		4	δέ		om.		X							
		4	περιβρανθέντων		περὶ θλασθέντων		(X)							
		5	ἐπὶ τ. γῆς καταπ.		ὥστε ὑπὸ τὴν γῆν καταπεσοῦσαν									
		7	ἐπιθυμίας		ῥαθυμίας		X							
		8	ἀπροσκέπτως		ἀπεριοκέπτους		X							(Mb Ca)
		8–9	λανθάνουσιν ... ἐσιέντες		σαυτοῖς εἰς ὄλεθρον βάλλουσιν		(X)							
303	Περιστερὰ καὶ κορώνη			205		203	198	109	–	60	113	127	–	
		1	περιστεροτροφείῳ		περιστερεῶν		(X)	(X)				(X)		Mb Ca
		1	ἐπί		ἐν							X		
		2–3	κορώνη ... λόγων		om.									
		3	τούτῳ		τούτοις							X		Mb
		4	σχῆς		ποιεῖς		ποιῆς							
		5	δουλείας		λύπης		λύπας X							
		7	om.		πολλὰ (at end)									
305	Πίθηκος καὶ ἁλιεῖς			206		204	199	–	–	–	–	128	–	
		1	καθίσας		καθεζόμενος		(X)							
		2	ἠϊόνος		ποταμοῦ		(X)							Mb (ποταμῷ Pb)
		4	om.		ὁ δὲ πίθηκος (before καταβὰς)		om. δέ							
		7	ἁλιεύειν		ἁλιεύς		X					X		

310	Πλούσιος καὶ βυρσοδέψης			207	βύρση παρακείμενος ἐπέκειτο αὐτῷ ἀνεβάλετο	205	200	—	—	—	—	—	(Ma Mb)
		1	Βυρσοδέψη παρῳκίσθη										Ma Mb
		1	διετέλει...ἐπικ.										Ma Mb
		2	ἀεί...διανεβάλλετο										
		3											
		5–6	συνέβη...διενοχλεῖν		τῆς δυσοδίας μηκέτι αὐτῷ ἐνοχλεῖν		(×)×						
311	Πλούσιος καὶ θρηνῳδοί			208			206	201	110	—	61	114	129	—
		2	τὰς λεγούσης		om.			××						Mb L etc.
		2	μηδὲν		λαλούσης μακρὸν			(×)						
		4	οὕτω		οὕτως			×						
		4	σφόδρα		σφοδρῶς							×		
		5–6	ἐκείνη...εἶπεν		καὶ ἡ μήτηρ ἔφη			××					××	
		6	οἰκτρῶς		om.									Mb
		9	καὶ		om.									Mb etc. Cf. L
313	Πομπὴν καὶ κύων			209			207	202	111	—	62	115	—	—
		3	εἰσελθούσης τῆς ποίμνης		εἰσελθὼν τῇ ποίμνῃ			×						Mb
		7	Πρός...εὔκαιρος		ὁ λόγος εὔκαιρος πρὸς ἄνδρα κόλακα			(×)						
312	Πομπὴν καὶ θάλασσα			210			208	203	—	—	63	116	130	—
		3	τὰ		αὐτοῦ τὰ			××					×××	Mb
		3	ἐπρίατο		ἀγοράσας			××				×		Mb
		7	ἠιόνος		γῆς									Mb

TABLE I—Continued

No.	Chambry Title	Line	Reading	G No.	G Reading	Pa	Pb	Pc	Pd	Pe	Pf	Pg	Ph	Other MSS Remarks
317	Ποιμὴν καὶ πρόβατα			211		209	204	112	–	–	117	–	–	
		1	εἰσελάσας (Pa Pc)		ἐλάσας		X				X			Mb Ca etc.
		2–3	τὸ ἱμάτιον		τὰ ἱμάτια		X	X			X			Mb etc.
		3	αὐτοῦ		om.		X	X						
		3	ἐπὶ		ὑπὸ									
		3	τὸν		om.									
		3	κατέσειε		ἀνέσειεν									
		5	συγκαταφαγόντα		σὺν καταφαγεῖν		(X)	X						Mb Ca
		7	ἐσθῆτας		ἐσθῆτα		X					X		(Mb Ca etc.)
		7	παρεχόμενα, ἐμοῦ		παρέχεται (for -τε) ἐμοῦ δὲ		(X)				(X)			
		7–8	τοῦ ... ἀφείλεσθε		τρέφοντος ὑμᾶς καὶ ἱματίων ἀφείλασθαι									
		9	πολλοί		πολλάκις	X		X						
314	Ποιμὴν καὶ λυκιδεῖς			212		210	205	–	–	–	119	–	–	Mb 187
		1	λυκιδεῖς, τούτους		λυκιδία, ταῦτα		X							
		3	τηρήσουσιν		φυλάξουσιν		X							
		3	ἕτερα		τὰ ἑτέρωθεν		(X)							(τὰ ἑτέρων Pb)
		4	ηὔξηθησαν		ἐγράφησαν		X							
		5	διαφθείρειν ἤρξαντο		διέφθηραν		X				X			Mb
		6	ταῦτα ᾔσθετο		om.									Mb etc.

136

			213		211	206	–	–	–	131	–	Mb 188
319	Πομπὴν παίζων	4	τῶν	om.	XX	XX	–	–	–	X	–	
		6	τῇ ἀληθείᾳ	ταῖς ἀληθείας								
		7	Ἀποτεμνομένου δὲ αὐτῶν	Ἀποτεμνομένου δὲ αὐτοῦ		X⁶						
		7–8	καὶ τοῦ...ἐπικα-λουμένου	καὶ αὐτὸς ἐπὶ βοή-θειαν βοῶν		XX				(X)		
		9–10	ἧττον ἐφρόντιζον	οὐδὲν ἐφρόντισαν		XX						
		10	τῶν προβάτων στε-ρηθῆναι	ἀπολέσθαι τὰ πρό-βατα		XX				X		Mb Ca
		12	ψευδολόγοι	ψευδόμενοι								
		13	om.	ὑπό τινος (at end)								
298	Παῖς λουόμενος			214	–	207	–	–	–	132	–	Mb 177
		3	ἐκάλει	ἐρώνει		XX						
		3	τῷ παιδὶ	τὸν παῖδα		XX						
		3	τολμηρῷ	τολμηρὸν		XX						
		5	μέμψῃ	μοι μέμφου		XX						
322	Πρόβατον κειρό-μενον			215	–	208	–	–	–	133	–	Mb 194
		2	ἔρια (Pb Ca)	ἔριον								
		5	προσφερομένους	περιφερομένους		X				X		Mb Ce Cf
		5–6	ὁ λόγος...ἐστι	om.								
325	Ῥοιὰ καὶ μηλέα, etc.			216	215	209	114	–	–	134	122	Mb 201
		1	καὶ ἐλαία	om.	X	X	X					
		3	φίλαι	φίλε						X		Mb
		6	τι εἶναι	om.								

⁶ Pb has βοήθειαν according to Schneider but βοήθειας according to Sternbach.

TABLE I—Continued

No.	Chambry Title	Line	Reading	G No.	G Reading	Pa	Pb	Pc	Pd	Pe	Pf	Pg	Mb	Other MSS Remarks
327	Σπάλαξ			217		219	210	—	—	65	124	135	—	Ma 131
		1–2	λέγει...μητέρα		λέγει τῇ μητρὶ αὐτοῦ									
		2	βλέπει		βλέπω		X					X		Ma Ca
		3	δοῦσα		δοῦσα αὐτῷ		X			X	X	X		Ma Me Ca
		3	ποτε		τοῦτο		X				(X)			Ma Me Ca
		4	ἔφη		καὶ ἡ μήτηρ εἶπεν		(X)				(X)	(X)		(καὶ om. Pb)
		5	ἀποβέβληται		ἀπώλεσας		(X)							(Ma Me Ca)
		7	κατεπαγγέλλονται		ἐπαγγέλλονται									
		7	ἐξελέγχονται		ἐλέγχονται		X					X		Ma Ca
330	Σφῆκες καὶ πέρδικες καὶ γεωργός			218		220	211	117	—	67	126	136	—	
		1	συνεχόμενοι		συνεχόμεναι	X				X		X		
		3	οἱ		αἱ					X				
		4	ποιήσειν		ποιῆσαι		X				X	X		Me Mf
		4	οἱ δὲ		αἱ δὲ σφῆκαι									
		6	εἶπεν		ἔφη		(X)				X	X		
		9	Πρός...εὔκαιρος		οὗτος ὁ λόγος πρὸς ἄνδρα ἀχάριστον		(X)							
331	Σφὴξ καὶ ὄφις			219		—	212	—	—	66 v. 2	125 v. 2	137	—	Ma 132
		1–2	τῷ κέντρῳ		τὸ κέντρον									Ce Cf
		5	Ὁ λόγος...συναποθνήσκειν		ὁ λόγος δηλοῖ πρὸς τοὺς συναποθνήσκειν τοῖς ἐχθροῖς ὑπομένοντας									(Ca)

138

101	Δένδρα καὶ κάλαμοι			220	inc. Τὰ δένδρα See no. [71]	221	213	–	–	–	–	Ma 133
		1	ποτε		om.		(X)					(ἑώρων Pb)
		2	ἑώρα		ἑώρων		X					Ma Ce
		2	ἀβλαβεῖς		ἀσινεῖς		X					Ma Ca Ce
		2	ἐπυνθάνετο		ἐπυνθάνοντο		X					Ma
		5	ἔφασαν		ἔφησαν							Ma ἥκομεν Ce Cf
		5	συνειδότες		συνιδόντες	X						(συμβολῇ Pb)
		6	εἴκομεν		ἥκομεν		(X)					Ce Cf
		6	ἐμβολῇ		συμβολῆς		X					Ma
		10	ἀνθίστασθαι		ἀντιτάσσεσθαι		X					
		10	om.		ἐστιν (at end)							
332	Ταῦρος καὶ αἶγες ἄγριαι			221		223	214	–	–	–	202	Ma 134
		1	τι		om.		XX					
		2	om.		ὁ ταῦρος (after αὐ- τῶν)							
		3	Ἀλλ'		om.		XX				XX	Ma Ce Cf
		4	τὸν δὲ		ἀλλὰ τὸν		XX				XX	Ma Ce Cf
		4	πρὸ... [λέοντα]		πρὸ τοῦ στόματος τοῦ σπηλαίου ἑσ- τῶτα							
		5–6	καὶ τὰς... ἡττόνων		om.		X					
308	Πιθήκου παῖδες			222	inc. Τοὺς πιθήκους	–	215	–	–	–	139	Ma 135
		3	ἀμελεῖν		ἀμελεῖσθαι		XX				X	Ma
		4–5	ἡδέως... ἀποστυγ- γεσθαι		ἀποθνήσκειν		XX					
		6	ἐκτελεῖσθαι		τελεοῦσθαι							

TABLE I—Continued

No.	Chambry Title	Line	Reading	G No.	G Reading	Pa	Pb	Pc	Pd	Pe	Pf	Pg	Mb	Other MSS Remarks
334	Ταὼς καὶ κολοιός			223	*inc.* Τῶν ὀρνέων	226	216	–	–	–	131	140	171	
		4	ἀετός		ὁ ἀετὸς ὅτι...φυλάττονται		X							*Cf.* Pg Mb
		5–6	ὅτι...φυλάττονται		ὅτι ἀεὶ τοὺς δυνατοὺς μὴ κάλλει ἀλλὰ δυνάμει κεκοσμέσθαι									
146	Κάμηλος καὶ ἐλέφας καὶ πίθηκος			224	*inc.* Τῶν ἀλόγων	–	217	–	–	–	132	141	60	
		1	Βουλευομένων		Βουλομένων		(X)				X	X	X	
		5	χολὴν οὐκ		χαλεπὸν		X							
		6	μὴ		καὶ		X							
		7	ὃ		*om.*									
		7	ἡμῖν ἐπιτιθῆται		ὑμῖν ὑποτίθεται						X	X	X	
		7	πολλοὶ...πραγμάτων		πολλάκις καὶ τὰ μέγιστα τῶν πραγμάτων									
123	Ζεὺς καὶ ὄφις			225	*inc.* Τοῦ Διός	–	218	–	39	–	–	–	34	
		3	ἔφη		εἶπεν εἴσω (at end)				XX				X	
		6	*om.*											

140

				226	227	220	118	–	–	133	–	211	
342	Ὗς καὶ κύων <ἀλ- λήλαις λοιδορού- μεναι>												
		1	ἀλλήλας		××	×	×××			××		××	
		2	ἐὰν										
		3	αὐτὴν		×	×××							
		3	ἀνατεμεῖν			××				×			Mf
		3	αὐτὴν		×		×						Me Mf
		4	μισεῖ			××				×			
		6	γε										Me Mf
		6	με			××	×					×××	
		7	θύῃ									×	θύσῃ Pf Me Mf
		9	προσφερόμενα		×	××						××	
		9	εἰς									×	
343	Ὗς καὶ κύων <περὶ εὐτοκίας>			227	228	221	119	–	70	134	143	212	Ma 136
		1	εὐτοκίας										
		1	εἶπεν			×				λέγεις	×××	××	Cf
		3	φράζῃ			λέγεις	×	×	×××	×	××	×	Ma Ca
		3	ἐν δὲ			×							Ma
		5	κρίνεται										Ma Ca
		6											
328	Σῦς ἄγριος καὶ ἀλώπηξ			228	217	222	116	40	64	123	142	210	
		1	Σῦς			××							
		2-3	ἐρομένης μηδενός...ἐφεστῶ- τος	inc. Ὗς		××		×				×	
			Ὗς ἐρωτώσης μήτε κυνηγῷ μήτε κινδύνου ἐνεστῶ- τος			(×)							
		4	ἔγωγε						××		×		
		5	τοῦ			×	×	×		×	×××	××	
		7	δεῖν			×							

TABLE I—Continued

No.	Chambry Title	Line	Reading	G No.	Reading	Pa	Pb	Pc	Pd	Pe	Pf	Pg	Mb	Other MSS Remarks
345	Φιλάργυρος			229	τις τῶν ἐργατῶν καὶ καταλαβὼν αὐτοῦ τὸν χρυσὸν ἀφείλατο	229	223	120	—	71	135	144	217	Ma 137
		4	ἐργατῶν τις											
		5–6	καὶ . . ἀνείλατο				X					X	X	Ma
		7	καὶ		τε καὶ									
		7	ἐσπάρασσεν		ἔτιλλεν		X				X		X	Ma
		8	ὑπερπαθοῦντα				X				X		X	Ca
		9	μὴ . . . λαβών		μὴ λυποῦ, ἑτέρᾳ, ἀλλὰ λαβὼν									
		12	καὶ		ὅτι.		X	X				X	X	
353	Χελώνη καὶ λαγωός			230		230	224	121	—	72	136	145	—	Ma 138
		4–5	ὁδὸν ἑαυτῇ βραδύτητα		τὴν ὁδὸν		X				X			Me Mf
		6	ἐπὶ		εἰς		X			(X)	X			Me Mf
348	Χελιδὼν καὶ δράκων			231		231	225	123	—	—	—	147	228	
		1	ἑξέστη		ἑξέστη		X							
		2	δράκων		ὄφις		X							
		5	πειρωμένης		βουλομένης		X							
		5	<ὅτι> οὐ		ὅτι.			X						
		6	συμβέβηκεν		συμβεβηκέναι		X					X	X	Ce Cf
		6	εἶπεν		ἔφη		X							
		8	β. τυγχάνουσιν		βοηθοῦνται		X							Ca
		9	πολλάκις		ὅτι.		X					X	X	Ce Cf
		10	ὅταν . . . ὑφίστωνται		ὅταν οἱ κριταὶ δι' αἰσχροκερδίαν προσωπολιπτοῦσι		(X)							C

142

354	Χῆνες καὶ γέρανοι			232		226	124	–	76	140	–	231	Ma 139
		2	αἱ										
		2	ἐλαφραὶ οὖσαι										Me Mf
		3	οἱ δὲ										Ma
		6–8	εὐπρόδροροι ῥᾳδίως...μετέχουτες					×	×		×		
		9	μένοντες...δουλεύουσιν		οἱ ἐλαφροὶ ὄντες αἱ δὲ ἔλαφροι ῥᾳδίως μεταβαίνουσιν ἀπὸ πόλεως εἰς πόλιν μένοντες ἀπόλλυνται									
282 v. 4	Ὄναγρος ⟨πατήσας σκόλοπα⟩ καὶ λύκος			233	inc. Χολός. Cf. supra, no. 189	227	–	–	–	–	148	232	
		1	ἐγκεκεντρισμένος αὐτῷ		ἐγκεντρισμένος αὐτὸν	×					×	×	
		3	βριαρός		ὅπ.	×							
		3	συναντήσας		ἀπαντήσας	×							
		4	θήραμα		εἰς θήραν	×							
		5	πρῶτον		ὅπ.								
		9	εἰς ὅρος		ὁ ὄνος	×					×		
349	Χελιδὼν καὶ κορώνη			234		228	–	–	74	–	–	225	Ma 140
		4	παρατείνεται		παρατάσσεται	×							Ma
		5	ἤ...παράτασις		ἡ παράταξις σώματος								Ma
352	Χελώνη καὶ ἀετός			235		229	–	–	73 v. 2	137 v. 2	149	230	Ma 141
		5	ἀναβὰς		ἀρθής							(×)	(Ma Ca)
		7–8	"Ὅτι...ἔβλαψαν		"Ὁ μῦθος δηλοῖ ὅτι πολλοὶ τῶν ἄνω ἐν ταῖς φιλονεικίαις αὐτοὺς καταβλάπτουσιν							(×)	

TABLE I—*Continued*

No.	Chambry Title	Line	Reading	G No.	G Reading	MSS of Class I Pa	Pb	Pc	Pd	Pe	Pf	Pg	Mb	Other MSS Remarks
357	Ψύλλα καὶ ἀθλητής			236		233	230 v. 3	—	—	—	141	150	234	Ma 142
		1	ἐπὶ...ἀνδρὸς		ἐπὶ πόδα ἀνδρὸς									
		2	νοσοῦντος...δῆγμα		om.							X	X	Ma
		2–3	Ὁ δ'...εὐτρεπίσας		ἐκεῖνος δὲ εὐτρεπί- σας									
		4	ὑφ' ὁρμῆς φυσικὸν		ὑφορμισθῆσα									
		5	ἀπαλλαγεῖσα		om.									
		5	Καὶ ὃς		Καὶ ὁ ἀθλητὴς							(X)		
		9	ἐπευθὺς		ἐπευθείαν							X	X	
		10	ἀνακαλεῖν		ἐπικαλεῖν									
336 v. 4	Μύρμηξ καὶ τέττιξ			237	inc. Ψῦχος	—	—	—	—	—	—	151	—	Ma 143 Ca 195
		2	ἐν ἀμητοῖς		om.									
		2	ἀπέθηκε		om.									
		3	ἐπὶ...ἐκδῦναι		ἐπόδυνος									
		5	μεταδοῦναι		om.							XX		Ma
		7	αὐτὸς γ. τινος		αὐτός γ. τινος γ.									
		7–8	ἐν ἀμητῷ		om.									
		8	Ὁ δὲ τέττιξ		Καὶ ὁ τέττιξ φησιν									
		9	τοὺς ὁδοιπορούντας		τοῖς ἀνθρώποις									
			γέλωτα π. κατα- χέας		γελάσας									
		10	om.		ἐπεὶ θέρος ἦδες (after ὀρχοῦ)									
		11–13	Ὁ λόγος...κωμα- σίαν		Ὁ μῦθος διδάσκει ὅτι οὐδὲν κρεῖττον φροντίζειν τῶν ἀναγκαίων τρο- φῶν καὶ μὴ ἀπο- σχολισθὲν εἰς ἀνω- φελεῖς προφάσεις.										

52 v. 4	Ἀνὴρ μεσοπόλιος καὶ ἑταῖραι		238	inc. Ὣν τις. See no. 31	–	–	41	–	–	152	–	Ma 144
		1		Ἦν								
		1		τρυφαῖς			ΧΧΧ					
		3		τὰς								om.
		4		ὁμοῦ μιγεῖσας								
		4–5		Ὡς...ἐνύγχανεν								
		5		ἥρατο			Χ			Χ		ἠνέσχετο Pg
		6		πρέσβεως								Ma
		6		νέας								
		7		Ὡς οὖν εἰσήρχετο								
		7–8		ἀπέσπα...τρίχας								
		9		τοῦτον δρᾶσθαι								
		11		ἐξέλεγε			Χ					Ma
		11		om.								
		12		om.								
		13		Οὕτως			(Χ)					(Ma)

b. The traditional content of the Augustana collection as it appears from a comparison of the manuscripts. Notes on the grouping of manuscripts within Class I (the Augustana)

In considering the content of the Augustana collection as far back as it can be traced, I have found it necessary to deal simultaneously, and somewhat incidentally, with the grouping of the manuscripts in Class I, since each subject is very closely connected with the other and little at present is known about either.

With the exception of nos. 237 and 238 [7] there are no fables or fable-versions in the Morgan manuscript which are not found in essentially the same form either in Pa or in Pb or in both. Since 237 and 238 come at the very end of the series, and are almost the only fables in the entire collection which appear in metrical or semi-metrical versions, it may be safely inferred that they did not belong to the Augustana tradition originally, but have been added to it from without. A further indication of this may be seen in the use of the word μῦθος in the epimythia in place of λόγος, which is regularly employed elsewhere.[8] No. 238, moreover, is a repetition in substance of no. 31, while no. 237 is found nowhere else in Class I except in Pg.[9]

A similar situation is to be noted in the other manuscripts of Class I, in so far as they include fables taken from near the end of the collection. The original series seems to have ended with no. 236, Ψύλλα καὶ ἀθλητής, since the one or two fables that follow it in Pa, Pb, Pf and Pg, as in G, show unmistakable

---

[7] The numbers given, unless otherwise stated, are those of G as they appear in Table I above.

[8] I find only two other exceptions to this rule, namely, in the epimythia of nos. 61 and 120 where, however, several good MSS read λόγος. The term μῦθος is regular in Class II, where it appears to have been taken over, along with some forty fables, from a collection of twelve-syllable verse fables no longer extant as such; further, see pp. 194f.

[9] It is also in Ma, Ca, and Cf (two lines only); but these MSS are of mixed contents, and none of them can be relied upon as independent authority for what was contained in the Augustana.

signs of being later additions. In Pa and Pf Ψύλλα καὶ ἀθλητής is followed by two fables, of which one, Μύρμηξ καὶ κάνθαρος, is merely a repetition with slightly different wording of no. 104 in Pa, and the other, Ψιττακὸς καὶ γαλῆ, is found nowhere else in Class I. Since Pf is a much later manuscript than Pa and elsewhere has many peculiarities in common with it, we are not surprised to find it dependent upon Pa in this instance also, whether directly or indirectly.[10] The original Augustana version of Μύρμηξ καὶ κάνθαρος is represented by Pa's 104, which is found also in the same alphabetical order (inc. Θέρους) in G, Pb, Pg, and Ca; but Pf contains only the later and altered form of this fable as it appears in Pa no. 235 (inc. Ὥρᾳ). The scribe, however, instead of reproducing faithfully the text of that version (Pa 235), has introduced some further, though minor, changes of his own, which in turn are reflected in the mixed manuscripts, Me, Mf, Mj. A similar dependence of Me, Mf (and Mj) upon the relatively late tradition represented by Pf [11]—a phenomenon which is widely manifested elsewhere—is evident also in the other odd fable, Ψιττακὸς καὶ γαλῆ, for which see Chambry no. 356. In Pb the last two

---

[10] Pf's partial dependence upon the Pa tradition, as opposed to that of GPbPg etc., is clearly revealed by the fact that it has eight fables in common with Pa which are found nowhere else in the other MSS of Class I. Seven of these are indicated in Table III below; the eighth corresponds to no. 194 in Chambry. Outside Class I these fables are confined almost entirely to the mixed manuscripts Me, Mf, and Mj, which elsewhere follow Pf; three of them, however, are found likewise in Ca and one of these three also in Ma. Furthermore, no. 112 in Chambry occurs only in PaPfPh (and Classes III and V); no. 226 only in PaPfPhMeMj; and no. 335 only in PaPfPeMeMf. Incidentally, Chambry's list (p. 7 of his edition) of fourteen fables in Pf that are not found in Pb includes two that are in Pb, namely Πλέοντες (= Pb 79) and Ὄφις καὶ γαλῆ καὶ μύες (= Pb 193). On the other hand, the basis of Pf's text was probably some MS of the GPbPg family, since the order of its fables at the beginning has not been affected by that of Pa, and it contains nine fables that are not found in Pa, although they are well represented in the other MSS; cf. Table II below. Chambry's count of ten fables in Pf that are not in Pa includes one fable that is in Pa, namely Ἀλώπηξ καὶ πίθηκος.

[11] See Chambry, pp. 21–22.

fables are merely variations of Ψύλλα καὶ ἀθλητής; the first belongs to Class III, having been substituted in place of the Augustana original;[12] and the second comes from the metrical version peculiar to Class II. Pg and Ma conclude their series with the same two spurious fables that we find in G, thereby revealing their dependence upon that particular branch of the tradition. Pd's 41 (no. 238 in Table I) follows the same tradition, and its last fable, no. 43 in verse (Chambry 139), comes from Class IV.[13]

I have dealt with this matter in detail because it throws some light upon the interrelationships of the manuscripts in Class I, a subject which will claim our attention as we proceed. For the present, however, it is important to note that previous to the date of our earliest manuscripts, i.e. in the tenth century or earlier, the Augustana fable-collection ended with Ψύλλα καὶ ἀθλητής; that the most complete and, for the most part, the oldest manuscripts of this collection are G, Pa, and Pb;[14]

[12] This is the only fable in Pb that belongs definitely to Class III. Marc's statement (409, n. 2) that nos. 206–219 and 231 in Pb are taken from the Accursiana recension is not true. All of these fables, except 231 which is from Class II, and 219 which is peculiar to Pb, are in G, and most of them are well represented in the other MSS of Class I as well; their text throughout is especially close to that of G. Eight of them have no representatives in the Accursiana at all, and the others have nothing in common with the textual peculiarities of the Accursiana redaction as such. Marc states that the fables in question are found on fols. 319 and 321, written in by a later hand. I have not examined the MS in this region and therefore cannot vouch for the accuracy of this statement. I speak only of the fables printed in Schneider's edition of Pb, to which, however, Marc himself obviously refers in the statement reported above: "Die auf diesen Blättern enthaltenen Fabeln (Schneider no. 206–219 und 230–231) gehören tatsächlich zur Redaktion der Accursiana." That the last two fables at least were written in by a later hand, I do not doubt.

[13] I am unable to identify Pd's no. 42. Pc, Pe, Ph, and Pi all end before 236.

[14] These MSS have in common nine fables (28, 106, 125, 142, 155, 183, 188, 190, 207) which do not recur in any other MS of Class I, excepting the mixed texts Ma, Mb, and Ca, in addition to peculiar versions of three others (31, 35, 39) which are found elsewhere only in Ma or in different

and that among these three manuscripts, G is not only the oldest,[15] but is, or was before the loss of its three leaves, the most complete; it is probably also the most faithful to the old tradition in respect to its choice and range of fables.

In order to gain a better idea of the original Augustana collection and to define the relation of the other manuscripts thereto, it will be useful to reconstruct, as well as we may, the corpus of fables that served as the common source of G, Pa, and Pb. From this corpus we have already deducted nos. 237 and 238 for various reasons and because they are not represented in either Pa or Pb. For similar reasons we should also eliminate no. 202, since it is not found in either Pa or Pb, and since it is merely a repetition in slightly altered form of no. 23. This leaves 235 fables or versions of fables that G had in common with either Pa or Pb, or both. Of these, 205 are extant in all three manuscripts, and may therefore be regarded as a group of fables certainly contained in the archetype. We have now to consider what other fables should be added to this group. The following table shows the testimony of the manuscripts with reference to the 30 fables in G that recur in either Pa or Pb, but not in both.[16]

recensions. They also have a score or more of unique textual variants in common though these may not be very significant in themselves. By this I do not mean to imply that G, Pa, and Pb represent a special family of manuscripts within Class I—on the contrary, there is, as we shall see, a partial division between G, Pb, and Pg, on the one hand, and Pa, Pc, Pf, Ph on the other—but only that they are, in respect to the fables mentioned above and by virtue of their antiquity, closer to the archetype than the other MSS.

[15] It is not later than the early 11th century, while Pa is of the 12th and Pb of the 14th or late 13th. Pa first became known to scholars generally through the publication of its text by Sternbach in 1894. The high value and antiquity of Pb's text has been recognized ever since Lessing.

[16] In the case of the mixed MSS (Ma, Mb, and Ca) I ignore those fables which appear in versions peculiar to Class II or III. Nos. 62, [71], 99, 173, and 233 are merely variations on 177, 220, 173, 99, and 189 respectively; hence in the following table they are grouped together at the end.

Table II

G	Pa	Pb	Pc	Pd	Pe	Pf	Pg	Ph	Ma	Mb	Ca
59	−	×	−	−	×	×	×	×	×	×	×
60	−	×	−	×	×	×	×	×	×	×	−
[72]	−	×	−	−	−	−	−	−	×	−	−
90	−	×	−	−	−	×	−	×	−	−	−
96	−	×	×	−	−	×	×	×	−	×	−
103	×	−	−	−	−	×	−	×	×	×	−
105	−	×	−	−	−	−	×	−	−	−	−
109	−	×	×	−	−	−	×	−	−	−	−
139	×	−	−	−	−	×	−	−	−	−	×
154	×	−	−	−	−	×	−	×	−	−	−
161	×	−	×	−	−	×	×	−	×	×	×
162	×	−	−	−	−	−	−	−	−	−	−
167	×	−	×	−	−	−	−	−	×	−	×
169	×	−	×	−	−	−	×	−	×	×	×
170	×	−	−	−	−	×	×	−	×	×	×
172	×	−	×	−	−	×	×	−	×	×	×
200	−	×	−	−	−	−	×	−	−	×	×
214	−	×	−	−	−	−	×	−	−	×	×
215	−	×	−	−	−	−	×	−	−	×	×
219	−	×	−	−	×	×	×	−	×	−	×
222	−	×	−	−	−	−	×	−	×	−	×
224	−	×	−	−	−	×	×	−	−	×	−
225	−	×	−	×	−	−	−	−	−	×	−
234	−	×	−	−	×	×	−	−	×	×	×
235	−	×	−	−	×	×	×	−	×	−	−
62	−	×	−	−	×	−	−	−	×	−	−
[71]	−	×	−	−	×	−	−	−	−	×	−
99	−	×	−	−	×	−	×	−	−	×	−
173	×	−	×	−	−	×	−	−	−	−	×
233	−	×	−	−	−	−	×	−	−	×	−

We may first consider the relation of Pa to the 235 fables that G had in common with Pa or Pb. Twenty of these are missing in Pa; but Pa has nineteen others that are not found in either G or Pb, plus one which recurs in Pb and Ca, but not in G, thus totaling 235 fables.[17] Now it is significant that the twenty fables that seem to have been omitted have a much better representation in the other manuscripts of Class I than do the nineteen or twenty which I assume to have been added by Pa, or by one of his forerunners, from other sources. The manuscript testimony in favor of the omitted fables is given in Table II above; and in this connection one should not overlook the fact that G and Pb represent a tradition that antedates Pa and is, therefore, presumably

[17] Not counting the accidental repetition of nos. 8 and 74 (in Pa) after 29 and 91 respectively; cf. Chambry, p. 5 and below, p. 169.

more trustworthy. The nineteen or twenty fables that appear to have been added in Pa are thus represented in the other manuscripts:[18]

TABLE III

Pa	Chambry		Elsewhere only in
63	98	Διογένης ὁδοιπορῶν	Ca (see note 42)
101	112	Ἑρμῆς καὶ τεχνῖται	—
(a repetition of no. 96 in slightly different form)			
124	184	Κύων κ. μάγειρος	Pg Mb Mh Classes II and III Syntipas 33
131	153	Καρύα	Pg Cd Mb (verse) IV Babrius
132	148	Κάμηλος ὀρχουμένη	Pg Mb Ch Cd (verse) Babrius
155	230	Λύκος κ. ποιμήν	Pf Ma Me Mf Mj Ca
157	191	Λαγωοὶ κ. ἀλώπεκες	Pb Ca III (Cf. Syntipas 22)
188	264	Ὄνον ἀγοράζων	Pf Mb Me
192	273	Ὄνος κ. ἡμίονος	Mb
193	286	Ὀρνιθοθήρας κ. πέρδιξ	(Cf. Babrius 124)
212	256	Ὁδοιπόροι κ. κόραξ	Pf Me
213	323	Προμηθεὺς κ. ἄνθρωποι	Pf Me Mf
214	304	Πῆραι δύο	Pc Mb IV (aliter) Babrius
216	33	Ἀλώπηξ κ. δράκων	Pc (Cf. Babrius 28)
218	329	Σῦς ἄγριος κ. ἵππος	IV Babrius
222	340	Ταινίαι	Pf Me Mf Mb (verse)
224	335	Τέττιξ κ. ἀλώπηξ	Pe Pf Me Mf
225	175	Κύκνος	Pf Me Mf
234	356	Ψιττακὸς κ. γαλῆ	Pf Me Mf Ca Mb (verse)
235	243	Μύρμηξ κ. κάνθαρος	—
(a repetition of no. 104)			

We have already noted the frequent dependence of Pf on Pa and of Me, Mf, and Mj on Pf. It is probable, therefore, that these manuscripts are indebted to Pa, directly or indirectly, for the fables mentioned above. Pc is also very closely related to Pa, as Chambry observes [19] and as may be seen from the collations given in Table I; but it is quite unlikely that Pc is descended in the main through Pa, since the order of its fables at the beginning agrees with that in GPb, etc. and is entirely independent of the peculiar order in Pa (cf. infra p. 169). This situation is perhaps best explained on the assumption that Pc comes more or less directly from one of the immediate sources of Pa; and if so we may suppose that nos. 214 and 216 in the list above owe their

[18] According to Chambry, as usual.

[19] P. 6: "Proximus omnium codici Pa est Parisinus 365, XIV saeculi, quem Pc appello." Furthermore see note 47.

presence in Pc either to crossing with Pa itself or to derivation from a source common to both manuscripts wherein these two fables stood in the place of others belonging to the corpus typified by GPb. No. 214 shows kinship with Babrius (no. 66), and no. 216 is a very brief and poor imitation of the well-known fable of the toad puffing herself up to equal a cow (= Babrius 28). Pg, which shares three of Pa's odd fables, usually agrees with GPb, but it is a 14–15th century manuscript which shows occasional mixing of sources in the *Fables*,[20] as well as in the *Life*, and may, therefore, be assumed to have crossed to some manuscript of the Pa family for nos. 124, 131, and 132 above. Mb and Ca are mixed manuscripts which elsewhere draw on both traditions and cannot, therefore, be relied upon as independent witnesses to the contents of either. We see that the fables in question are practically confined to Pa and a few closely related manuscripts. Some of them may have been added by Pa for the first time, but it is probable that most of them come from an earlier collection whose contents differed somewhat from GPb. To the same or a similar source we may perhaps refer also a few odd fables found in the other manuscripts of Class I. There is no reason to suppose that the contents of what we call the Augustana (i.e. the ancient as opposed to the Byzantine) recension of the prose fables were uniform in all the older texts. We have seen that even in the *Life* the ancient editions varied in respect to the episodes they contained; hence it is only to be expected that the fable collections which accompanied them should likewise differ, and perhaps even more widely. The source from which the odd fables in Class I were derived, may

[20] See Chambry, p. 8 and no. 350, where Pg stands with Pf and Pc against PaPb and G. In the *Life* Pg itself contaminates its main source (λ) with readings taken from the SBP family; and that source in turn (λ) was already elaborately compounded of the two families, MOR and SBP; see *Text Tradition*, 211ff. Moreover, there is reason to believe that the Augustana fables contained in λ were derived in part from a manuscript of the Pa family, since *Vita III*, which originated in λ (*infra* pp. 177f., note 2) is based upon the Aphthonian preface, which in turn is confined to the Pa group; see the diagram on p. 180.

possibly have been the same as that from which the archetype of SBP interpolated the Westermann version of the *Life*, since that source, as we have seen, differed in some notable particulars from the tradition represented by G and the archetype of the Westermann *Life*. It is certain that the prose fables of Class II (= SBP; *cf. infra* pp. 174ff.) have, like the *Life*, been interpolated from (not based directly upon) a text of Class I (*cf.* pp. 195 and 200f.), but these interpolations do not, so far as I have observed, reveal any definite kinship with the Pa tradition as opposed to that of GPb. Whatever may be the identity of the source from which the odd fables in Pa were derived, it is at any rate noteworthy that in the Augustana fables, as in the *Life*, there are traces of a double tradition, and that the tradition that is exemplified in G has survived in the majority of our manuscripts.

c. G in relation to Pb and Pa

Both in its text and in its choice of fables Pb stands closer to G than does Pa.[21] The details of this agreement may be consulted in the table of collations given above. If we except nos. 70 and 71, which were probably contained in G originally (see pp. 99f.), there are only seven fables in Pb which are not in G, and of these, six are absent also in Pa and in most of the other manuscripts of Class I:

TABLE IV

Pb	Chambry		Elsewhere only in
158	195	Λέαινα καὶ ἀλώπηξ	Ma Mb Ml Classes II and IV Babrius
159	223	Λύκος κ. ἀρνίον	Ma Mb Ca
160	191	Λαγωοὶ κ. ἀλώπεκες	Pa (157) Ca III
165	244	Μύρμηξ κ. περιστερά	Pf Pg Ma Mb Me Mf Mj II and III
219	333	Ταὼν κ. γέρανος	Mb IV Babrius
230	357	Ψύλλα κ. ἀνήρ	III
231	358	Ψύλλα κ. ἄνθρωπος	II

The alien character of nos. 230 and 231 has already been noted above (p. 148). Nos. 158 and 159 stand in the place

[21] The close connection of G (= Cryptoferratensis *A* 33) with Pb was inferred by Hausrath (*Philologus* LVIII [1899], 259) from the titles of the fables as listed in the 18th-century MS Cryptoferratensis *a* 27. His promise (*l.c.*), "totam syllogam quam maxime cum Augustani archetypo congruere alio loco demonstrabo," has not to my knowledge been fulfilled.

of Μάντις and of Παῖς καὶ κόραξ respectively, both of which are attested by G and Pa. No. 165 replaces Μυῖα found in G, Pa, and Pc; and 219 is apparently derived from Class IV or Babrius. The ten fables which Pb has omitted from the common stock are indicated in Table II. Since these have been only partially replaced by six or seven others of doubtful origin, so as to total 231 fables, it may be inferred that the manuscripts through which Pb is descended normally contained about 235 fables (235 − 10 + 6 = 231), thus closely approximating the number in Pa and in G.

In the variant readings we find PbG opposed to Pa far more frequently than PaG to Pb;[22] but in spite of this fact Pa has a somewhat larger number of obvious errors in common with G than has Pb.[23] This paradoxical circumstance may possibly be accounted for on the supposition that the scribe of Pa, or of one of Pa's immediate ancestors, copied his text alternately from two or more different manuscripts, one of which, as we shall observe in another connection, was particularly close to G. Further evidence of Pa's tendency to innovate, and of the desultory character of his procedure, will be described below (p. 169) in connection with the order of his fables and the substitution of the Aphthonian *Preface* in place of the old *Life*. Indeed, the difference in character between the two manuscripts (Pa and G) is very marked. Pa was written in an age of greater scholastic activity by an able and sophisticated, if not very alert penman, at some center of learning, probably Byzantium, where there were many books at hand,

[22] A rough estimate based upon the collations given above indicates that there are approximately 71 fables where Pb has more in common with G than has Pa, as against 14 where Pa stands closer to G than does Pb.

[23] See, in Table I, no. 2, line 7; 4,6; 6,17; 14,3; 25,8; 26,5; 28,6 and 10; 40,1; 57,4; 100,4 and 5; 111,4; 112,6; 120,2; 129,3 and 9; 136,3; 144,2 and 7; 145,9; 147,1 and 4–5; 159,4; 161,5 and 9; 183,3; 195,6; 201,3 (ὡς); 211,9; 216,3; 226,4. On the other hand, I note in passing only about a score of cases in which PbG is unquestionably in error as against Pa. As a rule, Pb follows the readings of G quite faithfully so long as they are intelligible, but he is wont to correct minor errors and is somewhat less likely than Pa to retain obviously corrupt or meaningless readings.

as is evidenced by the great variety of its contents; whereas G was faithfully copied out of a single mutilated manuscript by an ignorant, though well-intentioned scribe (see p. 78), who had no other books before him by which to correct or supplement his own text, and, unlike Pa, no learned affectations. Accordingly, the tradition of G must be considered more reliable on the whole than that of Pa, as being simpler and less likely to have been mixed or altered. There has been some interpolation in the ancestors of G (as in the *Life*), but apparently not very much.

G itself contributes only a few readings that are at once unique and valuable,[24] and it often fails to give help in passages where all the manuscripts seem to be corrupt.[25] Nevertheless, owing to its antiquity and to the apparent faithfulness of its tradition, G is very important for the recension, and in spite of numerous corruptions furnishes a valuable check upon the readings of other manuscripts.

d. Further notes on the various manuscripts of Class I

Among the other manuscripts of Class I, Pg is especially noteworthy for its kinship with G, being sometimes closer to it than is any other manuscript, and agreeing much more frequently with GPb than with PaPcPf. With the former group also, rather than with the latter, we must reckon Pd and Pe. A close relationship between Ph and Pf is evidenced in the order and choice of their fables as well as in the text.[26] The allegiance of the mixed manuscripts Ma, Mb, and Ca appears to be divided; sometimes they stand more or less alone with GPb or even G, while at other times they agree with Pa against GPb. Their testimony is valuable chiefly when it corroborates the readings of G, Pb, or Pa, to which traditions they may be regarded as useful witnesses. Indeed,

---

[24] *Cf.* 77, 6–7; 142,3; 145,11; 164,7; 223,5–6.

[25] As in 1,9; 8.2; 9,19; 13,5; 17,8; 46,7; 126,7; 171,8.

[26] Besides Table I above, see especially nos. 77, 78, 84, 95 and 108 in Chambry's text. This is not to deny that Ph may also have been influenced by the Pb group as Chambry suggests (p. 8).

it is evident that the majority of manuscripts in Class I represent traditions that are to some extent crossed with each other, and for that reason any attempt to draw up a stemma of their precise interrelationships would involve a great deal of painstaking tabulation, and might in the end prove futile. Here I have made only such observations about the manuscripts as seem to me to be justified by a comprehensive, though by no means exhaustive survey of the data furnished by Chambry, viewed in the light of the contents and readings of G, our oldest manuscript.

e. The supposed rhetorical character of the Augustana

The history of the prose fables of the Augustana previous to the tenth century is obscure. It is probable, however, that they represent, in large measure, an ancient recension or combination of recensions [27] dating from sometime between the death of Alexander and the third century after Christ. My reasons for so thinking are mainly subjective, but I note that Chambry defends the same view,[28] and not even Hausrath, if I understand him rightly, supposes that these fables were given their present form in Byzantine times. He lays stress —in my opinion, wrongly—upon their prevailingly rhetorical character. Surely the great majority of them are written in a simple, unaffected style that shows itself conscious of the matter rather than of the phrase, rhythm, or symmetry, and leaves unspoiled the native irony and wit that we are wont to associate with antiquity. The vocabulary, moreover, is Alexandrian and the thought always pagan. It is true that many fables in the collection cannot be regarded as genuinely popular and traditional Aesopic lore descended from pre-Alexandrian times; some of them look like artificially expanded

[27] The variety of formulae in the epimythia may possibly reflect a corresponding variety of sources. The most common formulae are Οὕτως or Οὕτω and Ὁ λόγος δηλοῖ. We also find, though much less frequently, Πρὸς...ὁ λόγος εὔκαιρος, or Ὁ λόγος εὔκαιρος πρὸς, Τούτῳ τῷ λόγῳ χρήσαιτο ἄν τις, Ἀτὰρ οὖν καὶ ἡμᾶς and others.

[28] *Ésope*, Paris, 1927, XLIV ff.

proverbs, or it may be combinations and variations of older motifs, or stories invented to illustrate a philosophical principle. But the presence of such matter in the Augustana does not prove that it is Byzantine or professionally rhetorical in origin. Many analogous tendencies appear as early as Phaedrus. Indeed they are only to be expected in the handling by ambitious, if not very gifted authors, of the loosely defined popular material. The *Life* which accompanies the *Fables* in the Morgan manuscript, even in the form in which we have it, certainly goes back to the second century after Christ (see p. 26); and it is natural to suppose that both texts belonged to the same ancient edition and that they have been transmitted together from the beginning. Whether the prose fables known to have been published by Demetrius of Phalerum in early Alexandrian times are preserved in whole or in part among those of the Augustana, is a proposition that can neither be proved nor disproved. I see nothing very unlikely in such a supposition, however, and Demetrius' use of the term λόγοι instead of μῦθοι in his title (Λόγων Αἰσωπείων Συναγωγή) accords with the regular designation of the fable as λόγος both in the epimythia of the Augustana fables and in the old *Vita*.[29] But if Demetrius' fables have been incorporated in the Augustana, it is probable that they have been more or less recast.

Hausrath's contention,[30] that the Augustana fables are in large part the product of the schools of rhetoric, seems to me to rest upon very weak foundations. He begins by calling attention to the indisputable fact that Aesopic fables were regularly employed in the schools as a *corpus vile* for rhetorical exercise, the pupils being encouraged to rewrite a given fable in several different ways, as by expanding or contracting it, or by embellishing it with ἐκφράσεις or ἠθοποιίαι. Likewise, the

[29] All the manuscripts of the fables, including those of the Augustana, use the term μῦθοι in the title; λόγος, which first appears in Herodotus, seems to be an early term that later went quite out of fashion; *cf. infra*, p. 171.

[30] *Neue Jahrb. f. Klass. Alt.* I (1898), 312–322.

pupil was asked to make up fables of his own which should illustrate a given principle, or, conversely, to invent several epimythia for the same fable. Having outlined the procedure in the schools of rhetoric, Hausrath proceeds to discover examples of the same sort of activity in Halm's collection of Aesopic fables. When a fable is unusually short he regards it as a technical school exercise in abbreviation; when it happens to be somewhat longer than usual, he sees in it a school exercise in expansion. But schoolboys and their teachers are not the only ones who may be presumed to write concisely or copiously; and for my part I fail to see that any of the fables cited by Hausrath from the Augustana collection, as συστελλόμενα or ἐκτεινόμενα are either so short as to be obscure or ineffective, or, with the exception of no. 72 (Table I), so long in proportion to the matter that one might justly call them verbose. Ἐκφράσεις are quite rare in the *Aesopica*, and Hausrath cites examples only from the fables in Babrius, Libanius, Dio Chrysostom, and Gregory of Nazianzus—whose writings are presumably not technical school exercises. As for ἠθοποιΐαι, there is one good example in the Augustana, namely no. 72, but this, owing to its insipid and purely technical character, is unique and so conspicuously different from all the others, that its presence in the collection should lead to the very opposite conclusion to that which Hausrath would draw from it; for if the majority of fables in the Augustana are mere school exercises, why is it that there are not many more like no. 72, or at least others equally insipid? Does Hausrath suppose that only the best products of the school have been preserved? That would not square very well with another statement of his,[31] that the scholastic origin of the Augustana is evidenced by the presence of false epimythia.

But I must not attempt to discuss here all the rhetorical categories that Hausrath finds illustrated in the *Aesopica*. It is his method to which I object most. Even if it could be shown that every fable in the Augustana collection had been

[31] *Phil. Woch.* XLVII (1927), 1513.

composed in accordance with some definite technical procedure taught in the schools, it would still be unsafe to conclude that no one but a professional rhetorician or his pupils could have produced them. For it is not technique *per se* that betrays scholastic origin but, if anything, *preoccupation* with technique; and that, it seems to me, is conspicuously absent in the collection as a whole.[32] The influence of rhetorical theory and practice is widespread in all post-Alexandrian literature, even in poetry; it is only natural therefore that it should have left its mark upon the fable also, at least to the extent that a man can find it there if he tries to do so. The same rhetorical influence is discernible in the poetic versions of Phaedrus and Babrius; it is all the more to be expected in prose fables, though they are addressed to the general reading public. The texts of the Aesopic fables that were used, along with those of Homer and the Attic prose writers, as a *corpus vile* for experimentation in the schools, were in all probability the same texts that circulated among the public at large. There is no good reason for supposing that they were different. It is true that the Augustana collection as a whole has admitted many rhetorical inventions in Hausrath's sense, as well as a certain amount of rhetorical coloring here and there that would probably not be found in a popular collection

[32] *Cf.* Chambry, *Supplément Critique*, I, p. 183: "Mais à part la sotte fable de *L'avare qui a trouvé un lion d'or* (62 de mon édition), reproduite uniquement dans deux manuscrits, je ne vois rien de spécifiquement entaché de rhétorique, ni dans nos trois classes de manuscrits, ni dans les tablettes de Palmyre, ni dans la paraphrase bodléienne." How the Augustana recension differs in style and content from a genuine rhetorical handbook may be gauged by comparing it with the fable collection from cod. Brancaccianus recently published for the first time by F. Sbordone in the *Rivista Indo-Greco-Italica* XVI (1932), 35ff., along with a new edition of the fables of Aphthonius. In both these collections we find explicit reference to teaching the young, a feature that nowhere appears in the Augustana, nor, to my knowledge, in any of the other recensions published in Chambry. Compare also the fable of the lamb and the wolf as told by Nikephoros Kallistos in his *Progymnasmata* (ed. J. Glettner in *Byz. Zeitschr.* XXXIII (1933), 7ff.) with the same fable in Chambry (107); the difference is wide and instructive.

written down in the time of Aristophanes; but if one assumes that a collection of popular fables, say that of Demetrius, once formed the nucleus of the Augustana, the accretions thereunto and the presumable textual alterations which appear in our oldest tradition, may very naturally be due to ordinary editing and compiling in ancient times. Since there was probably never, at least in later times, any standard text of the Aesopic fables, it was inevitable that both their range and their style of composition should change in accordance with the literary fashions of the day and the fancy of individual authors. Many of Phaedrus' departures from his Greek original [33] are no doubt the same in kind, if not in amount, that we may assume to have been made by the various unknown Greek editors and compilers. The distinction that Hausrath and Marc draw between *Volksbücher* on the one hand and *rhetorische Lehrbücher* on the other is artificial and overdrawn. The two qualities 'popular' and 'rhetorical' are not mutually exclusive, but may exist side by side in the same piece of literature. The didactic character of the fable with its epimythium is congenial to the common man, who finds it edifying, as well as to the schoolmaster, who wants to be instructive; and a naïve and thoroughly popular book may at the same time be either *lehrhaft*, like the *Physiologus* and *The Seven Wise Masters*, or full of rhetorical mannerisms and technique like *Chaereas and Callirhoe*.[34] Unlike the biography of Aesop, the fables, though common literary property, were thought of as belonging to a more formal type of literature,

---

[33] Compare the Prologue of Book II in Phaedrus:
        Equidem omni cura morem servabo senis (*sc.* Aesopi)
        Sed si libuerit aliquid interponere,
        Dictorum sensus ut delectet varietas,
        Bonas in partes, lector, accipias velim.

and the Prologue to Book III:
        Ego porro illius semita feci viam
        Et cogitavi plura quam reliquerat.
The fifth book professes to be entirely independent of Aesop.

[34] See my article on Chariton in *A. J. P.* LI (1930), 93–134.

thereby becoming subject in a greater degree to rhetorical experiment on the part of various authors and editors. And yet, even that biography, which Hausrath regards as a folkbook *par excellence*, and which was presumably not used for experimental purposes in the schools, has not entirely escaped the influence of rhetoric; in its oldest form, in the Morgan manuscript, it contains an elaborate ἔκφρασις in the passage where Aesop lies down to sleep in the garden (see p. 13), though the style is elsewhere, on the whole, quite simple.

On another occasion [35] Hausrath declares that a glance into Chambry's edition, with its numerous alternative versions, is enough to convince one that the fables of the Augustana collection come from the schools of rhetoric: "Wie will man sich sonst überhaupt die Existenz von oft 6–8 Variationen derselben Geschichte erklären, deren Autoren das oft krampfhafte Bestreben haben, in Kleinigkeiten—direkte Rede statt der indirekten, Änderung der Reihenfolge der Geschehnisse, Beifügung ausschmückenden Details, Auffindung einer neuen Moral (Daher die sinnlosen Epimythia!) usw.—zu ändern und die doch im ganzen genau nach demselben Schema arbeiten?" This argument does not seem to apply to any one recension in particular but in some vague and unintelligible way to all of them combined. The Augustana collection in its oldest form contains only five duplicate versions in a total of approximately 235 fables. These are easily accounted for by the activity of later scribes. It is exceptional when more than one version of the same fable occurs in a single manuscript. The great mass of variant versions in Chambry's edition are contributed jointly by the four different recensions of the fables and in a few cases by different manuscripts within the same recension. Since the greater part of them are either later than the Augustana, or unrelated to it, they prove nothing about the origin of that collection. If all the versions presented by these different recensions (Classes I–IV) could be traced to a common archetype, then that archetype might be

---

[35] *Phil. Woch.* XLVII (1927), 1575.

regarded as a rhetorical handbook, or something of the sort. But that is not the case; according to Hausrath himself, Class II comes from I, III from I and II, and Class IV derives from Babrius. We have a certain number of popular editions; that is the full extent of the variation in our texts. The authors of these separate Byzantine recensions do indeed make use of schoolboy methods in the recasting of the fables, but that is no proof that they were writing exercises in or for the schools. Even the ordinary copyist likes to paraphrase now and then, and not a few of them make their experiments in verse—a practice not much in accord with elementary instruction in rhetoric. Moreover, the same methods that have been employed in recasting the fables in Classes II and III—direct discourse for indirect or vice versa, change of word order, abbreviation, expansion, paraphrase, substitution of synonyms—all these are likewise found, and at corresponding stages, in the different versions of the *Life;* yet no one supposes that *that* text was employed in the schools for the purpose of rhetorical exercise. It ought to be obvious that the successive changes in the text of the *Aesopica* are due to essentially the same impulse toward willful alteration on the part of individual editors that confronts us elsewhere in the history of popular lore, in the *Physiologus* for example, or in the story of Syntipas. There is no need of invoking the schools of rhetoric in order to explain such phenomena. The four different recensions of the *Fables* do not account for *all* the variant versions in Chambry, but the relatively small remainder that are peculiar to this or that manuscript may be attributed to the same sort of scribal activity. Not every copyist was ambitious enough to rewrite all the fables, though he might be inclined to experiment with a few of them. Furthermore, one must not overlook the probability that there existed other special editions of the Aesopic fables that have not come down to us as such, but have been laid under contribution here and there by the compilers of our Byzantine manuscripts.

The short notice about the life of Aesop that is ascribed to Aphthonius,[36] which Marc more appropriately calls a *Prooimion* —I shall call it the *Preface*—is of a thoroughly learned and rhetorical character. Accordingly, Hausrath [37] does not hesitate to follow Marc (410–411) in regarding it as the original and proper introduction to the Augustana collection: a rhetorical edition of the fables would naturally be accompanied by a rhetorical preface, and vice versa. But this prop to Hausrath's theory is easily removed when one examines Marc's argument in detail and in the light of the new evidence afforded by G. The issue depends entirely upon the manuscript tradition of the *Preface*, and Marc rests his case upon the fact that the *Preface* in question is found only in manuscripts containing fables of the Augustana recension, the list of which he gives as follows:

1. Florence, Laur. conv. soppr. 627 (= Ca in Chambry)
2. Copenhagen, Add. 275
3. London, British Mus. Harl. 5543
4. Milan, Ambros. gr. 481 (L43 sup.) (= Me)
5. Paris, suppl. gr. 105 (= Cd)
6. Paris, suppl. gr. 126 (= Mf)
7. Paris, suppl. gr. 690 (= Pa)
8. Rome, Vat. Pal. gr. 156 (= Pf)
9. Rome, Vat. Pal. gr. 195 (= Ma)
10. Vienna, phil. gr. 178

The list is not quite accurate; no. 5 does not contain the Aphthonian *Preface*, but only a curiously interpolated version of Eberhard's *Vita III*.[38] The contents of nos. 1 and 9 are

[36] Printed in Eberhard's *Fabulae Romanenses* 306–308, as *Vita II*.
[37] Pauly-Wissowa, *R. E.* vi. 2, 1734.
[38] The text reads as follows at the beginning (f. 34ʳ): Αἴσωπος ὁ μυθοποιὸς Φρὺξ μὲν ἦν τὸ γένος τῇ τύχῃ δὲ δοῦλος· μέλας ὑπάρχων κακοειδὴς (sic) ὑπερβολὴν, σφόδρα φωξὸς τὴν κεφαλὴν...σιμὸς καὶ παντελῶς ἀνείδεος, ὀνηθεὶς δὲ παρά τινος Ξάνθου τοῦ φιλοσόφου, καὶ εἰς τὴν ἀγρὸν αὐτοῦ χάριν θεωρίας τῶν ἐργατῶν ἐν τῷ σκάπτειν πεμφθείς, ἤδη μεσημβρίας οὔσης καὶ τῷ καύματι χαυνωθείς, κτλ.—The same version is found also in cod. 1408 in the Library of Trinity College, Cambridge, but nowhere else to my knowledge. The interpolations are from the Planudean and Westermann *Lives*. Marc's error is evidently taken over from Hausrath, *Untersuchungen* 293.

drawn from diverse sources,[39] and there is reason to believe that both of them are indebted directly or indirectly to Pa (= no. 7);[40] they cannot, therefore, be trusted as independent witnesses to the Augustana text prior to Pa. Nos. 3, 4, 6, 8, and 10 form a closely interrelated group by themselves, which is recognized as such by Hausrath,[41] and, as we have shown above (p. 147) depends in part upon Pa or one of its immediate kin. I include no. 10 in this group not because I know anything about the sources of its fables, but because the text of its *Preface*, as reported by Eberhard, clearly reveals its kinship with the others and especially with Me Mf.[42] Another manu-

[39] See above, p. 155 and Chambry, pp. 10 and 19. Marc and Hausrath both recognize the thoroughly mixed character of no. 1 (Ca).
[40] See below, note 42.
[41] *Phil. Woch.* XLVII (1927), sp. 1541.
[42] The following variants illustrate the general alignment of the MSS:

Eber.	Pa Ca	Me Mf. Vind. 178. Harl.
306,6	Τιμάρχῳ	Ζημάρχῳ
306,8	om.	τοῖς τρόποις
306,10	ἠτιᾶτο	εἰστιᾶτο
306,12	ὠφελίμους	ὠφελιμωτάτους (ὠφελίμους Harl.)
306,15	ἄθετα Pa	αὐθαίρετα
	ἀθέμιτα Ca	
307,1	om.	δὲ
307,19–20	Αἴσωπος εὗρεν	εὗρεν Αἴσωπος
308,1–2	om.	καὶ τῶν λύκων (τῶν om. Vind.)
308,7	καὶ προσομοιούσας	om. omnes praeter Mf
308,8	προκεχειρισμένας	προσκεχρημένας

Corruptions common to all these MSS are: ἀπιστεῖν εἰς (307,8), ἄγειν καὶ (307,18), ὑπὸ (308,6). Note that Pa and Ca agree against the others. The following considerations also strengthen the probability that Ca has at times drawn upon some MS very closely akin to Pa, and that his *Preface* comes from the same source: (1) Pa and Ca are, according to Chambry, the only manuscripts which contain Διογένης ὁδοιπορῶν (Cham. 98), and herein Ca omits Pa's unintelligible πρὸ τὰς σίλβας, words which, though corrupt, probably represent a genuine reading, perhaps πρὸς τῇ βαλβῖδι, as Chambry suggests; (2) Λύκος καὶ ποιμήν (Cham. 230) is found only in Pa, Ca, Ma and the Pf group mentioned above, and here the text of Ca is aligned with PaMa against the others; (3) Ψιττακὸς καὶ γαλῆ (Cham. 356) occurs only in PaCaPfMeMf, and Ca regularly agrees with Pa in opposition to PfMeMf; (4) Λάρος καὶ ἰκτῖνος (Cham. 194) is confined to PaCaPfMeMj. But Ca's dependence on the Pa tradition is only occasional and incidental, as is further evidenced by the fact that the *Preface* is inserted at the end of

script, which was overlooked by Marc, though it contains the *Preface* and belongs to this same group, is described by A. Cosattini in his *Index Codicum Graecorum Bibliothecae Archiepiscopalis Utinensis*.[43] Cosattini states that this manuscript, which is of the 15th century, contains the same number of fables (i.e. 151) as Mf, and in the same order; close kinship between the two is therefore very probable. Still another manuscript not on Marc's list is cod. Alexandrinus 57, of the 16th century, formerly at Cairo. This has been examined recently by W. G. Waddell,[44] who reports that it contains 140 fables from Classes I and III; that the fables of Class I show numerous resemblances to Pf, Me, Mj, and Mf, but especially to Me and Mj; and that the *Preface* agrees in its readings with Me. The Alexandrian manuscript is therefore merely another representative of the PfMeMf recension which, as we have seen, is a later development within Class I, being in part dependent upon Pa. I cannot be absolutely sure about the identity of the manuscript at Copenhagen, but I suppose that it is none other than the Hauniensis 215 which Hausrath (*l.c.*) assigns to the PfMeMf family; 215 is presumably a misprint for 275, or vice versa, and neither Marc nor Hausrath mentions both. The Holkham manuscript also contains the *Preface*, but it is merely a copy of Ca.[45]

the Westermann *Life*. The author of this MS had three different codices before him in making his text of the Westermann *Life*, and at least two others from which he took his Augustana fables. His sporadic use of the recension that I call λ (p. 177) is revealed by his copying the first line only of λ's peculiar preface (Eberhard's *Vita III*). The fact that he shows absolutely no acquaintance with the original (Augustana) *Life*, although he copies two other versions and part of a third, is presumptive evidence that his sources in Class I are relatively late—that he used MSS which, like Pa, had dispensed with the old *Life*; cf. *infra* p. 174.

Ma's partial indebtedness to the Pa tradition is seen most clearly in the order of its fables at the beginning (Table I); it is the only manuscript that agrees with Pa in this respect.

[43] In *Studi Italiani di Filologia Classica* v (1897), 395ff.

[44] *Byzantion* vi (1931), 327–331.

[45] A 16th century MS at Einsiedeln (no. 19 in the catalogue by P. G. Meier) contains one of the short biographical notices about Aesop; but whether this is the Aphthonian *Preface* or the *Vita III* printed by Eberhard (*infra* p. 177) I do not know.

We are now left with Pa as the only known manuscript whose testimony in favor of the presence of the Aphthonian *Preface* in the early Augustana tradition may be regarded as independent; but this testimony, as it happens, is of no value.

In Pa, the *Preface* takes the place of the old *Vita* extant in G; whereas neither text is found in Pb, Pc, Pd, Pe, or Pg [46]—manuscripts which, with the exception of Pc,[47] are all, as we have seen, more faithful to the tradition of G than to that of Pa. In general, we have here to choose between the authority of Pa on the one hand and that of G on the other, having already concluded on other grounds that the tradition of G is the simpler and more trustworthy of the two. But apart from this consideration it is more probable that G's kindred (Pb Pg etc.) have intentionally omitted the long *Life*, than that they have omitted merely the short *Preface;* and since the *Preface* was not only superfluous when accompanied by the *Life*, but also contradictory to it,[48] it is quite unlikely that both of them stood together in the archetype of the recension. On the other hand, it is not surprising that Pa, who is otherwise somewhat inclined to make changes, should substitute a two-page introduction in place of a much longer biography. So much for general *a priori* considerations. When we come to compare the first page of the *Fables* in Pa with the first page in G (Plate IV), three points emerge clearly: (1) that Pa at the beginning must have had a manuscript before him whose first page exactly, or almost exactly, resembled G; (2) that

---

[46] Pg's fables belong to the Augustana tradition, but the Westermann *Life* which accompanies them has been taken from Class II; *cf. infra* p. 180.

[47] The close agreement of Pc with Pa is confined chiefly to that part of the text which is common also to G and Pb, whereas, with the exception of the two fables mentioned above (p. 151), it shares none of Pa's innovations in the choice of fables or in the order of them at the beginning. If we are right in supposing that Pc and Pa are derived from a common source, then the absence of the *Preface* in Pc points—somewhat negatively—to its absence in Pa's source as well. As we shall see presently, Pa did not get the *Preface* from the MS which he began to copy.

[48] In the *Life*, Aesop is a Phrygian by birth and becomes the servant of Xanthus of Samos, whereas in the *Preface* he is a Lydian by birth and later serves Timarchus at Athens.

that manuscript, Pa's main source, contained the old *Life;* and (3) that the *Preface* in Pa was added as an afterthought. In G, the *Life* ends on the same page (f. 67ᵛ) on which the *Fables* begin. The space between the two texts is occupied by two separately enclosed lines of writing relating to the preceding *Life,* followed by an ornamental design coming immediately above the title Αἰσώπου μῦθοι κατὰ στοιχεῖον ὠφέλιμοι: μῦθος ᾱ. Like this title, the first of the two lines of writing above begins with Αἰσώπου. A scribe intending to copy the *Fables* might easily begin with the wrong Αἰσώπου (i.e. the first one), especially since the first line of writing was also preceded by a decorative line in such a way as to suggest a hasty glance that a new text, the *Fables,* or an introduction to them, immediately followed. Of the two subscriptions following the *Life* and referring back to it, the first reads Αἰσώπου γέννα, ἀνατροφὴ, προκοπὴ, καὶ ἀποβίωσις and the second, Τὰ μετ' εὐκολίας εὑρισκόμενα καὶ εὐκαταφρόνητα πολλοῖς εἶναι δοκεῖ—which is apparently a philosophical comment, perhaps a quotation, by some earlier person upon the fictitious character of the preceding *Life of Aesop.* Turning to Pa, the first thing we read is (f. 155ʳ) Αἰσώπου γέννα· ἀνατροφὴ· προκοπὴ· ἀποβίωσις· ἔτι δὲ καὶ μῦθοι σοφοὶ καὶ ἐπιλύσεις αὐτῶν:[49]—We see that Pa misunderstood the subscript in G; he supposed that it was the title of what followed, that it looked forward instead of backward. Inadvertently, no doubt, he had begun with the wrong Αἰσώπου; but after copying the line and realizing that it said nothing about fables, he proceeded to make up the deficiency by adding ἔτι δὲ καὶ μῦθοι κτλ., thus awkwardly leaving the impression that the fables were some kind of appendix to a complete biography of Aesop—a biography which, however, he had omitted. It is clear that the long *Life of Aesop* stood in Pa's main source, because the words Αἰσώπου γέννα κτλ., which occur in no other known manuscripts of the *Aesopica,* can refer (as in G) only to the long *Life* and are in no way applicable to the Aphthonian *Preface* that follows after the

[49] After this a word has been erased, but I cannot make out what it was.

first fable. Having written down his title, Pa was next confronted, not with a biography nor with a fable, as one might expect, but with the strange sentence Τὰ μετ' εὐκολίας κτλ. Obviously something was wrong. Perhaps Pa suspected that this gnomic sentence was the epimythium of some lost fable which it would be desirable to restore; at any rate, I believe that at this point he began looking about for some fable whose meaning would approximate the thought in Τὰ μετ' εὐκολίας κτλ., and that he chose G's no. 10 for that purpose. The fable in question tells how the fox almost died of fright when she saw a lion for the first time, but upon the third meeting became so bold as to go all the way up and converse with him. The analogy between this fable and the *gnome* in G does not walk on all fours. Nevertheless, the words εὐκολίας and εὐκαταφρόνητα may very well have suggested to Pa the choice of this particular fable as being the most suitable thing he could find with which to match the apparently isolated epimythium in his archetype. In this way also we can account for the unique order of the fables in Pa, as will be seen presently. After he had copied out G's no. 10 as his first fable, Pa noticed that his title promised a biography of Aesop which was not forthcoming; whereupon, in order to make good his title, he added the short notice about Aesop which we have referred to as the Aphthonian *Preface*. We now see why the *Preface* in Pa comes after the first fable; it was due to an afterthought. The scribe began copying in the wrong place before he realized what he was doing. Having made a bad start and that too in what was intended to be an *edition de luxe*,[50] he could not erase but had to go ahead. The peculiar words Τὰ μετ' εὐκολίας...δοκεῖ distracted his attention from the meaning of the title for the time being only, but after he had copied in his first fable in response to that stimulus, he noticed the unfulfilled promise which he had unintentionally made in his title and proceeded to make up for it by inserting the *Preface*.

---

[50] "Scriptura autem est pulcherrima, atque epimythia litteris aureis efficta sunt"—Chambry.

THE FABLES

We cannot know where Pa got the *Preface*, nor does it matter much; but it is certain that he did not find it in the manuscript from which he began to copy, unless possibly in some other part of that manuscript, in which case it would have been decidedly out of place and as much open to the suspicion of having been later interpolated as it is in Pa.

The order of the fables in Pa differs from that in G and all the other manuscripts of Class I [51] principally in the first 42 entries, as follows:

Pa	G	Pa	G	Pa	G
1	= 10	8	= 27	24	= 17
2	9	9	32	25–29	22–26
3	16	10	42	29ª (i.e. 8 *bis*)	27
4	18	11–18	1–8	30–33	28–31
5–7	19–21	19–23	11–15	34–42	33–41
				43	43

This order is not so entirely arbitrary as it appears to be at first sight; rather it is due to the same kind of indecision on the part of the scribe that we have seen him display on the first page. He begins with fable no. 10 and follows it with no. 9, perhaps with the intention of setting down in reverse order the nine fables that he had so far omitted. But he changes his mind and skips to no. 16, making thereafter only a *selection* of the fables in G up to no. 42, which is the last of the fables beginning with A. At this point he again changes his mind and decides that, instead of merely excerpting his archetype, he will copy out *all* its fables; and so he proceeds to fill in, in regular order, all the gaps that he had left between 1 and 42. After copying no. 26 he should have skipped to 28, inasmuch as he had already excerpted no. 27 as his eighth fable; but, inadvertently, he went on with 27, thus writing down the same fable twice in almost exactly the same words.

At the earliest stage that we can trace in our manuscripts the Augustana collection of fables is introduced, not by a learned rhetorical preface, but by a thoroughly popular biography. This fact, if it means anything at all, means that the *Fables* have been transmitted from antiquity in company

[51] Except Ma, which is dependent in part upon the Pa tradition; see pp. 155, 164f., note 42.

with the *Life;* that both texts were intended for the general public; and that the former was no more the peculiar property or product of the rhetoricians than was the latter.[52]

There remain three other arguments by which Marc seeks to strengthen his theory that the Augustana recension comes from the rhetoricians. The first relates to the use of λόγος (= fable) in the epimythia, and of λογοποιός in the Aphthonian *Preface.* Marc (411) asserts that these are specifically rhetorical terms.[53] That is very misleading. In the old *Life,*

[52] Marc (415f.) believed that the long *Life,* which was known to him only in the Westermann recension, had been transmitted from antiquity in an environment totally independent of any body of fables, and that it was joined with the *Fables* for the first time in the archetype of the Class II ("Vindobonensis") recension, a corpus which, in contradistinction to the "rhetorical" Augustana and to the learned Accursiana, he arbitrarily designates *das Byzantinische Volksbuch.* This theory ignored the significant fact, known to both Marc and Hausrath, that in the lost Cryptoferratensis A 33 (= G) the long *Life* (of which the Westermann recension is merely a Byzantine edition) was accompanied by the Augustana fables, and that the Aphthonian *Preface* was absent. Class II, moreover, is no more *volkstümlich* than Class I (the Augustana); Marc considered it so merely because, being prepossessed by the idea that the Augustana was rhetorical and traditionally associated with Aphthonius, he regarded the presence of the popular *Life* in Class II as an exceptional and significant phenomenon. According to his view, Class II is a *Volksbuch* chiefly because it contains the *Life.* The fables of this corpus, in spite of the fact that they show very poor editing as compared with those of the Augustana, are no less and no more "rhetorical" than the latter.

[53] "Durch stilistische Beobachtungen, wie die folgende, könnte das rhetorische Element in der augustanischen Recensio wohl nachgewiesen werden: in ihren Epimythien wird die Fabel als λόγος und im Prooimion Äsop als λογοποιός bezeichnet, während in den andern, letzten Endes von Babrios abhängigen Redaktionen mit derselben Konsequenz μῦθος und μυθοποιός gebraucht werden; nun aber sind λόγος und λογοποιός die Termini gerade der Rhetoren, die das Lehrhafte der Fabeln dem Erzählerischen (μῦθος) gegenüber betonen." For proof of this statement we are referred to the passages cited by Grauert, *De Aesopo,* p. 86, and by Hausrath in Pauly-Wissowa VI, 1705; but the few passages there cited testify to nothing more than that λόγος is more congenial to prose writers than to poets, and that it has a certain rational meaning which is absent in μῦθος. As for λογοποιός, its mere presence in the old *Vita* shows that it is not an exclusively rhetorical term; but, as we have seen, the *Preface* in which Marc finds this word had nothing to do with the Augustana originally.

which Marc would certainly have considered a *Volksbuch*, since he applies that term to the West. *Life*, λόγος is employed almost exclusively, although μῦθος also occurs in a few such expressions as λόγων εὕρημα καὶ μύθων Ἑλληνικῶν πλοκήν, or τοὺς ἰδίους λόγους καὶ μύθους. The fable is also called λόγος by Herodotus, Aristophanes, Plato, Aristotle, Demetrius of Phalerum (*supra* p. 157), Plutarch in the *Banquet of the Seven Sages*, and, according to Theon's testimony, by ancient prose writers generally.[54] But not all prose writers are professional rhetoricians; and, as a matter of fact, the latter, including Theon, use μῦθος much more frequently than they do λόγος; so Hermogenes in Spengel II.3; Theon (*l.c.*); Nicolaus (III.451ff.); and Aphthonius (II.21), who explicitly labels each one of his forty fables a μῦθος.[55] As a rule these rhetoricians use the term λόγος in connection with the fable only when they are defining what they habitually call μῦθος. In the Aphthonian *Preface* the use of λόγος in the sense of 'fable' (once), along with μῦθος (thrice), may be intentionally antiquarian. μῦθος is also the favorite term with the poets, if we may judge by the remarks of Theon and by the use of this word in the epimythia of the metrical fables of Class II and of Babrius. So far as I can see, there are only two inferences that one might reasonably draw from the fact that λόγος is the regular word for fable in the Augustana recension: (1) that the fables were written in prose, as we already know; and (2) that the composition of their basic stock antedates the authors of *Progymnasmata* and reaches well back into Alexandrian times, when λόγος still survived as a common term for prose fables, as in Aristotle and Demetrius of Phalerum. In later times μῦθος became so common that it supplanted λόγος even in the title of the

[54] Spengel, *Rhetores Graeci* II, p. 73: προσαγορεύουσι δὲ αὐτοὺς τῶν μὲν παλαιῶν οἱ ποιηταὶ μᾶλλον αἴνους, οἱ δὲ μύθους. πλεονάζουσι δὲ μάλιστα οἱ καταλογάδην συγγεγραφότες τὸ λόγους ἀλλὰ μὴ μύθους καλεῖν, ὅθεν λέγουσι καὶ τὸν Αἴσωπον λογοποιόν. By συγγεγραφότες Theon may mean the compilers of prose fables such as Demetrius; in any case there is not the slightest reason to suppose that he refers to rhetoricians only.

[55] For the fables of Aphthonius, see the new edition by Fr. Sbordone in *Rivista Indo-Greco-Italica*, XVI (1932), 47–57.

Augustana. There can be little doubt that the use of λόγος in the *Life* dates back to the fifth century B.C., since each of the six fables that Aesop relates to the Delphians, in that oldest part of the biography, is explicitly called a λόγος, and λόγος is the term that Aristophanes uses in referring to one of the same fables, that of the eagle and the beetle, told under the same circumstances.[56] Indeed, Aristophanes uses λόγος several times in referring to Aesop's fables,[57] but never μῦθος. Now if λόγος in the *Life* has come down from early times without owing anything to rhetoric, why may not its use in the epimythia of the fables be due to an equally old and popular tradition? We do not know when epimythia were first attached to Aesopic fables. We find them in Phaedrus and Babrius (which, incidentally, invalidates Marc's second argument),[58] but their origin may be considerably earlier. In any case, it is probable enough that the use of λόγος in the epimythia was suggested by, if it did not come directly from, the popular tradition surviving in the *Life* and attested by the title of the collection edited by Demetrius of Phalerum.

Marc's last argument is also worthless. He says that the Augustana fables are never found in a *Volksbuch*, but are always accompanied in the manuscripts by texts of a learned or rhetorical character.[59] That is partially true of some rela-

---

[56] *Vespae*, 1446: Φι. Αἴσωπον οἱ Δελφοί ποτ'—Βδ. ὀλίγον μοι μέλει,
Φι. φιάλην ἐπῃτιῶντο κλέψαι τοῦ θεοῦ·
ὁ δ' ἔλεξεν αὐτοῖς, ὡς ὁ κάνθαρός ποτε...

Pax 129: ἐν τοῖσιν Αἰσώπου λόγοις ἐξηυρέθη
μόνος πετεινῶν ἐς θεοὺς ἀφιγμένος. (sc. ὁ κάνθαρος).

[57] Cf. *Vespae* 1258 and 1399; *Aves* 651.

[58] Namely, that epimythia *per se* are unquestionably rhetorical elements. Even if they are—which I doubt very much—their presence in the Augustana collection need mean no more than it does in Phaedrus or in Babrius; any editor, if not the authors themselves, may have added them. Phaedrus certainly writes his own epimythia as well as promythia, and, like the schoolboys, even draws more than one moral from the same fable; is he, therefore, a rhetorician, and his book a *Lehrbuch*?

[59] On page 412: "Auch die Umgebung, in der die Augustana in den Hss sich findet, spricht für ihren rhetorisch-gelehrten Charakter: sie begegnet niemals in einem Volksbuch und ebenso wenig in einer richtigen Klassikerhs;

tively late manuscripts, but it is much less true of those which we have seen to represent the earliest tradition. In G, which is the oldest of all our manuscripts, and whose contents were known to Marc as those of Cryptoferratensis A 33, the Augustana fables are accompanied by the *Life*, the *Physiologus*, fragments of *Kalilah and Dimnah*, Babrius, and the *Philogelos;* in Pa's archetype they were accompanied by the old *Life*, in Pg by a *Physiologus* and the Westermann *Life* along with various theological texts, and in Pd by Pseudo-Kallisthenes. True, the Augustana fables are often found in company with learned or semi-learned writings; but the contents of such manuscripts are usually so heterogeneous and their sources so diverse that no sound inference can be drawn with regard to the original environment and character of any one of their texts. Not only the Augustana but the Class-II recension as well, which Marc calls a *Volksbuch*, is often bound up with learned, especially theological, writings; such is the case in Baroccianus 194, Pal. 269, Vat. 695 and 1192, and Par. 2894. Likewise the Moscow codex (436), which Marc calls *ein reines Volksbuch* because it contains a series of popular texts, nevertheless includes besides these a wealth of theological, philosophical, historical, and scientific lore. In short, among all the known manuscripts containing *Aesopica*, there is only one that can be said to be a folk-book in any real sense, and that is the very one in which we find the Augustana fables for the first time, namely G. The later manuscripts have been affected by the learned and scholastic activity that became dominant in the eleventh and succeeding centuries.

sie ist vielmehr inmitten von poetischen, theologischen, rhetorischen, grammatischen, historischen (darunter die Πάτρια Κπόλεως) und juristischen Stücken byzantinischer Provenienz überliefert, mehrfach in nächster Nachbarschaft der Fabeln des Aphthonios und der Tetrasticha des Ignatios; von klassischen Texten pflegen diese Hss nur rhetorisches und paränetisches Gut zu enthalten."

3. MONACENSIS 525 AND CLASS II

a. The manuscript tradition of the Westermann *Life* and the identity of Class II in the *Fables* with a branch thereof (i.e. with the SBP, or *B* group). Remarks upon the individual manuscripts of Class II

The old *Life*, which is extant only in G, and which had presumably been transmitted from antiquity in company with the Augustana fables, was probably a rare book even as early as the thirteenth century; for, with one exception,[1] Pa in the twelfth century is the last scribe who shows any acquaintance with it. Thereafter the copyists of Augustana fables either omitted the *Life* entirely or, following the example of Pa, they substituted the Aphthonian *Preface*. Thus the *Life* passed entirely out of the Augustana tradition. But it did not perish entirely; sometime previous to the thirteenth century, probably as early as the eleventh, it was, as we have seen (p. 26), recast into a new and syncopated form typified by the Westermann text; and this new form of the *Life* was henceforth accompanied by a new recension of the *Fables*, that of Class II, which was likewise derived in large part from the Augustana. It is natural to suppose that both of these new recensions came from the hand of the same redactor, or at any rate, that they originated at the same time and place, since the manuscript tradition of the Westermann *Life* is identical in its main outlines with that of the *Fables* of Class II. In order to make this point clear and to show what light the tradition of the *Life* throws upon that of the *Fables*, it will be necessary to summarize the results of my study of the manuscripts of the Westermann recension. In the stemma given below I have made use of Chambry's symbols in so far as his list of manuscripts corresponds with those of the Westermann *Life;* the symbols for manuscripts not appearing in Chambry are Marc's and my own. The manuscripts are:

---

[1] Aesop's sermon to Ainos as given in Vind. theol. gr. 128 (14th cent.) is an isolated excerpt from the old *Life*.

The Fables

Group A

M Monacensis graecus 525, *s.* xiv. Contains both *Life* and *Fables*.
O Baroccianus 194 (Bodleian Library), *s.* xv. This ends in the passage corresponding to p. 44, line 24 of Westermann's text. It has no fables.
R Vaticanus gr. 1192 (ff. 189^r–198^v), *s.* xiv, a fragment supplementing O and Lo and containing no fables.
Par Parisinus gr. 2894, *s.* xiii. This is a fragment consisting of one leaf only.
Lo Lollinianus 26 (Belluno), *s.* xiv, in Latin. This manuscript, which contains no fables, leaves off at the same point in the *Vita* at which R begins; it is probably a translation of the first part of R (*Text Tradition* 201).

Group B
(designated SBP in Part I)

Cb(P) Vat. Palatinus gr. 269, *s.* xv. *Life* and *Fables*.
Cf(B) British Museum, Add. 17015, *s.* xv. *Life* and *Fables*.
S Mosquensis 436, *s.* xiv (*olim* 285 and 298, a double codex). Besides the *Life* this manuscript contains fables not seen by Chambry, for a brief account of which see Urban Ursing, *Studien zur griech. Fabel*, Lund 1930, pp. 1–6.
Pl The vulgate *Life* belonging to the Accursiana recension and ascribed to Maximus Planudes.
Rin The Latin version of the *Vita* and *Fabulae* by Rinuccio da Castiglioni. See *Class. Phil.* xxix (1934), 53–62.

Mixed Group

Ca(W) Laurentianus conv. soppr. 627, *s.* xiii. *Life* and *Fables*.
H Holkham 278; see p. 71, note 1. This is a copy of Ca.
L Leidensis vulc. 93, *s.* xv. *Life* and *Fables*.
Mc (F) Laur. 57.30, *s.* xvi. This is probably a copy of L; the differences between the two in the *Life* are few and minute.
Pg (V) Vat. gr. 695, *s.* xv. This is the only manuscript in which the Westermann *Life* is accompanied by fables belonging to Class I.
λ Lost archetype of LMcPg (LFV).

176   THE LIFE AND FABLES OF AESOP

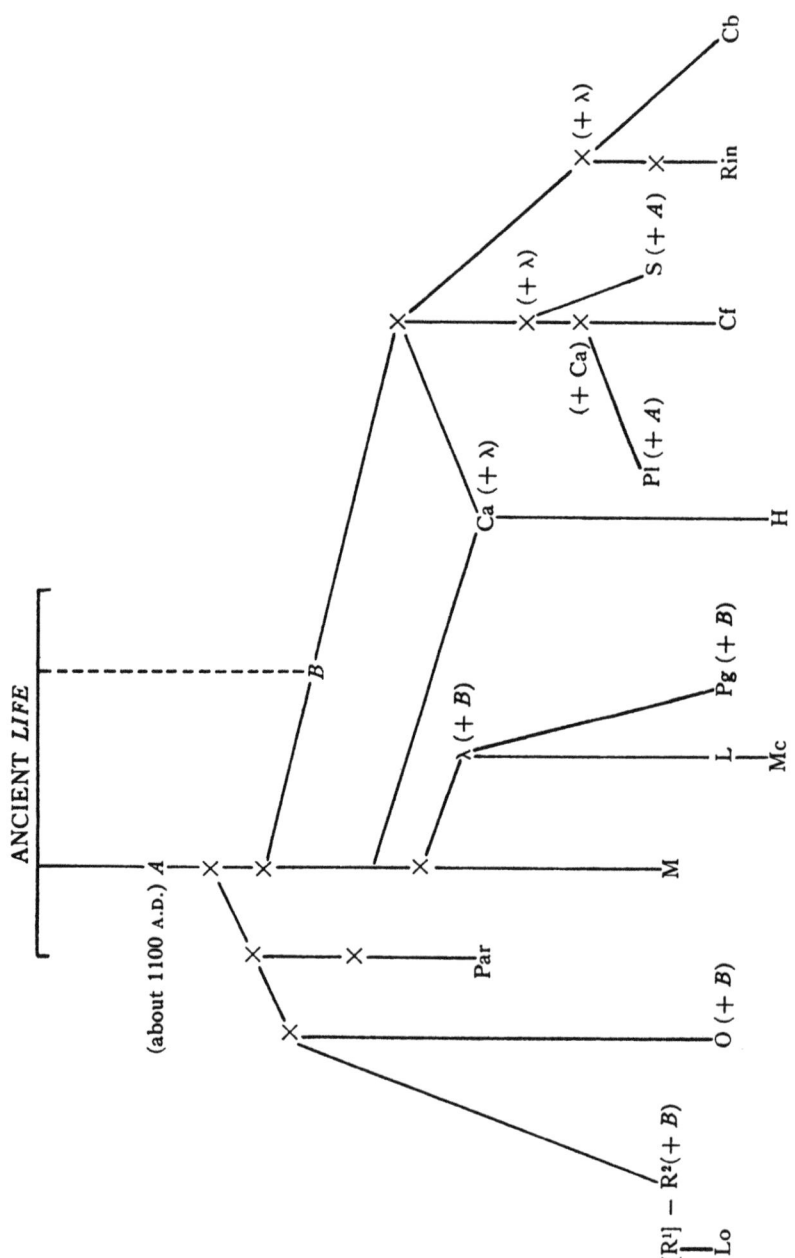

Classified according to the great majority of their readings throughout, these manuscripts fall into two principal groups, which I have here labeled A and B for the sake of convenience in reference. B (the archetype of SBP) comes from an imperfect copy of A and has been slightly rewritten. It has also interpolated three episodes and a number of smaller readings from an ancient version of the *Life* similar to G and belonging to Class I; cf. *Text Tradition* 226–230 and *supra* pp. 29–31. The other texts, Ca and λ with their descendants, are compounds painstakingly put together in almost equal proportions of A and B; they make, however, a few insignificant verbal additions and alterations of their own. With the partial exception of M, all the principal manuscripts have been crossed in some degree with others of a different family, especially near the beginning. In the diagram on p. 176 these crossings are indicated by plus marks (+), except that the partial indebtedness of B to an ancient version of the *Life* is shown by a dotted line. [R[1]] refers to the lost part of R, which has been translated by Lo, and R[2] to the part that is extant in Greek.

Before entering upon a discussion of the larger aspects of this stemma, and especially of the significant relation between the groups A and B, I wish to make a few observations upon the individual manuscripts belonging to Class II.

In Chambry's list there are five manuscripts (Cc, Cd, Ce, Cg, and Ch) which do not appear above because they do not contain the *Life*. Four of them indeed do not have any biographical notice at all, while Cd has an interpolated version (see p. 163, note 38) of the short preface printed by Eberhard as *Vita III*. This *Vita III* is, as Marc says, merely an abbreviated and somewhat altered version of the Aphthonian *Preface;* and I may add that it must have originated in, and is probably peculiar to, the family of manuscripts that I call λ.[2]

[2] The earliest trace of this text is in Ca, where the first line of it is taken over, along with various other readings in the Westermann *Life*, from λ. The entire text is found in L, Mc, Cb, Par. gr. 2902 (*s.* xv), Mon. gr. 551 (*s.* xv), Upsaliensis 8 (*s.* xv), and a 16th-century MS at Salamanca (see

Cd is therefore indebted to some manuscript of the λ family, whether directly or indirectly, and the same is true of the Cambridge manuscript no. 1408 (see p. 71, note 1) which has the same peculiar form of *Vita III*. But the kinship of Cd with the λ family as represented by LMc is not confined to the biographical preface; it is also apparent throughout the text of the *Fables*, where its readings very frequently stand alone with those of LMcCb plus one or two of the mixed manuscripts, usually Mk.[3] The agreement of Cd with Cb in Graux et Martin, *Notices Sommaires des MSS grecs d'Espagne et de Portugal*, Paris 1892). In Cb it is merely one of the numerous borrowings of that MS from the λ family. Concerning the relationships of the three MSS last mentioned, I have no knowledge, but they are all relatively late and there is no reason to suppose that their tradition antedates λ. The text of the preface in Mon. gr. 551 collated by Eberhard, and in Par. 2902 collated by myself, are both inferior on the whole to that of LMc, and in some respects apparently later. Moreover Par. 2902 (= Mk) very clearly shows kinship with λ (i.e. L and Mc) in the *Fables*, as anyone may see who cares to look up the references given below in note 3. Marc, however (415), observing that this preface was found in a few MSS of Class II, without any further consideration of the manuscript tradition, concluded that it belonged in the archetype of the recension, and that its creation on the basis of the Aphthonian *Preface* was coincident with the revision of the Augustana prose fables by the original redactor of Class II. I am convinced, however, that *Vita III* originated in λ. In the first place, it is absent in all the better-known representatives of Class II except those particular MSS which have elsewhere drawn on λ; secondly, there is no trace of it in the *A* group which antedates λ, nor in SCf, which in this case, owing to the contamination in Cb, is the best witness to the archetype of the *B* group also; and finally, λ is just the kind of scribe who would make an innovation of this sort, since his whole text of the Westermann *Life* is conflated and inanely altered on the basis of *A* and *B*. The motive for changing some of the statements about Aesop found in the Aphthonian *Preface* was no doubt to bring them into line with the substance of the Westermann *Life*, as Marc observes; but this motive is as much to be expected from λ as from the author of the archetype. Believing that the prose fables of Class II had been modeled directly upon those of the Augustana, Marc evidently wished to trace a parallel evolution in the *Vitae*, and for that purpose erroneously chose the Aphthonian *Preface* as original with the Augustana recension and *Vita III* as its successor in the archetype of Class II. The real parallelism is quite different and more complex; see pp. 229f.

[3] For CbCd alone in agreement with L or Mc or both, see for example Chambry's apparatus in no. 4, line 10; 12,1; 13,2; 13,12; 23,5; 34,5; 38,13;

numerous readings taken from LMc, together with the fact that Cd and Cb are often unique by themselves, seems to indicate that these two manuscripts come, in large part at least, from a common source,[4] and that that source was already contaminated with LMc. Cd represents a peculiar recension in that it contains 28 original versifications, 11 or more fables taken from Class I, probably from either λ or Pg, and the curiously and stupidly interpolated version of *Vita III* which appears elsewhere only in the Cambridge manuscript. The latter's textual agreement with Cd, in so far as I have been able to test it, is almost absolute except for additional errors in orthography; but it is unlikely that either of the two is the archetype of its kind, since both have many corruptions in common which appear to be due to carelessness in copying or to misunderstanding of the original text. The Cambridge manuscript contains only about half as many fables as Cd, and for reasons that need not be described here, I am inclined to believe that it was copied from the latter rather than from a source common to both. The complex relationships here described are shown in the diagram on p. 180, which I believe to be correct in outline, although it involves a few uncertainties centering about the immediate source of Cd. Concerning LMc's independence of λ in the *Fables*, see below p. 184; for Ca's relation to λ, p. 182.

Although Cd does not contain the Westermann *Life*, it nevertheless stands in very close relation to manuscripts of the

41,5; 61,10; 66,15; 83,7; 87,12, 14–15 and 17; 103,9; 115,12; 163,12; 179,1 and 12; etc. For the same MSS standing alone with Mk (= Par. 2902): 23,1; 30,4; 31,2; 66,10; 103,8 and 11; 115,2; 179,3 and 21 (+ Lf); etc. There are a few instances in which Cd stands alone in agreement with LMcMk but these are not numerous. Cb's indebtedness to LMc appears to be more extensive in the *Fables* than in the *Life*. Chambry does not cite L, but its readings, with a few exceptions, are the same as those of Mc; see below p. 183.

[4] For Cd alone in agreement with Cb, see Chambry 35,4–5; 43,4; 55,7; 87,3, 16, 17 and 19. The close kinship between Cd and Cb is further evidenced by the omission of certain fables in both, and by the order of nos. 19, 25, and 22; see Table VII.

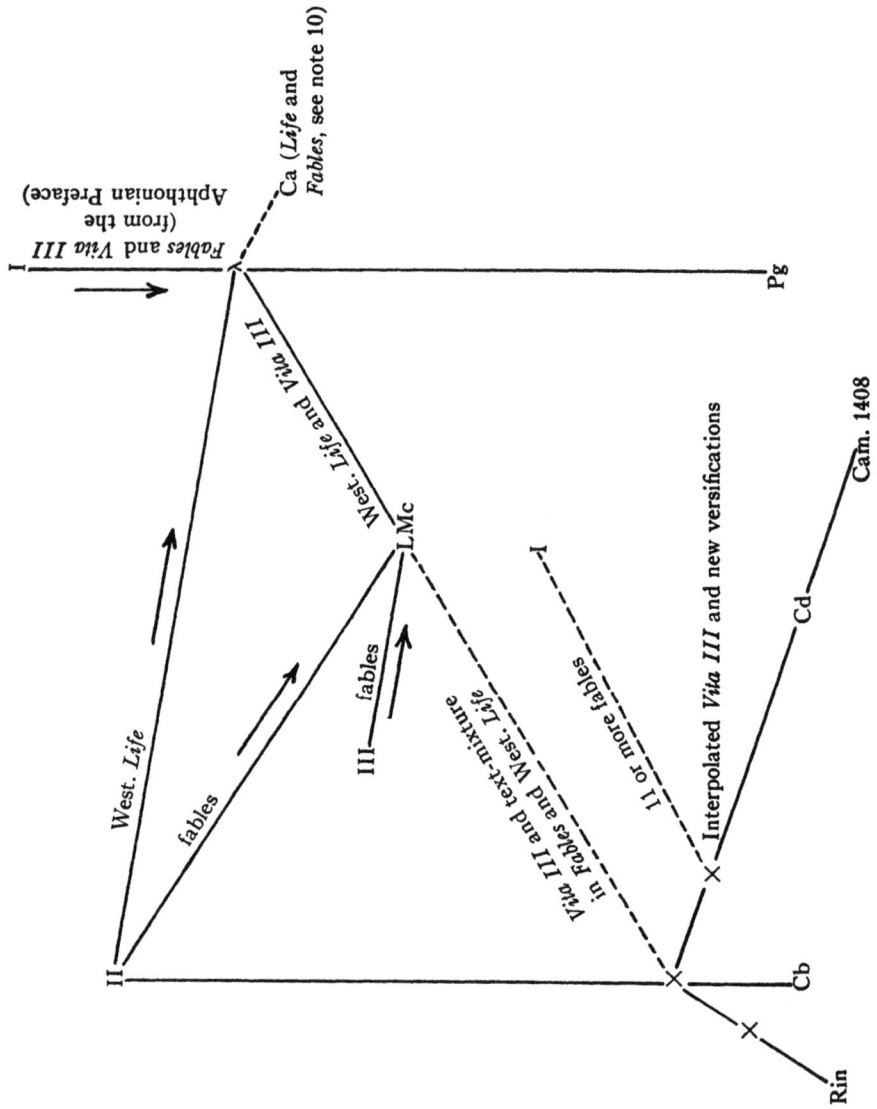

B group that do contain it; and that is true also of all the other manuscripts of Class II.

Ce is especially close to Cf and is no doubt derived in large part from a common ancestor.[5] Cg and Ch sometimes stand by themselves,[6] but whatever their precise interrelationships may be, their constant agreement with Cb, Cf, and the other manuscripts of Class II, against M, leaves no doubt that their tradition lies entirely within the B family of manuscripts indicated above in the stemma of the *Life*. This touches upon an important point that will claim our attention later on. Cc contains only 30 fables that sometimes show a close affinity to Ca,[7] but in general what has been said of Cg and Ch is true likewise of this manuscript. As in the *Life*, so in the *Fables*, Cf has been crossed to a slight extent with Ca,[8] although some of this crossing must have taken place in one of the immediate ancestors of Cf, inasmuch as the borrowings from Ca are also in part reflected by Planudes in the *Life* and by Ce in the *Fables*.

Ca, which Chambry treats as the *chef de file* for Class II, is almost the worst manuscript he could have chosen for that purpose. Not only are its contents mixed, in the sense that

[5] *Cf.* Chambry, p. 11, and nos. 81, 235, 244, 298, 301, 310, 314, 317, 345, and 352, in all of which Ce and Cf have so many variants peculiar to themselves that their text in each case is printed by Chambry apart from the others as a separate version. But these are only the more conspicuous points of agreement between Ce and Cf; as a matter of fact their close kinship is apparent throughout the *Fables*. The archetype of these MSS has drawn on Class I also (see Table VII below) and upon Ca (see note 8).

[6] E.g. in the fables numbered by Chambry 250, 261, 269, 284, 297, 301, and 253. Cg has only 41 fables.

[7] See for example nos. 61, 63, 142, and 179 in Chambry.

[8] See Chambry, no. 336 (p. 534) where Cf and Ca, the former fragmentary, are alone with Pg and Ma; and nos. 343 and 348, where Ca, Ce, and Cf are the only MSS in Class II that contain Ὗς καὶ κύων and Χελιδὼν καὶ δράκων respectively. The same situation, namely, Cf and Ce alone in Class II with Ca, is also to be noted in no. 101 (p. 202, top) and in no. 322. Chambry says that in no. 235 Cf is contaminated from Ce and Ca, but I cannot find any justification for that statement in his apparatus. The crossing of Cf to Ca in the *Life*, likewise toward the end, is also clearly revealed; see *Text Tradition*, 235.

some of the fables come from the Augustana recension and others from Class II, but the text of the individual fables, more often than not, is either compounded out of Classes I and II, or arbitrarily altered to suit the fancy of Ca himself. The prose fables of Class II had already been rewritten on the basis of Class I (Augustana), and Ca contaminates the text of these once more with phraseology taken from the original Augustana.[9] Moreover his fables from Class I can be traced to two different sources: a manuscript closely akin to Pa, if not Pa itself (see p. 164, note 42) and λ.[10] Since Ca draws upon *A* in the *Life*, it is natural to suppose that he has done so likewise in the *Fables;* but the traces of such borrowing are so meager that it may be doubted whether or not it has actually taken place. The various sources of Ca are represented graphically in the accompanying figure.

[9] The following statement by Marc (416f.) is true in every respect and could be abundantly illustrated from Chambry's edition: "Da auch die Volksbuchfabeln (those of Class II), wie gezeigt, aus versifizierten babrianischen und aus vulgarisierten augustanischen sich zusammensetzen, so ist das Durcheinander in der Fabelsammlung des Casinensis das denkbar verwirrendste: reine augustanische zwischen Versfabeln und überarbeiteten augustanischen. Aber der Kompilator hat sich damit noch nicht begnügt, sondern seine Volksbuchfabeln selbst noch aus den augustanischen interpoliert, bald durch Ergänzungen, bald durch leise Änderungen, bald durch grobe Eingriffe: also überarbeitete augustanische Fabeln aus rein-augustanischen interpoliert!"

[10] For Ca's indebtedness to λ in the *Life*, see *Text Tradition*, 219–221, where I use the symbol W for Chambry's Ca. In the *Fables*, Ca's use of λ is betrayed by the presence of numerous readings occurring elsewhere only in Pg, which is here the sole representative of λ (see p. 184), or in Pg and Mb. For noteworthy readings peculiar to Pg and Ca, see Chambry's apparatus on no. 96, line 1; 192,2; 258,4; 82,1,2,4 (*bis*) and 7; 14,4; 84,6; 89,11; 282,8. For Ca alone with Pg and Mb, 95,4 and 5; 108,2 and 3; 132,2; 205,5,7 and 8; 215,8 and 9; 252,2 and 7; 258,7; 267,1,2 and 3; 302,4 and 5. In no. 336 (p. 534, bottom) Ca has a peculiar version of the fable about the ant and the grasshopper that is found elsewhere only in Pg, Ma, and Cf; the latter, which breaks off near the beginning, comes from Ca (see note 8) and Ma disagrees with PgCa eight times in twelve lines. If Ca's sources in Class I were confined to Pa (or one of its near kin) and to λ, we can the more readily understand why he shows no familiarity with the ancient *Life* in spite of the fact that he interpolates abundantly from various other *Vitae* and from the parallel (Class I) edition of the *Fables;* for neither Pa nor λ contained the ancient (Class I) version of the *Life*.

THE FABLES

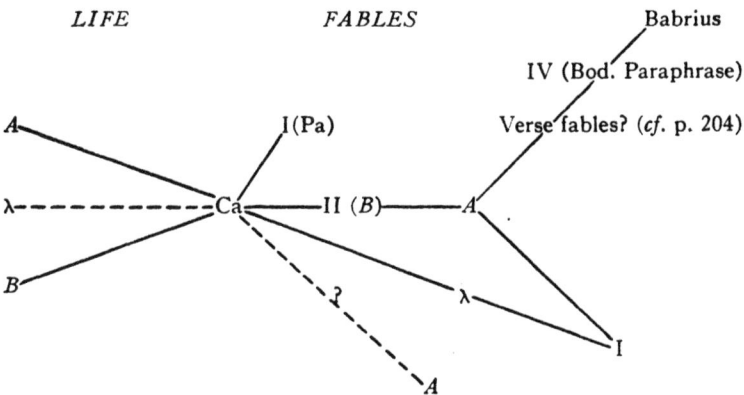

The archetype of the λ family is represented in the *Fables* only by Pg; while L and Mc, which follow λ in the West. *Life* and *Vita III*, have substituted an entirely new and later collection. Mc's readings are reported by Chambry, but L has apparently never been used by the editors of Aesop, although Eberhard collated the text of its *Vita III*. I have compared L's text throughout with Chambry's apparatus and have found it to be extremely close to Mc. The two manuscripts have a very large number of variant readings and errors peculiar to themselves or shared with a few other manuscripts of the mixed group, especially Mk (see note 3), and the order and identity of the fables in both is the same with only a few exceptions.[11] In L, 78 of the fables belong to

[11] I am unable to discover from Chambry's edition the identity of nos. 41, 87, and 101 in Mc, but otherwise the correspondence is as follows:

L	Mc	L	Mc
1–2	1–2	45	41?
3	—	46–86	42–82
4–37	3–36	87	83?
38–40	—	88–104	84–100
41–44	37–40	105	101?

The agreement between these two MSS is so close that one must infer either that Mc was copied from the immediate parent of L or else that Mc copied from L and made some emendations and alterations of his own, perhaps with the aid of other texts. The latter hypothesis is in my opinion much the more probable in view of the situation in the *Life; cf. Text Tradition* 218.

Class II, 26 to Class III (Accursiana), and 1 to Class IV (Bodleian paraphrase). The fables from Class III do not come in a separate series at the end, as if they had been added later, but are scattered about singly or in small groups among the others. There is also, in two cases at least, mixture of II and III within the limits of a single fable,[12] although such mixture is apparently quite rare. From these facts we may reasonably infer, I think, that the Accursiana fables in LMc owe their presence in the collection to the original compiler of the archetype of LMc (which may have been L itself), and that this archetype must therefore be later than that of the Accursiana recension. Since the Accursiana was probably not in existence before the 14th century (see p. 208), and since λ antedates the 13th-century manuscript, Ca, it is clear that, unlike the *Life*, the fables in LMc do not go back to λ. On the other hand, there is every reason to believe that the Augustana fables contained in Pg come from the same source as its text of the Westermann *Life* and *Vita III*, that is, from λ. Likewise the presence of *Vita III* in λ (see note 2) is an indication that λ's fables belonged to the Augustana, since the Aphthonian *Preface*, upon which it is based, is confined to certain manuscripts of that recension. Moreover, as we have seen, Ca, which dates from the 13th century, shows the influence of λ as represented by Pg in the *Fables*, as well as in the Westermann *Life*. The unique combination of Augustana fables with the Westermann *Life* in λ is quite in character when we consider the elaborate mixing of *A* and *B* in λ's *Life*. The method of compilation displayed is the same that confronts us in Ca, and it is not unlikely that the two texts, λ and Ca, were the products of approximately the same time and place, perhaps southern Italy or Sicily in the middle or the early part of the 13th century.

[12] See Chambry, nos. 40,4 (p. 102) and 248,1, in both of which passages Mc's readings are the same as those of L.

b. The dependence of *B* upon *A* in the *Life* indicates a similar relationship in the *Fables*

Up to this point we have been dealing with individual manuscripts of the fables in Class II, all of which are seen to belong to the same family and to be intimately related either to those of the *B* group in the *Life*, or to the mixed texts Ca and LMc, while none of them individually shows any direct kinship with the *A* group represented by M. Now this identity of Class II with *B* suggests very forcibly, when considered in the light of the tradition in the *Life*, where *B* depends much more on *A* than on I, that the fables of Class II in the main do not come directly from the Augustana and from an unknown collection of twelve-syllable verse fables, as has hitherto been supposed, but from an *intermediate recension corresponding to* A *in the* Life *and preserved only in* M *and, to some extent at least, in* S.[13] A comparison of the text of M with that of Class II will bear this out and will tend to show that the relationship between the two recensions is in fact the same in the *Fables* as in the *Life*. But before making this comparison, there are some important considerations of a more general nature to be mentioned which point to the same conclusion, and which indeed are more convincing than the textual evidence itself; it will be necessary also to give some account of the contents of M and of its relation to S, since neither manuscript, so far as I know, has ever been used by the editors of Aesop.

c. The antiquity of the *A* tradition in M and S. The probable eastern origin of the various texts peculiar to this tradition. The fables of Pseudo-Syntipas in relation to the archetype of the *A* recension

In the *Life*, S is frequently indebted to one of the direct ancestors of M, although his text comes mainly from *B*. That, however, is only one of the significant points of contact between S and M; their close kinship is further revealed by

---

[13] See below, pp. 191ff.

the series of peculiar texts which they have in common.[14] They are the only manuscripts known to contain the κοσμικαὶ κωμῳδίαι ascribed to Aesop;[15] and the four texts, *Life* and *Fables* of Aesop, *Cosmic Comedies*, and the *Fables* of Syntipas, all come in the same order in both, as in no other codex. Moreover, both manuscripts contain *Stephanites and Ichnelates* and the *Book of Syntipas* (i.e. *The Seven Wise Masters*), the latter in a recension which is *older* than the vulgate *Retractatio* and which is known to be extant elsewhere only in cod. Vat. 335, where the variant readings stand regularly opposed to the consensus of SM,[16] and in an unexplored manuscript at Strassburg (no. 5) mentioned by Krumbacher in his *Geschichte der Byzantinischen Litteratur*[2] 893. The one manuscript of Class II that contains this text, namely Cd, has it in the later version (*Retractatio*). Puntoni did not use either S or M in editing the *Stephanites;* hence it still remains to be seen whether or not we have there also, as in *Syntipas* and in the *Life of Aesop*, a recension older than that represented by the majority of manuscripts.[17] It is an interesting fact sug-

[14] *Cf.* Krumbacher, "Die Moskauer Sammlung mittelgriechischer Sprichwörter," in *Sitzb. d. bayer. Akad.*, Phil.-Hist. Classe (1900), 382–3. In summing up, Krumbacher remarks: "Die Aehnlichkeit ist so gross, dass man sogar einen engeren verwandtschaftlichen Zusammenhang des zweiten Teiles des Mosq. 298 (ff. 351–576) mit dem Monac. 525 annehmen muss."

[15] These and kindred texts are discussed in the Appendix, p. 231.

[16] See the edition of the *Liber Syntipae* by Jernstedt, in *Mémoires de l'Acad. impériale des Sciences de St. Pétersbourg* XI (1912), especially pp. *iii* and *iv–ix* of the *Praefatio*. To the three manuscripts of the *Retractatio* mentioned by Jernstedt must be added cod. Marcianus 605 (Krumbacher, *Byz. Lit.*[2] 893) and the manuscript at Urbana described by W. A. Oldfather and M. Madden in *Speculum* II (1927), 473–475. Apparently no one knows whether cod. Harleianus 5560 (Krumbacher *l.c.*) belongs to the older version or to the *Retractatio*. The *Liber Syntipae* is found also in Vind. 166 (*s.* XVI); and since it is there accompanied by *Stephanites* (8 chapters) and the fables of Pseudo-Syntipas, we may surmise that it comes directly from S or M, probably S. Cod. Sinaiticus 1208 (*s.* XV) also has some excerpts from the *Seven Wise Masters*, according to V. Gardthausen, *Catalogus Codicum Gr. Sinaiticorum* 253.

[17] For Puntoni's edition of *Stephanites and Ichnelates* see *Pubblicazioni della Società Asiatica Italiana*, vol. II, Firenze, 1889. M contains only the first five of the fifteen chapters.

gestive of the relative antiquity of the texts found in M and S that the former was written in the 14th century by a native of Trebizond [18] and contains, like S, the oldest known Greek version of *Syntipas*, and that the latter (S) is the only manuscript of *Syntipas* that preserves the prefatory verses of Michael Andreopulus,[19] who translated this book from the Syriac and lived near Melitene, some 200 miles south of Trebizond toward the end of the 11th century. In other words, we have in M and S a tradition that is more definitely and more directly associated with the time and place in which *Syntipas* was first translated into Greek than is to be found elsewhere. And what about the fables ascribed to the philosopher Syntipas? No one supposes that these have been translated from an oriental tongue; on the contrary, they are manifestly and by common consent a purely Byzantine creation, partially indebted, though indirectly, to Babrius as well as to other Greek sources known and unknown.[20] And yet the manuscript tradition of these pseudonymous fables is to all appearances just as old and just as peculiar to M and S [21] as is that of the oriental *Syntipas*, the *Life of Aesop*, and

[18] Namely, the geographer Andreas Libadenus, whose signature appears on the manuscript; see Krumbacher "Die Moskauer Sammlung," p. 382, and *Byz. Lit.*² p. 422. S was brought to Moscow in the 17th century from the (once Georgian) monastery Iveron on Mt. Athos.

[19] See Jernstedt, *op. cit.* p. 3 and Eberhard's Teubner text, *Fabulae Romanenses Graece Conscriptae*, Leipzig 1872, p. viii; both are indebted to D. Comparetti's *Ricerche intorno al libro di Sindibād* (Milan 1869).

[20] See Crusius' edition of Babrius p. *xxi*; Hausrath, *s.v.* "Syntipas" in Pauly-Wissowa IV.A2, 1470.

[21] I know of only three other MSS that contain the fables ascribed to Syntipas, but all of them are later than M and S, and only one of them (Vind. 166) includes the genuine *Syntipas;* Marcianus x.9 (see p. 72, note 1) is of the 15th century and, as I recall, has only a few excerpts; Athous 1025 is also of the 15th century, and Vind. 166 is of the 16th. Hausrath in his article on Syntipas mentions Vind. 152; but that, I suppose, is only a mistake for Vind. 166, since the fables in the latter manuscript begin on fol. 152 and Hausrath makes no mention of Vind. 166. The Moscow manuscript, which combines two different codices, one of the 15th century (fols. 1–350) and one of the 14th (351–576), contains the fables of Syntipas in both parts.

the *Cosmic Comedies;* and their vogue in Asia Minor and the East is well attested by the fact that they have been taken over into the Arabic collection ascribed to Lokman and into the Aramaic of the so-called Sophos.[22] In short, it would appear that this whole group of texts, copied down by Andreas Libadenos at Trebizond in the 14th century, had its origin in eastern Asia Minor near the end of the 11th century;[23] and that the "Fables of Syntipas," created amid the same scholastic activity that brought forth the Westermann version of the *Life* (*A* branch) and the fables of M, were ascribed to Syntipas, not by an arbitrary choice or by accident, but owing to the immediate presence and popularity of the genuine *Syntipas* among the books of that time and in that part of the world. The man who sought to win fame or general acceptance for his own collection of Greek fables by ascribing them to the famous oriental philosopher Syntipas was probably someone engaged in editing or copying both the Aesopic fables and the oriental *Syntipas*. And indeed the similarity in

[22] For a brief account of these oriental collections see the able monograph on the history of the Aesopic fables by O. Keller in *N. Jahrb. f. Phil. und Paed.*, Supp. IV (1861–67), 328–332; Crusius, *Babrii Fabulae xxii*; and the references given by Krumbacher, *Gesch. d. Byz. Lit.*² 895.

[23] The stemma of the *Life of Aesop*, as well as the translations of the *Syntipas* and of *Stephanites and Ichnelates* (ca. 1080 A.D.), points to that date. There is also some reason to believe that the Αἰσώπου λόγοι (see Appendix) and the somewhat later gnomologion of Georgides come from approximately the same region. For, apart from the kinships described in the Appendix, the former text, unique as it is, was brought to Moscow from the Vatopedi monastery on Mt. Athos, whose near neighbors at least, the monks of Iveron and the Grand Laura, had close connections in the early days with Georgia and Trebizond: Iveron (from which, incidentally, S comes) was settled by a colony of Georgians (Iberians) in the latter part of the tenth century under the leadership of John Tornikios who, being called away from Athos shortly after his arrival there, had afterwards returned laden with the spoils of his conquests against the rebel Phokas in Armenia and Georgia; and the Great Laura was founded in 963 by Athanasius of Trebizond. As for Georgides, one of the best of the four eleventh century manuscripts containing his gnomologion, namely Par. suppl. 1246, was brought from somewhere in the Levant by Minoides Menas in the middle of the last century.

terminology between the title of the Syntipas-fables and that of both the *Life* and the *Fables* of Aesop suggests quite plainly that the same author or redactor was responsible for all three texts. The title of the fables ascribed to Syntipas in M and S is Συντίπα τοῦ φιλοσόφου, ἐκ τῶν παραδειγματικῶν αὐτοῦ λόγων; of the *Life of Aesop*, Βίος Αἰσώπου τοῦ φιλοσόφου;[24] and of the fables in M, Μῦθοι Αἰσώπου σοφιστοῦ καὶ λογομυθοποιοῦ, μεταπεποιημένοι μὲν ὡς ἐν παραδείγμασιν· ὀνησιμώτατοι δὲ τῷ ἀνθρωπείῳ βίῳ τὰ μάλιστα (Plate V). The application of the words φιλόσοφος and παραδείγματα to Aesop and his fables is very unusual, if not altogether unique, and I know of no other manuscript in which they recur.[25] Accordingly, in the absence of any evidence to the contrary, one can scarcely avoid the conclusion that all three titles were invented by the original redactor of these texts, who thought of Aesop as a "philosopher" after the analogy of Syntipas and of the Indian author of *Stephanites*, and chose to describe the fables as παραδείγματα in both cases. Further evidence that both collections of fables (Pseudo-Syntipas and Aesop) were edited, not merely copied, by the same man may be seen in the very peculiar style of epimythium, Οὗτος δηλοῖ or simply Δηλοῖ, which is found in both collections and nowhere else, and which was probably due to the redactor's uncertainty whether a particular fable should be called λόγος or μῦθος, since he, the original compiler of the M recension, had drawn from two earlier collections one of which used λόγος and the other μῦθος.[26]

At a later period and farther west the Trapezuntian or

[24] No title is given in O.

[25] We probably have a reminiscence of these words in the Latin version of the *Vita* from Belluno (Lo), the first line of which reads as follows: *Incipit vita vel acta qualiter Esopus nomine gessit, eo quod omnia in parabolis posita sunt acta illius quia amator sapientie fuit*. As noted above, Lo belongs to the A group entirely, and it has an older text of the *Life* than M itself; cf. *Text Tradition* 222–226, and the stemma given above, p. 176. Terms equivalent to φιλόσοφος and παραδειγματικοὶ λόγοι are also frequent in the introduction to *Stephanites and Ichnelates* (Puntoni v–vi).

[26] See pp. 194f. In the fables of Syntipas, Vind. 166 and M have the bare Οὗτος δηλοῖ. S (in the later text, fols. 232ff.) adds μῦθος.

Asiatic recensions,[27] so to speak, fell into neglect, being supplanted in other centers of learning by other recensions derived from them; Class II of the *Life* and *Fables* of Aesop eclipsed in popularity the older *A* recension, and the *Syntipas* of Andreopulus was succeeded by the *Retractatio*. This may account for the rarity of the texts contained in M and S. We may now turn our attention to the fables in these manuscripts.

d. Description of the fables in M and S

The leaves of M had evidently become loose and misarranged and some of them lost before they were given their present numbers, since this numbering is not consecutive with the text, either in the *Life* or in the *Fables*, and the latter

[27] It is a curious coincidence, which may or may not be significant, that Minoides Menas found, or claimed to have found, in a monastery near Trebizond, a fragmentary manuscript containing the following, apparently unique, metrical fable:

Ἵππος διαύλων ἅμ' ὄνῳ καὶ νικήσας
Οὐκ ἔσχε δόξαν, αἰσχύνην δέ γε πλείω
Ὡς ἀμιλληθεὶς ἀφανωτέρῳ ζῴῳ.
Οὕνας (sic) δὲ τοῦτον παρελὼν ἐθαυμάσθη
Ὡς ὑπερισχύοντι συνδραμὼν ζῴῳ.
Οὕτω τι θαῦμα οὐδὲν εἴπερ νικήσει
Ὑπέρβιός τις τὸν πένητ' ἢ δυνάστης·
Ἡνίκα πένης δὲ τὸν δυνάστην νικήσει
Θαυμαστὸν ὄντως τοῦτο καὶ θείας μοίρας.

For this announcement we are indebted to Boissonade (*Pachymeris Declamationes XIII*, Paris 1848, 317) who says that Menas sent him a transcript of this fable in the year 1844 and that he, Menas, had found another version of it (also printed by Boissonade) on a torn and isolated leaf of the same manuscript. One fears that Menas found too much; and it is well known that he was capable of forging documents of this kind, as well as of discovering really new and valuable manuscripts. The fable in question is stylistically quite unworthy of Babrius and too definitely choliambic to be typical of the Byzantine 12-syllable verse fables which appear in M and Class II. It is not impossible, however, that this fable is a genuine relic surviving from a lost collection of metrical fables imitative of Babrius. For the thought, which appears to have been proverbial in Byzantine times, cf. M. Planudes *Epist.* 66 (ed. Treu, p. 81): νυνὶ δὲ τοῖς ὄνοις ἀνάγκην ἔχει συνθεῖν, εἰ τὰ ἴσα τοῖς ἄρτι ἐκ θηλῆς εἰς διδασκάλου βαδίζουσι διδαχθήσεται.

are by no means completely extant. The real order of the leaves containing the fables is 21ʳ–22ᵛ, 26ʳ–27ᵛ, 25ʳ and 25ᵛ, 24ʳ and 24ᵛ, 28ʳ and 28ᵛ. Folios 23ʳ and 23ᵛ are taken up with fables of Syntipas and should follow 33ᵛ. In its present state the manuscript contains only 52 fables ascribed to Aesop, two of which are fragmentary owing to the loss of leaves, but the original total was 95, as appears from the numbering of the fables in the margin. The several lacunae come at the end of 22ᵛ, 26ᵛ, and 25ᵛ respectively. In the first of these lacunae, 17 fables beginning with Α–Ε have been lost;[28] in the second, 18 beginning with Κ–Μ, and in the third, 8 beginning with Ο and Π. Of the 52 fables remaining, 31 are in prose and 21 in 12-syllable verse. Table V shows the order and identity of the fables extant in M as compared with S on the one hand and with Class II, as represented by Ch and Cb, on the other. I am dependent upon Urban Ursing's *Studien zur griechischen Fabel* (Lund, 1930), p. 110, for information about the fables in S.

We see that in the order of the fables M and S are in close agreement against Class II at the beginning, and that only about one half as many fables intervene between nos. 15 and 33 in M and S as between the same fables in Ch and Cb. As for the text, since I have no photographs of the fables in S, and since Ursing reports only a few of its readings that disagree with II, I can make no comprehensive comparison. Nevertheless even the scanty information at hand affords proof that, in a few instances at least, S and M represent a common archetype opposed to all of Class II. According to Ursing (p. 6), no. 89 in S (Chambry 312) breaks off in the middle with the word ἀπώλεσε and is followed by the unique

---

[28] Owing to the torn margins only one numeral is extant opposite the fables in the region between the first two lacunae, and even that is not complete but cut off in the middle. Comparison with the contents of S and Class II shows, however, that that numeral (ϛ′, f. 26ᵛ) must have been λϛ′, and this hypothesis proves to be correct in the light of data furnished by the other serial numbers in the margins.

Table V

Cham.	(A) M	S	(II) Ch	Cb	Cham.	(A) M	S	(II) Ch	Cb
42	1	1	6	6	240	62	69	91	75
41	2	2	8	8	249	63	70	92	76
26	3	3	9	9	250	64	—	94	77
35	4	4	11	11	254	65	72	95	78
34	5	5	12	12	274	66	73	96	79
12	6	6	7	7	284	67	74	97	—
21	7	7	13	13	192	68	75	98	80
61	8	—	15	15	269	69	76	99	
179	9	8	16	16	147	70	77	100	—
6	10	9	17	17	282	71	78	101	81
142	11	10	18	—	81	72	80	104	84
63	12	11	19	—			Lacuna		
45	13	12	20	—	312	81	89	115	94
51	14	13	21	—	327	82	90	118	96
46	15	14	22	—	330	83	91	119	97
	Lacuna				334	84	92	120	—
107	33	33	55	48	123	85	93	121	98
163	34	34	56	49	308	86	94	122	99
326	35	35	57	50	296	87	95	123	100
129	36	37	59	52	328	88	96	124	101
133	37	38	60	53	345	89	97	125	102
135	38	39	61	54	354	90	98	126	103
154	39	41	63	56	352	91	99	127	104
319	40	42	64	57	358	92	100	128	105
	Lacuna				357	93	101	129	106
238	59	65	87	73	336	94	102	130	107
245	60	66	88	—	52	95	103	—	108
235	61	67	89	74					

epimythium ὁ μὴ ἐπαρκῶν εἰς ὃ ἐπέχει, ἀλλὰ μείζονος δεῖται, καὶ αὐτοῦ ἀφίσταται. In M likewise the fable ends at the same point with ἀπώλεσε πάντα and the epimythium reads, more correctly, Οὗτος δηλοῖ ὅτι ὁ μὴ ἐπαρκούμενος εἰς ὃ ἔχει, ἀλλ' ἐφίεται μείζονος, καὶ αὐτοῦ ἀφαιρεῖται. None of the manuscripts of Class II have anything like this, and in Class I, whence this fable was originally derived, Pe, though it ends at the same point and with almost the same words, has no epimythium. This passage is significant in more ways than one, for it seems to show that the SM recension in the prose fables was based upon an archetype in Class I that is more nearly represented by Pe than by any other manuscript. Further evidence on this point will be cited below. In the Pe tradition this fable was simply defective, but the editor of the SM archetype was ingenious enough to give a different, though suitable, interpretation to the story and to supply his own epimythium. The redactor of Class II on the other hand did not follow the SM recension all the way through in this case, but turned to some manuscript of the Augustana. As we shall see, Class II in the prose fables, as in the *Life*, builds alternately upon SM and upon Class I (Augustana). Fable no. 101 in S has the reading τῷ νύγματι ἔνυττε and in M τῷ δήγματι ἔνυττε. Class II, on the other hand, reads δῆγμα ἐκέντα although Ca, which Chambry follows, has substituted ἐνῆκε δῆγμα from Class I. A more thorough canvass than I have made of the readings of S incidentally mentioned by Ursing, would doubtless yield other examples of this kind; but enough has been said, I think, to show that S drew upon the M line at least for some of his text, and the absence of the first five fables of Class II at the beginning suggests that an *A* text, like M, was his first source, however often he may have resorted to Class II (*B*). It is natural that S should follow an *A* text at the beginning of the *Fables* because, in the latter part of the *Life* which immediately preceded, he was already leaning on that recension in preference to *B* (= II = SBP); *cf. Text Tradition* 229 and 234. As indicative of S's close affinity to Class II, Ursing cites fable 36 (Chambry 346), which agrees almost word for word with Ch: but Ursing himself states that this is not typical,[29]

[29] *Op. cit.* p. 5: "Nicht immer herrscht aber eine solche Übereinstimmung zwischen Ci (S) und Ch wie im erwähnten Beispiel. Grosse Unterschiede kommen auch vor, wobei Ci in der Regel die vulgärere Version hat. Dies gilt besonders von den Prosafabeln, die in Ci mitunter eine äusserst nachlässige Form haben. Das Entgegengesetzte kann auch vorkommen, dass nämlich Ci eine klassische, Ch eine unklassische Konstruktion hat." The stylistic differences between S and Class II here mentioned by Ursing are also characteristic of the *A* group in the *Vita* as compared with *B*; but I am somewhat surprised by Ursing's statement that the prose fables in S are more corrupt than those in verse, for in M the situation is just

and the absence of this particular fable in M may mean that it was absent also in the common parent of SM and that S got it from Class II.

Judging by the tradition in the *Life*, the source common to M and S in the *Fables* must be very old; for in the former text it antedates the archetype of λ and M (*Text Tradition* 234), which itself is two stages earlier than the thirteenth-century manuscript Ca.

e. Further evidence pointing to the M recension as the source of Class II

The relative antiquity and isolation of the various texts common to M and S, of which we have spoken above, creates a strong presumption in favor of the view that the unique recension of Aesopic fables found in M is not derived from Class II but antedates it and served as one of its sources. Another argument pointing to the priority of M's fables may be drawn from the use of the word λογομυθοποιός in the title (*supra* p. 189).[30] This word, which seems not to have survived anywhere in Class II, is just what we should expect of the *original compiler* of the fables common to M and Class II, since these fables are taken partly from the Augustana recension where they are called λόγοι in the epimythia and partly from a lost collection of 12-syllable verse fables where they were presumably called μῦθοι, as they are everywhere else

the opposite: the verse fables are more corrupt than the prose fables. This leads me to believe that in the *Fables*, as in the *Life*, S has drawn from both the *A* and the *B* families and that many of his verse fables, including no. 36 mentioned above, have been taken from Class II (*B*), where they are preserved in a more correct form, on the whole, than in M (*A*). The verse fables in M, as we shall see later, have evidently undergone many corruptions in the course of transmission from the early copy of the *A* recension upon which the archetype of Class II was based.

[30] It is also in the *Life* of Baroccianus 194 (= O), showing that it is considerably older than M itself, in fact older than the archetype of *B*; see the stemma (p. 176).

outside Class I (Augustana), especially in metrical fables. In Class II, moreover, the fables, whether in prose or in verse, are regularly, though with some exceptions, called μῦθοι in the epimythia; whereas in M they are very rarely designated by either term.[31] This means, if I am not mistaken, that the redactor did not wish to commit himself to a decision whether a particular fable should be called λόγος or μῦθος and hence studiously avoided using either. His noncommittal policy in this matter matches his invention of the noncommittal compound, λογομυθοποιός. If the M recension had come from Class II instead of having been put together for the first time from the two diverse recensions mentioned above, it would be more difficult to explain this hesitation on the part of the redactor, for Class II would have given him ample authority for the use of μῦθος as applied to both prose and verse fables. As it was, his two sources, the Augustana and the collection of verse fables (or the Bodleian Paraphrase, cf. p. 204), contradicted each other in this matter.

The first five fables in Class II are not found in SM; but they are all in prose and, as may be seen from Chambry's text (nos. 3, 5, 4, 8, 40), they are considerably closer to their counterparts in the Augustana than are most of the other prose fables of Class II. This, I think, is best explained on the assumption that for these particular fables Class II was entirely dependent upon Class I, whereas in most of the other prose fables, which are found also in M, the text of Class II is either *two* stages removed from Class I (through having copied the M text) or else a composite of the M recension and Class I. Moreover the ingenuity that is responsible for the differences between the text of M and II on the one hand, and Class I on the other, is more in accord with the talent of the M redactor as we know it from the *Life* and from his many

[31] Μῦθος is used only three times; elsewhere we always find either the bare Δηλοῖ without any expressed subject (especially near the beginning) or Οὗτος δηλοῖ, and once or twice Οὗτος ἐλέγχει.

unique, sometimes interesting, readings in the *Fables*, than with that of the redactor of Class II, whose changes in the *Life* are slight, and whose variants in the *Fables* are rarely of any interest or consequence except when they agree with either I or M. There are only two instances in which a prose fable common to M and II is absent in I, and in those cases (Cham. 308 and 107), as we should expect, the agreement of II with M is unusually close.[32]

f. The text of M compared with that of Classes II and I

A comparison of the text of the two recensions will demonstrate the following points: (1) that M and Class II are so close to each other and so different from the other recensions that one of the two must have served as a chief source for the other; (2) that M sometimes preserves readings of Class I in the prose fables and of Class IV in the verse fables[33] that have

---

[32] Variants in no. 308 (ignoring Ca): ἀποστρέφεσθαι M, ἀμελεῖν or καταφρονεῖν II; τύχην θείαν M, θείαν τ. II; ἐπιμελείας ἀξιούμενον M, ἐπιμελούμενον II; ζωογονεῖσθαι καὶ M, om. II. Only the epimythium of no. 107 is extant in M, and II is in exact agreement. Both fables are found in Pg and Ma, and no. 308 is also in Pb; but because they are absent everywhere else in Class I, it is probable that these manuscripts have taken them from II or M. Their source appears to be the Bodleian paraphrase.

In Class II, as represented by Ch, there are two verse fables (Chambry 288 and 239) which are absent in both M and S. It may be that Ch or the archetype of Class II drew these fables from the same source that was used by the original compiler of the SM recension, but it is equally possible that these two fables and perhaps a few others, such as S's no. 36, had dropped out of the SM tradition at some time after Class II was created. As for the other verse fables in Ch, as compared with M and S, 12 of them are extant in S but missing in the lacunae of M; 3 others are absent in S but may have been lost in the lacunae of M; and 3 are in S but were never apparently in M. It is not to be supposed that either M or S is entirely faithful to the 11–12th-century recension that they represent; for that is far from being the case with either text in the *Life*, and S must often have followed II in the *Fables* as it does in the *Life* (*Text Tradition* 234).

[33] The verse fables of M and Class II are derived ultimately from Babrius through the medium of the Bodleian paraphrase (Class IV); see Fedde, *op. cit.* (see p. 73, note 2) 16–17; Hausrath, *Untersuchungen* 297; Marc 412–13; and below, p. 204.

disappeared in Class II, thus showing that of the two M stands nearer to the original source in such cases than does II; (3) that the readings of M are at times superior to those of II or have been corrupted by the latter; (4) that the redactor of Class II frequently substitutes οὖν for δὲ in the *Fables* just as he does in the *Life*, where he is certainly dependent on the M recension; and (5) that the prose fables of the M recension were built upon a manuscript of the Augustana that is best represented by Chambry's Pe.

The difference between M and Class II is illustrated by the following examples. I give Chambry's text of Classes I, II, and IV except where he erroneously follows Ca (see pp. 181ff.). Some of the more important variants are indicated when they agree with either M or II, but for further details the reader is referred to Chambry's apparatus.

I (Augustana) Cham. 254	II [34]	M No. 65
Ξυλευόμενός τις παρά τινα ποταμὸν τὸν πέλεκυν ἀπέβαλε· τοῦ δὲ ῥεύματος παρασύραντος αὐτόν, καθήμενος ἐπὶ τῆς ὄχθης ὠδύρετο, μέχρις οὗ ὁ Ἑρμῆς ἐλεήσας αὐτὸν ἧκε. Καὶ μαθὼν παρ' αὐτοῦ τὴν αἰτίαν δι' ἣν ἔκλαιε, τὸ μὲν πρῶτον καταβὰς	Ξυλευόμενός τις παρά τινα ποταμὸν τὸν ἑαυτοῦ πέλεκυν ἀπεβάλετο. Ὑπὸ πολλῆς οὖν θλίψεως συσχεθείς, καθήμενος παρὰ τὰς ὄχθας τοῦ ποταμοῦ ὠδύρετο. Ἑρμῆς δὲ ὁ τοῦ ποταμοῦ θεὸς ἐλεήσας αὐτὸν ἧκε μαθεῖν παρ' αὐτοῦ τὴν	<Ξ> υλευόμενός τις παρά τινα ποταμὸν τὸν ἑαυτοῦ πέλεκυν ἀπεβάλετο. Ὑπὸ πολλῆς οὖν θλίψεως συσχεθείς, καθήμενος παρὰ τὰς ὄχθας τοῦ ποταμοῦ ὠδύ<ρετο>. Ἑρμῆς δὲ ὁ τοῦ ποταμοῦ θεὸς ἐλεήσας αὐτόν, ἐπεὶ μεμαθήκει παρ'

(*Continued on page 198*)

[34] The text here given follows that of Chambry in the main, except that the peculiar Ca readings are rejected in favor of those found in the majority of other MSS. In this fable Ca mixes all three recensions. Noteworthy variants: Τοῦ δὲ ῥεύματος παρασύραντος αὐτόν, ὑπὸ πολλῆς συσχεθεὶς θλίψεως Ca (I + II)   ἧκε μαθεῖν θέλων Ca   αἰτίαν δι' ἣν ἔκλαιε Ca (I)   ποταμοῦ, καὶ ἐπυνθάνετο Ca (I)   ὁ δὲ πένης...τοῦτο] ἀρνησαμένου δὲ αὐτοῦ Ca   οὖν *post* δευτέρου *om*. Ca   καὶ πάλιν] ὁ δὲ πάλιν Ca   ἐπηρώτησε δὲ τοῦτον καὶ πάλιν, εἰ ταύτην ἀπώλεσεν Ca   ἔφη·   " Ἀληθῶς τ. ἀπώλεσα"] ὁ δὲ " Ἀληθῶς ταύτην ἀπώλεσα" εἶπεν Ca   Εἷς... αὐτῶν] Εἷς...αὐτῶν τοῦτον ἐπιφθονήσας Ca   ἐβουλήθη τῶν ἴσων...ξυλευόμενος] *sic fere* Ch Cg   ἐπιφανέντος...ἀνήνεγκε] ἐπιφ. καὶ τὴν αἰτίαν τῶν θρήνων πυνθανομένου (*cf*. M), ἔφη ὅτι πέλεκυν ἀπώλεσα ἐν τῷ ποταμῷ· ὅπερ ἀκούσας ὁ Ἑρμῆς καταβὰς...ἀνήγαγε Ca   ἰδὼν δὲ] ἰδὼν οὖν Ca   ψεῦσμα Ch Ca Mc   ψεῦδος Cg   ψευδὲς Cb   τὸν ἴδιον Ca Cg   δηλοῖ] διδάσκει Ca   ἡμᾶς διδάσκει Ch

(Concluded from page 197)

I (Augustana) Cham. 254	II	M No. 65
χρυσοῦν αὐτῷ πέλεκυν ἀνήνεγκε καὶ ἐπυνθάνετο εἰ οὗτος αὐτοῦ εἴη. Τοῦ δὲ εἰπόντος μὴ τοῦτον εἶναι, ἐκ δευτέρου ἀργυροῦν ἀνήνεγκε καὶ πάλιν ἀνηρώτα εἰ τοῦτον ἀπέβαλεν. Ἀρνησαμένου δὲ αὐτοῦ, τὸ τρίτον τὴν ἰδίαν ἀξίνην ἀνεκόμισε. Τοῦ δὲ ἐπιγνόντος, ἀποδεξάμενος αὐτοῦ τὴν δικαιοσύνην πάσας αὐτῷ ἐχαρίσατο. Καὶ ὃς ἐπανελόμενος, ἐπειδὴ παρεγένετο πρὸς τοὺς ἑταίρους, τὰ γεγενημένα αὐτοῖς διηγήσατο. Τῶν δέ τις ἐποφθαλμιάσας ἐβουλήθη καὶ αὐτὸς τῶν ἴσων περιγενέσθαι. Διόπερ ἀναλαβὼν πέλεκυν παρεγένετο ἐπὶ τὸν αὐτὸν ποταμὸν καὶ ξυλευόμενος ἐπίτηδες τὴν ἀξίνην εἰς τὰς δίνας ἀφῆκε καθεζόμενός τε ἔκλαιεν. Ἑρμοῦ δὲ ἐπιφανέντος καὶ πυνθανομένου τί τὸ συμβεβηκὸς εἴη, ἔλεγε τὴν τοῦ πελέκεως ἀπώλειαν. Τοῦ δὲ χρυσοῦν αὐτῷ ἀνενεγκόντος καὶ διερωτῶντος εἰ τοῦτον ἀπολώλεκεν, ὑπὸ τοῦ κέρδους ὑποφθὰς ἔφασκεν αὐτὸν εἶναι. Καὶ ὁ θεὸς αὐτῷ οὐ μόνον οὐκ ἐχαρίσατο, ἀλλ' οὐδὲ τὸν ἴδιον πέλεκυν ἀποκατέστησεν. Ὁ λόγος δηλοῖ ὅτι ὅσον τοῖς δικαίοις τὸ θεῖον συναγωνίζεται τοσοῦτον τοῖς ἀδίκοις ἐναντιοῦται.	αἰτίαν. Τοῦ δὲ εἰπόντος αὐτῷ, καταβὰς ὁ Ἑρμῆς χρυσοῦν πέλεκυν ἀνήνεγκεν ἐκ τοῦ ποταμοῦ· ἐπυνθάνετο οὖν εἰ τοῦτον ἀπώλεσεν. Ὁ δὲ πένης ἔφη μὴ εἶναι τοῦτο. Ἐκ δευτέρου οὖν καταβὰς ἀργυροῦν ἀνήνεγκεν· καὶ πάλιν ἠρνήσατο κἀκεῖνον μὴ εἶναι αὐτοῦ. Καταβὰς δὲ ἐκ τρίτου τὴν ἰδίαν ἀξίνην ἐκόμισεν. Καὶ ἐπηρωτηθεὶς εἰ τοῦτο ἀπώλεσεν, ἔφη· "Ἀληθῶς τοῦτο ἀπώλεσα." Ὁ δὲ Ἑρμῆς ἀποδεξάμενος αὐτοῦ τὴν δικαιοσύνην καὶ τὸ ἀληθὲς πάσας αὐτῷ ἐχαρίσατο. Παραγενόμενος οὖν πρὸς τοὺς ἑταίρους αὐτοῦ, διηγήσατο αὐτοῖς τὰ συμβάντα αὐτῷ. Εἷς δέ τις ἐξ αὐτῶν ἐβουλήθη τῶν ἴσων περιγενέσθαι. Διόπερ ἀναλαβὼν πέλεκυν παρεγένετο πρὸς τὸν ποταμὸν ξυλευόμενος, καὶ ἐπιτηδείως τὴν ἑαυτοῦ ἀξίνην ῥίψας ἐν τῷ ποταμῷ ἐκαθέζετο κλαίων. Αὐτίκα οὖν τοῦ Ἑρμοῦ ἐπιφανέντος τὴν αἰτίαν τῶν θρήνων ἐπυνθάνετο καὶ μαθὼν καταβὰς χρυσοῦν πέλεκυν ἀνήνεγκε. Καὶ δὴ φήσαντος αὐτοῦ εἰ τοῦτον ἀπώλεσεν, ἔφη μετὰ χαρᾶς "Ναί, ἀληθῶς οὗτός ἐστιν." Ἰδὼν δὲ ἐκεῖνος τὴν ἀναίδειαν καὶ τὸ ψεῦσμα αὐτοῦ, οὐ μόνον τοῦτον οὐκ ἐδωρήσατο αὐτῷ, ἀλλ' οὐδὲ τὴν ἰδίαν ἀπέδωκε πέλεκυν. Ὁ μῦθος δηλοῖ ὅτι ... ἐναντιοῦται.	αὐτοῦ <τὴν> αἰτίαν, καταβὰς χρυσὸν ἀνήνεγκε ἀργυροῦν (sic) ἀπὸ τοῦ ποταμοῦ· ἐπυνθάνετο δὲ αὐτοῦ εἰ τοῦτο ἀπώλεσε. Ὁ δὲ πένης ἔφη μὴ εἶναι τοῦτο. Ἐκ δευτέρου δὲ καταβὰς ἀνήνεγκεν ἀργυροῦν, καὶ πάλιν ἠρνήσατο μὴ εἶναι τοῦτο. Καταβὰς δὲ ἐκ τρίτου τὸν ἴδιον ἀνεκόμισε πέλεκυν· ὁ δὲ πένης ἅμα τῷ ταύτην θεάσασθαι ἔφη· "Ἀληθῶς ταύτην ἀπώλεσα." Ὁ δὲ Ἑρμῆς ἀποδεξάμενος τὴν δικαιοσύνην αὐτοῦ καὶ τὸ ἀληθές, πάσας ἐχαρίσατο αὐτῷ τὰς ἀξίνας. Παραγενομένου δὲ πρὸς τοὺς ἑταίρους αὐτοῦ καὶ διηγησαμένου αὐτοῖς πάντα, εἷς ἐξ αὐτῶν ἠβουλήθη παθεῖν τὰ ὅμοια· καὶ λαβὼν τὸν ἑαυτοῦ πέλεκυν ἀνῆλθε κατὰ τὸ χεῖλος τοῦ ποταμοῦ ξυλευόμενος, καὶ ἐπιτηδείως τὴν ἑαυτοῦ <ἀξί>νην ἐν τῷ ποταμῷ ῥίψας, ἐκαθέζετο κλαίων. Αὐτίκα δὲ τοῦ Ἑρμοῦ <φαν>έντος αὐτῷ καὶ τὴν αἰτίαν πυνθανομένου, ὁ ἄνθρωπος τὸ συμβὰν ἔλεγε· καὶ δὴ < > ὁ Ἑρμῆς καταβὰς χρυσοῦν ἀνήνεγκε πέλεκυν, καὶ εἰ τοῦτο δὴ ἀπώλεσεν ἠρωτήκει. Ὁ δὲ μετὰ χαρᾶς "Ναί," φησιν, "ἀληθῶς αὕτη ἐστὶν ἡ ἀξίνη ἣν ἀπώλεσα." Ἰδὼν δὲ ὁ Ἑρμῆς τὴν ἀναίδειαν καὶ τὸ ψεῦδος αὐτοῦ, οὐ μόνον ταύτην αὐτῷ οὐκ ἀπέδωκεν, ἀλλ' οὔτε τὴν ἰδίαν παρέσχε αὐτῷ. Οὗτος δηλοῖ ὅτι ὅσον τοῖς δικαίοις συναγωνίζεται τὸ θεῖον τοσοῦτον τοῖς ἀδίκοις ἐναντιοῦται.

The Fables

Class IV (Bod. paraphrase) Cham. 129	II Variants from M	M
Ἡμίονος ἐκ κριθῆς παχεῖα γενομένη ἔτρεχε σκιρτῶσα καὶ ἔλεγεν· "Ἵππος ἐστί μοι μήτηρ· ἐγὼ δὲ οὐδὲν αὐτῆς εἰς τὸν δρόμον ἐλάττων." Ὅτε δὲ ἔπαυσε τοῦ δρόμου, ἐσκυθρώπασεν· ὄνου γὰρ εὐθὺς πατρὸς οὖσα ἀνεμνήσθη.	ἐκ κριθῆς (recte)	Ἡμίονός τις ἀπὸ κριθῶν παχυνθεῖσα Ἀνεσκίρτησε καθ' ἑαυτῆι βοῶσα·
	Πατήρ μου (falso)	"Μήτηρ μοί ἐστιν ἵππος ὁ ταχυδρόμος, Κἀγὼ δὲ αὐτῷ ὅλῳ ἀφω‹μοι›ώθην." Καὶ δὴ ἐν μιᾷ ἀνάγκης ἐπελθούσης Ἠναγκάζετο ἡ ἡμίονος τρέχειν.
	πέπαυται (Cb Cf Ch)	Ὡς δὲ τοῦ δρόμου πέπαυτο σκυθρωπάσασα †
	σκυθρωπάζουσα πατρὸς τοῦ ὄνου εὐθὺς	Εὐθὺς τοῦ ὄνου ‹πατρὸς› ὑπανεμνήσθη.
Ὅτι, κτλ.	Ὁ μῦθος δηλοῖ, κτλ.	Οὗτος δηλοῖ, κτλ.
Cham. 319	Text of Ch	
Παῖς τις νέμων πρόβατα συνεχῶς ἐπὶ τὸ χῶμα ἀνιὼν ἐβόα· "Λύκος, βοηθεῖτε." Οἱ δὲ ἀγρόται τρέχοντες ἐκεῖσε εὕρισκον ψεῦσμα. Τοῦ δὲ λύκου ἀληθῶς ἐλθόντος καὶ τοῦ παιδὸς βοῶντος, οὐδεὶς ἐπίστευσε καὶ ἀπῆλθε πρὸς βοήθειαν. Ὁ δὲ λύκος τὰ πρόβατα διέφθειρε. Ὅτι κτλ.	Καί που παιδίον ποίμνια νέμων ὄρει Ἀνακέκραγε· "Βοηθεῖτέ μοι, λύκος." Οἱ δὲ... ποίμνην Τοῦτον εὕρισκον μὴ ἀληθεύειν ὅλως. Ὃ καὶ πολλάκις... πραξαμένου Εὕρισκον τοῦτο ψευδὲς ὑπάρχειν πάλιν. Μετὰ... προσέλθοντος Καὶ τοῦ νέου βοῶντος· "Ἔλθετε, λύκος," Οὐκέτι οὐδεὶς πεπίστευκε τῷ νέῳ Εἰς... ἐπορέξαι. Εὐθὺς δ' ὁ λύκος εὑρηκὼς ἐπ' ἀδείας Τὴν ποίμνην πᾶσαν διέφθειρεν εὐκόλως. Ὁ μῦθος δηλοῖ κτλ.	Καί που παιδίον τὰ ποίμνια ποιμαῖνον Καὶ ἀνερχόμενον ἐφ' ὑψηλοῦ τόπου, Ἀνακέκραγε· "Βοηθεῖτέ μοι, λύκος." Οἱ δὲ ἀγρῶται τρέχοντες εἰς τὴν ποίμνην Εὕρισκον αὐτὸν ὅλως μὴ ἀληθεύοντα Ὅπερ πολλάκις τοῦ παιδὸς πραξαμένου Εὕρισκον πάντως ψευδὲς ὑπάρχειν τοῦτο. Μετὰ δὲ ταῦτα τοῦ λύκου ἐπελθόντος Καὶ τοῦ παιδίου βοῶντος· "Δεῦτε, λύκος," Οὐκέτι οὐδεὶς ἐπίστευσεν αὐτῷ Εἰς τὸ ἀπελθεῖν ‹καὶ χεῖ›ρα ἐπορέξαι. Εὐθὺς δὲ ‹ὁ› λύκος εὑρηκὼς ἄδειαν Πᾶσαν ἀδεῶς διέφθειρε ‹τὴν πο›ίμνην. Οὗτος δηλοῖ κτλ.

The foregoing comparison shows plainly that one of the two versions, M and II, has been built upon the other. Sometimes M is nearer to the original Augustana or to Class IV, as the case may be; sometimes Class II is nearer. In the latter case it is *logically* possible, when considering these phenomena alone, to assume either that II represents the first reworking of the original, which in turn has been altered by the M archetype, or that the M archetype is the older and that II has deserted it by crossing to I or to M's ultimate source in the verse fables that were built on IV. We have also to reckon with the probability that in some cases II, being extant in numerous manuscripts, has preserved the reading of the archetype of the M recension when that reading has been lost or altered in M itself, for M is an isolated and relatively late representative of its class. But when M stands closer to I or to IV than does II, it is not likely to be due to crossing, since there is little of this type of mixing in M either in the *Life* or in the *Fables*, whereas II shows clear evidence of having mixed I with M, both in the numerous substantial passages in which it appears to desert M for I,[35] and in that its agreement with I is much closer in the first five fables, where M has no equivalent, than elsewhere where both are extant. But the probability that II has interpolated the M recension by drawing supplementary material from I (instead of vice

[35] Thus the entire epimythium of no. 163 in Chambry is essentially the same in I and II, but very different in M: ...οὕτως οἱ πολλοὶ τῶν ἀνθρώπων ἐπὶ τοῖς ἀλλοτρίοις ἐγκαυχῶνται καὶ ἐναμβρύνονται (sic) πράγμασι, δοκοῦντές τινες εἶναι· ἐπὰν δὲ τούτων στερηθῶσιν, ὁποῖοι καὶ πρότερον ἦσαν γίγνονται πάλιν. Likewise in no. 330, II has M's text except for the epimythium (πρὸς ἄνδρα ἀχάριστον) which is taken from the Augustana; whereas M has a unique epimythium which is an improvement upon the Augustana: Οὗτος δηλοῖ ὅτι ἄμεινόν ἐστι τοὺς οἰκείους ἀγαθοποιεῖν ἢ τοὺς πέλας καὶ ἀχρήστους. These epimythia are typical of M's originality, which is relatively more vigorous than that of II. But the best proof that II has used both the M recension and Class I is seen in the fable cited above (p. 193), where M (and S), following a defective prototype in Class I, breaks off in the middle and adds a new and suitable epimythium; while II, though agreeing with M against I in the first half, takes the latter part of the fable and the epimythium from a MS of Class I.

versa) is enormously increased by the fact that this very phenomenon has taken place in the Class II version of the *Life* (the archetype of SBP, or *B*); see *Text Tradition* 226–230 and *supra* pp. 29ff. It would be strange indeed if *B* (= II) had copied *A* in the *Life*, while *A* (= the M recension) had copied *B* in the *Fables*. In order to make way for that proposition it would be necessary to show that the *Fables* in M were a later addition which did not stand in the archetype of *A*; whereas we have seen that these fables reach far back into the *A* tradition and were therefore in all probability present at the beginning.

In addition to the examples underlined above, the following passages may also be cited in which M is either closer to I than is II, or else has the older and better reading.

Cham.	I	II	M
51,2	ἀποδημήσας ποτὲ καὶ μετὰ χρόνον ἐπανελθών, ἀλαζευόμενος ἔλεγεν	ἀποδημήσας ἦκε πάλιν εἰς τὴν ἰδίαν χώραν. Φρυαττόμενος δὲ ἐκαυχᾶτο μεγάλως [36]	ἀποδημήσας καὶ αὖθις εἰς τὴν ἰδίαν χώραν ἐπαναλύσας ἐκαυ<χᾶτο μεγ>άλως
51,3	ἐν ἄλλαις πόλεσιν	εἰς διαφόρους τόπους	διαφόροις ἔν τισι τόποις
163,4	— —Ὡς δὲ ἐνέστη	Συνέβη οὖν ἐκ τούτου εὐειδέστερον πάντων ᵞγεγονέναι. Ἐπέστη οὖν	Συνέβη οὖν... γενέσθαι Ἐπέστη δὲ
163,5	μέλλοντος δὲ αὐτοῦ (μ. δ. τοῦ Διὸς Pf Ph Ma)	τοῦ δὲ Διὸς μέλλοντος	μέλλοντος δὲ αὐτοῦ
249,2	ὡς ἐθεάσατο χελιδόνα παρὰ καιρὸν ὀφθεῖσαν (ἐλθοῦσαν Chambry ἐλθοῦσαν καὶ ὀφθεῖσαν Ca)	εἶδε χελιδόνα παρὰ καιρὸν ὀφθεῖσαν καὶ (ἐπεὶ δὲ ἴδεν Ce ἐπεὶ εἶδε Cf Ml)	ὡς οὖν ἐθεάσατο χελιδόνα παρὰ καιρὸν ὀφθεῖσαν
274,9	παρὰ τοῖς προτέροις δεσπόταις ἀχθοφοροῦντα λιμώττειν	παρ' ἐκείνοις τοῖς δεσπόταις εἶναι	παρὰ τοῖς προτέροις εἶναι δεσπόταις
284,3	καὶ μικρὸν ὑποχωρήσαντος	ὑποχωρήσας (-σασα Ce; Ca = I)	καὶ μικρὸν ὑποχωρήσας
328,1	Σῦς ἄγριος ἑστὼς παρά τι δένδρον τοὺς ὀδόντας ἠκόνα (Ὗς G Pb PdPg; περὶ Pb Pc; τινι δένδρῳ Pe)	Ὗς ἄγριος ἑστὼς ἐπὶ τινος δένδρου τοὺς ὀδόντας ἔθηγε (παρά τι δένδρον... ἠκόνα Ca, from I)	Ὗς ἄγριος ὑπό τινι δένδρῳ ἑστὼς τοὺς ὀδόντας ἔθηγε

[36] ἀποδημήσας καὶ πάλιν εἰς τὴν ἰδίαν χώραν ἀφικόμενος ἐκαυχήσατο μεγάλως Ce Cf.

In no. 235, vs. 16, all the manuscripts of II are badly corrupted and Chambry has patched up the verse out of Cg and Ch; the most nearly right is probably M's καὶ σοι προσκρούσει ἵν' ἐκεῖνον ἐκπλήξῃς, which is easily emended to καὶ σὺ προσκρούσεις κτλ. The future indicative here is coordinate with the ὅστις ἥξει which precedes. This reading is likewise superior to the ὅστις (or ὥς τις) ἥκει given by all manuscripts of II except Ca, and to Ca's ἄν τις ἥκῃ. Again in 192,7, where M reads καὶ μὴ κακίστ<ως> οὕτως ἐν βίῳ ζῆν μετὰ φόβου, the right reading may probably be restored by striking out ἐν βίῳ and perhaps changing οὕτως to οὕτω.

The most convincing illustration of the connection between Pe in Class I and the prose fables of the M recension is seen in Chambry's no. 312, which has already been cited in another connection (p. 191). The following readings of M are also found only in Pe among the manuscripts of Class I: Chambry 42,1 μήπω; 328,1 τινι δένδρῳ; 328,6 ἀλλ' ἑτοίμοις; 330,6 βόες δύο instead of δύο βόες; 352,2 πετασθῆναι; 345,1 οὐσίαν αὐτοῦ (also in Ma). This is a very meager list, to be sure, but it becomes more significant when one considers that only ten of Pe's selection of seventy-six fables are represented among the thirty-one prose fables extant in M, and that the latter rewrites quite freely.

It is possible that some of the manuscripts of Class II have taken readings here and there directly from the M recension instead of from their own archetype, although, having made no search for them, I have noted only a few possible instances of this sort. Such crossings, if they exist, may be looked for especially in those manuscripts which show a similar contamination in the *Life*, namely Cf (and therefore Ce) and S.

Since M represents the original recension from which Class II is in large part derived, its text may often serve as a guide where the other manuscripts are divided. Thus in 123,1 (Chambry) we should read ἀνήνεγκαν with Cb and Ch, because it is supported by M; and for the same reason παραμυθίαν is to be preferred to παρηγορίαν in 192,18; πρώην to πρῶτον in 282,19; τὸν μὲν ἕνα τρέφειν καὶ περιποιεῖσθαι καὶ ἀγαπᾶν, τὸν δὲ ἕτερον (Cb Cd Ce Cf Ch Mc L M) to Ca's τὸ μὲν ἓν τῶν γεννημάτων στέργειν καὶ μετ' ἐπιμελείας τρέφειν, τὸν δὲ ἕτερον followed by Chambry in 308,1-2; ἐν θαλασσίῳ τόπῳ to Ca's ἔν τινι τόπῳ παραθαλασσίῳ; γαληνιῶσαν to γαληνήν τε καὶ πραεῖαν, ibid. 2; πωλήσας οὖν τὰ πρόβατα αὐτοῦ to Ca's διόπερ κτλ., ibid. 3; ἔθηγε to Ca's ἤκόνα in 328,1; ἐρομένης to ἐρωτησάσης, ibid. 2; ὁ δὲ γεωργὸς ἔφη to κἀκεῖνος ὑποτυχὼν ἔφη in 330,6; and ibid. 8, δοῦναι ὕδωρ to ποτὸν παρέχειν. These are merely a few passages cited at random from a long list where Chambry's choice of variants is shown to be wrong according to the testimony of M in conjunction with that of two or more of the other manuscripts. In many of these cases Chambry errs in following Ca against the consensus of all the other manuscripts including M; but there are also numerous instances in which M's agreement with this or that manuscript or group of manuscripts within Class II enables one to make a rational choice between variants of equal plausibility, when otherwise the choosing would be mere guesswork. A few cases in which M provides a clue to the right reading, where all the other manuscripts fail, have already been cited above; but such passages are probably not very numerous. On the other hand, it sometimes happens that M shares a corruption in common with the majority of the other manuscripts; and from such cases we may infer that Class II was not derived from the archetype itself of the recension but, as in the *Life*, from a somewhat later and more corrupt descendant of that archetype. For example, in 284, 1-4, M and all manuscripts of Class II except Ca read, with a few unimportant variants, Ὀρνιθοθήρας πτηνοῖς παγίδας ἴστη. Κορύδαλος δὲ τοῦτον θεασάμενος ἠρώτα μακρόθεν ἑστώς· " Τί ἐργάζῃ; " Τοῦ δὲ εἰπόντος " Πόλιν κτίζω," ὑποχωρήσας ἐκρύβη. Ὁ δὲ κορύδαλος πεισθεὶς κτλ. Ca emends by reading καὶ μικρὸν ὑποχωρήσαντος καὶ κρυβέντος, apparently by reference to the Augustana version. Likewise the repeated error in the gender of ἵππος in no. 129 already cited (p. 199) is shared by M and the archetype of Class II.

Before leaving the M recension, it may be noted that a new problem arises in connection with the source of the verse fables common to it and to Class II. Hitherto we have assumed, in conformity with the theory of Hausrath and Marc, that these fables were taken from some lost collection made up entirely of verse fables. That is a plausible hypothesis and may be true; but it is equally possible that the fables in question were versified for the first time by the author of the M recension, both in view of his inventive capacity as elsewhere demonstrated in the *Life*, and in the *Fables*, and of the fact that in the prose fables also he has apparently made some direct use of the Bodleian paraphrase (see note 32) from which the verse fables are derived.

4. THE ACCURSIANA RECENSION (CLASS III)

a. Date and sources

The Accursiana may be described as the modern vulgate recension of the Aesopic fables. It was the first collection to be published after the invention of printing; and from the *editio princeps* by Bonus Accursius (about 1479) down to the beginning of the nineteenth century its vogue was supreme, while the other recensions, though partially represented in a few unusual collections such as those of Nevelet and Hauptmann, remained otherwise practically unknown. The *Life of Aesop* which accompanies this popular collection and which is undoubtedly the work of the same redactor, is ascribed in several manuscripts [1] to the learned monk Maximus Planudes, who died at the age of 50 about the year 1310. Consequently, both *Life* and *Fables* have often passed under his name, although some deny that Planudes had anything to do with

---

[1] That is, in Parisinus 2899 ("m. altera saec. XV"—Eberhard), Vaticanus 949 (= Le in Cham.), Par. 2900, and in Eberhard's K and Z. In the manuscript at Modena (Estensis gr. III B 3) which Marc (p. 398) reckons among those representative of the oldest tradition, the *Life* and *Fables* of Aesop, though anonymous, follow directly after a dialogue on grammar by Planudes. The Accursiana fables are explicitly ascribed to the editorship of Planudes in cod. Borbonicus 118; see p. 217.

the Accursiana recension, and at the most he was not the author in any real sense either of the *Life* or of the *Fables* but merely the editor who recast them on the basis of the earlier recensions. But the question whether Planudes was or was not the redactor of the Accursiana texts is best considered in the light of what can be established, on independent grounds, concerning the date and sources of this recension; and it is with the latter problem that I am, for the present, primarily concerned. On this subject an astonishing difference of opinion exists between Chambry on the one hand and Fedde, Hausrath, and Marc on the other; the latter, with whom I agree, hold that the Accursiana is a relatively late Byzantine redaction and that it is heavily indebted both to the Augustana and to Class II; whereas Chambry [2] maintains, on purely aesthetic or sentimental grounds, that it is ancient, perhaps as early in origin as the third century after Christ, and that it owes nothing to Class II.[3] If it were not for this latest pronouncement by Chambry, it might be considered unnecessary to reopen the question here; but since I am convinced that Chambry is greatly mistaken and since neither Fedde nor Hausrath nor Marc have defended their position with sufficient comprehensiveness and detail to convince a skeptic who is unfamiliar with the problem, I propose here to state the evidence as clearly as possible and at the same time to extend and modify the conclusions reached by Hausrath and Marc.

The late origin of the Accursiana fables is indicated in the first place by the age of the manuscripts which contain them, no one of which is older than the latter half of the 14th century, and only a very small proportion of which can claim to be even as old as that. This fact would be less significant than it is, were it not true that the manuscripts in question are much more numerous than those that contain fables belonging

[2] *Ésope*, Paris 1927, pp. XLVII–XLVIII.

[3] According to Chambry, Class II is the latest of all the recensions and dates from the fourth or the fifth century.

to any one of the other three recensions, and that each of the latter is nevertheless represented by two or more manuscripts older than any of those that contain any of the Accursiana fables.[4] This situation might be explained as due to a remarkable accident of fortune, in case one chose to explain it in that way instead of making the more natural inference that the uniform lateness of the manuscripts points to the lateness of the recension; but the supposed accident begins to take on the aspect of a miracle when one considers (1) that the chronological relation between Classes I, IV, and II, as admitted by Chambry and deduced on entirely different grounds by Fedde and others, is accurately reflected in the proportion of older manuscripts belonging to these three recensions respectively; and (2) that the text of the Accursiana, in spite of the numerous manuscripts that represent it, is far more uniform and consistent with itself and less burdened with variant readings than is any of the other recensions.[5] If the Accursiana had been transmitted from antiquity, or even from the twelfth century like Class II, its text would undoubtedly have undergone more numerous and more substantial alterations than it has as a matter of fact undergone. Its remarkable uniformity is best explained as due to the brief period of time represented by the course of its transmission from the archetype and to the learned, humanistic environment in which it

[4] Taking into account only the MSS mentioned in Chambry's edition, Accursiana fables are found in 36, of which all but two are of the 15th century or later; those of Class I in 21 MSS, of which one is of the 12th century, one of the 13th, and three of the 14th; those of Class II in 21 MSS, of which one belongs to the 13th century and one to the 14th; and those of Class IV in 6 MSS, of which two date from the 13th century and one from the 14th. Among the MSS not used by Chambry, M and S, which stand in very close relation to Class II, are both of the 14th century; the Morgan manuscript representing Class I is of the late 10th or early 11th century; and the New York manuscript (no. 100) representing the Accursiana is of the late 14th century, if not of the 15th.

[5] Class IV is no exception, since Bc and Bd are written in forms that differ widely from each other and from Ba and Bb; hence Chambry usually prints their texts separately instead of recording their variants in the apparatus to BaBb.

was created and propagated. The text of the Accursiana recension, both in the *Life* and in the *Fables*, does indeed show some tendency to change, but the process has by no means been carried so far as in the other recensions; the tendency is rather toward learned emendation than toward the willful and often stupid sort of meddling that is typical of scribal activity from the eleventh to the fourteenth centuries. Moreover the great popularity of the Accursiana recension in the fourteenth and fifteenth centuries would indicate that it was made to suit the taste of that age; the mere fact that contemporary scribes supposed Planudes to have been its editor shows that this recension was then regarded as a fairly recent production.

The Byzantine origin of the Accursiana collection is further evidenced by the presence in at least two of its best representatives, and probably also in most of the others, of three fables in quatrains from the hand of Ignatius Diaconus who lived in the ninth century.[6] Chambry does not print these fables in his edition because he regards them as later interpolations; but that is an arbitrary assumption, being supported only by the consideration that such interpolations are easily made,[7] and by the preconceived opinion that the recension as a whole dates from antiquity. But in the absence of any evidence to the contrary, it is certainly more natural and more reasonable to suppose that the fables of Ignatius were merely one of several different sources that were used by the

[6] These three fables are in the New York MS mentioned above (p. 71, note 1) and therefore probably in Lf (Ambrosianus 7) also. Chambry, who excludes them from his edition, testifies explicitly that they are in La, which he regards as the best manuscript of this class; and I infer from his comments on the recension in general (p. 16) that he found them likewise in other MSS. In any case, their presence in La and N gives them a sufficiently reliable pedigree so far as the manuscripts are concerned.

[7] But they are usually added at the *end* of a manuscript or of an alphabetical series, as Chambry himself incidentally makes plain (*Ésope*, p. XLVIII), whereas in the Accursiana the fables from Ignatius come in the midst both of the series as a whole and of a smaller group (nos. 73–79, see p. 215) that has been taken from various unusual sources.

original compiler of the Accursiana recension; these include Aphthonius (see p. 215) and some unknown sources in addition to Classes I and II.

I pass now to an argument of more weight than anything so far mentioned, namely, that the Planudean *Life*, which is always found in company with Accursiana fables,[8] when not transmitted separately, and which shows unmistakably the same sort of learned and judicious innovation on the part of the redactor as do the *Fables*, is not only derived from the Westermann *Life* belonging to Class II, as Marc showed (pp. 400–405), but furthermore from a certain manuscript within that recension which was later than the 13th-century text Ca.[9] Accordingly, if the *Fables* are by the same author as the *Life* which accompanies them, they must be dated in the lifetime of Planudes, or shortly thereafter. However, it is not necessary to rely upon the analogy of the *Life*, significant though it is; for the case can be clearly proved with reference to the *Fables* alone. We shall see that the latter text comes in part from the same late manuscript source as the *Life*.

The Accursiana collection is made up of fables drawn from varied sources; only the first sixty-two can be said with certainty to have been derived from Class II. Of these sixty-two fables all but one are found in Cf, all but two in Ch, all but five in Ce, and all but eleven in Cb; the other manuscripts show a smaller degree of correspondence. By this I do not mean to imply that the redactor of the Accursiana recension modeled all these fables upon the lost archetype of Cf (which for convenience we may call β) but only that the number, order, and identity of the fables in that manuscript (β) must have corresponded sufficiently well with those of the Accursiana to have served as a guide to the latter in the selection

---

[8] That is, either in MSS made up entirely or almost entirely of Accursiana fables, as Lb, Le, Lf, Lh and others, or in MSS of mixed contents which include a substantial portion from that recension, as Md, Mi, etc.

[9] For a graphic representation of this relationship, the reader may consult the stemma given above on p. 176. See also *Text Tradition* 236ff.

of fables.[10] Although in the *Life*, β served as the principal source of the Accursiana version from beginning to end, while other manuscripts were consulted only upon occasion, in the *Fables*, on the other hand, it is apparent that the redactor of the Accursiana, finding β either corrupt or perversely original, often abandoned it entirely in favor of other manuscripts, though at other times he appears to have emended the text of β either by his own composition or by comparing other codices. These points, however, are of minor consequence. The partial indebtedness of the Accursiana fables to a manuscript of Class II most nearly represented by Cf and Ce (for the relation between these two see p. 181) will be apparent from the following list of variant readings. In this list the fables are cited by number and line of Chambry's text in the version from Class III, and in the order in which they appear in the manuscripts of Class III.

TABLE VI

Chambry	Accursiana (Class III)	β (= Cf or Cf Ce)	Other MSS of Class II
42,3	θεασαμένη	θεασαμένη Cf Ce	περιτυχοῦσα Ca Cc Cd Ch τυχοῦσα Cb
248,1	Δύο νεανίσκοι μαγείρῳ παρεκάθηντο La Lb Lc Ld Le Lf Lg Lh Me Mf Mg Mj Ml and N	Δύο νεανίσκοι μαγείρῳ παρακαθήμενοι Ce	Δύο ν. ἐν ταὐτῷ κρέας ὠνήσαντο
38,12	δυστυχήμασι περιπίπτουσι	ἐπὶ τὸ δυστυχεῖν πίπτουσι Cf Ce	ἐπὶ τῷ δυστυχεῖν καὶ γέλωτα ὀφλισκάνουσι [Cb, Cd, Mc, Mh, and Ch present variants of the same reading, in all of which some form of γέλωτα ὀφλισκάνειν appears]
135,7	ὅτι δεῖ τοὺς φίλους ἐν καιρῷ ἀνάγκης τὰς βοηθείας παρέχειν	ὅτι δεῖ τοὺς φίλους ἐν κ. ἀνάγκης τ. β. π. Cf Ce (= III)	ὅτι δεῖ τοῖς φίλοις ἐν κ. ἀ. τ. β. π.
185,9	καὶ στὰς	καὶ σταθεὶς Cf Ce	Ὁ δὲ σταθεὶς

[10] The complete details of this correspondence may be seen in Table VII below.

TABLE VI—Continued

Chambry	Accursiana	β	Other MSS of Class II
181,5	φωνήσαντος	ἐφώνει Cf Ce	μεγάλα ἐκεκράγει
201,9	Ὁ μῦθος δηλοῖ ὅτι ἄλλων κοπιώντων ἄλλοι κερδαίνουσιν ['Ο μῦθος ὅτι κτλ. Lb 'Ο μ. τῶν ἄλλων κτλ. Le]	Ὁ μῦθος δηλοῖ ὅτι (ὅτι om. Cf) ἄλλοι κοπιῶντες καὶ (καὶ om. Ce) ἄλλοι κερδαίνουσι Cf Ce	Ὁ μῦθος δηλοῖ ὅτι πολλοὶ κόπον καὶ μόχθον ποιοῦνται (ὑφίστανται Ch) εἰς ἑτέρων κέρδος Cg Ch [Ca has two epimythia of which the first, taken from Class I, bears no resemblance to the others, and the second is essentially that of Cg Ch]
234,4	ἀφῃρημένα	ἀφῃρημένα Cf Ce [and Me Mf]	ἐκπεφορημένα Cb Cg Ch Mh ἐκφορημένα Ca
Ibid. 5	Τρέχοντα δέ τις αὐτὸν θεασάμενος	ἐπεὶ δρομέως ἔτρεχεν, θεασάμενος τις (τὶς θ. Cf) Cf Ce	ᾔει (ἀπῄει Cb) δρομαίως τὸ γεγονὸς ὀψόμενος. Τῶν δὲ ὑποτυχόντων τις θεασάμενος Cb Cg Ch; and similarly all the others.
251,13	Ὁ μῦθος δηλοῖ ὅτι περὶ ἃ σπουδάζομεν, τούτοις ἐς ὕστερον περιπίπτομεν (which is meaningless in this connection)	Ὁ μ. δ. ὅτι περὶ ὧν σπουδάζομεν, ὕστερον περιπίπτομεν Cf (obviously the source of the error in the Accursiana)	Ὁ μ. δ. ὅτι περὶ ταῦτα μᾶλλον (μ. om. Ch) σπουδάζομεν ὕστερον, περὶ ἃ (ὧν Ch) πρότερον πέσωμεν (πταίομεν Ch) Ca Ch. This gives the right sense and is very close to the Augustana version. In Cg this epimythium is omitted, and no other MSS of Class II have the fable.
250,1	ὅπως διετηρήθη (nonsense) Lb Le Lf Lh Mc Mg Ml Mm Mn and N [ὅπως διετέθη La Md ὁ. διετίθη Ld. These are obviously emendations]	ὅπως (πῶς Ce) διετηρήθη (nonsense) Cf Ce	πῶς ἐτηρήθης Ca Cg π. ἐτυλήθης Cb π. ἐτηρήθη Ch πῶς ἔχεις Cd
284,7	τοιαύτην πόλιν	τοιαύτην πόλιν Cf Ce	τοιαύτας πόλεις Ca Ch τὰς πόλεις Cg
297,2	ἤνεγκε τῇ μητρί	ἔφερε τῇ μητρὶ αὐτοῦ Cf Ce	τῇ ἑαυτοῦ μητρὶ ἐκόμισε Cb Cg Ch τῇ ἑαυτοῦ μ. ἐπιδέδωκε Ca
330,2	ἦλθον	ἦλθον Cf Ce	ἥκασι Cb Cd Ch Mc ἧκον Ca
334,3	κολοιὸς ὑπολαβὼν ἔφη	κολοιὸς ὑπολαβὼν ἔφη Cf Ce	κολοιὸς αὐτῷ εἶπεν Ca κ. ἔφη αὐτῷ Ch

THE FABLES

TABLE VI—Continued

Chambry	Accursiana	β	Other MSS of Class II
328,1	Μόνιος ἄγριος	Μόνιος (ὄνυος Cf) ἄγριος Cf Ce	Ὗς ἄγριος Ca Cb Cd Ch Ὗος ἄγριος Mc (ὗς and σῦς Class I)
Ibid. 7	παρασκευάζεσθαι	παρασκευάζεσθαι Cf Ce	τὰς παρασκευὰς ποιεῖν Ca Cb Cd Ch Mc
170	This fable (Κορυδαλός) is found only in the Accursiana, in Ce Cf, and in four mixed manuscripts, where it appears in a unique metrical form. The text of the Accursiana here agrees exactly with Cf except for a few misspellings, while Ce, which contains more variants, is printed by Chambry as a separate version.		
352,3–4	ἐκείνη μᾶλλον τῇ δεήσει προσέκειτο. Λαβὼν οὖν αὐτὴν τοῖς ὄνυξι	ἐκείνη...ὄνυξι Cf Ce (a paraphrase of Class I)	omitted
	But for the epimythium to this fable, the redactor of the Accursiana draws upon Ch Cb Mc, or perhaps upon Class I which is similar.		
357	Here Cf and Ce agree so closely with the Accursiana version that Chambry uses them in his apparatus of that version; while the version contained in Ca, Cb, Cd, Ch, and Mc is very differently worded and about three lines longer.		

The fables that follow no. 62 of La are taken in large part from Class I, but nos. 83, 84, and 87 are among the exceptions; for here the Accursiana text is definitely aligned with CfCe against Class I, as may be seen from Chambry's classification of the manuscripts, and Cf and Ce are the only manuscripts in Class II that contain these fables.

The dependence of the Accursiana upon Class II generally is also evidenced by changes in the opening words of fables, whereby the correct alphabetical order of Class II is destroyed; see nos. 2, 23, 33, and 51 in Table VII below.

Among the first 127 fables of the Accursiana—to leave out of account the last 21 in La, which may be a later addition, as Marc says—about 45 of those following no. 62 are taken from Class I, and, with four or five exceptions, in the same order in which they appear in PaPb. I have made no attempt to discover to which of the various manuscripts of Class I the Accursiana fables most nearly approach as regards their text; yet it is evident that the editor of the Accursiana had a text before him that was more complete than any of the manuscripts of Class I except G, Pa, and Pb. Of the 45 fables in question, five are missing in Pa but present in Pb, while two are in Pa but not in Pb.

As it happens, these fables have undergone less revision on the part of the Accursiana editor than have most of those in the early part of the collection that are modeled upon Class II. But this fact need not mean, as Marc implies (p. 419), that the Augustana fables following no. 62—or according to his different division of the corpus, nos. 90–127—are by a different editor; for the same man may be presumed to have grown weary by this time of rewriting his original, just as in the *Life* his opening paragraph is more ambitious than anything that follows; and among the first 62 fables from Class II some are much closer to the original than others. Moreover, the need of altering his original was considerably less when dealing with the fables of Class I than when dealing with those of Class II, which are more corrupt and written in a more debased style.

Marc has a theory concerning the gradual growth of the Accursiana collection of fables which may be stated somewhat as follows: The entire collection is to be divided into four parts consisting of (I) nos. 1–62 in La; (II) nos. 63–89; (III) nos. 90–127; and (IV) nos. 128–148; and this division, based upon the alphabetical order of the fables, must represent at least three cumulative stages in the growth of the entire collection, because, in the first place, parts I–II have been transmitted separately in Laur. conv. soppr. 69 (= Md) and in Par. 2899 (Mi), part III in Laur. 55.10, and parts I–III in Par. 2901 (and elsewhere); and because, in the second place, these divisions coincide with similar divisions based upon the varied sources of the collection, part I being from Class II, part II from mixed and partly unknown sources outside the four principal recensions of the Aesopic fables, part III from the Augustana, and part IV from Classes II and IV. From these supposed facts the conclusion is then drawn that parts I–II, found separately in Md and Mi, represent the *Urform* of the Accursiana, to which parts III and IV were added later; and finally, that no doubt may remain in our minds on this point, we are assured that the text of the *Fables* in Md and Mi, as in the *Life*, does as a matter of fact stand closer to Class II than the other manuscripts and therefore represents the oldest tradition in both cases.[11]

For reasons which need not be explained here, I am inclined to believe that Marc is right in regarding part IV as a late addition to the corpus; and though I am not familiar with the evidence, I am also willing to believe that Md and Mi may represent the oldest tradition in so far as the *text* of certain fables is concerned, though not in regard to the number and identity of the fables contained in the Accursiana archetype. For it is just as easy to account for the antiquity of the tradition in Md and Mi on the supposition that their fables have been *excerpted* from a relatively old text, as it is to assume that their range of fables represents an original nucleus which has been added to by later copyists, especially since these two manuscripts do not contain the same number of Accursiana fables (as Marc loosely implies),[12] and since the contents of both are made up not merely of Accursiana fables but also of substantial blocks *excerpted* from Classes II and IV and from other sources. It is hardly to be expected that a special recension of the *Fables* like the Accursiana should have been taken over into these fifteenth-century anthologies—for that is just what Md and Mi are—in its entirety.

[11] I doubt whether Marc had seen many of the other MSS. What he actually says (p. 420) is that the text of Md and Mi stands midway between that of Class II and the printed editions. It is only fair to Marc, and to Hausrath also, to remind the reader that these scholars did not have access to any such abundant storehouse of information about the MSS as is available to the present writer in the elaborate and well-classified edition by Chambry; instead they had to work almost entirely with their own collations (often only *Stichproben*) and with such unsystematic compilations as those of Halm and Koraes.

[12] According to Chambry who has collated both MSS, Md has the first 92 fables of the Accursiana collection, and Mi only the first 78.

But the greatest weakness in Marc's argument lies in his arbitrary division of the Accursiana into parts which will match those sections of it that appear separately in a few manuscripts, and in the fact that the division according to sources does not, as he says, correspond with that which would be indicated by the separate series in Md and Mi and in Laur. 55.10. In order to make these points clear it will be necessary to tabulate the facts. I omit reference to the manuscripts Cc and Cg, since they contain relatively few fables. The numbers of these fables in N, La, and Lf, which I regard as the best manuscripts of Class III, correspond exactly up to 127.

TABLE VII

Chambry no.	Initial letter	La Lf N	Cf	Ce	Ch	Cb	Cd	Chambry no.	Initial letter	La Lf N	Cf	Ce	Ch	Cb	Cd
3	α	1	1	1	1	1	1	138	ι	32	62	58	62	55	53
4	λ	2	3	—	3	3	3	154	ο	33	63	59	63	56	54
8	α	3	4	.3	4	4	4	184	κ	34	65	61	67	—	58
40	α	4	5	5	5	5	5	185	κ	35	66	62	68	59	59
42	α	5	6	6	6	6	6	181	κ	36	68	64	—	—	—
12	α	6	7	7	7	7	7	202	λ	37	73	69	73	62	73
41	α	7	8	8	8	8	8	210	λ	38	76	72	76	65	76
31	α	8	11	10	10	10	10	201	λ	39	77	73	77	—	77
35	α	9	12	11	11	11	11	234	μ	40	82	78	85	71	85
21	α	10	14	13	13	13	13	244	μ	41	83	79	86	72	86
43	α	11	15	14	14	14	14	251	ν	42	88	—	93	—	93
56	α	12	59	55	26	19	19	250	ν	43	89	84	94	77	92
23	α	13	19	17	32	25	25	254	ξ	44	90	85	95	78	94
51	α	14	22	19	21	—	—	274	ο	45	91	86	96	79	95
46	α	15	23	20	22	—	—	284	ο	46	92	87	97	—	96
50	α	16	24	21	24	—	—	261	ο	47	93	88	106	86	100
22	α	17	27	24	29	22	22	297	π	48	100	94	113	93	107
55	α	18	28	—	30	23	23	312	π	49	102	96	115	94	109
68	β	19	30	26	34	27	27	325	ρ	50	115	—	117	95	111
78	γ	20	35	31	39	32	32	327	ο	51	117	109	118	96	112
87	γ	21	36	32	40	33	33	330	σ	52	118	110	119	97	113
83	γ	22	25	22	25	18	18	334	τ	53	119	111	120	—	—
80	α	23	37	33	41	34	—	328	μ	54	81	77	124	101	116
90	γ	24	39	35	43	36	—	170	κ	55	69	65	—	—	—
178	δ	25	43	38	44	37	34	238	ν	56	—	—	87	73	87
248	δ	26	45	41	46	39	36	192	ο	57	94	89	98	80	97
115	δ	27	46	42	47	40	37	269	ο	58	95	90	99	—	—
13	ε	28	50	46	51	44	41	345	φ	59	126	118	125	102	118
38	ε	29	51	47	52	45	42	354	χ	60	128	120	126	103	119
133	θ	30	60	56	60	53	51	352	χ	61	130	121	127	104	—
135	ι	31	61	57	61	54	52	357	ψ	62	131	122	129	106	120

TABLE VII—Continued

Chambry	Initial letter	La Lf N	Class II	Class I [13]	Elsewhere extant
106	ε	63	—	76	Ca and Class V [14] (= four or more mixed MSS)
105	ε	64	—	77	Ca, V
104	ε	65	—	78	Ca Ma Mb
270	ο	66	—	83	Ca, V
156	κ	67	Cd 66 —	119	Ma Mb Mj
300	γ	68	—	95	Ca Ma
342	υ	69	—	220	Mb Me Mf
343	υ	70	Cf 125 Ce 117	221	Ca Ma Mb Me
291	ο	71	—	192	Mb Me Mf
315	π	72	—	(Cf. 205, = Cham. 314)	(Ba Mb, *aliter*)
206	λ	73	—	—	— [15]
88	γ	74	—	—	—
—	μ	75	—	—	Ignatius Diaconus I, 8
—	φ	76	—	—	" " I, 19
—	π	77	—	—	" " I, 22
174	α	78	—	—	Aphthonius no. 2
11	α	79	—	—	" " 6
349	χ	80	—	228	Ca, V
75	β	81	—	48	Ma Me Mf
173	γ	82	—	54	—
89	γ	83	Cf 41 Ce 37	55	Ca Ma Mb
91	γ	84	Cf 40 Ce 36	56	Ca Me Mf
77	γ	85	—	59	Ca Ma Mb (Mh unique)
84	γ	86	—	61	Ca Ma Me Mf
257	δ	87	Cf 42 Ce 39	67	Mb Me Mf
67	δ	88	—	69	Ma Me Mf
236	ε	89	—	73	Ma Me Mf
28	α	90	—	25	Me Mf
27	α	91	—	26	Me Mf
306	ε	92	—	74	Ma Mb
241	ε	93	—	81	Ca Ma
109	ε	94	—	89	—
111	ε	95	—	90	—
176	ε	96	—	93	Me Mf
49	ε	97	—	96	Mb
108	ε	98	—	98	Ca, V
151	κ	99	Cd 64(= I)	115	V
157	κ	100	—	120	V
159	κ	101	Cd 67(= I)	121	V
171	κ	102	—	124	Ma

[13] The numbers in this column are those of Pb except where otherwise stated. In Class II all the MSS are mentioned that contain the fable.

[14] The mixed manuscripts referred to in this column all present the text of Class I unless otherwise indicated, and no account is taken of those which belong with the Accursiana.

[15] This fable is mentioned by ancient authors; cf. Hausrath, *Untersuchungen* 261.

TABLE VII—Continued

Chambry	Initial letter	La Lf N	Class II	Class I	Elsewhere extant
172	κ	103	—	126	Mb Mj
168	κ	104	Cd 69(= I)	127	Ma Mh
164	κ	105	—	128	—
165	κ	106	—	130	Mj
112	ϛ	107	—	Pa 96	V
119	ϛ	108	—	108	—
126	ϛ	109	—	105	Ca Ma
232	λ	110	—	157	Me Mf Mj
191	λ	111	—	160	Ca Me Mf Mj
242	μ	112	—	164	Ca Mb
252	ν	113	—	Pa 169	Ca Ma Mb Mj
259	o	114	—	172	V
265	o	115	—	179	Ca V
263	o	116	—	181	Ca V
268	o	117	—	184	Ca V
272	o	118	—	185	Ca V
275	o	119	—	186	Ca V
271	o	120	—	187	Ca V
287	o	121	—	188	Ca V
149	o	122	—	191	Ca
292	o	123	—	194	Ca V
302	π	124	—	197	Ca Mb Me Mf
303	π	125	Cf 107 Ce 100	198	Ca V
311	π	126	Ce 102	201	Ca V
317	π	127	Cf 111 Ce 104	204	Ca Mb Me Mf

Nos. 1–62 form an alphabetical series by themselves. They are all represented in Class II and, with a few possible exceptions, are derived from that source. On the other hand, nos. 63–89, which constitute Marc's part II, do not have any unity of their own as a group, either with respect to their alphabetical order or with respect to the sources from which they come. No. 90 comes in the middle of an alphabetical series and, in spite of its beginning with α, does not, as Marc says, stand at the commencement of a new series. Neither is there any new division according to sources at no. 90, but the fables that follow in Marc's part III (90–127) come in general from the same source as nos. 80–89, that is, from Class I. The real divisions, according to the sources, are such as I have indicated above: nos. 1–62 from Class II; nos. 63–71 from Class I; nos. 72–79 from various sources, partly unknown; and nos. 80–127 from Class I. In addition to the three manu-

THE FABLES 217

scripts mentioned above (Md, Mi, and Laur. 55.10), to which Marc attributes so much significance because they contain isolated portions of the Accursiana collection, Chambry (pp. 12–16, 19–24) describes 17 or 18 others which also contain separate blocks of the collection, but whose boundaries, so far as I can see, do not correspond in a single case either with those set up by Marc on the basis of Md Mi and Laur. 55.10, nor with those which are indicated in the table above. Part I, on the other hand, appears to stand alone in several manuscripts (see p. 72, note 1); but no. 62, at the end of an alphabetical series, was a natural place for an excerptor to leave off.

In the light of the facts stated above, it will be seen that there is no support for Marc's theory that the original Accursiana contained *ca.* 89 fables and that two separate parts consisting respectively of nos. 90–127 and 128–148 were successively added by later editors. On the contrary, we have every reason to believe, in view of the manuscript tradition, of the uniformity of text in so many copies, and of the short period of time intervening between the composition of the archetype and the copying of our most complete manuscripts, that the original collection contained at least 127 fables.

b. The Planudean Editorship of the Accursiana *Life* and *Fables*

Hausrath (*Byz. Zeitschr.* x [1901], 91–105) imagines that he has settled the question of Planudes' relation to the Accursiana recension by calling attention to a glossed and grammatically annotated school edition of the Accursiana fables in cod. Borbonicus 118, which bears the title Μῦθοι Αἰσώπειοι κατὰ στοιχεῖον διορθωθέντες ὑπὸ τοῦ πανσόφου κυροῦ Μαξίμου τοῦ Πλανούδη. He would have us believe that the commentary which accompanies these fables and which shows a few cases of misunderstanding of the *original* Accursiana text (not of the particular text upon which the commentary is based; see pp. 95–96) is by Planudes and that the text recension (διόρθωσις) is by someone else! But the title, which Hausrath does not venture to discuss, explicitly contradicts this interpretation; for μῦθοι ...

διορθωθέντες κτλ. can mean only that the *text* of the fables was revised, emended, or recast by Planudes (who himself uses the word in this sense; e.g. *Ep.* 68, line 24, ed. Treu), while nothing whatever is said about either the commentary or its author. What we have in this Neapolitan manuscript is therefore plainly nothing more than an inferior copy of the widely current Accursiana text, which as such is ascribed to Planudes. It has, however, been annotated by an unknown schoolmaster. Furthermore, even if Hausrath's interpretation of the title were correct, it would by no means follow that the ascription to Planudes is right in this one particular case and therefore wrong in the case of the five or more manuscripts which assign the *Life* to him, for Hausrath admits that *Life* and *Fables* must be by the same redactor. Nor does the anonymous commentary in this manuscript (in so far as it is published and indexed by Hausrath) show any noteworthy resemblance to the commentaries of Planudes. In the 364 pages of Planudes' scholia on Hermogenes (Walz *Rhet. Gr.* v, 212–576) there is not, according to Walz's index, a single reference to Aphthonius, Aristarchus, the Bible, Hippocrates, Libanius, Plutarch, Ptolemy, or Synesius; yet all these authors are cited in the brief anonymous commentary on the fables in codex Borbonicus—Synesius four times, Libanius twice, and the others once each. Conversely, four of the authors most frequently cited by Planudes in his commentary on Hermogenes are not mentioned at all in the Borbonicus, namely Aeschines, Demosthenes, Plato, and Hermogenes himself. We may therefore dismiss the codex Borbonicus as totally insignificant for the present inquiry, except in so far as it confirms the tradition pointing to the Planudean editorship of the Accursiana fables.

Equally superficial and uncritical is Hausrath's argument from the language and style of Planudes (*Untersuchungen* 264–265). After citing Treu's observation that in his *Letters* Planudes writes in two styles, the one an ornate atticism in which the sentences are sometimes piled one upon another in long-winded fashion, the other an affected λακωνισμός that is sometimes brief to the point of obscurity, he declares that if the Accursiana recension had been the work of Planudes the style of the *Life* and *Fables* would have been altogether different from what it is. That, however, does not follow. The numerous narratives that Planudes introduces by way of illustration into his commentary on Hermogenes, and indeed many passages in the *Letters* themselves, are as simple and straightforward as anything in the Accursiana. Here and elsewhere in the writings of Planudes we observe a natural adaptation of style to subject matter and to tradition. Ordinarily one does not write fables or objective biographical narratives in the elaborate style traditionally associated with the epideictic epistle, nor would it have been possible for Planudes to do so in this case without totally discarding the traditional text which served as the basis of his διόρθωσις. In other words, such broadly generalizing statements as Hausrath makes concerning the style of Planudes in the *Letters* as compared with that of the Accursiana editor are beside the point for two reasons: (1) because the style of the Accursiana recension is not entirely that of its editor but is often determined by the words and structure of the traditional text, and (2) because the subject matter of the *Life* and *Fables* is of a very different character from that of the *Letters* and therefore calls for a somewhat different style. The only part of the Accursiana text that can properly be compared in general terms with the *Letters* of Planudes is the philosophical preface which precedes the *Life*, and which is entirely the work of the Accursiana redactor. What do we find here? Obviously the same kind of writing that characterizes the *Letters:* an involved, highly sophisticated and subjective style, full of learned mannerisms and classical allusions. The sentences are so loaded with distinctions and antitheses that they are more difficult to read at a glance than the simple, objective narrative of the remainder of the *Life* and of the *Fables*.

So much for the generalities of style. When Hausrath and

Keller (*Jahrb. f. kl. Phil.*, Suppb. IV, 362) make mention of particular points in order to show that the style of Planudes is not that of the Accursiana editor, they are still less felicitous. Hausrath mentions Planudes' fondness for anaphora and for the grouping together of words beginning with the same or similar letters, as if he thought that these phenomena were not to be found in the Accursiana recension. But they do occur there, and probably as often as the editor found it convenient to introduce them. For anaphora see Eberhard's edition of the *Life*, p. 261, 3ff. (δι' αὐτῆς...δι' αὐτῆς...δι' αὐτῆς...δι' αὐτῆς), and 262, 9ff., where the interrogative formula οὐ...δι' αὐτῆς is repeated four times in succession. In both these cases, as well as in all the citations made below, the words in question have been added or substituted by the Accursiana editor. Further, compare the sentence ἀλλὰ σοῦ νῦν δέομαι, εἴ τις ξύνεσις, εἴ τις δεινότης καὶ ἐμπειρία, ξυμπαρίστασο (Eb. 270,3f.) with the words of Planudes in *Epistle* 13 (ed. Treu, lines 25–27): ἄγε οὖν, εἴ τις φιλίας δύναμις, εἴ τις χάρις μαθημάτων κοινῶν, εἴ τις ὀνόματος ἐπιθυμία χρηστοῦ—μίμησαί μοι τὸν Σαμαρείτην. In this connection note also ὤνησαί με, καὶ εἴ τίς ἐστι πίστις κτλ. at Eb. 235,3. For the grouping together of words of similar sound and spelling on the part of the Accursiana redactor in the *Life*, cf. πολλὰ καὶ πολλαχόσε at 227,14; ἀπεστάλην παρὰ τοῦ θεοῦ μου πεῦσίν τινα πυθέσθαι σου at 295,1–2; ἡμεῖς δι' ἡμέρας γλώττας ἐσθίοντες τὰς ἡμετέρας ἠλγήσαμεν at 260,13; περὶ πολλοῦ ποιοῦμαι παρὰ τοὺς πόδας ἀφικέσθαι at 282,13; and τὰς...γωνίας τέτταρας τοὺς τέτταρας τῶν ἀετῶν at 292,13f. (cf. the Byzantine proverb: οἱ τέσσαρες τοὺς τέσσαρας καὶ ἐνίκησεν ἡ θύρα). As an example of non-Planudean usage in the Accursiana *Life*, Keller cites τοῖς ὅλοις which occurs five times, coupled with the verbs ἀπορέω (twice), ἀμηχανέω (twice) and ἐπαπορέω: the expression is indeed quite unusual; but unfortunately for Keller's argument, it happens to be one of which Planudes is conspicuously fond; I have noted six examples in the *Letters* (52,8; 79,38; 98,40; 99,121; 114,40; 119,163). Again, we may grant the truth of Keller's assertion that the phrases τοῦ χυδαίου τούτου καθάρματος (237,2) and βαβαί, πῶς ἡδέως κεκοίμημαι (232,4) are without parallel in the writings of Planudes; but there is no point in this argument because every word in these phrases, except βαβαί, which has been substituted for οὐαί, comes from the traditional text and therefore does not belong to the language of the Accursiana editor. We are certainly not justified in assuming that Planudes, were he the editor, would have been at pains rigorously to exclude every word and grammatical usage that did not conform to the purest standard of ancient Greek. He would not have taken his task quite so seriously. In all probability he would have worked hastily and would have let some things stand as they were. That, at any rate, is what the editor of the Accursiana texts has done, in spite of the fact that he has made hundreds of corrections and alterations, and that vulgarisms in his edition are very rare; this editor, if we may judge by the nature of his corrections, substitutions, and additions in the *Life* and *Fables*, was every bit as learned, as sophisticated in matters of taste, and as fond of ancient, especially Attic and poetic, diction as Planudes himself. Indeed, the question at issue resolves itself to just this: were the Accursiana *Life* and *Fables* edited by Planudes or by an equally learned, though unknown, contemporary? Obviously the only way to reach an intelligent decision in this matter, if one is not content with the tradition, is to study the language and style of the Accursiana editor *in detail* and to compare it with that of Planudes. But before any such study can be made it is necessary to compare the Accursiana recension line for line with the original text upon which it was based (or with the closest available representative thereof, *supra* pp. 209ff.), in order to find out just what features the editor himself is responsible for. Following this method in his doctoral dissertation, a pupil of mine, Mr. C. C. Hower, has brought together an imposing array of linguistic and stylistic phenomena which have been introduced into the *Life* and *Fables* for the first time by the Accursiana editor, and which show a remarkable agreement with the language and style of Planudes. Since Mr. Hower's dissertation will probably not be published for some time yet, I venture to summarize the chief results and to put before the reader some extracts from his interesting collection of parallels. Mr. Hower finds that the language of the Accursiana editor is the same as that of Planudes in respect to the following noteworthy details of morphology and syntax: crasis in such words as ἅτερος and θάτερος, κἀγώ, κἄν, κἀκεῖνοι, προὔτρέπετο, ταὐτόν, τοὔνομα, τοὐντεῦθεν; the forms ἄττα, ἔνι, νυνί (especially frequent both in the Accursiana and in Planudes), οὑτοσί, ἐκεινοσί, etc.; τήμερον; ττ for σσ in such words as γλῶττα, θαλάττιος, πάτταλος, περιττός, φυλάττω; comparative endings in -ιω and -ιους; the superlative followed by ὅσος (e.g. πλεῖστον ὅσον); various forms of the dual number; the frequent use of adjectives in the predicate position; the use of compound verbs in place of simple verbs followed by a preposition; the preposition ὡς; the frequent use of the genitive of the whole in such phrases as ἀνδράποδα τῶν πολυτίμων, τὸν ἕνα τῶν ποδῶν, τὰ πεμπόμενα τῶν προβλημάτων; the comparison of the subject with itself as in καλλίους ἑαυτῶν (probably imitative of Herodotus; examples are cited below); the accusative absolute; the cognate accusative; final clauses introduced by ὡς ἄν; a certain partiality to the aorist forms of ἔχω and οἶμαι; the infinitive of result introduced by ὡς instead of by ὥστε; ἐφ' ᾧ τε with the infinitive to express purpose; the absolute infinitive; the extended use of supplementary participles (examples cited below); the participle introduced by ἅτε and οἷα δή; fondness for participles used as substantives; the joining of a participle to a verb at the end of a clause or sentence as in παρέδωκαν φέροντες (Eb. 226,2); fondness for phrases involving the ellipsis of ὁδόν; fondness for play on words; certain peculiarities of word order (examples below); the frequent use of parenthetical sentences. In contrast to the Westermann *Life* and the *Fables* of Class II, the archaizing editor of the Accursiana employs a great variety of particles and adverbial expressions which are unusual in late Greek but are all found in the *Letters* of Planudes, where

THE FABLES

some of them (starred below) occur with great frequency. Here we may mention ἄλλως τε καί, ἄρα*, αὖθις*, γε* (especially ὅ γε, ἡμεῖς γε, σύ γε), γοῦν, δή*, δῆθεν, δήπου, δῆτα, δέ γε, εἶτα*, καὶ δή, καὶ δὴ καί, μὲν οὖν*, μέντοι, νυνί*, οὐδ' (μηδ') ὁτιοῦν, πάνυ μὲν οὖν, πλήν, που, πως, τάχα, τε...καί*, τηνικαῦτα*, τί ποτε, τί (ὅτι) δή ποτε*, τοίνυν*, τοιγαροῦν, τοῦ (ὅτου, τοῦδε, τούτου) χάριν, τοῦτο μέν...τοῦτο δέ (adverbially).

In the following table of unclassified parallels the *Life of Aesop* is cited by reference to page and line of Eberhard's edition, the fables by number and line in Chambry's text, and the *Letters* of Planudes according to number and line in the edition by Treu. Occasional citations from Walz (*Rhetores Graeci* v, 212–561) are from Planudes' *Commentary on Hermogenes*; *V.G.* has reference to the writings of Planudes contained in C. F. Matthaei's *Varia Graeca*, Moscow 1811, pp. 91–182 (the commentary on Macrobius), 183–204 (the translation of *Scipio's Dream*), and 205–221 (translation of a part of the *Auctor ad Herennium*); and Migne is short for the *Comparison of Winter and Spring* contained in Migne's *Patrologia Graeca* 147, 1170–1176.

Accursiana editor	Planudes
ὅπερ οὐ πάνυ τί με πειθόμενον ἔχει Eb. 290,12; ἑαυτὸν παρεῖχεν πειθόμενον Cham. 291,4	ἐμὲ δὲ πειθόμενον ἔχῃ (= me persuasum habeat) *Ep.* 52,23. ἐμὲ δ' οὐκέθ' ἕξει πειθόμενον *Ep.* 52,25. οὐ πάνυ τι *Ep.* 99,130. οὐδ'...πάνυ τι πιστεύειν ἔχω Migne 147,1171A
ἄλλου καὶ ἄλλου Eb. 260,9. καὶ μάλα αὖθις καὶ αὖθις Eb. 262,4	καὶ μάλα ἄλλο καὶ ἄλλο *Ep.* 99,43
ὡς ἀρραβῶνα τὴν κλῆσιν ἁρπάσασα Eb. 245,14–15	ὥσπερ ἐπαγγελίαν τὸν λόγον ἥρπασα *Ep.* 48,23–24
καὶ γὰρ φοξὸς ἦν Eb. 227,18	The phrase φοξὸς ἔην κεφαλήν (*Il.* 2,219) is cited by Planudes to illustrate ψόγος: Walz v, 558
ἀμηχανήσαντος τοῖς ὅλοις Eb. 239,20 ἀμηχανήσας τοῖς ὅλοις Eb. 302,10	ἀμηχανεῖν με τοῖς ὅλοις *Ep.* 52,8. Further references are given above
ἅλις ἔχει σοι Eb. 266,11; ἅλις σοι Eb. 246,9; ἅλις ἔχων Cham. 269,2	ἅλις ὑμῖν ἔχειν *Ep.* 76,28; ἅλις ἔχει 8,27; ἅλις with other forms of ἔχω: 17,34; 94,7; *V.G.* 152

Accursiana editor	Planudes
πληγὰς τῷ Αἰσώπῳ ἐντείνειεν Eb. 263,18	πληγὰς ἐνέτεινεν Ep. 72,12
καλλίους ἑαυτῶν τοὺς νεανίσκους φανῆναι Eb. 239,7; χείρων σαυτοῦ γέγονας Cham. 88,14	καλλίων ἑαυτοῦ φαίνεται Ep. 11,39; εὐπορώτερος αὐτὸς ἑαυτοῦ Ep. 6,6; similarly 9,25; 10,30; 69,33; 102,22; 119,210
τῶν δέ τις αὐτῷ συνήθων Eb. 238,9; τῶν τις συνανακειμένων Eb. 262,15. Apparently another imitation of Herodotus	τῶν τινα προσεστώτων Migne 147, 1173A
ἦρος διαγελάσαντος Eb. 290,17	ἔαρ ἡμῖν προσγελάσει Ep. 1,89; ἔαρ ἡμῖν ἐπιλάμψῃ 86,46; τῆς τύχης ἡμῖν προσγελώσης 19,31
Σκύλλῃ καὶ Χαρύβδει περιπεσεῖν καὶ ταῖς ἐν 'Αφρικῇ Σύρτεσιν Eb. 305,2-3	Χαρύβδεις καὶ Σύρτεις Ep. 12,59
ὅ τι δήποτε βουλομένῳ σοί ἐστι Eb. 234,2; οὐ βουλομένῳ μοι ἦν τοῦτο πρᾶξαι; Eb. 272,3-4	ἐμοί...γράφειν ἦν βουλομένῳ Ep. 12,19; similarly, with βουλομένῳ, Ep. 33,9; 46,21-22; 99,61; with ἡδομένῳ 12,154
ὁ δὲ ἀκούων μὲν καὶ συνιεὶς ἦν Eb. 230,3; γράμματα...κελεύοντα 281,1-3	τὰ γράμματα...κελεύοντα ἦν Ep. 67,31-32
δόγμα κεῖται Eb. 240,17	γνώμην κεῖσθαι Ep. 28,17
συνελόντι φάναι Eb. 261,6	ὡς συνελόντα φάναι Ep. 5,17; συνελόντα εἰπεῖν 7,28
τοῦτ' αὐτό Eb. 299,16; Cham. 41,3; 138,10	τοῦτ' αὐτό Ep. 67,33; 68,2; 94,9; 51,1 (τοῦτο δ' αὐτό)
τὸ κάλλος τοῦτο τεθήρακας Eb. 248,1; cf. ἀγρεύει ψυχάς, 226,11	προφάσεις...θηρεύω Ep. 16,2-3; 17,23
ἔργοις μᾶλλον ἢ λόγοις φιλοσοφήσας Eb. 227,4	ἔργῳ καὶ λόγῳ Ep. 3,44; 67,21; λόγῳ καὶ ἔργῳ 32,11; λόγῳ μόνῳ καὶ ζήσομεν καὶ φιλοσοφήσομεν Migne 147, 1171C
εἰς ἀθυμίαν ἐνέβαλε Eb. 287,7	εἰς ἀθυμίαν ἐμβάλλειν Ep. 39,6; εἰς ἀμήχανον ἀπορίαν συνέκλεισε 18,7
οὐκ ἀγεννῶς Eb. 245,11	οὐκ ἀγεννῶς Ep. 9,28; οὐκ ἀγεννής 5,16
περὶ πολλοῦ ποιοῦμαι Eb. 282,13	περὶ πλείστου ποιούμενος Ep. 103,30

The Fables

Accursiana editor	Planudes
δεῦρο κἀκεῖσε (substituted for ὧδε κἀκεῖσε) Eb. 236,13; 237,7	δεῦρο κἀκεῖσε Ep. 4,41; 32,28; V.G. 185
μάλιστα πάντων τῶν πεζῶν ζῴων Cham. 343,2	μάλιστα πάντων, without a following substantive however, is very frequent in the Letters, e.g. 41,24
χαίρειν εἰπὼν τῷ λυπεῖσθαι Eb. 278,8	πολλὰ χαίρειν εἰπόντα τοῖς ἡμετέροις πίλοις Ep. 12,107
καλῶς ἅμα καὶ ἀληθῶς Eb. 227,8	πλείοσιν ἅμα καὶ καλλίοσι Ep. 11,13
οἰμώζειν ἰσχυρῶς ἐνεστήσατο Eb. 300,5	γράφειν μὲν ἐνεστησάμην Ep. 28,8
διὰ ταχέων Eb. 253,3	διὰ ταχέων Ep. 100,23; διὰ βραχέων V.G. 136 and 139
ἐταλάνιζεν (for ἠλέει) Cham. 269,7	ταλανίζω Ep. 81,22
ἐσκίρτα Cham. 40,10; ἐσκίρτων 23,2	σκιρτῶ Ep. 29,29; σκίρτα 10,28; σκιρτητέον 17,57
ἀνακαγχάσας Eb. 234,11	ἀνεκάγχασαν Ep. 114,37
ἐπιμελῶς Eb. 248,16; 250,4; 275,7; Cham. 269,2	ἐπιμελῶς Ep. 25,7; 39,23; V.G. 134 and 218
σελαγεῖ Eb. 292,5	σελαγεῖ V.G. 119; σελαγούντων ib. 191
ῥύμης (for ὁρμῆς) Cham. 133,3; 133,4	Various forms of ῥύμη: Ep. 5,15; 14,37; 17,41; 86,46; V.G. 182; 196; 204
ἀποτινάξασθαι Eb. 302,16; Cham. 4,18	ἀπετινάξαντο Ep. 100,11
ἀσχάλλοντος Eb. 265,4	ἀσχάλλειν Ep. 17,41
ἐμφορηθῶμεν...τῶν σύκων Eb. 229,6	πόματος ἐμφορεῖσθαι Ep. 66,5
θρέμμα (= beast of burden) Eb. 234,6; θρέμμασι (= προβάτοις) 282,17	θρέμματα (= πρόβατα) Ep. 12,142; 78,13 (gen. pl.); V.G. 178 (dat. pl.)
πολυάνδριον (sepulchre) Cham. 88, 4 and 7 (gen. sing.) [16]	πολυάνδριον Ep. 31,50

[16] The fable in which this word occurs (γυνὴ καὶ ἀνὴρ μέθυσος) is found nowhere in the Aesopica outside the Accursiana collection, and Hausrath (Untersuchungen 362, note 3) shows good reason for believing that it has been taken over from the Italian Novellistik. The motif is essentially the

Accursiana editor	Planudes
εὐπροσώπῳ λόγῳ Eb. 263,18; εὐπροσώπων ἀπολογιῶν Cham. 12,11	εὐπρόσωπα Ep. 85,54
ἀτενίζων Eb. 238,20	ἀτενίζειν Ep. 16,6; 17,24; ἀτενίσαντες 80,33; ἀτενίζοντες V.G. 140
δοίδυκι (for κοχλιαρίῳ) Eb. 252,7	δοίδυκα Ep. 12,84 and 86
τὸ τῆς εἰσόδου μεσαίτατον Eb. 267,8	τῷ μεσαιτάτῳ τούτων τόπῳ V.G. 111; τοῦ κύκλου τὸ μεσαίτατον ib. 129
λειτουργίαν (for διακονίαν) Eb. 241,1	This is a favorite metaphor in Planudes: λειτουργίαν Ep. 3,39; λειτουργήματος 3,27 and 12,161; λειτουργῆσαι 94,32; λειτουργοῦντας 90,59
πενιχρόν Eb. 243,15	πενιχροῦ Ep. 28,38
διέδρα Eb. 227,1; διαδρᾶναι Eb. 244,14; διαδρᾶσα Cham. 41,2	διέδρα Ep. 46,39; 67,107; διαδρᾶναι 12,130
συχνά Eb. 268,16	συχνούς Ep. 3,38; other forms of the same word: 8,9; 80,52; 88,8
εὐμετάδοτον (for μεταδοτικόν) Eb. 289,1	εὐμετάδοτος Ep. 28,62
προπηλακίσαι Eb. 274,5	προπηλακίσωμεν Ep. 14,44
τεταμίευται Eb. 276,6; ἀποταμιεύου (for ἀποθησαύριζε) 289,16	Planudes is fond of ταμιεύομαι and often uses it figuratively, cf. Ep. 12,205; 38,10; 46,35; 64,44 (ταμιεύων); 98,51; V.G. 157

Finally, Mr. Hower notes a remarkable agreement between Planudes and the Accursiana editor in certain matters of word order. Both are particularly fond of placing participles or verbs in the penultimate position within a compact word group; and the verb itself is often, contrary to normal Greek

same as in Boccaccio's story of Ferondo (*Decameron* III,8). If Planudes were the editor of the Accursiana fables, it would be easy to understand how this Italian novella, if such it is, got into the collection; for he spent some time in Italy as an ambassador, and he was one of the very few Byzantines of his day who had any acquaintance with Latin or with the culture of the West. Since his embassy began in 1296 it is likely that his edition of the *Life* and *Fables* of Aesop was made in the early years of the fourteenth century.

usage, postponed until the end. The latter phenomenon attracted the attention of Chambry in spite of the fact that he believed the Accursiana fables to have antedated Planudes by a thousand years.[17] Examples: ἐπὶ τῷ τῆς ὀπώρας ἡσθεὶς ὡραίῳ Eb. 228,19; μερίδας ἐκ τῶν παρακειμένων ἀνελόμενος ἐπιλέκτους Eb. 254,14; τὸν τῶν ἀετῶν μετέθηκε τοκετόν Cham. 4,26; ὑπό του τῶν μεγίστων διωκόμενος ἰχθύων Cham. 22,3. Mr. Hower finds fifty-five examples of this word order in the first 127 fables of the Accursiana, and in every instance except one the order is due to a *change* from that of the traditional text of Classes II and I. There are many examples of this phenomenon in the *Life* also, and one or more may be found on almost every page of Planudes' *Letters;* cf. τῶν ἐν ἀλλοτρίοις τρυφώντων δάκρυσιν *Ep.* 3,36; τὴν αὐτοῦ καὶ ὑμῶν ποθεῖν ὁμολογοῦμεν ἐπάνοδον 4,4–5; ἡ σὴ περὶ ταῦτά με ἀναπείθει σπουδή 5,2; τὸ τῆς ἐπιστολῆς ἀκούσας προοίμιον 7,8. At Eb. 236,15–16 the Accursiana editor has changed ὃν ἔμελλον δύο βαστάζειν (Cf) to ὃν καὶ δύο β. ἔμελλον; and similar changes occur elsewhere, e.g., Eb. 253,9–10 (ὡς...ἑώρακε) and 263,20 (τοὺς...νίψον). At Cham. 271,4 ὑπέσχετο παραδώσειν αὐτῷ τὸν ὄνον (Class I) is changed to π. αὐτῷ τ. ὄνον ὑπέσχετο; and in 254,5 ἐπυνθάνετο εἰ τοῦτον ἀπώλεσεν (Class II) becomes εἰ οὗτός ἐστιν ὃν ἀπώλεσεν ἤρετο. In the *Letters* likewise the verb is often postponed until the end of the sentence or colon when the sense of the words seems not to require it; cf. *Ep.* 10,19 and 37; 12,59 and 143.

Most of the Planudean idioms cited above are taken from the *Life* because that text has been more freely rewritten by the Accursiana editor than have the *Fables*. Nevertheless, we have noted many peculiarities of Planudean usage which are common to both texts, and there are some in the *Fables* which do not occur in the *Life*. But no one has seriously challenged the natural assumption that the *Fables* are by the

[17] *Ésope*, (Paris 1927) p. xlviii: "... la phrase ... se rapproche par sa contexture de la phrase latine; le complément s'y trouve la plupart du temps avant la mot complété, et le verbe est presque aussi souvent qu'en latin à fin de la proposition." For this reason Chambry believes that the editor of the Accursiana recension knew Latin.

same editor as the *Life* which accompanies them in the manuscripts; and it would be easy to show that the style and diction is the same in both with respect to other points not mentioned above.[18]

Except for the fact that the editor's name is omitted in many manuscripts of the Accursiana recension (though it has been omitted in *all* the manuscripts of the other three recensions), there has never been any good reason to question the fifteenth-century tradition which says that Planudes was responsible for it. The skeptical attack upon this tradition, arising in an age when atheticism was highly fashionable, was fostered partly by the erroneous idea that Planudes must be the inventor, not merely the editor, of the fabulous biography of Aesop, partly by a very superficial stylistic comparison of the *Life* and *Fables* with the *Letters* or other writings of Planudes, and partly by the irrelevant fact that there existed at least one manuscript of the *Life* (the Casinensis, which of course belongs to an earlier recension) which apparently antedated Planudes.

[18] Hausrath, for example, calls attention to the fact that the fable about the eagle and the beetle has almost exactly the same wording in the *Life* (Eb. 301–302) that it has in the *Fables* (Cham. 4), where it differs in many notable variants from Classes I and II.

SUMMARY

It would be impractical to attempt to recapitulate here the numerous conclusions reached in the preceding pages. Nevertheless, the main outlines of the Aesopic tradition as unfolded above, and the parallelism that exists between the successive stages in the history of the *Life* and in that of the *Fables* may be outlined somewhat as follows:

Successive recensions	Approximate date of origin (*Life* and *Fables*)	Title or identity of the *Life*, and chief representative MSS	*Fables*, and their chief representative MSS	Sources of the *Life*	Sources of the *Fables*
I (Augustana)	Second century P.C.? (*cf.* p. 26)	Βίβλος Ξάνθου φιλοσόφου καὶ Αἰσώπου δούλου αὐτοῦ G and papyri	About 230 prose fables G Pb Pa etc.	In part a folkbook of the 5th cent. A.C.	Ancient editions of the *Fables*, *cf.* p. 156
Ia	14–15th cent.?	Aphthonian Preface (*Vita II* Eber.) Pf Me Mf	Μῦθοι κατ' ἐκλογήν Pf Me Mf	Aphthonius, through the medium of Pa or a kindred manuscript	Pa and other manuscripts of I
II	*ca.* 1100 A.D.	Βίος Αἰσώπου τοῦ φιλοσόφου M O R	95 or more fables, partly in prose, partly in 12-syllable verse M Συντιπα τοῦ φιλοσόφου, ἐκ τῶν παραδειγματικῶν αὐτοῦ λόγων M and S	I, as typified by G (*cf.* p. 26)	I, and either the Bod. paraphrase directly or an unknown collection of verse fables (*cf.* p. 204) Babrius and other sources

Continued on page 230.

SUMMARY—Continued

Successive recensions	Approximate date of origin (*Life* and *Fables*)	Title or identity of the *Life*, and chief representative MSS	*Fables*, and their chief representative MSS	Sources of the *Life*	Sources of the *Fables*
IIa (hitherto known as Class II)	12th cent.	Διήγησις Αἰσώπου S B P (i.e. S Cf Cb)	Fables in prose and verse Cb Ch Cd Cf Cg (S)	II, with interpolations from I, *cf.* pp. 29–31	II, except for sporadic interpolations and five or more fables taken from I
IIb (= λ)	Early 13th cent.	Βίος τοῦ βιωφελεστάτου Αἰσώπου and *Vita III* Pg, L, and Mc for the βίος, and L and Mc for *Vita III*	*Ca.* 150 prose fables from I (unaltered) Pg only	II and IIa for the long *Life*, and Pa or Ia for *Vita III* (from the Aphthonian *Preface*)	I
IIc (= Ca)	13th cent.	Βίος τοῦ πανθαυμάστου Αἰσώπου and the Aphthonian *Preface* Ca	199 fables of thoroughly mixed text Ca	For the βίος II and IIa with slight admixture of IIb; for the *Preface*, Pa	IIa and I
III (Accursiana)	1300 A.D., or somewhat later	Βίος Αἰσώπου τοῦ μυθοποιοῦ by Maximus Planudes La Lf N etc.	127 or more fables edited by Planudes La Lf N etc.	A late text of IIa best represented by Cf	I, and the same source in IIa from which the *Life* is derived

APPENDIX

Note on the Corpus of Proverbs ascribed to Aesop (see p. 186)

The *Cosmic Comedies* (i.e. proverbs) ascribed to Aesop in M and S come, in part at least, from the same source as the unique collection published by Krumbacher (*op.cit.*) from cod. Mosquensis 239 (*s.* XIV), though they lack the metrical epimythia (ἑρμηνεῖαι). Krumbacher's edition is incomplete owing to the loss of two or three leaves in the Moscow manuscript; but the first of these leaves, which contains the interesting title Αἰσώπου λόγοι, was later discovered by V. Jernstedt in the Royal Library at Dresden (cod. Dresdensis Da 35, f. 20), whither it had been brought, along with the preceding nineteen folios containing the text of Palaephatus, by C. F. Matthaei in the early part of the 19th century. The fourteen new proverbs together with their metrical ἑρμηνεῖαι, which are contained on this leaf, were published with a Russian commentary by Jernstedt in *Vizantijsky Vremennik* (1901), 115–130, and reprinted in the author's *Opuscula*, St. Petersburg 1907, 217–234. This Moscow collection in part shows an intimate kinship on the one hand with the *Cosmic Comedies* and the proverbs ascribed to Aesop in cod. Laur. 58,24 (Leutsch, *Corpus Paroem. Gr.* II, 228–230), both of which series are without epimythia, and on the other hand with certain apothegms ascribed to Aesop in the gnomologion of Georgides, which consist of metrical epimythia to proverbs without the proverbs themselves. Among the 144 proverbs extant in the Moscow manuscript as published by Krumbacher and Jernstedt, one finds eight of the forty *Cosmic Comedies*, four of the sixteen (not seventeen) proverbs ascribed to Aesop in Laur. 58,24, and twelve of the sixteen isolated ἑρμηνεῖαι which Georgides assigns to Aesop. From these facts we may reasonably infer that at some time previous to the eleventh century—

Georgides is not later and may be earlier—there existed a corpus of nearly 200 proverbs which went under the name of Aesop and had been furnished with metrical epimythia somewhat after the analogy of the fables in Babrius. For it is clear that the isolated epimythia in Georgides, some of which are corrupt in all the manuscripts as compared with their counterparts in Krumbacher, are *excerpts* from a collection similar to that of the Moscow manuscript, rather than part of the source material out of which the latter was compiled; and the same is true of the proverbs which appear without epimythia among the *Cosmic Comedies* and in the Florentine group.

The connection between these proverbs as a whole and the traditional Aesopic lore of antiquity as we know it appears to be slight; yet a number of them are reminiscent of Aesopic fables (*cf.* nos. 4, 6, 35, 42, 54, 67, 101, 118, 120 in Krumbacher with his commentary on the same), and two or three may be related to the ancient *Life of Aesop*. Thus at Westermann p. 17, line 14, the right reading, instead of ἐπί τινων λαλεῖν κτλ., is probably εἰ πετεινὸν λαλεῖ πολύτιμον εὑρίσκεται (εἰ πτηνὸν λαλοῦν π. εὑρίσκεται O), which in substance is exactly what Aesop should have said, considering that he was being sold at auction and that Xanthus had just asked him why he was so loquacious (πολύλαλος). Since the Westermann version has probably been rewritten, as usual, in this passage, and since this one sentence has accidentally fallen out of G, we may be sure that in the ancient texts of the *Life* Aesop's reply was more or less identical with the proverb τὰ πολύλαλα (or λαλοῦντα) στρουθία πολλοῦ πωλεῖται (= Krumbacher no. 94, *Cosmic Comedies* 15). Again, in the Moscow collection (Krumbacher no. 87) we find the proverb τὸ οὐκ οἶδα εἰς φυλακὴν οὐ βάλλει, which must be either the basis of the episode related in chapter 11 of the *Life* (West. p. 32) or, more probably, a derivative from it. In like manner we find apothegms taken from the *Life of Aesop* in other mediaeval Greek anthologies and in Stobaeus; and since Georgides himself has some excerpts from the *Life* which bear no relation to the proverbs mentioned above, it is clear that in compiling his anthology he made use, whether directly or indirectly, both of the corpus that is entitled Αἰσώπου λόγοι in the Moscow-Dresden manuscript, and of the *Life of Aesop*—a fact which suggests that the two texts, *Life* and *Proverbs*, circulated in the same (probably eastern) environment; see p. 188, note 23.

The gnomologion of Georgides was published by Boissonade in the first volume of his *Anecdota Graeca* from cod. Parisinus 1166, but that manuscript omits some material that is found in certain of the others, especially in Par. suppl. 1246, which is also of the eleventh century. Thus, for example, the epimythium to Krumbacher's no. 95, which is incomplete in the Moscow manuscript, may be partially, if not accurately, restored by reference to Par. suppl. 1246:

Krumbacher	Par. suppl. 1246 (Georgides)
Ἐν ἀν<άγ>κης καιρῷ < >	Ἐν καιρῷ ἀνάγκης καιρῷ δυσκαίρῳ ληφθείς,
Τοὺς θηριώδεις ἄνδρας π<ατέ-ρας> κάλει	Καὶ τοὺς τυχόντας ἄνδρας τοκέας λέγε.

The first verse, containing thirteen syllables, is probably corrupt (*cf.* Maas. *Byz. Zeitschr.* XII, 364ff.); perhaps ἐν should be omitted.

GENERAL INDEX

Aeschines 218
Aesop, his conversation with the gardener 4; teaches Xanthus how not to give orders 6, 37 n. 10; deceives Xanthus by a quibble 6′, 37 n. 10; boils one lentil seed 6; offends his mistress by obtaining vegetables free of cost 7; his sexual prowess 8–10; befriends a priestess of Isis 12; is given power of speech by Isis and inventive talent by the Muses 14; as protégé of the Muses 14–16; is likened to Marsyas 15; discourses on the evils of delegated authority 17, — on the wanton behavior of Xanthus' wife *ibid.*, — on why dreams are sometimes deceptive 17 f.; freed from prison 19; dissuades Xanthus from suicide 20; tries to find a man who can mind his own affairs 21, 46–51; relates fables to the Delphians 25 n. 1, 34 f., 62–65, 172; reconciles Xanthus' wife 35 f.; defends himself when falsely accused of eating the figs 41–43; outwits Nektanebo and his wise men 53 f.; insults the Delphians 60 f., 67; plotted against and condemned at Delphi 61 f., 64, 67 f.

 Epithets applied to Aesop: φιλόσοφος 58, 189; λογοποιός 170, 171 n. 54; μυθοποιός 170 n. 53; λογομυθοποιός and σοφιστής 189. Cf. *Life of Aesop* and *Fables*.

Agathopus 41, 44
ἄγειν = agere 25 n. 2
Ahikar VII, 28 n. 5, 32
Ainos, adopted son of Aesop 32, 174 n. 1
Αἰσώπου λόγοι (proverbs) 188 n. 23, 231–233
ἀκουμβήσομεν 25 n. 2
Alexander, romance of 1, 173 (Ps. Kallisthenes)
Alexios Komnenos 26
Allen, T. W. 72 n. 1
Andreopulos, Michael 26, 187, 190
Aphthonius 159 n. 32, 171, 208, 215, 218; see also under *Life of Aesop*
Apollo, ὁ προστάτης τῶν Μουσῶν 14 n. 19, 18; ὁ μείζων τῶν Μουσῶν *ibid.*; offended by Aesop 15; his enmity at foundation of legend of Aesop 15 f., 65; connives at conspiracy against Aesop 16, 61; offends Zeus by his arrogance and is humbled 18
Apollonius of Tyre 35
Apuleius 25
Aristarchus 218
Aristophanes 160, 171 f.
Aristotle 171
Armenia 188 n. 23
Artemis 12 n. 11
Athanasius of Trebizond 188 n. 23
Athens 23, 166 n. 48
Athos, Mt., 187 n. 18, 188 n. 23
Ἀτλαντικὸν πέλαγος 24

Babrius VIII, 25, 73, 151–154, 158 f., 162, 171–173, 183, 187, 190 n. 27, 196 n. 33, 231
Babylon 55 f.
Balzac, *Contes Drolatiques* 10 n. 9
Bible 218
Boccaccio, *Decameron* III 8, 226 n. 16
Bodleian Paraphrase, see under *Fables*
Boissonade 190 n. 27, 233
Bonus Accursius 204
Byzantine copyists and editors, their methods of handling the *Fables* 73, 161 f., 167–169, 206
Byzantine renaissance 26

Chambry, E. VIII, XI, 71 f. n. 1, 74, 147 n. 10, 151, 155 n. 26, 156, 159 n. 32, 168 n. 50, 181, 203, 205, 213 n. 11 and 12, 227; and often elsewhere in Part II
Chariton 160
Charybdis 24, 224
χρεία 80
Collart, P. 40 f., 44 f.
Comedy 24
Comparetti, D. 187 n. 19
Cosattini, A. 72 n. 1, 165
Cosmic Comedies (κοσμικαὶ κωμῳδίαι) 186, 188, 231 f.
Croesus 24
Crusius, O. VIII, 40, 187 n. 20, 188 n. 22
Cypris 24

Delphi 15, 55, 60, 64, 67
Delphians 16, 23, 25 n. 1, 27 n. 3, 34 f., 60–65, 67 f., 172

Demetrius of Phalerum, his edition of Aesopic fables 157, 171 f.
Democritus, as byword 24
Demosthenes 17, 218
δερματοκόπτης 78
Dio Chrysostom 158
Diogenes, the philosopher 80
Dreams, why some are true and others false 18
Drinking up the sea 23, 36 n. 9

Eberhard, A. 163 n. 36, 164, 178 n. 2, 183, 187 n. 19, 223–227
ἔκφρασις 13, 158, 161
Epimythia, various forms of, 156 n. 27, 189, 195; origin of, 172; isolated epimythia 231 f.
ἑπτασφόνδυλα ῥήματα 24
ἠθοποιία 80, 157 f.

Fables, aetiological 18; use of in schools 157–159; terminology, see λόγος and μῦθος, παραδείγματα; eagle and beetle 16, 25 n. 1, 172, 228 n. 18; Zeus and Apollo, or why dreams are sometimes deceptive 18; the man who fell in love with his own daughter 34 f.; the widow consoled 62 f., 67 f.; the stupid girl 63 f., 68; the frog and the mouse 65; the fox and the lion 168; the horse and the ass (racing) 190 n. 27; Hermes and the woodcutter 197 f.; the boasting mule 199; the shepherd boy 199; the wife and her drunken husband 225 n. 16; other fables briefly alluded to, Part II *passim*
Fables (as text): nature of their tradition 71–73, 160–162; principal recensions and their interrelations 73, 75 f., 162, 229 f.; parallelism of their tradition with that of the *Life* and the short biographical notices 74, 76, 170 n. 52, 174, 178 n. 2, 229 f.; unknown recensions of 162
  Augustana recension (Class I): contents 82–154; branch represented by PfMeMf etc. 147, 164 f.; double tradition in 152 f.; date of origin 156 f.; unconnected with rhetoricians or schools of rhetoric 156–173; originally accompanied not by the Aphthonian *Preface* but by the old *Life* 163–170
  M recension: relation to Class II 174–204; time and place of origin 187–189, 194; characteristics 189, 193 n. 29–195; contents 191 f.; kinship with Pe in Class I 192 f., 202; sources 194 f., 196 n. 33, 204; specimens of 197–199, 201; character of epimythia 200 n. 35
  Fables ascribed to Syntipas 26, 72 n. 1, 151, 186–189
  Class II: its archetype identical with that of SBP in the *Life* 177–185; derived mainly from the M recension with interpolations from Class I 185–190, 194–202
  Mixed recension of Ca 181–183
  Recension of Cd 178–180
  Accursiana recension (Class III): date and sources 204–217; popularity 204, 207; uniformity of its tradition 206; Marc's theory concerning its component parts 212–217; Planudean editorship 217–228; school edition of, 217 f.
  Bodleian Paraphrase (Class IV) 73, 162, 183 f., 195 f., 204, 206 n. 5, 230
Fedde, F. 73 n. 2, 75, 196 n. 33, 205 f.
Fortune, see Τύχη

Gardthausen, V. 13 n. 12, 186 n. 16
Gaselee, S. 72 n. 1
Georgia 188 n. 23
Georgides, Johannes 188 n. 23, 231–233
Glettner, J. 159 n. 32
Golenischeff, W. 58. Cf. Papyri (under *Life of Aesop*)
Grauert, W. H. 170 n. 53
Greene, Belle da Costa VIII f.
Gregory of Nazianzus 158
Grottaferrata VIII
Guggenheim Memorial Foundation IX

Hamilton, Arthur 10 n. 9
Harris, J. Rendel 28 n. 5
Hauptmann, J. G. 204
Hausrath, A. XI, 15 n. 21, 16, 18 n. 28, 52, 59 n. 5, 71 f. n. 1, 74 f., 77, 153 n. 21, 156–165, 170 n. 52, 170 n. 53, 187 n. 20 and 21, 196 n. 33, 204 f., 213 n. 11, 215 n. 15, 217–220, 225 n. 16, 228 n. 18
Helicon 14, 23
Helios (for Ainos) 32
Hellas 23 (τὸ κοινὸν τῆς Ἑλλάδος), 55
Hermas 42
Hermippus 22, 24
Hermogenes, rhetorician 171, 218 f.
Herodotus 157 n. 29, 171, 222, 224

Hesiod 1
Hippocrates 218
Homer 158; life of 1, 25; *Il.* 6. 146: 23, 59; *Il.* 2. 219: 223
Hower, C. C. 221 f., 226 f.
Hunt, A. S. 46, 52
Husselman, Elinor VIII, 7 n. 5

Ignatius Diaconus 207, 215
Indifferent man (ἀπερίεργος) 21 f., 34, 46–51
Isis, prayer to· 12; gives power of speech to Aesop 14; as mother or mistress of the Muses 14, 25; in an oath 14 n. 18; cult of 25
Iveron, monastery on Mt. Athos 188 n. 23

James, C. W. 71 n. 1
—— M. R. 71 n. 1
Jernstedt, V. 186 n. 16, 231
Judaea 34 f.

Kalilah and Dimnah VIII, 173; translation by Symeon Seth (= *Stephanites and Ichnelates*) 26, 186, 188 n. 23, 189
Keller, O. 188 n. 22, 220
Koraes, A. 213 n. 11
Krumbacher, K. 186, 188 n. 22, 231–233
Kumaniecki, C. F. 59, 66

Lake, Kirsopp VIII
Latin words in the *Life of Aesop* 25
Laura, the Great 188 n. 23
λέντιον 25 n. 2
Lessing 149 n. 15
Libadenos, Andreas 187 n. 18, 188
Libanius 158, 218
Life of Aesop, character of 1 f.; double tradition of in ancient times 26, 37–39; serious tone in later part of 37 n. 10
 Ancient version preserved in G 2–66; general comparison with W 4–24; new material in 4–8, 11–24, cf. 46–50, 53–55, 60–65; lacunae 4–11, 20, 34 f., 40, 42, 60; glosses and variant readings 4, 11, 13 f., 18 n. 25, 20, 27 f. n. 3, 29; text emended 5, 11, 13 f., 15, 18, 20, 23, 27 f. n. 3, 232; importance of Muses 14–16; style compared with that of W 22–24; date of composition 24–26, 172, 229; diction 24 n. 35; sources 24 n. 35, 25, 229; relation to W 26, 28–36; omitted in MSS of Class I after the 12th century 26, 165 n. 42, 166–169, 174; compared with papyri 30–33, 37 f., 42 f., 46–50, 53–55, 60–65; contains one interpolated or misplaced episode 37 n. 10, 38; present in Pa's source 167; cf. G, under Manuscripts
 Various ancient editions 27–39: as evidenced by double readings in G 27–30, 58; by SBP 27–31, 34–36, 39; by cod. Vind. 128, 27, 28 n. 5, 32 f., 38; by the text of Ahikar 32. Two main traditions distinguished 35–39
 Papyrus fragments of the *Life* XI, 2, 24, 27, 37–67: Golenischeff papyrus 15 f., 31, 33, 37–39, 60–67; Berlin papyrus 24, 26, 30, 38, 53–55, 57 f.; Oxyrhynchus papyrus 27, 32, 37 f., 45–50, 52; PSI no. 156: 40–42, 44 f.
 Westermann version (*W*): manuscripts and text tradition XI, 39 f., 57 f., 174–177; date of composition 2 n. 1, 26; source 2 n. 1, 26, 34, 38; relation to G and other texts 2 n. 1, 26–39; relation to the Planudean version 2 n. 1, 19 n. 29, 175 f., 208; compared with G 4–24; defective motivation 6, 14–16, 19 n. 29, 21 f., 35; effect of syncopation and omissions 6, 17, 22–24, 27 n. 3; corrected by reference to G 22; popularity 26; its abbreviation sometimes older than the archetype 27 f.; supplements G 34; its text compared with papyri and G 42 f., 50 f., 55 f., 67 f.; portions of the text critically edited 42 f., 50 f., 55 f., 67–70; textual comments 44 f., 52, 57 f., 65 f.; Westermann's edition 39, 44 f., 52
 SBP recension: readings cited 12 n. 11, 29–31, 43 f., 51, 53, 56 f., 69 f.; emends W 19 n. 29; kinship with Berlin papyrus 26, 30, 38, 53, 57 f.; interpolates material from a version older than W 27–31, 34–39, 57, 153, 230; derived mainly from W 28, 38, 176, 230; kinship with Golenischeff papyrus 31, 37–39, 66
 Planudean (Accursiana) version: source 2 n. 1, 19 n. 29, 57 f., 175 f., 208, 230; valueless for restoration of papyri 44 f., 52, 65; its source contaminated with W (Ca) 176, 181; its linguistic and stylistic features compared with the writings of

Planudes 218–227; no ground for questioning the tradition that this recension is the work of Planudes 228

Short biographical notices: Aphthonian *Preface* (*Vita II* in Eberhard) 26, 154, 163–169, 170, 174, 177 f., 180, 184, 230; *Vita III* 165 n. 42 and 45, 177–180, 183 f., 230; interpolated version of *Vita III* 163
Linos (for Ainos) 32
λογομυθοποιός 189, 194 f.
λογοποιός 170, 171 n. 54
λόγος and μῦθος as terms for fable 146, 156 n. 27, 157, 170–172, 189, 194 f.
Lokman 188
Lucian 25
Luxor 40
Lycurgus, king of Babylon 15, 22, 24, 53–55
Λυκῆρος, Λυκοῦρος, and Λυκῶρος for Λυκοῦργος 57 f.

Maas, P. 233
Madden, M. 186 n. 16
Manuscripts: classified lists with symbols xii f., 175; supplementary list of MSS containing fables 71 f. n. 1; MSS containing the Aphthonian *Preface* 163–165; diagrams showing relationships 38, 176, 180, 183; comparative tables (with or without collations) 29–33, 82–145, 150 f., 164 n. 42, 169, 183, 192, 197–199, 201, 209–211, 214–216; heterogeneous contents of Aesopic MSS 172 f.; MSS of Class I, 82–156; of Class II, 175–184, 202 f.; of the M recension 185–204; of Class III, 204 n. 1, 205 f., 212 f., 217 f.

Individual MSS of the *Life* (arranged according to recensions): **G**, identity with Cryptoferratensis A 33, viii, 170 n. 52, 171 f.; description of, 3 f., 7 f., cf. Plate III; character of its tradition 3 f.; corruptions in text 3 f., 11, 13 f., 15, 18, 23 n. 34, 27 n. 3; as *Volksbuch* 173; further, see under *Life of Aesop*. **Vind. theol. gr. 128**: 27, 28 n. 5, 32 f., 174 n. 1. **M** xii, 8, 12 n. 11, 39 f., 43, 51 f., 56 f., 68–70, 175–177, 185–190. **O** xii, 8–12 n. 11, 39 f., 43, 51 f., 173, 175 f., 189 n. 24. **R** xii, 39 f., 56 f., 68–70, 173, 175–177. **Lo** xii, 8–10, 11 n. 10, 43, 175–177, 189 n. 25. **Parisinus 2894 (Par.)** 173, 175 f. **MO** and **MR** best witnesses to archetype of W 40, 176. **S** xii f., 12 n. 11, 39, 43, 51 f., 56 f., 68–70, 173, 175 f., 185–189. **B (Cf)** and **P (Cb)** xiii, 12 n. 11, 39, 43, 51, 56 f., 68–70, 173, 175 f. **P** 58. **SBP**, see references under *Life of Aesop*. **L** and **F (Mc)** xiii, 40, 43, 51 f., 56, 175 f. **L** 68–70. **V (Pg)** xii, 40, 43, 51 f., 56, 58, 68 f., 152 n. 20, 173, 175 f. **λ** xiii, 8, 12 n. 11, 39, 43, 51, 152 n. 20, 165 n. 42, 175–177, 182 n. 10, 183 f. **W (Ca)** xiii, 39, 43, 51 f., 56 f., 68–70, 165 n. 42, 175 f., 182 n. 10, 183 f. **Holkhamicus 278 (H)** 175 f. **Le (Vat. 949), Mi (Parisinus 2899), Mj (Paris. 2900), K (Bernensis 629), Z (Turicensis C 136)**, and **Estensis III B 3**: 204 n. 1. **Constantinopolitanus** 72 n. 1.

Individual MSS of the *Fables*: **G** viii, xii; description 77–80, 167, cf. Plate IV; character of tradition 78 f., 155; lacunae 79 f., 94, 99 f.; collated 82–145; inventory of its fables compared with that of other MSS of Class I, 146–154; kinship with Pb and Pa 153 f., with Pg 155; value for text of *Fables* 155; similarity to source of Pa 166 f. **Cryptoferratensis a** 27 153 n. 21. **Pa** xii, 81–155, 166–169; influence on PfMeMf 147, 164; on Pg 152; on Ca 165 n. 42, 182 f.; on Ma 165 n. 42; substitutes 19 or 20 fables of unknown origin 150–153; kinship with Pc 151, 166 n. 47; errors in common with G 154; method of scribe 154 f.; inserts Aphthonian *Preface* in place of the old *Life* 167 f.; why the *Preface* comes after the first fable 168; peculiar order of its fables explained 169. **Pb** xii, 73, 81–155; especially close to G 80, 153; odd fables in, 153 f. **Pc** xii, 82–145, 150; kinship with Pa 151, 166 n. 47. **Pd** xii, 82–145, 148, 150, 155, 172. **Pe** xii, 82–145, 148 n. 13, 150, 155, 192 f., 197, 202. **Pf** xii, 82–145, 147, 150 f., 155, 163–165. **Pg (V)** xii, 82–152, 155, 175 f., 180, 182 n. 10, 183 f. **λ** xiii, 177–180, 182 n. 10, 183 f. **Ph** xii, 82–137, 150. **Pi (Vat. 112)** 84, 148 n. 13. **M** and **S** xii, 175 f., 185–196, 202, 206 n. 4, 230 f. **M** 196–203. **Cf (B)** and **Ce** xiii, 137–139, 142, 181, 201, 208–211, 214–216. **Ce** 87. **Cf**

146 n. 9, 174, 229. **Cb (P)** xiii, 82, 87, 113, 175 f., 178–181, 191 f., 197, 199, 202, 208, 210 f., 214, 229. β (lost archetype of Cf and Ce) 208–211. **Cc** xiii, 82, 177, 181, 210, 214. **Cd** xiii, 82, 87, 111, 114, 116, 151, 163, 177–180, 186, 210 f., 214–216, 230. **Cantabrigiensis 1408** (Coll. Trin.) 71 n. 1, 163 n. 38, 178–180. **Cg** xiii, 177, 181, 197, 202, 210 f., 214, 230. **Ch** xiii, 73, 82, 113, 151, 177, 181, 191–193, 196 n. 32, 197, 199, 202 f., 208, 210 f., 214 f., 230. **La** xiii, 207 n. 6, 209, 211 f., 214–216, 230. **Lb (Laur. 58.23)** 208 n. 8, 209 f. **Lc (Laur. 59.33)** 209. **Ld (Palatinus 122)** 209 f. **Le (Vat. 949)** 204 n. 1, 208 n. 8, 209 f. **Lf** xiii, 71 n.1, 207 n. 6, 208 n. 8, 209 f., 214–216, 230. **N** xiii, 71 n. 1, 205 n. 4, 207 n. 6, 209 f., 214–216, 230. **Lg (Ambros. 340)** 209. **Lh (Paris. 2077)** 209 f. **Bononiensis 2839:** 72 n. 1. **Borbonicus 118:** 204 n. 1, 217 f. **Chisianus** 72 n. 1. **Constantinopolitanus** 72 n. 1. **Estensis II.33:** 72 n. 1. **Estensis III B 3:** 204 n. 1. **Laur. 55.10:** 212, 214, 217. **Paris. 2901:** 212. **Patavinus** 72 n. 1. **Ba (Bodleianus Auct. F. 4.7)** 71 n. 1, 206 n. 5, 215. **Cantabrigiensis 1158** (Coll. Trin.) 71 n. 1. **Bb (Palat. 367), Bc (Paris. 1277),** and **Bd (Vat.949 bis)** 206 n. 5.

Mixed MSS of the *Fables:* **Ca (W)** xiii, 91, 93, 95, 97 f., 101–104, 106 f., 110, 117–119, 121, 123–132, 134, 136–139, 141–143, 146 n. 9–153, 155, 163–165, 181–183, 194, 197 n. 34, 201–203, 208–211, 215 f. **Holkhamicus** 71 n. 1, 165, 175 f. **Ma** xiii, 82–106, 108 f., 111 f., 114, 116–119, 121, 123–130, 132, 135, 138 f., 141–145, 146 n. 9–151, 153, 155, 163–165, 182 n. 10, 201, 215 f. **Mb** xiii, 82, 84 f., 87, 92, 94, 96, 98, 101–104, 106 f., 110–116, 119, 121, 123–145, 148 n. 14–153, 155, 182 n. 10, 215 f. **L** and **Mc** xiii, 178–180, 183 f. **Mc** 197 n. 34, 209 f. **Md (Laur. conv. soppr. 69)** 209, 212–214, 217. **Me** and **Mf** xiii, 83, 85–89, 91 f., 101, 103, 105, 108, 110–112, 116, 122, 124, 127, 133, 138, 141–143, 147, 151, 153, 163–165, 209 f., 215 f., 229. **Me** 72 n. 1, 82, 106 f., 113, 119 f., 130. **Mf** 131. **Mg (Paris. 994)** 209 f. **Mh (Paris. 2494)** 209, 215. **Mi (Paris. 2899)** 204 n. 1, 212–214, 217. **Mj** xiii, 92 f., 107–109, 112 f., 116, 120, 124 f., 146, 150, 152, 164, 204 n. 1, 209, 215 f. **Mk (Paris. 2902)** 178 n. 2, 179 n. 3, 209. **Ml (Vind. 152)** 109, 201, 209 f. **Mm (Laud. 10)** 210. **Mn (Ambros. 91)** 210.

Other MSS mentioned or commented upon (unless otherwise indicated these contain the *Fables* with or without the Planudean *Life* or one of the short biographical notices): **Alexandrinus** (*olim* **Caerensis**) 165. **Argentoratensis 5** (at Strassburg, contains *Syntipas*) 186. **Athous 1025** (*Fables of Syntipas*) 187 n. 21. **Brancaccianus 159** n. 32. **Cantabrigiensis 1032** (Coll. Trin.) 71 n. 1. **Dresdensis Da 35** (Αἰσώπου λόγοι) 231. **Einsiedlensis** 165 n. 45. **Harleianus 5543:** 163 f. **Harl. 5560** (*Syntipas*) 186 n. 16. **Hauniensis** (275 or 215?) 163, 165. **Laur. 58.24** (proverbs ascribed to Aesop) 230. **Lucensis** 72 n. 1. **Marcianus X.9** (*Fables of Syntipas*) 72 n. 1, 187 n. 21. **Marc. 605** (*Syntipas*) 186 n. 16. **Mon. 551:** 177 f. n. 2. **Mosquensis 239** (Αἰσώπου λόγοι) 231. **Oliverianus** (at Pesaro) 72 n. 1. **Tabulae Palmyrenses** 159 n. 32. **Paris. 1166** (Georgides) 233. **Paris. suppl. 1246** (Georgides) 188 n. 23, 233. **Salamanticensis** 177 f. n. 2. **Sinaiticus 1208** (*Syntipas*) 186 n. 16. **Trapezuntius** (reported by Menas) 190 n. 27. **Upsaliensis 8:** 177 n. 2. **Urbanensis** (*Syntipas*) 186 n. 16. **Utinensis** 72 n. 1, 165. **Vat. 335** (*Syntipas*) 186. **Vind. 166** (*Syntipas, Stephanites* etc.) 186 n. 16, 187 n. 21. **Vind. 178:** 163 f. **Vind. suppl. 99:** 72 n. 1, 25 n. 2.

Marc, P. xii, 10 n. 9, 52, 71 n. 1, 74–76, 148 n. 12, 160, 163–165, 170–173, 182 n. 9, 204, 208, 211–214, 216 f.
Marsyas 15
Matthaei, C. F. 223, 231
Matthidia 35
Maximus of Tyre 25
Mazzatinti 72 n. 1
Meier, P. G. 165 n. 45
Melitene 26, 187

General Index

Menas (or Minas or Mynas), Minoides 188 n. 23, 190 n. 27
Mnemosyne 15
Morgan Library, see Pierpont Morgan Library
Muses, their importance in the life of Aesop 14–16; shrine of 16; ἡ Μοῦσα κρίνεται ἐν θεάτροις, ἐν δὲ κοιτῶσιν Κύπρις 24
μυθοποιός 170 n. 53
μῦθος, see λόγος and μῦθος

Nektanebo, king of Egypt 53 f.
Nemesis 24
Nevelet 204
Nikephoros Kallistos 159 n. 32
Nicolaus, rhetorician 171
Nicostratus, collection of fables by 25
Novellistik 10 n. 9, 225 n. 16

Oldfather, W. A. 186 n. 16
Omens and portents 11, 19–21, 23, 27 n. 3, 36 n. 9
Oracle concerning Aesop's death 16

Palaephatus 231
Papyri, see Life of Aesop
παραδείγματα and παραδειγματικοὶ λόγοι 189
Parallel tradition of Life and Fables, see under Fables
Phaedrus 157, 159 f., 172
Philogelos 173
Philoxenia 12
Phocis 61, 67
Phoenicia 34 f.
Phokas, Byzantine rebel 188 n. 23
Physiologus 162, 173
Pierpont Morgan Library VII f.
πιθήκων πριμιπιλάριος 23
Planudes, Maximus 190 n. 27, 204, 217–228, 230; language and style of, 218–227; knowledge of Latin and sojourn in Italy 225 f. n. 16; editor of Accursiana Life and Fables 228, 230; see also under Life of Aesop
Plato 18 (Phaedo 60 C), 218
Plutarch 218; Banquet of the Seven Sages 1, 171; On Isis and Osiris 14 n. 16
Post, L. A. IX, 13 n. 13
Potente, F. 59
Progymnasmata 171
Promythia 172 n. 58
Proverbs 19 f., 23 f., 186 n. 14, 220, 231–233; cf. Cosmic Comedies and Αἰσώπου λόγοι
Ps.-Kallisthenes 173

Ptolemy 218
Puntoni, V. 72 n. 1, 186 n. 17, 189 n. 25

Recognitiones of Ps.-Clement 35
Reiske, J. J. 2, 45
Rhetoric 156–163 and 170–172 passim; schools of 157–161; terminology of 170–172
Rinuccio da Castiglioni 175 f., 180
Robertson, D. S. 71 n. 1

Samians 14, 19 f., 23 f., 37
Samos 61, 166 n. 48
Sbordone, F. 159 n. 32, 171 n. 55
Schneider, J. G. 45, 81, 117, 137 n. 6, 148 n. 12
Schubart, W. 24, 53, 58
Scylla 224
Seven Wise Masters, see Syntipas
Sicily 35
Slavery, evils of 17
Sophos, Aramaic fables of 188
σπινθῆρσι λόγων 24
Spoils, consecration of, to Apollo 60 f., 67
Stephanites and Ichnelates, see Kalilah and Dimnah
Sternbach, L. 81, 108 n. 4, 129 n. 5, 137 n. 6, 149 n. 15
Stobaeus 232
Symeon Seth, see Kalilah and Dimnah
Syncretism 14
Synesius 218
Syntipas, Book of, or Seven Wise Masters 10 n. 9, 26, 160, 162, 186–190
Syntipas, see under Fables
Syria 34 f.
Syrtes 224

Theon, rhetorician 171
Timarchus, Athenian master of Aesop 166 n. 48
Tornikios, Johannes 188 n. 23
Trebizond 26, 187 f., 190 n. 27
Treu, M. 190 n. 27, 218 f., 223
Τύχη 12

University of Illinois IX
Ursing, Urban 191, 193
ὗς τροχάζων 23

Vatopedi monastery 188 n. 23
Volksbücher 1 f., 160 f., 170 n. 52, 172 f.

Waddell, W. G. 165
Walz, C. 218, 223

Weil, H. 58, 65 f.
Westermann, A., his edition of the *Life of Aesop* XI, 2 n. 1, 33, 36 n. 9, 39, 41, 44 f., 52; cf. *Life of Aesop*

Xanthus, Aesop's master: errs in giving orders to Aesop 6; arbitrates between Aesop and his mistress 9 f.; as professional philosopher 18–21, 23 f.; ὃν ὅλη ἡ Ἑλλὰς οἶδε 19; resolves on suicide but is dissuaded by Aesop 20; prepares to drink up the sea 23

Xanthus, wife of: destroys vegetables brought by Aesop 6 f.; promises Aesop a cloak in return for personal services 9; desires a beautiful man-servant 17, 21; deserts X. and is reconciled by Aesop 35 f.

Zeitz, H. XI, 40, 44 f., 52, 57 f., 65 f.
Zemarchus for Timarchus 164 n. 42
Zenas 16 f., 22 f., 27 n. 3, 44
Zereteli, G. 58 f., 65–67
Zeus (and Zeus Xenios) 16; humbles Apollo 18

Plate I

P. Oxy. 2083 Recto
(By permission of the Egypt Exploration Society)

Plate II

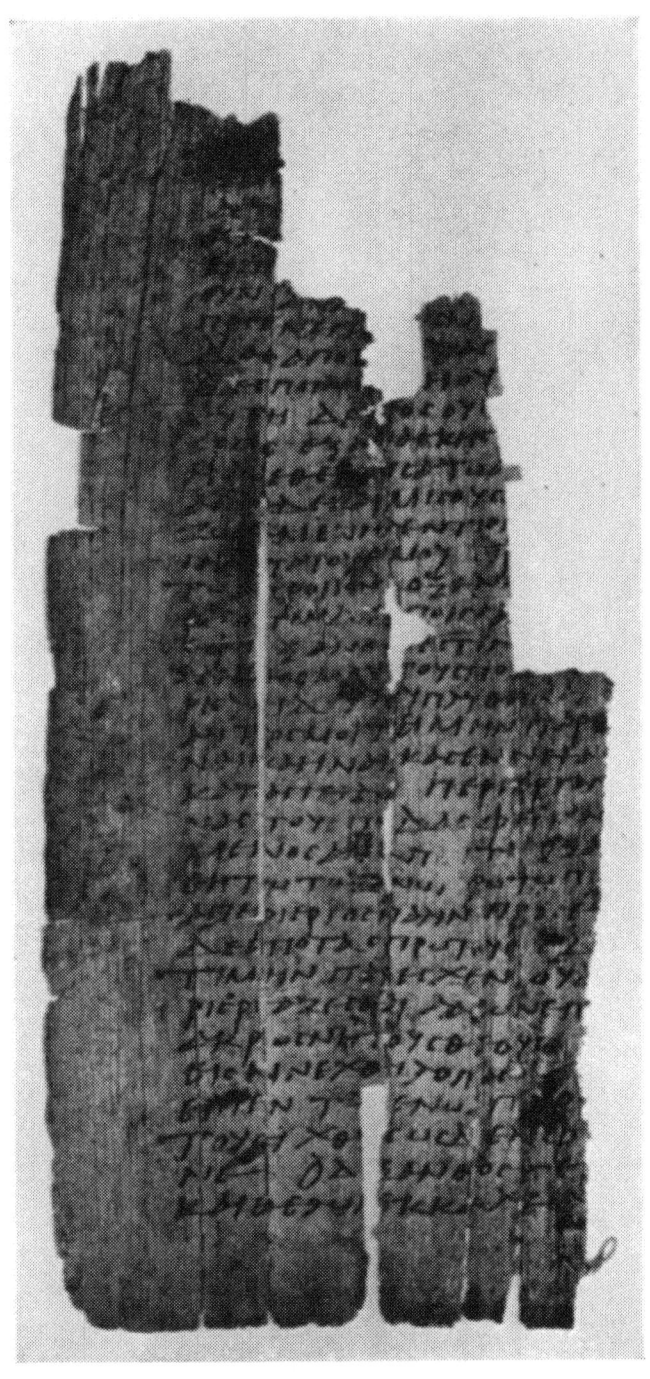

P. Oxy. 2083 Verso
(By permission of the Egypt Exploration Society)

PLATE III

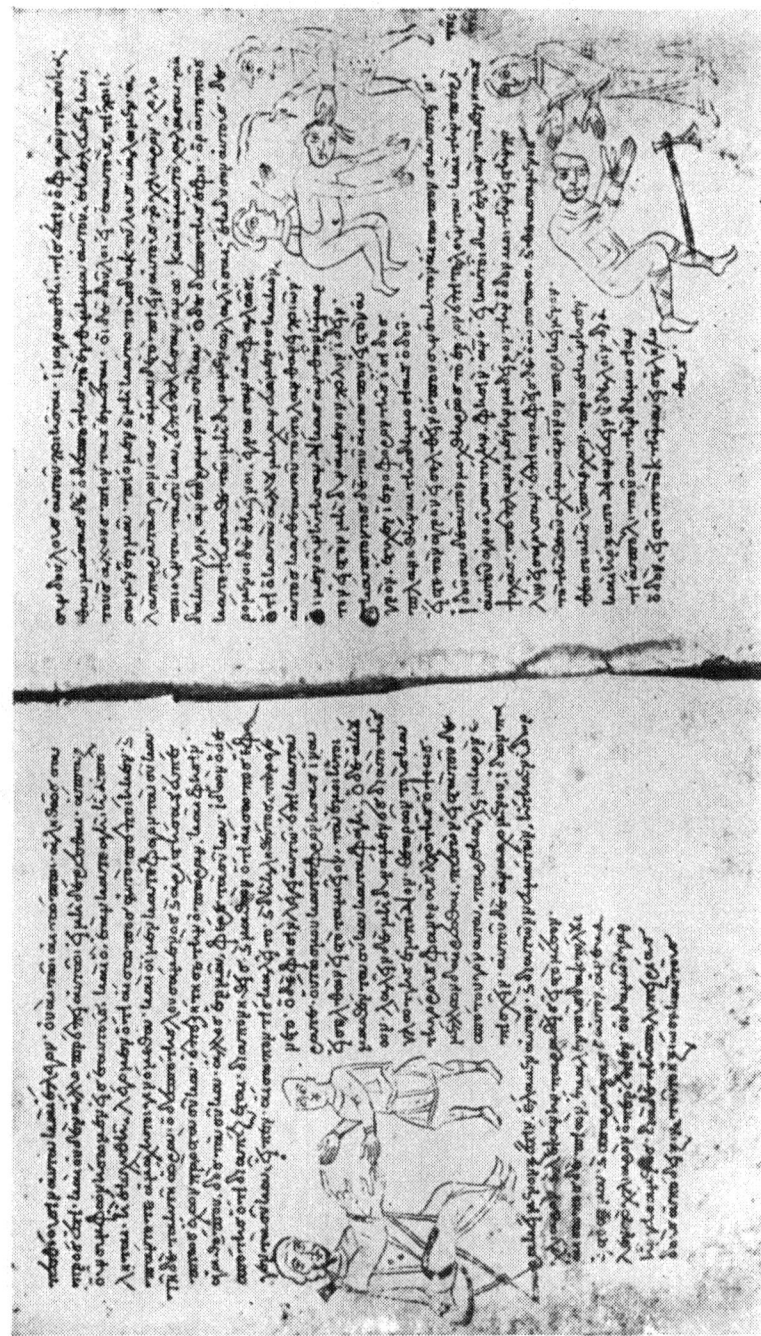

Morgan manuscript no. 397. Folios 22v and 23r

Morgan manuscript no. 397. Folios 67ᵛ and 68ʳ

Plate V

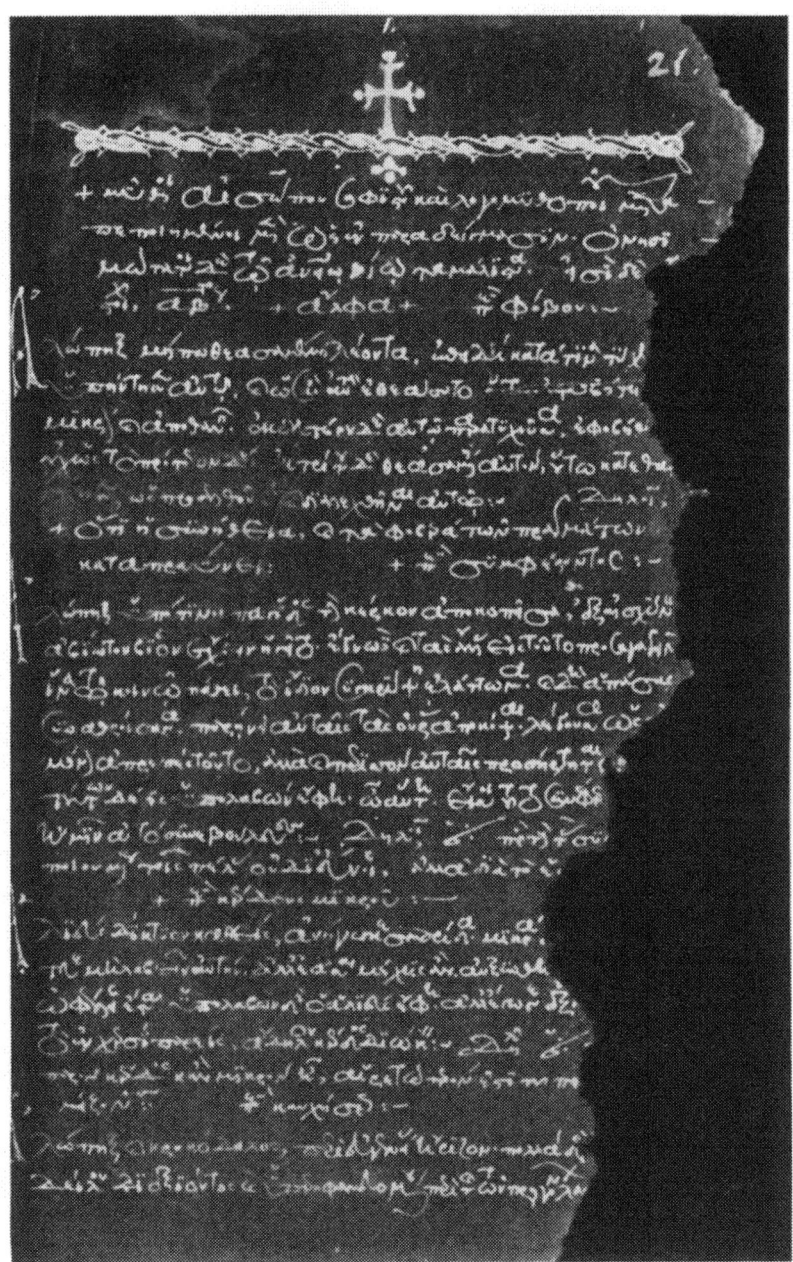

Cod. Mon. 525. Fol. 21ʳ

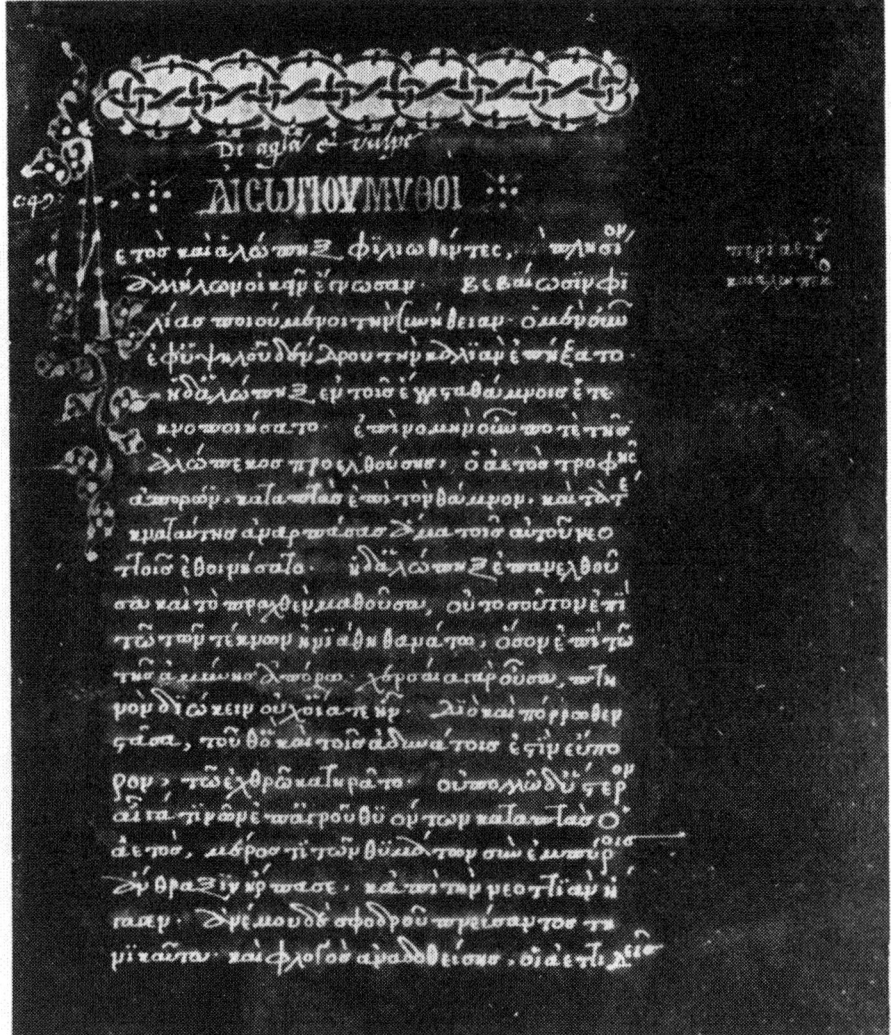

Manuscript no. 100 of the Astor Collection,
New York Public Library

www.ingramcontent.com/pod-product-compliance
Ingram Content Group UK Ltd.
Pitfield, Milton Keynes, MK11 3LW, UK
UKHW041431180426
11947UKWH00007B/379